Killing Civilization

KILLING CIVILIZATION

A Reassessment of Early Urbanism and Its Consequences

JUSTIN JENNINGS

University of New Mexico Press • Albuquerque

First paperback edition, 2021
Paperback ISBN: 978-0-8263-6273-5

LIBRARY OF CONGRESS CATALOGING-IN-PUBLICATION DATA
Names: Jennings, Justin, author.
Title: Killing civilization : a reassessment of early urbanism and its consequences / Justin Jennings.
Description: Albuquerque : University of New Mexico Press, 2016. | Includes bibliographical references and index.
Identifiers: LCCN 2015019428 | ISBN 9780826356604 (cloth : alk. paper) | ISBN 9780826356611 (electronic)
Subjects: LCSH: Cities and towns, Ancient. | Civilization, Ancient. | Human settlements. | Urbanization.
Classification: LCC HT114 .J46 2016 | DDC 306.7609/01—dc23
LC record available at http://lccn.loc.gov/2015019428

Designed by Lila Sanchez
Composed in Minion Pro

For my parents, Kay and Dick Jennings

CONTENTS

ILLUSTRATIONS

PREFACE

EVER SINCE ANATOMICALLY MODERN HUMANS EVOLVED SOME 200,000 years ago, there have been long stretches during which people have lived in a similar manner. This relative stasis has been punctuated by much shorter periods of change within which social, political, and economic organizations were radically reorganized. The most rapid of these changes was likely the shift from rural to urban society. These transitions, often occurring in the space of just a few hundred years, are virtually instantaneous blips when placed against the backdrop of humanity's first 200,000 years; their swiftness makes us prone to seeing cities, states, craft specialists, peasants, and bureaucrats as suddenly appearing fully formed, like Athena from Zeus's head, on the timeline of human history—seemingly unfurling together when civilization was finally achieved.

A seductive concept, civilization has long been used as a heuristic device to make sense of a dizzying landscape of cultural variation. By placing groups that share certain broad characteristics into distinct societal types, we bring order to chaos and allow for comparative analysis. Humanity has a bad habit of misconstruing heuristics for reality, however, and hundreds of years of relying on stages in our models of cultural development has warped our understanding of the past. Bundling together a group of characteristics that often, but importantly far from always, appear at around the same time has not surprisingly led us to often consider these characteristics as parts of a single civilization package. We make assumptions about how societies *should* change, which shapes our interpretations of what happened during transition periods that are often just rapid enough to be difficult to see archaeologically.

We know civilization's flaws of course, and so by now, yet another argument against the concept might seem passé to many readers. As one reviewer of this manuscript noted, there is already a growing literature on the alternate paths to social complexity, as well as widespread recognition that there are many different ways of being complex. It is widely acknowledged that even the term itself is fraught with racist and ethnocentric undertones. Surely we have moved well beyond this antiquated concept? This book suggests that, to the contrary, civilization still very much lingers in our models, unconsciously shaping how we view many of the world's first urbanizations, colonizations, state formations, and cultural horizons. I argue that the relationship between these four processes—all long associated with the idea of civilization—has been consistently misrepresented because data that go against our deeply ingrained assumptions have been downplayed or ignored. Eliminating the civilization concept by refusing to think in stages of cultural development would allow for a far more accurate understanding of the relationships between these four processes over time.

This book argues that much of what is considered as "civilization" can be better understood as the often-unintended consequences of actions addressing the challenges of rapid settlement aggregation. I suggest that the accumulation of many people in one place demands societal change. Resources need to be provided, and, just as importantly, individuals in these large groups need to find new ways to get along with each other. The on-the-fly changes that people make during the first years of aggregation can have long-term ramifications as people, ideas, and products circulate across a wide region. The earliest state formations, when they occurred at all, came years after the establishment of cities, colonies, and cultural horizons. The first states were thus grudgingly accepted—and often short-lived—replacements for the more bottom-up, decentralized, and less hierarchical regional polities cobbled together as the world's first cities grew.

This book uses case studies from across the modern and ancient world to develop this countermodel of incipient urbanism and its broad consequences. Our interpretations of what life was like during these periods of transition have long been guided, often unconsciously, by the idea of civilization as a stage of cultural development. Fortunately, the available excavation and survey data from places like Harappa, Tiahuanaco, and Monte Albán can be used to create a more accurate picture of the turbulent social, political, and economic conditions that were occurring in and around our earliest cities. Scholars have long recognized that the data do not jibe with the sudden arrival of a "civilization," but we still hesitate to accept the implications of our own research. Too often, we allow fully formed cities, states, colonies, and cultural horizons to pop out of civilization's head.

ACKNOWLEDGMENTS

AS WITH MOST BOOKS, THERE ARE MANY PEOPLE WHO PLAYED pivotal roles in this one's writing. Let me begin by thanking Jonathan Tam, who raised his hand in class when I asked who might be willing to illustrate a golem for an archaeology manuscript I was working on. (I actually said "Gollum," confusing my monsters at this early stage in the writing.) Jonathan would go on to work with me to create other illustrations for the book. His golem crashes through an office in chapter 1, but you will also find his work in the header illustrations that begin each chapter. His illustrations proved evocative for me, and I hope that they prove useful to readers.

Jennifer Birch, Paul Duffy, Tim Earle, and Craig Fredrickson were kind enough to read early versions of a chapter or two of the manuscript. The book benefited enormously from their thoughts. Others provided encouragement and insights in casual conversations. Kevin Vaughn, for example, shared his thoughts over a long car drive, Heather Miller did so on the way to a bar, and Sally Lynch, Edward Swenson, and Andrew Roddick did so in a different bar. Editors John Byram, Alyson Carter, and Anastasia Graff provided insightful feedback, as did several anonymous reviewers. Michael E. Smith and Mark Allen's reviews of the last version of this manuscript proved particularly useful in shaping the final outcome. MJ Devaney's careful copyediting helped to smooth the rough edges of my argument. The book is a reflection of these and other colleagues' considerable generosity and intelligence, and I hope that they will forgive any of my missteps or errors.

Whatever insights this book may have, it is because of the work of some of archaeology's giants. This book draws on an incredibly rich array of global scholarship on early urbanism and, in particular, would not have been possible without the multiyear excavation projects at Çatalhöyük, Cahokia, Harappa, Jenne-jeno, Tiahuanaco, and Monte Albán. Urban sites are incredibly difficult to dig and understand, and I hope that I have done the data from these projects justice, even as I occasionally differ from the excavators in my interpretations.

Finally, I would like to thank my family members for their help. My wife, Adrienne Rand, and my mother, Kay Jennings, read every page of the earliest version of this book. Their comments were often grudgingly accepted, but the changes that they invoked made my argument crisper and more intelligible. My father, Dick Jennings, read an early draft of the first chapter and provided insightful comments that clarified my thinking on critical issues. My daughters, Isla and Poppy, are still too little to read, but they played their own vital role in keeping me afloat during the long months of writing. This book is dedicated to my parents. Their love and support began before I can remember and continue to this day. It is only now as a father that I fully realize the many gifts that they have given to me over all these years. A book dedication is not much of a thank-you, but perhaps it is a start. Thanks, Mom and Dad!

CIVILIS

1

CIVILIZATION, OR MORGAN'S GOLEM

LEWIS HENRY MORGAN SPENT THREE YEARS WRITING A BOOK that nearly killed him. Curled over his desk hour after hour in the mid-1870s, he obsessively marshaled data from his ethnographic observations, voluminous library, and wide-ranging correspondences, using this data to create a model of cultural evolution in which humans were propelled forward from the lowest stages of savagery to civilization. When *Ancient Society* was finally finished in 1877, Morgan wrote to his publisher that he was in a "state of usedupness" (quoted in Resek 1960:146). His handwriting was now so shaky that it alarmed many of his correspondents, and he was often grumpy, upset, and depressed at home (Resek 1960:146). The energies that Morgan had invested into the book would be rewarded with critical acclaim—its publication led in large part to his election as president of the American Association for the Advancement of Science in 1879. His health, however, never recovered from the three years of intense scholarship. By the fall of 1881, Morgan had become too feeble to write, and he died in December, a month after his sixty-third birthday (Moses 2009:264–265).

The stages of cultural evolution that Morgan developed were heuristic signposts in a "gradual" and "protracted struggle" (1963:3 [1877]). This gradual process, however, was pitched as a series of buildups in pressure within stages that slowly strained a community's social fabric until a rupture occurred. These all-encompassing ruptures catapulted humanity from one stage to the next in an upward trajectory that began in the lowest depths of savagery and ended at the heights of civilization. Each stage was thus a well-defined, distinct plateau—a tread on the staircase of cultural evolution—that was punctuated after years of stability by a riser of sudden transformative change (fig. 1.1). Humanity's gradual struggle, by the end of the book, would be likened to geologic strata, each lasting "many thousands of years" (1963:506–507 [1877]).

I sometimes imagine Morgan in his study literally pouring his life-force into an evolutionary theory that he hoped would long outlast him. His hopes were seemingly in vain. Few people today talk about the "savages" and "barbarians" that populated *Ancient Society*, and ever since the 1890s, critics have rightfully critiqued the models offered by Morgan and his contemporary evolutionists as too rigid, too comparative, too dismissive of other mechanisms of culture change, and too wedded to the idea of progress (Sanderson 2007:35). Little more than a century later, Morgan's crowning achievement is most often cited only as a deeply flawed idea of human progress—referenced in passing by contemporary writers as a broken, harmless relic of a bygone era.

The accounts of *Ancient Society*'s demise, however, have been greatly exaggerated (e.g., Yoffee 2005). Although few people today would agree with Lewis Henry Morgan's assertion that all of humanity progressed

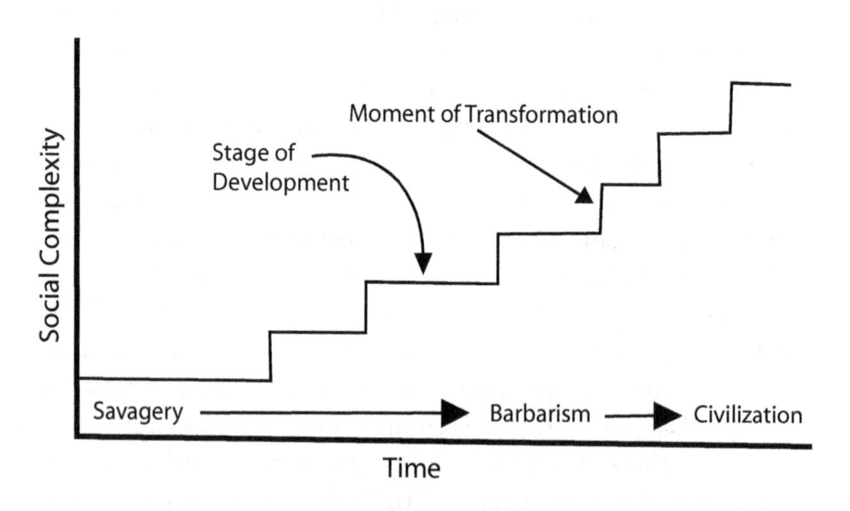

Figure 1.1. The staircase of classic cultural evolution (Justin Jennings).

through the same set of narrowly defined evolutionary stages, his conceptualization of civilization remains in widespread use. For example, the online *American Heritage Dictionary* that I use echoes Morgan and other late nineteenth-century thinkers in describing civilization as "an advanced state of intellectual, cultural, and material development in human society, marked by progress in the arts and sciences, the extensive use of record keeping, including writing, and the appearance of complex political and social institutions." The term remains in widespread use in academia—one department at the university where I teach has "civilizations" in its name, and our library contains 494 books published in the last two years alone with "civilization" in the title—and it is employed, in broad stroke, in the same ways that it was almost 150 years ago.

The continued influence of the civilization stage comes at a time when the other treads and risers in the staircase of classic cultural evolution have come increasingly under fire (e.g., Birch 2013; Yoffee 2005; Pauketat 2007). Recent research, for instance, has demonstrated a long and "bumpy ride to village life" (Belfer-Cohen and Bar-Yosef 2000:19), and those who argue for sudden, sweeping societal changes after the introductions of agriculture and settled life do so now in contravention of widely available data and current interpretations. Instead of a staircase, we now therefore recognize that there are many windy paths to greater social complexity (e.g., Price and Feinman 2012; Vaughn et al. 2010).

The civilization stage, however, still remains. By this, I do *not* mean to suggest that we remain mired in a narrow nineteenth-century construct of what constituted a civilization—one of the great achievements of the last half century has been the recognition of "considerable variation" in the organization of early states and regional polities (Smith 2004:73). I am arguing only that we continue to think of civilization as arriving at a pivotal moment in a region's history, a moment when a sudden step is taken toward a greater level of social complexity. This temporal conceit lingers because it seems to be well supported—after all, accumulating data are confirming that many of civilization's traits *did* indeed appear for the first time together during eras of rapid cultural change. The concept therefore helps underscore some of the possible links between processes such as urbanization, state formation, class stratification, craft specialization, colonization, and the creation of broad cultural horizons while also emphasizing that these processes often emerged around the same time and in the same place.

With our data seemingly meshing with our long-held assumptions about the rise of civilization, it should come as no surprise that scholars today have become comfortable talking about the emergence of the world's first cities, rulers, and peasants as something akin to a unified step, leap, or sea change even as they argue against such a punctuated transition in the creation of less complex societies. No one actually believes that the first cities and states magically appeared fully formed on the landscape, but there remains a curious tendency to treat their creation as something akin to a phase change—an "implosion," as Lewis Mumford notes in a seminal urban history volume, caused by the "very pressure" of so many people packed together into a limited space (1961:34). Scholars might not use the term "civilization" when they talk about the rise of more complex societies in their writings, but they often tacitly accept the idea of a coevolving moment within which all of the processes associated with civilization came into being near the beginning of a new stage of development (fig. 1.2).

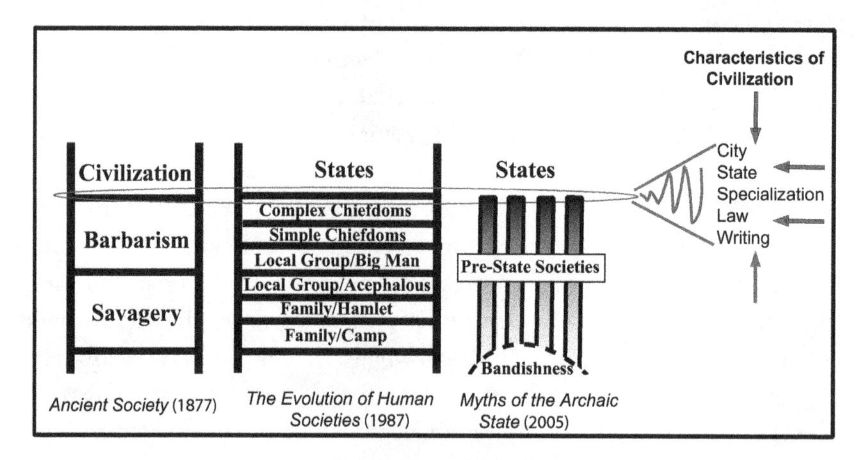

Figure 1.2. Though the terms have changed over time, the idea remains of a civilization threshold that is reached when a community acquires certain characteristics. These characteristics vary in the models developed in these three books, but each author argues that these characteristics emerge together when a certain threshold is reached (Justin Jennings).

The steplike transition to civilization that began as an undesired byproduct of classic cultural evolutionists' insistence on creating clearly defined societal types—the treadlike stages in their sequences had necessitated riserlike moments of punctuated change—has thus become an integral, if often unstated, part of a civilization concept that still structures our interpretations of the emergence of more complex societies. The mythical creation of civilization in a single steplike transition is reified in our maps and bracketed within our chronologies when we color in vast areas as Olmec, Tiwanaku, or Uruk at the outset of a new period (fig. 1.3). A society, all too often, is labeled a "chiefdom" or as "middle-range" in one period, and by the next it has suddenly become a "civilization" or, if you prefer, a "state-level" or "urban" society. Instead of looking at generations of people struggling to navigate wholly new ways of life, we instantaneously create *Homo civilis.*

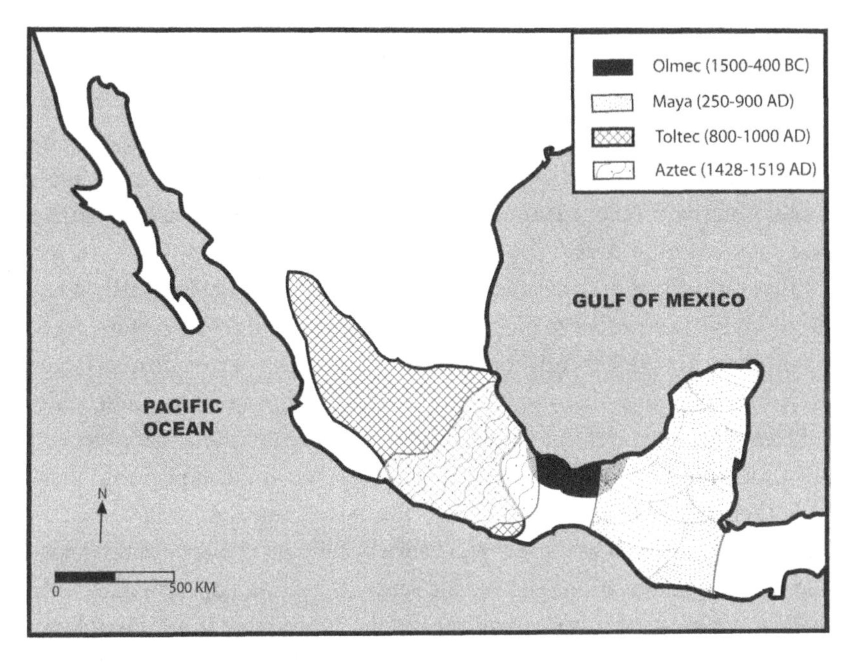

Figure 1.3. A map of Mesoamerican "empires," as defined by the *Oxford Companion to Archaeology* (1996:799). The Olmecs, the first society commonly called a civilization in Mesoamerica, is included in this map. The overlaid culture areas not only equate four very different types of societies but also bracket these societies in time and space (Justin Jennings).

Everyone knows that this is a simplification of what happened in the past, but collapsing a multitude of tangled, rapidly occurring processes into a single step to civilization is nonetheless seductive because it is often hard for scholars to detail the first decades of early cities, states, colonies, and cultural horizons. What after all is actually lost by using the civilization concept and its steplike transition to understand the emergence of more complex societies? If it is only the messiness of reality, then perhaps one might argue that we are missing little of import. Models, after all, are supposed to simplify in order to promote better understanding. Yet I argue in this book that there are at least two fundamental problems with the structure imposed on the past by the civilization concept.

The first problem is that the idea of a steplike transition to civilization leads to models that are inherently overly mechanistic and atemporal—a religion perhaps is introduced, an art style reinforces that religion, and a sacred ruler takes the throne in a tidy hypothetical scenario that is often filled with vectors, structures, agents, and feedback loops. Rapid change is not the same as instantaneous change, and by too often equating the two types of changes in our models we have had a tendency to fuse together an array of conflicting, and at times even unrelated, processes into a single transformative moment at the beginning of a societal stage (e.g., Drennan and Peterson 2006, 2012).

The second, and perhaps more important problem, is that our adherence to the civilization concept inclines us to assume both that a certain set of traits emerged together fully formed at the beginning of a civilization stage of development and that the structural relationships between these traits held steady throughout this stage. If craft specialization and writing were on our trait list for civilization, for example, then we would expect that these and other traits on our list came into being at the same time. Following this logic, we would then assume that a cadre of bureaucrats always ran a city and that colonial relations were stable across centuries. Few would actually make these kinds of extreme arguments, but I argue that thinking of more complex societies as stable plateaus in societal development nonetheless leads us to deemphasize the cultural changes that occur within the stages that we have manufactured.

Thinking in stages is particularly deleterious when evaluating shorter periods of widespread change. Focusing on the challenges and opportunities faced by those struggling for decades to turn a settlement into a city and a region into a countryside, this book argues that our often-unconscious adherence to a staged model of civilization has fundamentally distorted our understanding of the emergence of more complex societies. According to my alternative model, much of what has been previously lumped together in civilization's steplike rise is better seen as the often-unintended by-products of rapid settlement aggregation. The world's first cities took centuries to form, a process that left its mark across broad regions. By acknowledging the multigenerational struggle to create an urban way of life, I argue that we can gain a better understanding of how colonies, cultural horizons, and states were all possible, but far from assured, outcomes of the decisions made within settlements that quickly grew far too big to sustain their populations with locally available resources.

Tearing Apart Civilization

How can we rid ourselves of a civilization concept that skews our vision of the past? The concept cannot be destroyed by fleeing from the word or by retreating to a narrow historical particularism where every society is unique. Offering new typologies of civilization is only a minor improvement since it still leads to the construction of parallel periods of relative stasis produced via parallel moments of seismic change—the exclusionary and inclusionary states of dual-processual theory, for example, remain stages of development (Blanton et al. 1996). To kill civilization, we need to first tear the concept apart and then reevaluate the relationships between the traits that have long been associated with the term. This book looks at the relationships between a few of these traits—the city, colony, state, and cultural horizon. These words have been so tightly linked together within the civilization concept that it is often hard to think of one term independent of the others.

In order to demonstrate how we might move beyond the civilization concept and its steplike transition, I need to be clear in how I define these words in this book. Let us begin by returning to a discussion of the definition of the concept that we are seeking to eliminate. The word "civilization," derived from the Latin word "civilis" and related to the terms for citizen, city, and city-state, was first used during the Enlightenment (AD 1650–1800).

Civilization was a state of being thought to have been brought about by people living together in cities and was juxtaposed by the philosopher Montesquieu to the categories of both savages (those living in a state of nature) and barbarians (those who have entered into some kind of society) (1951 [1748]). Enlightenment thinkers thought that civilization was the highest form of social life, and scholars during the period strove to uncover the processes that moved humanity from one state of development to another.

Lewis Henry Morgan was among the group of early anthropologists who built on these Enlightenment beginnings to offer evolutionary models that identified specific characteristics of different stages of development and investigated how improvements in such areas as technology, religion, and subsistence regimes propelled a society from one stage to the next. The existence of cities and states were almost always among the most important of criteria that these scholars used to identify civilization, and colonies and long-distance trade would later be seen to be among the most critical of the mechanisms through which civilization spread.

Definitions of civilizations that have been offered over the last century have tended to follow in broad stroke those that were given by Morgan and his colleagues during the second half of the nineteenth century. They tend to be enumerative, defining civilization as a type of society that contains A, B, C, and D. Cities and states are almost always the anchors of these lists and thus the critical indicators that a group had reached the civilization stage of development. Although they waffle a bit on naming specific traits, the editors of the *American Heritage Dictionary* that I cited earlier follow this enumerative tradition by suggesting that civilization is an "advanced stage of development" marked by achievements in the arts, sciences, record keeping, and politics. The dictionary's editors are likely aware of the wide-ranging debates regarding both what characteristics should be on the list that is used to identify a civilization—writing, high art, or a monopoly on force, for example—and regarding what evidence is required to demonstrate each of these traits.

I refer back to these trait lists, but in this book, I follow Bruce Trigger's more functional definition. In *Understanding Early Civilizations*, Trigger attempts to show how the traits commonly associated with civilization "were required for societies of this degree to function" (2003:44), and then he succinctly suggests that the first civilizations were "the earliest and simplest form of class-based societies" (2003:46). He argues that the critical aspects of civilization were those that created and reinforced class ties, and he shows how the specific organization of these ties changed depending on historical, social, and environmental conditions. Jettisoning the idea of progress through time in his definition—there was no "advanced stage of development"—he nonetheless still both offers up civilization as a stage and uses cities and states as the primary markers of this stage (2003, 2008). The following chapter traces the development of the civilization concept over time in greater detail.

The close association of cities and states with civilization since the inception of the term means that determining when a population center becomes a "city" and a society a "state" has long been tantamount to determining whether or not a group can qualify as a "civilization." One of the best definitions of a city is Louis Wirth's: cities are permanent settlements that have a large population size, a dense population nucleation, and a high heterogeneity in the social roles of inhabitants (1938:8). Cities in this definition are defined relative to other settlements within a particular cultural context (1938:3–8). This definition can be improved on by adding the functional element Michael E. Smith provides when he asserts that cities are "centers whose activities and institutions—whether economic, administrative, or religious—affect a larger hinterland" (2007:4). Combining Wirth's and Smith's descriptions provides us with a working definition for the kinds of settlements that have often been used as markers for the arrival of civilization.

Definition for cities and states tend to significantly overlap since cities are often taken as indicators of states (finding a city, then, would be evidence for both the existence of a state and a civilization). A good definition of the state and the one that I use in this book comes from combining that offered by Joyce Marcus and Gary Feinman (1998b:4) with that given by Allen Johnson and Timothy Earle (1987:246). These scholars see states as regionally organized societies with a professional ruling class, commoner class, and a highly centralized and internally specialized government. The institutions that run the city are regarded by these scholars as closely related to those that run the state, and, in this definition, a state has a significant degree of control over a surrounding region just as a city is seen to "affect a larger hinterland" (Smith 2007:4). A state is only one solution to the problem of how to organize a region. I use the term "regional polity" as a broader term that encompasses not only states but also less hierarchical, more decentralized means of governance.

Though cities and states have long been subsumed under the term, "civilization" is also commonly used to refer to sets of relationships that extend far beyond the boundaries of these particular entities. The "cultural seepage," to use Lewis Mumford's evocative phrase (1961:101), of people, objects, and, most importantly, ideas from cities can create ties between groups living hundreds of kilometers away from each other. On occasion, the interaction network created by these flows become dense enough that a cultural horizon—albeit a fractured, hybrid, and often contentious one—emerges within it, a new landscape where people negotiate shared conceptions of how to live and view their world (Jennings 2011:28). These cultural horizons extend far beyond the boundaries of the linguistic, political, economic, and/or social groups that first trigger them. Though these groups produce many of a horizon's innovative ideas in urban environments (and the regional polities that often formed around them), they thus often have very limited control over these ideas as they spread across far-reaching interaction networks.

Civilizations are also often seen as being spread at least in part as the result of state efforts to influence long-distance interaction through the establishment of colonies (Algaze 1993a; Gosden 2004:3; Stein 2005:13). Following Gill Stein, colonies can be defined as permanent settlements that are founded in foreign lands by individuals who identify with their homeland and distinguish themselves from surrounding communities (Stein 2002:30). Although the terms "colonization" and "colonialism" are sometimes used to describe political domination of a territory (Deitler 2005:54), in this book the terms are used only to refer to the act of founding and maintaining colonies.

These sites can be settled for a wide variety of reasons, and colonists can have very different kinds of relationships with local groups (Stein 1999). Getting to a far-off location was often far easier than maintaining close connections with one's homeland once there. Early colonies were sometimes able to impose their will on local groups, but in most cases colonists struggled to maintain only the most tenuous of footholds in far-off regions (e.g., Deitler 2010). These footholds would have been particularly shaky, if, as I argue in this book, a city's first colonies were founded before states and other kinds of regional polities were well entrenched.

The definitions of states, cities, cultural horizons, and colonies that are described here represent the end result of social, economic, and political processes that bring people together into new kind of societies. This may sound obvious, but thinking in terms of processes unfolding over time is an essential step toward creating an alternative to civilization. In this book, urbanization is defined as a group of processes that draw large groups of people into new kinds of relationships out of which emerge the roles, responsibilities, and institutions that create a city and countryside. Though urbanization is never fully completed (a city will continue to change throughout its occupations), settlements that match the city definition provided by Wirth and Smith will often emerge after only several generations of change. The same social, economic, and political processes that create the city can also lead to the formation of states or other kinds of regional polities. Colonization is another group of related processes that often, but not necessarily, occurs during periods of urbanization and polity formation. The founding of colonies is often part of a broader suite of interregional interactions that can sometimes lead to the creation of a cultural horizon.

The Civilization Golem

Most readers of this book are likely already uneasy with the civilization concept. Much of this unease comes from the word's ugly and divisive history. The term has been tainted by the atrocities of the "civilizing" missions of European (and later American) colonialism, and so even those who might want to argue that human history is composed of stages of cultural evolution would likely prefer to avoid the word. Yet I would argue that we are also discomfited by the fundamentalist interpretation of stable stages bookended by transformative moments of cultural change. We recognize, as scholars did in the past, that there was never really a staircase (or even staircases) of cultural evolution but rather incremental, and even sometimes stochastic, cultural change over time (e.g., Friedman 1982; Upham 1990).

Thinking in stages nonetheless helps to make sense of the past, and so there has been a consistent trend over the years of sharply dividing more complex societies from the varying degrees of less complex ones.

We thus recognize that change is ongoing, and yet we often study this change as a series of before and after pictures, reifying, albeit often subconsciously, the hard borders of the various societal stages that we have inherited (Peregrine 2012:167). This is particularly true in the case of civilizations where, in a couple hundred years, a region of isolated villages is integrated into a broadly influential state anchored by a capital city. These swift transformations are hard to *see*—writing or other recording systems were only beginning to emerge in these places, and radiocarbon dates and ceramic seriations at their best tend to deliver history in century-long increments. Time thus comes back us in great chunks during these early eras of rapid change, and this chunkiness reinforces thinking in terms of stages, as we often uncritically toggle back and forth between a precivilization and civilization period.

This critique about civilization is *not* a new one. The limitations of thinking about human history in stages have been recognized by at least seven generations of scholars who have alternately attempted to reform, limit, ignore, and sometimes destroy the civilization concept that was reluctantly offered by Lewis Henry Morgan and his contemporaries. Diffusionists and historical particularists began an assault on the idea at the turn of the twentieth century (e.g., Boas 1989; Ratzel 1898), and just since the 1960s civilization has been submerged beneath the debates on the origins of the state (e.g., Haas 1982), decentered through culture contact studies (e.g., Cusik 1998), sliced up into different kinds of complex societies (e.g., Feinman 2008, 2012), punctured by the insertion of "gender, class, and faction" into its operational mechanisms (e.g., Brumfiel 1992), and had its roots shattered through attacks on the idea of chiefdoms (e.g., Yoffee 1993). On top of all of this, the Darwinian evolutionists have been doing their best to rip apart classical cultural evolution for 40 years (e.g., Dunnell 1970; Mesoudi and O'Brien 2009).

With all of this effort, one might expect that the civilization concept would be dead and forgotten by now. But, on the contrary, these assaults only seem to lead to the creation of more civilizations, the identification of more ways to become a civilization, and the uncovering of more of the complex inner workings of civilizations. Though these critiques have modified the concept, every blow seems to only entrench the idea of civilization deeper into our understanding of the past. With the concept's resilience in mind, I am tempted to label the civilization concept a factoid—"a speculation or guess that has been repeated so often it is eventually taken for hard fact" (Yoffee 2005:7). Civilization, however, is no mere factoid. We *know* that the civilization concept is deeply flawed, and yet we continue to rely on it despite our better judgment.

I suggest that civilization's resiliency is linked in large part to the acceptance of its steplike rise. Few would argue that cities, regional polities, colonies, and cultural horizons emerged in lockstep in an instantaneous phase change. Yet I would argue that the idea of a step-like transformation to civilization nonetheless continues to shape our thinking when we suggest that ancient cities go "hand-in-hand" with ancient states (Manzanilla 1997:5) or that civilization is "inextricably intertwined" with state formation (Yoffee 2005:17). Step-like thinking also lies underneath those books that compare ancient fourth-millennium Mesopotamian cities to modern early nineteenth-century sub-Saharan African cities (e.g., Marcus and Sabloff 2008) or that relate the states of Bronze Age Crete to those of Pharaonic Egypt and Classic-period Mexico (e.g., Feinman and Marcus 1998). If we think in stages, then the foggy beginnings of one civilization can be filled in by what we know of the Roman Empire. After all, they all are "civilizations" that share the same stage of cultural development.

The concept seems to lumber ever forward whether we like it or not, and, after more than a century of critiques, it seems that many of us have grown frustrated and tired of the fight. We are now apt to avoid the term "civilization," leave it undefined in our writing, or hide the concept behind the edifice of the "state" or "complex society." Ignoring civilization, however, does not mean that the concept has gone away. On the contrary, the basic premise of civilization continues to shape our understanding of the past, and I would argue that our conviction in a steplike transition to civilization is more deeply held than ever before. Even the term itself is in the midst of an alarming 30-year resurgence.

Civilization's resurgence can be linked in large part to the introduction of world-systems approaches into the study of the ancient world during the 1980s (to be discussed in more detail in chapter 2). These approaches stimulated scholars to explore in greater detail the formation, maintenance, and decline of often-neglected interaction spheres that extended beyond political, economic, and geographic boundaries. These scholars and their critics needed a word for this higher order of interaction. I offer "cultural horizon" for these large-scale interaction networks in this book, since this term has long been used by archaeologists, but some scholars have begun using "civilization" for these networks without first untangling the term from its additional associations with cities, states, and the other traits that have been traditionally assigned to it (e.g., Kohl 2007; Sanderson 1995; Wallerstein 1990).

Civilization's revival via the world-systems approach is disturbing enough, but I am even more concerned about the new support for the concept's steplike transition that has come from two unlikely sources (see chapter 2). In 1972, Niles Eldridge and Stephen Jay Gould published an influential paper on punctuated evolutionary change. Although they applied their theory to the fossil record, other scholars have since used the theory to argue that civilizations arise "in a transformational or punctuational—not gradual—fashion" (Spencer 1990:11). The second source of support for civilization's steplike transition is the theories of complex adaptive systems. Pioneered by physicists and mathematicians in the mid-twentieth century, these theories have been used to study how complex organizations in the ancient world, such as states, suddenly emerged from simpler systems (Lansing 2003). The transition to civilization in these theories is often compared to the shift in thermodynamics from one state of matter to another.

In his best seller of the same name, Malcolm Gladwell defines a tipping point as "the moment of critical mass, the threshold, the boiling point" (2000:10). Buoyed by work on punctuated evolutionary change and the self-organization of complex systems, archaeologists, historians, and other scholars seem increasingly willing to regard the rise of civilization as a tipping point in world history—the moment, as described by Norman Yoffee, when cities "crystallized" in a phase change (2005:230). When Yoffee, one of the most vociferous critics of cultural evolutionary models, equates social change to a chemical reaction, you know that the belief in a phase transition to civilization has become an almost unquestioned assumption.

Cities, states, colonies, and global cultures often emerged very rapidly, but couching this shift in terms of a tipping point tends to absolve us from the duty of studying the details *within* these periods of transition. We are content instead to look at what happened before and after the tipping point and thus allow the myriad of processes subsumed within the civilization concept to remain bound together in a neat and tidy transition from one stage to the next. No one really thinks, of course, that villages literally boiled over to become cities or that a state crystallized from a chief's house, and there is no reason to think that all of this was happening at the exact same time. Yet we cannot seem to shake our reliance on a steplike transition to civilization. Our vision appears destined to be skewed forever by the concept's ever-onward march through our imaginings of times past.

Based on our long-standing, if often reluctant, embrace of the concept, civilization might therefore seem more akin to an addictive drug that we cannot quite shake—Morgan's morphine?—or perhaps to a mildly debilitating disease that we have learned to ignore. I prefer, though, to think that the years that Lewis Henry Morgan spent alone in his library yielded a monster alongside his masterpiece: a civilization golem formed from a congealed mass of nineteenth-century thought that still lives in the recesses of our minds long after the death of its original master. Thinking of civilization as a golem is admittedly over the top, but doing so makes me more motivated to get rid of it.

Figure 1.4. The civilization golem ruins another day at the office (Jonathan Tam).

Whatever metaphor might be used for civilization, the point is that we need to acknowledge that the concept still continues to shape our understanding of how such entities as cities, states, craft specialists, and rulers first arose. Whether in the field, office, or classroom, we are dogged by a concept that will not go away (fig. 1.4). Yet simply attacking the civilization concept once again is of little use without also offering alternative explanations to explain the rise of some of the world's more complex societies. My alternative presents a cascade of processes that were triggered by the challenges and opportunities faced by those living through the earliest urbanizations. There is nothing earth shattering presented in this alternative explanation—data supporting my claims are found throughout the literature on early cities and states—but I suggest that the full implications of these data have often been ignored because of our unconscious insistence on a civilization stage of development.

An Alternative to Civilization

My alternative to the civilization concept posits that people commonly reacted to the process of early urbanization by forming regional polities, colonizing, and spreading cultural horizons (fig. 1.5). This model, summarized below, hinges on the recognition of the problems that are created by having too many people living in one place. Solving these problems takes time, and founding colonies, creating extensive networks, and regularizing connections with neighboring communities were all means through which urbanites sought to sustain their growing settlements. The bulk of this book discusses in detail this alternative model with the help of six case studies taken from around the world.

In a recent essay comparing the societal trajectories of a dozen regions, Christian Peterson and Robert Drennan argue that the "path towards large-scale social formations" often begins with a population surge (2012:88, 116–121). Why people came together is often unclear and likely varied from one region to the next. In some cases, people coalesced to protect themselves from increasing violence. In other cases, they came together largely because of the attraction of a sacred place or scarce resource. More often than not, these population concentrations were short-lived since the most common reaction to an increase in the size and density of settlements in a location is fission—as tensions rose, people left, sometimes quite literally, for greener pastures (Bandy 2004; Fletcher 1995).

Long-term aggregation made little sense in societies composed of self-sufficient producers used to living in small communities. Among other consequences, such coming together led to an increase in infectious disease rates, exacerbated social conflicts, curtailed individual freedoms, and strained local subsistence resources (Bandy 2010). Despite these negatives, people in the past occasionally decided to stay together and work through the difficulties of living together in a large group. Cultural evolutionary models tend to offer up charismatic, if ruthless, rulers or a collection of elites who imposed their will on these nucleated groups through a combination of force, subterfuge, and gifts. The reality in the first decades of these settlements, however, was more complicated, as "multiple and potentially conflicting rationalities of individuals and groups" intersected "in complex ways" (Blanton and Fargher 2008:14). Since no one had done this before, everyone was clumsily feeling their way.

In rare cases, people continued to stream into a settlement, and the population could climb in little more than a century from the hundreds into the tens of thousands (Cowgill 2004:534). The social mechanisms required to coordinate this crush of inhabitants needed to be assembled on the fly, and the process was likely just as ad hoc and chaotic as that seen in the early growth of most cities today (Cowgill 2003:48; Shen 2003:304–305).

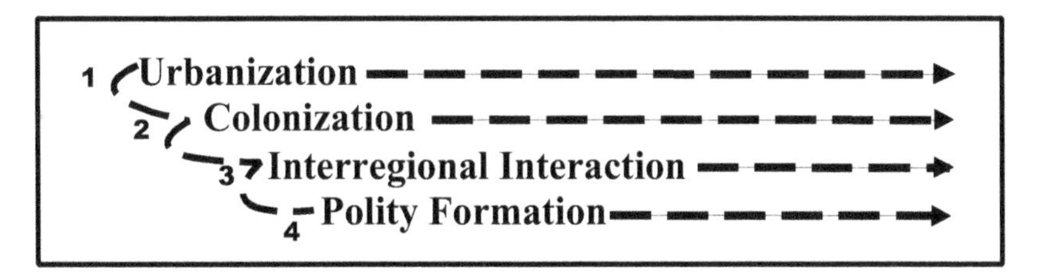

Figure 1.5. A model for the cascading impacts of early urbanization. As a city begins to form, colonization often occurs as long-distance interaction increases, and this increasing interaction sometimes leads to the creation of a cultural horizon. State formation is a common reaction to the instability of the wider interaction networks created by urbanization (Justin Jennings).

Residents came into these urbanizing centers with the skills and traditions of villagers. They were farmers and herders who were used to having considerable autonomy, interacting with other people in person, working through kin connections, and making most everything that they needed. From this stock of people would need to come the priests, bureaucrats, shopkeepers, and craft specialists whom one often associates with city life (Cooper 2006; Creekmore 2014; Smith 2003; Ur 2014). This transition could happen in as little as a couple of generations, but it was often a difficult transition for those living through it (Pauketat 2007:163).

Our understanding of the chaotic first decades of these cities is necessarily hazy. We often have trouble breaking up time even into century-sized blocks, and the scant remains of these initial years are often buried under meters of detritus from subsequent occupations. We could look to a city's later periods for insights, but our best window into what life was really like during these early years might not be what these settlements were like after an urban society had fully formed within them a couple hundred years later. Our best sense of these transformative periods might instead come from more recent examples of urbanization. We have eyewitness accounts from these settlements, making it possible for us to track on a year-by-year basis the emergence of a city from a village or small town (e.g., Gugler 1997). Ancient urbanization unfolded differently, of course, without cars, concrete, computers, and capitalism, but these recent case studies can nonetheless make clear many of the immense challenges that large groups face when they come together.

Creating a countryside was one of the biggest challenges that those living in urbanizing centers faced. Since cities tend to be too big for residents to provide for themselves (Johnson and Earle 1987:247; Schwartz and Falconer 1994:3), a breadbasket region dedicated to producing the food needed to feed cities was required. The surrounding villages that might produce a surplus, however, were often depopulated as a result of residents moving to growing cities, and the farmers and herders that remained at these sites initially had few incentives to intensify production in order to feed those living elsewhere. Small-scale producers, after all, are notoriously hesitant to adapt new technologies and practices if they seem too risky (Isik and Khana 2003; Kuznar 2001; Netting 1993; Nmandu et al. 2012), and so villagers needed to be convinced or coerced to shorten their fallow periods, drain swamps, and clear-cut forests in order to intensify production so that other people could live together in a city. New roads, irrigation canals, storehouses, and corrals were also required, and a bureaucratic structure and accounting system had to be put in place to track the flow of goods (e.g., Bandy 2005; Hastorf 1993; Zeder 1991).

If a ruling class developed through this process of regional integration, then the creation of a countryside would have been tantamount to the formation of a state. Other ways of organizing the countryside, however, were also possible and could lead to the construction of other kinds of regional sociopolitical organizations that were less hierarchical (Feinman 1998:102). My critical point is that the creation of a well-functioning city and countryside, no matter how it was orchestrated, took *time*. Maintaining order in the first decades of urbanization would have been difficult enough inside these cities, as everyone adjusted to a radically different, and seemingly ever-changing, settlement (Yoffee 2009). While civic leaders struggled to both legitimize their positions and organize city life, they would have been hard pressed to also meet soaring demands for food, drinks, raw materials, and prestige items.

The demands of city residents needed to be met decades before a regional polity could be put into place, and so the initial economic, political, and cultural interaction that occurred between a growing city and its outlying regions would have been on an ad hoc basis that depended in large part on the previous connections of many parties (Adams 2001, 2004; Oka and Kusimba 2008:356–357). A family, for example, might be supplied with meat from an aunt that visited over the summer; an entrepreneur might strike up a partnership to bring copper ore down from the mountains in donkey caravans.

A dense network of interactions that would support a swiftly growing city was therefore needed *before* the state or any other kind of regional polity could be fully formed. Since ad hoc connections often fail and are often in flux—an aunt can get sick and an entrepreneur can have a falling out with his partner—city residents were often scrambling to increase and maintain connections both within the city and with outside groups. People could not sit back and rely on production from the countryside to meet their basic needs, since it too was also only beginning to come into existence. They needed to provide for themselves in the interim both by spending considerable time trading, farming, and herding outside the city and by developing relationships with more and more distant groups. Colonial outposts were one means by which the city's increasing demands could be met.

Colonies are often seen as state projects (Goldstein 2005; Stein 1999). Yet colonization often occurred almost contemporaneously with the beginnings of urbanization in many regions. The first colonies were therefore likely founded just as both the city was beginning to organize and the countryside was still forming. Civic leaders likely advocated for the dispersal of groups into important trading corridors, but the bureaucracy to centrally manage these colonies across distances was still at best nascent. Early colonies instead were likely run through clans or other groups that could lean on preexisting relationships to maintain links between the city and those who were living in a colony. Even with these more familiar connections facilitating interactions, these first colonies often failed or lost touch with their homeland when distance became too difficult a hurdle to routinely overcome (see, e.g., Stein 1999:59).

Colonies, of course, were only a small part of the growing network of interactions that brought goods, people, and ideas into and out of the city. Cities required imports in order to function, and as the population got larger and more specialized, these imports were paid for by both the mass production of items and the creation of unique works of art for export (Stanish 2004). People left the city to work in outlying areas, but more and more people also came into the city to visit in order to ply their wares or to worship at newly built temples (White et al. 2004). Ideas flowed back and forth with these people and objects (Sherratt 2004), and these ideas sometimes ignited discussion across a wide region on the proper ways of doing things like making a pot, burying the dead, or sowing a field.

The interaction networks that urbanization gave rise to were not centrally controlled. Administration over the city was superficial and still widely contested during those first decades of growth, and the flow of most ideas, people, and objects even directly into and out of the city would have been largely unregulated. Controlling these flows farther afield—such as the trading of obsidian or a discussion of a new way of honoring the gods—would have been virtually impossible. Expanding networks created new opportunities for rural groups to exchange people, objects, and ideas among each other as well as with urban populations (Kohl 2007; Sherratt 2004).

These new connections in turn created still more connections in a cascade of interactions that had the potential to link together previously disparate groups into a cultural horizon.

Cities cannot survive for long without regulating and simplifying external interactions (Yoffee 2005:17). With the countryside still taking shape, it was necessary for those living in the cities to found colonies and extend interaction networks farther and farther afield because they could not routinely depend on those living close by to meet their needs. Colonization and the creation of cultural horizons in these contexts is therefore a reflection of the early *weakness* of incipient states and other sociopolitical formations that sought to organize regional affairs (cf. Algaze 1993b). Expanding outward was necessary in the absence of a well-functioning countryside, but as this countryside formed through the development of a state or other regional polity, the need for many of a city's broader, though less stable and intelligible, interactions faded. The creation of a well-functioning regional polity thus often meant declining investment in colonies and the erosion of the cultural horizons that had been initially fueled by escalating interregional interaction.

This novel model for the emergence of the earliest cities, states, colonies, and cultural horizons contains elements that can be found in many recent discussions of the rise of more complex societies (e.g., Algaze 2008; Pauketat 2007; Stein 1999; Yoffee 2005). Although the authors of these accounts are often critical of aspects of cultural evolutionary theory, they do not fully explore the implications of civilization's steplike transition on their thinking. Creating a city from a collection of people is an alternately terrifying, intoxicating, exhausting, and mind-bending experience. It takes time to figure things out, especially when *no one* has done this before. To arrive at a more accurate understanding of the past, we need a deeper appreciation of what generations of people went through as the first cities, regional polities, colonies, and cultural horizons were coming into being.

Living without Civilization

In 1973 Jann-Erik Olsson robbed a bank in central Stockholm and took four people hostage for five days before releasing them unharmed. The hostages later expressed sympathy for their captor, and a local criminologist coined the term "Stockholm syndrome" for what he thought was a more general psychological phenomenon. Sometimes I think that we have a similar kind of unhealthy attachment to the civilization concept. When I first attempted to write this book, I hoped to find a way to try to save the term by rehabilitating it (e.g., Hann 2011). Like others before me, I was painfully aware of the shortcomings of the concept, but for some reason I could not bear to let it go.

Thinking of civilization as a golem is perhaps my way of putting some distance between the concept and me. Others might choose a different metaphor for civilization (or no metaphor at all), but I think that most people would agree with me that the concept is deeply flawed. Yet living without it would not be easy. We are used to the well-worn term, and civilization's fingerprints are all over our chronologies, maps, models, and comparative studies. The disciplinary foundations of archaeology and ancient history are based in no small measure on the concept. Avoiding the use of the term will not change its pervasive influence, nor can we just promise to avoid civilization's pitfalls in future work. We need to expunge the concept.

Living without civilization would require a methodical housecleaning to repair the damage to our conceptualizations of the past. But who wants to do housecleaning? Faced with all of this work, we might be tempted to argue that civilization is not that bad. We might convince ourselves that the term works well enough, that we have dealt with enough of its negative connotations, or that battling against civilization's resurgence really is quite tangential to our own interests. This book was written to convince you otherwise. The next chapter demonstrates how this concept has continually warped our understanding of the past since even before the term was coined during the Enlightenment. I argue that our often-unconscious adherence to civilization and its steplike transition has distorted the true story of the emergence of the world's first cities, regional polities, colonies, and cultural horizons. The bulk of this book then uses case studies from around the world to present an alternative to the construct of the rise of civilization that, though certainly inadequate in many ways, hopefully brings us closer to what happened during the frenetic first decades of societal change that was precipitated by the world's earliest urbanizations.

2

THE GOLEM'S MARCH

WHEN GODZILLA ATTACKED TOKYO, THE MONSTER LEFT A TRAIL of squashed buildings and molten steel that captivated moviegoers. King Kong, the Stay Puft Marshmallow Man, and the 50 Foot Woman caused similar mayhem in the streets. The civilization golem—if you will continue to begrudge me my metaphor—has also blazed a path of destruction, but the damage that has occurred is to our understanding of the past. This damage is unfortunately more difficult to recognize because the civilization concept has so thoroughly burrowed itself into our subconscious. The leap to civilization makes intuitive sense to us, even though we also recognize that the concept does not fit particularly well with our own data on how more complex societies first emerged. So instead of jettisoning the concept, we often downplay divergent data or treat these data as exceptions to the rule. Old habits die hard. We cleave to the civilization concept and its steplike arrival, even while knowing that it does not really work.

This chapter traces the development of the civilization concept and describes how it has distorted our interpretations of the emergence of the world's earliest cities, states, colonies, and cultural horizons. Since archaeology first developed as a discipline in the Western world, this chapter concentrates more on European, and later American, conceptions of civilization. Special attention is paid to the Enlightenment, the period when the term was first used, as well as to the work on civilization by the evolutionary theorists of the nineteenth century. I then go on to consider how aspects of this concept, especially its steplike transition, have continued to distort the ways that we currently think about the past.

CHAPTER 2

Pre-Enlightenment Conceptions of Civilization

In its broadest sense, the civilization concept likely predates the emergence of *Homo sapiens*, since intergroup preference among humans—a bias toward those within one's group and against those outside of one's group (Mahajan et al. 2011:387)—has been prevalent throughout history (Prentice and Miller 1999). The ubiquity and longevity of intergroup preference suggests a deeply rooted, evolutionary origin to this behavior, and recent work among rhesus macaques demonstrates that these kinds of biases are not unique to people (Mahajan et al. 2011:387). The concept of civilization likely maps on to this long-standing predilection toward intergroup preferences, since civilization tends to be an us-versus-them proposition, according to which we are civilized and they are not.

The criteria used to elevate a group above others have varied enormously, but there has been a propensity to link a group's superiority to such attributes as their language, physical makeup, customs, and cuisine (Barth 1969). These and other traits are often used to draw distinctions between the natural and the cultural: those who routinely cook their food or conduct their rituals in a certain way are seen as more cultured, and thus superior, to other groups (Lévi-Strauss 1983). The Nuer of Sudan, for example, position themselves above others based on their mastery of cattle (Evans-Pritchard 1940), while the Yąnomamö rely on details of body decorations to distinguish themselves from both animals and others human groups that are considered closer to a state of nature (Chagnon 2012).

Writing, legal codes, monetary systems, agriculture, organized religion, and urban living are some of the attributes of a society that are commonly held up as cultural achievements and were also often used as wedges to separate the civilized from the uncivilized in the ancient world. One of the most developed concepts of civilization before the Enlightenment arose in China during the first millennium BC. The Chinese distinguished between China, called Hua, and all other groups that collectively lived in other regions called Yi (Pines 2005). The boundaries of China were defined by the existence of a collection of traits, and predominant among these was agriculture and cities. Although a group could theoretically become Chinese if it adopted Hua traits, the distinctions were in practice starkly drawn between superior Chinese and inferior non-Chinese. In *Records of the Grand Historian*, the historian Sima Qian in the first century BC, for example, describes the nomadic Xiongnu (inaccurately) as without writing, rituals, or even respect for their families (Chin 2010).

These Chinese distinctions were echoed in the classical world. The English word "barbarian" is derived from the ancient Greek word "barbarous" for a person that babbles or speaks incoherently. The word was opposed to "politis," a person who lived within a polis or city-state (Hall 1989). By the fourth century BC, "barbarous" was clearly a derogatory term that Greeks used to refer to those they saw as "servile, ugly, effeminate, and always defeated" (Huang 2010:563). Greek superiority was furthermore envisioned as innate to the particular kind of city-state found in Greece, and thus Greek culture and institutions were considered better than those found elsewhere. The Egyptians and Persians might also have cities, but, according to Aristotle, they suffered under the yoke of despotic rulers and therefore lacked the elevated spirit of Greeks (1999:156).

The Romans inherited the word "barbarian" from the Greeks (the Latin term is "barbarus"), and continued to oppose this word to that used for people living in cities (the Latin term is "civitas"). Civitas meant more than just a place of residence. It was a group of citizens that were united under law and charged with a set of sacred rights and duties. One of these duties was to spread the benefits of civitas to other groups (although often without offering the full rights of citizenship) that were classified into "bands of progressively more degenerate character" based on their religion, writing systems, residence patterns, and other characteristics (Mattingly 2010:34). Like the Chinese, Greeks, and many other societies, the Romans created negative stereotypes of barbarian groups that either ignored or downplayed those traits that could be used to argue that these outside groups were in fact civilized (Shaw 2000:374–375).

Although the differences between civilized Romans and barbarian groups were often seen by the former as an inherent superiority ordained by the gods, a group of philosophers called Epicureans argued instead that all societies progressed over time through a uniform set of human achievements (Mazlish 2004:3). These philosophers all agreed that Roman society's laws, city life, agriculture, and writing represented the highest level of progress in the world; they disagreed on the exact steps that elevated humans from the state of nature to the state of civitas. In *Satires* 1.3, Horace, for instance, offers a scenario of progress tinged with violence:

> When [rude] animals, they crawled forth upon the first-formed earth, the mute and dirty herd fought with their nails and fists for their acorn and caves, afterward with clubs, and finally with arms which experience had forged: till they found out words and names, by which they ascertained their language and sensations: thenceforward they began to abstain from war, to fortify towns, and establish laws: that no person should be a thief, a robber, or an adulterer. (1863:153)

Lucretius, in contrast, argues in book 5 of *On the Nature of Things* that the discovery of fire and the creation of the family led to language and the building of houses. The creation of wealth in these houses then precipitated the rise of tyrants and eventually gave birth to the rule of law. Despite their disagreements, all Epicureans believed that they could reconstruct stages in human progress not only by studying their own history but also by observing living populations that still remained in earlier stages of development.

To summarize pre-Enlightenment conceptions, people in the distant past, like today, had a tendency to categorize individuals into different groups and then rank these groups relative to each other using various sets of criteria. Separating out the "civilized" from the "uncivilized" (no matter what specific terms might be used) has thus long been a common means of ranking groups, and typically the group doing the ranking used characteristics from their own societies to create the measuring stick. For those living in urban settings, civilization was thus often equated with city life. The origin of civilization for these urbanites was generally equated with mythical events that occurred at the creation of the world or a new age (Trigger 1989:27). The Epicureans, in contrast, were one of the few groups of early thinkers that offered ideas, albeit coarsely drawn, for how humanity may have moved from hunter-gatherer to urban lifestyles. Enlightenment scholars would develop these ideas further.

Enlightenment Conceptions of Civilization

The Epicurean debates on the mechanisms that propelled societies through progressive stages of development did not survive the fall of Rome. Christian polemicists maligned the Epicureans as seekers of transient pleasures, and for the next thousand years the idea of human progress was replaced in the Western world by strict biblical interpretations that posited that humanity had fallen from a state of grace. This idea and other religious orthodoxies were destabilized during the Protestant Reformation of the sixteenth century, when many people began to question the church's broader role in society. Among these reformers was a group of thinkers who formed an intellectual movement in Western Europe that brought back the idea of human history as the gradual triumph of reason. This movement became known as the Enlightenment (Jacobs 2000).

Enlightenment thinkers believed in God but felt, as John Locke argued, that the mind started as a "white paper, void of all characters, without any idea," that was filled across generations by experiences that created the "vast store which the busy and boundless fancy of man has painted on it" (1956:1:122 [1690]). They felt that the ways in which the mind developed over time followed divinely ordained natural laws (e.g., Montesquieu 1951:1:1 [1748]) and that it was their job to uncover these laws. With these laws in hand, they would be able to both reconstruct the past and predict the future (or at least what should happen in the future if reason finally prevailed).

Enlightenment thinkers such as Kant, Locke, and Smith constructed their arguments using what they perceived as common sense and suggested that the first step in uncovering divine laws was to identify the stages of development as humans progressed further and further from a state of ignorance. Most believed that those living in Western Europe had moved through these stages the most rapidly and that therefore their lives represented the pinnacle of human progress. Since these philosophers tended to live in growing cities with a surging middle class, wide-ranging mercantile connections, and broad support for the arts, they often suggested that reason could triumph if the transition to a more urban society was completed in Europe. This same yardstick for relative progress was used even by social critics—such as by Voltaire (1759) in his assertion of Chinese superiority—to demonstrate how the West was lagging behind other urbanized regions.

With the top of the progression typically defined by their own kinds of societies, Enlightenment thinkers sought to identify previous stages of development elsewhere. Other living groups were often used to identify these stages because it was thought that these groups had progressed more slowly because of geographic isolation, temperament, religion, aptitude, or other factors. The marquis de Condorcet (1933 [1795]), for example, divided history into nine epochs that begins with a first epoch of "men united in hordes" and ends with a predicted tenth epoch of individual freedoms, moderation, lawfulness, and compassion. Jacques Turgot (1973 [1750]), meanwhile, used living groups to help identify the successive stages of hunting, pastoralism, and farming that preceded eighteenth-century Europe. These writers then distilled the natural laws that allowed for the creation of legal codes, commerce, monetary systems, and other markers that they used to define the development of more advanced societies.

Progress, for most of these philosophers, was lineal—as humans gained experience they gained intelligence and left behind an original condition that Thomas Hobbes famously described as "solitary, poor, nasty, brutish, and short" (2010:212 [1651]). Jean-Jacques Rousseau was one of the few thinkers of the era that challenged Hobbes's vision of the life of "savages." Rousseau painted a far rosier picture of the life of hunters and gatherers and felt that much of what his contemporaries labeled as "progress" was instead that of "despotism gradually rearing up her hideous crest, and devouring . . . all that still remained sound and untainted" (2007:94 [1755]). Instead of an arrow of progress, Rousseau envisioned an almost full-circle return to savagery's era of "primitive equality" in the near future—this time around leavened with the law, morality, and reason that he felt was now being acquired in urban societies (2007:94 [1755]).

There was a fierce rebuttal to Rousseau's challenge to the narrative of progress in the late eighteenth century (Pagden 1988). Those opposed to Rousseau seized on an obscure word, "civilization," and placed it as a stage of development that stood firmly on top of savagery and barbarism. "Civilization," at that time, was a seldom-used legal term for a society within which civil law replaced military law. The word first made its way into Enlightenment debates when it was employed in a 1756 treatise authored by Victor Riqueti Mirabeau. Like other thinkers in the period, Mirabeau suggested that humans progressed from a state of nature through what he called greater and greater levels of "civility"—a term combining eighteenth-century vernacular associations of politeness and proper manners with the term's deeper Latin roots in "civitas" as a community formed by the creation of a city ruled by law (Pagden 1988). The highest level of civility, according to Mirabeau, was "civilization."

Though he coined the term "civilization," Mirabeau was ironically often critical of urban environments, and he argued instead that civilization was first attained with the advent of agriculture. Most scholars, however, disagreed with Mirabeau, and the word quickly came to be widely used to refer to the stage of human development attained through the creation of cities (e.g., Carli 1792, Condorcet 1933 [1795], and Grimaldi 1958 [1799]). Urban life was seen by these writers as transformative, enabling a group of savages in the forest to attain civilization if they were to gather "in a city, namely, in an enclosed area of houses endowed with a common defense to protect themselves against pillage from outside and disorder from the inside" (Constantin-François de Volney, quoted in Mazlish 2004:15). Change was thus viewed as punctuated: all one needed was a change in address. Such a sudden increase in civility was possible for all humans because the mind and body were seen as elastic. A savage could be civilized if educated, brought into urban societies, and ruled by laws.

The French Revolution's reign of terror from 1793 to 1794 momentarily shattered the belief of many in reason and progress, and philosophers and artists increasingly turned to romanticism and its celebration of the individual, nature, and the imagination. Romanticism was strongly linked to the rise of both nationalism and the culture concept in Europe (Simpson 1993). Building off the work of Johann von Herder ("Another Philosophy of History Concerning the Development of Mankind" [1774]), for example, Germans increasingly saw themselves as the Volk, a unique people forged through similarities in land, language, blood, and history. Before long, the perceived differences between Germans, English, French, and other nationalities came to be seen as biologically rooted, and Europeans began to be held up as members of a race that was inherently superior to all others (e.g., White 1799). As the nineteenth century unfolded, a new generation of thinkers critiqued the Enlightenment's single track of human progress, arguing for multiple racial and cultural tracks that reached different stages of development.

Most Enlightenment thinkers, in sum, believed that Europe had attained the highest degree of civilization in the world. They debated the particular characteristics of their current stage of civilization, argued about what the next stage of civilization would look like, and sought the best ways to move to this higher stage. Scholars were thus interested in earlier stages of human progress, but they sought to elucidate these stages largely to provide themselves with clues as to how to improve their own society and safeguard it from decay. The movement from savagery to civilization was seen as a natural progression that had occurred over the few thousand years allotted to humanity in the biblical chronology. Some groups advanced slower than others, but simple exposure to civilized cities, books, and manners in the West or elsewhere would be enough to allow their rapid transition to civilization.

Classic Cultural Evolutionary Conceptions of Civilization

European disillusionment with the idea of human progress and the triumph of reason lasted only a few decades. By the mid-nineteenth century, Europe controlled large swaths of Africa and southern Asia, Chinese power was eroding, and the United States had expanded across the North American midcontinent. There was therefore renewed confidence in Western superiority, as well as a need to both legitimate colonial expansions and better understand the rich diversity of people with whom these nations were coming into contact. The civilization concept inherited from the Enlightenment filled both of these needs while also meshing well with the culture concept that had become popular earlier in the century. Authors now divided the world's population up into distinct cultures, but they pigeonholed each of these cultures as savage, barbaric, or civilized.

Scholars of the period were thus willing to consider the development of unique civilizations—note the "s" now added to civilization—each with its own defining characteristics. They grudgingly accepted China as a contemporaneous, if not decadent, civilization and more enthusiastically accepted the civilization status of Egyptians, Babylonian, and other ancient circum-Mediterranean groups that had boasted cities, writings, and monarchies (Bahn 1996:94–107). Others groups, however, were not so lucky (e.g., Lubbock 1865:44). Spectacular ruins in Mexico (Stephens and Catherwood 1841), the United States (Squier and Davis 1848), and Africa (Mauch 1971) were often dismissed as the work of barbarians, treated as the colonies of known civilized groups or assigned to a now-vanished race.

Thinking in terms of a broad range of distinct cultural groups became easier in the nineteenth century because the earth had gotten far older. Scholars like Charles Lyell (1830–1833) and Boucher de Perthes (1847–1864) were using geologic evidence, extinct fauna, and artifact associations to dismantle the biblical chronology that had guided research for almost two millennia. By pushing humanity's origins far past the 6,000-year mark asserted in the Bible, this work opened up the possibility of cultures changing very slowly over time. Yet this radically slower pace of culture change also led to pessimistic reconsiderations of the civilizing projects that had been trumpeted during the Enlightenment. If it took thousands of years for some groups to advance past others through the introduction of new inventions and institutions, then was it not difficult, if not impossible, to bridge the yawning gaps between developmental stages in the space of just a few generations?

Some scholars emphatically suggested that the uncivilized would never catch up. The deeper past that made it possible for Charles Darwin (1859) to suggest that humans and apes evolved from a common ancestor was used by these writers to argue for the evolution of multiple human species (for example, Joseph de Gobineau in *The Inequality of Human Races* [1856]). Multilineal evolution, mixed with popular understandings of natural selection, led to racialized conceptions of the past. John Lubbock's widely read *Pre-Historic Times, as Illustrated by Ancient Remains, and the Manners and Customs of Modern Savages*, for example, draws sharp, often ugly, distinctions between groups based on innate characteristics. He suggests that "evil hangs like a thick cloud over savage life, and embitters every pleasure" (1865:571) and also dismisses those groups still living in tribal societies, calling them depraved cannibals who were morally bankrupt and incapable of abstract thought.

Since Lubbock felt that savages could not be civilized, he was largely indifferent to the civilizing process. He tended to be more interested in classifying groups according to their evolutionary stage than with studying the possible movement of these groups from one stage to the next. Many of Lubbock's contemporaries, however, were very interested in how such progression might take place. The other major theorists of classic cultural evolution—Herbert Spencer, Edward Burnett Tylor, James Frazer, and Lewis Henry Morgan—departed from thinkers like Lubbock by arguing that differences between groups were cultural because all humans shared the same basic mental capacity (Erickson and Murphy 1998:45). They argued that people *could* change, albeit slowly.

A war had just been fought in the United States over slavery, and many writers, such as Dickens (*Oliver Twist* [1867]) and Marx and Engels (*The Communist Manifesto* [1848]) were seeing signs of moral decay in what was considered the civilized world. With more people questioning if Western society had made a wrong turn, there was an increasing nostalgia for a purer past and even occasional doubts of the inherent superiority of Europeans. Scholars like Tylor, Frazer, Spencer, and Morgan sought to move beyond earlier explanations of culture change that ended to be based strictly on divine will or racial aptitude. Though they were not as virulently racist as Lubbock, it should be emphasized that their justification for categorizing other groups as inferior was, at best, paternalistic. They felt a duty to serve as caretakers to those groups who had not yet attained the greater intelligence and moral rectitude that was concomitant with civilization.

Late nineteenth-century cultural evolutionists used an expanding corpus of ethnographic and archaeological data in an effort to better understand how humans progressed from a state of nature. They continued to use stages in their models—often keeping or slightly modifying the Enlightenment sequence from savage to civilization—but they offered far more detailed discussions of the expected attributes for each stage and the mechanism through which each of these stages were maintained. The major works of Spencer (*The Principles of Sociology* [1876]), Tylor (*Primitive Culture: Researches into the Development of Mythology, Philosophy, Religion, Art, and Custom* [1871]), and Frazer (*The Golden Bough: A Study in Magic and Religion* [1890]) concentrate on the development of religion, magic, and science. Lewis Henry Morgan's *Ancient Society* (1963 [1877]), in contrast, provides a more sweeping discussion of how interrelated shifts in social, political, and economic institutions created the first civilizations and specifically addresses the relationship of cities and states to civilization. It is this book more than any other that led scholars to advocate for the steplike transition to the civilization stage that continues to plague our understandings of the past. Therefore, I go into Morgan's argument in greater detail.

In *Ancient Society*, Morgan identifies seven stages of "ethnical status" beginning with a lower stage of savagery and ending with civilization. His principal concern is with the changing makeup of seven institutions—

subsistence, government, language, the family, religion, house life and architecture, and property—and how they come together in each of his stages to create "obstacles which delayed civilization" (1963:6 [1877]). Morgan thought that inventions and discoveries were catalysts that overcame these obstacles to progress—a change in one institution triggered by such advancements as the introduction of pottery or metallurgy would lead to a series of changes in other institutions that broke the stalemate and ushered in the next stage of development. Yet these same transformative inventions and discoveries also created a new stage by inciting the development of new sets of stable, mutually reinforcing institutions (1963:4 [1877]).

Morgan recognized that environmental shifts, long-distance trade, and other factors could lead to social change, and he thought that these factors led to the "wide vicissitudes" between groups within a single stage of development (1963:563 [1877]). Yet he fundamentally believed that "the results of the human experience have been substantially the same in all times and areas in the same ethnical status" (1963:562 [1877]) and thus felt justified in using a handful of case studies to represent a particular stage. For modeling the attainment of the civilization stage of development, Morgan relied largely on data from classical Greece and Rome. He connected civilization to the emergence of "political society"—his term for the state—and linked this shift to the development of agriculture and the domestication of animals.

Morgan argues in *Ancient Society* that the tending of crops and herds led to territorial ties becoming more important than kinship relationships and that this shift in focus toward land holdings led in turn to the creation of private property and the retention of this property through patrilineal decent. He associates these transformations with the creation of cities, the development of social classes, and the formation of the state (1963:263–264 [1877]). Just like the Enlightenment thinkers before him, Morgan maintains that cities are the most important driver of civilization: "The development of municipal life and institutions, the aggregation of wealth in walled cities, and the great changes in the mode of life thereby produced, prepared the way for the overthrow of gentile society, and the establishment of political society in its place" (1963 [1877]:224). He also felt confident that the existence of cities in and of themselves was an indication that all of his conditions for civilization had been met. Cities, he notes, "imply the existence of a stable and developed field agriculture, the possession of domestic animals in flocks and herds, and of property in houses and lands. The city brought with it new demands in the art of government by creating a changed condition of society" (1963:264 [1877])

Like his contemporaries, Morgan did not actually think that civilizations formed overnight. He suggests instead that the need for judges, soldiers, and bureaucrats "gradually arose" and that the transition to the state was a "step by step" process away from chiefly power (1963:264 [1877]). He posits that 15,000 years of middle- and upper-level barbarism had paved the way for writing, which in turn brought about the other sweeping changes that were associated with the civilization stage (1963:38 [1877]). State formation for Morgan thus "was gradual, extending through a long period of time, and was embodied in a series of successive experiments by means of which a remedy was sought for existing evils" (1963:263 [1877]).

Morgan's discussion, though now dated, of the stuttering steps toward the state in Greece and Italy actually fits quite well with this book's argument regarding the process of urbanization and its broader impacts. Yet despite all of Morgan's assertions of gradualism in *Ancient Society*, the bulk of the book argues for punctuated, wholesale change. In presenting his thesis, Morgan argues that "the most advanced portion of the human race were halted . . . at certain stages of progress, until some great invention or discovery, such as the domestication of animals or the smelting of iron ore, gave a new and powerful impulse forward" (1963 [1877]:39). This "powerful impulse" is rendered into a steplike transition between stages that he compares near the end of his book to "successive geological formations" that sat one layer above the next (1963:506 [1877]).

Morgan's contemporaries shared his ambivalence toward the moments of transformative change that were inherent in their stages model. E. B. Tylor, for example, persuasively argues in *Anthropology: An Introduction to the Study of Man and Civilization* that

> on the whole, it appears that wherever there are found elaborate arts, abstract knowledge, complex institutions, these are results of gradual development from an earlier, simpler, and ruder state of life. No stage of civilization comes into existence spontaneously, but grows or is developed out of the stage before it. This is the great principle which every scholar must lay firm hold of, if he intends to understand either the world he lives in or the history of the past. (1881:20)

This insistence on gradualism, however, was no match for the rigid framework of Tylor's model. Just as Morgan finds himself referring to evolutionary strata as discrete, superimposed geologic strata, Tylor argues two pages earlier in the same book that the progress toward civilization often "remains stationary for long periods" until suddenly propelled forward by new inventions and institutions (1881:18).

Nineteenth-century cultural evolutionists therefore recognized the problems inherent in the model that they had inherited from Enlightenment thinkers. With the recognition that humanity was older than the Bible suggested, scholars like Morgan and Tylor could now allow that changes occurred very slowly. Yet their nod to gradualism was ultimately overwhelmed by their desire to continue the Enlightenment's grand classification project. By emphasizing the stability of the bundled set of mutually reinforcing institutions and discoveries that were associated with each stage, these scholars found themselves in the uncomfortable position of compressing the "gradual development" that they believed led from one stage to the next into the slivers of time that occurred between their evolutionary stages.

Lewis Henry Morgan and his contemporaries thus ultimately followed a long tradition of cramming the creation of cities, states, social stratification, writing, and the arts into the first moments of a civilization stage. In so doing, they not only ended up implying that these shifts happened quickly but also, just as importantly, that they happened together as part of a single, civilizing process. The messy, decades-long transition periods that Morgan and others explicitly acknowledged were collapsed into risers that separated each stage of cultural evolution from the next. At the top of this evolutionary staircase stood civilization's cities and states, and below them was barbarism and savagery.

Culture History and the Decline of Classic Cultural Evolutionism

Classic cultural evolutionism lost favor in the last decade of the nineteenth century. With archaeological and ethnological data rapidly accumulating, scholars were finding the neatly defined stages of the evolutionary staircase too constricting (Sanderson 2007:35). The savage and barbaric stages of development were the most heavily scrutinized—anthropology, after all, was founded as an encounter with the "other" (Asad 1995)—and books began to identify and celebrate the rich complexity of the groups placed in these two stages (Baker 2004; Cole 1999).

One scholar who played a particularly influential role in the decline of classic cultural evolutionism was Franz Boas. Boas thoroughly discredited the idea of an inferior primitive mind and also placed far greater emphasis on both the variation between cultures and the myriad of reasons why this variation could occur. Believing that each culture was unique because of its distinctive history and environmental setting, Boas suggested that a culture could only be understood after long periods of ethnographic fieldwork (Boas 1940).

This did not mean, however, that Boas disavowed cultural evolution—he simply argued that that there were different paths to civilization in different parts of the world. Like the earlier cultural evolutionists, Boas was happy to talk about stages and to separate out primitive from civilized groups (e.g., *The Mind of Primitive Man* [1911]). He also followed previous scholarship in both associating civilization with writing, domesticated plants and animals, the state, a division of labor, and organized religion and in considering that these traits arrived together as part of the "the bloom of civilization" that "bursts forth now here, now there" in world history (1911:7, 8). Boas, however, strenuously objected to the sweeping generalizations of the earlier generation of scholars. To understand how each region evolved to civilization (or why it did not), he argued that one needed to take the time to reconstruct ancient cultures and trace the relationships between them.

Boas's students were among the most important archaeologists of the first half of the twentieth century, and their work often offered further critiques of classic cultural evolutionism. Robert Lowie, for example, wrote *Primitive Society* (1920) as a direct rebuttal to the work of Lewis Henry Morgan. He found "mottled diversity" in the world's cultures instead of the "dull uniformity" expected in Morgan's model (1920:427), and Lowie suggested that any uniformity that was found could be attributed to historical connections. Alfred Kroeber, another student of Boas, also critiqued the cultural evolutionists by arguing in *Configurations of Cultural Growth* (1944) that each civilization followed its own trajectory. Most archaeological work until the mid-1960s followed the lead of Lowie and Kroeber by tracing these different evolutionary trajectories via careful reconstructions of the shifts in regional artifact assemblages over time.

Although early twentieth-century scholars largely opposed the cultural evolutionists' argument that all of humanity was climbing a universal staircase of progress (Trigger 1989:205), they still talked about cultures moving through stages to reach civilization. They also continued the tradition of arguing that culture change was gradual, even as they retained a steplike transition that suddenly propelled a group from one stage to the next. Civilization therefore remained a bundled set of fully formed traits, and its creation, according to Kroeber, could be described as "the *moment* that the old political order proved insufficient and was superseded by a more tightly organized one" (1944:72, emphasis added).

The most influential archaeologist of the mid-twentieth century, V. Gordon Childe, spent the 1920s doing the kind of detailed culture history work that would have been lauded by Boas and his students (e.g., *The Dawn of European Civilization* [1925], *The Aryans: A Study of Indo-European Origins* [1926], *The Most Ancient Near East: The Oriental Prelude to European History* [1928], and *The Danube in Prehistory* [1929]). Childe, however, grew dissatisfied with simply assembling chronological and cultural sequences, and in the 1930s he attempted to integrate Marxist approaches to culture change into his research. Marx and Engels had been inspired by a close reading of *Ancient Society*—their book *Origins of the Family, Private Property, and the State* (1884) was a reworking of Morgan's evolutionary sequence—and they were more comfortable than the classic cultural evolutionists with the idea of sudden, sweeping societal change between stages of development. Marx and Engels inspired Childe to see change as being driven by fundamental shifts in social relations (e.g., *Social Evolution* [1951] and "Prehistory" [1954]), and in his writing Childe chose to further emphasize the transitions to agriculture and city life by referring to them as the neolithic and urban *revolutions* (Greene 1989).

Childe believed that the gathering of people into cities at the beginning of the urban revolution caused civilization. In *Man Makes Himself*, he calls the periods before the revolutions "preludes," and, like Lewis Henry Morgan before him, he maintains that the groundwork for the urban revolution was slowly laid over centuries: "Science, techniques, and beliefs were being widely diffused; knowledge and skill were being pooled. . . . [T]he exclusiveness of local groups was being broken down, the rigidity of social institutions was being relaxed, self-sufficing communities were sacrificing their economic independence" (1951b:114 [1936]). "Thereby equipped . . . for urban life," agricultural societies were primed for the rapid transition to civilization (1951b:87 [1936]). Suggesting that the city was the "symbol" of civilization, Childe believed that "civilization, wherever and whenever it arose, succeeded barbarism" (1950:2), enumerating a now-famous list of 10 characteristics of civilizations: 1) cities, 2) occupational specialization, 3) taxation, 4) monumental construction, 5) a ruling class, 6) writing, 7) mathematics and astronomy, 8) sophisticated art, 9) regular foreign trade, and 10) the state (1950).

In his research on the rise of civilization in Mesopotamia, Egypt, and the Indus Valley in *Man Makes Himself*, Childe argues that the urban revolution occurred sometime between 4000 and 3000 BC (1951b:114–115 [1936]). Like other archaeologists of his day, Childe was struck by the sudden emergence of some of the earliest cities suggested by the evidence in the field: an excavation layer of "modest huts" gave way to a subsequent layer of "truly monumental buildings" (1951b:117 [1936]). Without greater chronological detail, however, he could only toggle back and forth between the ends of a millennium-long moment of time that began with "communities of simple farmers" and ended with "states embracing various professions and classes" (1951b:114 [1936]).

To summarize this period of scholarship, the classical cultural evolutionism came under attack just a quarter century after Lewis Henry Morgan's death, when scholars like Max Weber offered spirited critiques of the "violence to reality" effected by these theoreticians (1949:103 [1904]). These critics were not against slicing history into stages—Weber, for instance, was willing to argue that the first cities formed through "the *fusion* of fortress and market" at the beginning of civilization (1958:77 [1921], emphasis added)—but rather were against adhering to the idea a single staircase of progress upon which all groups had to climb. In its place, early twentieth-century scholars suggested a wide variety of evolutionary trajectories that were shaped by cultural differences, exchange patterns, types of warfare, local environments, and other factors. These new trajectories nonetheless maintained the idea of punctuated moments of systemic change that drove society from one stable organizational plateau to the next in different regions of the world.

Neoevolutionism and Processualism

Since early twentieth-century writers never fully abandoned the structural framework of the classic cultural evolutionists, it is perhaps unsurprising that more explicit cultural evolutionary approaches would enjoy a renaissance after World War II (White 1945, 1947, 1959). The return of these approaches corresponded with renewed confidence in both the idea of progress and the power of new technologies to effect positive social change. As the intellectual climate shifted, luminaries who had been hostile to evolutionary approaches earlier in their careers like A. R. Radcliffe-Brown reconsidered their positions and began to argue that "social evolution is a reality which [we] should recognize and study" (1952:203).

The return to avowedly evolutionary approaches was particularly exciting to those working across the long time spans of the past, and many were eager to explore the potential of comparative research now that regional cultural histories had become better defined in the intervening years (e.g., Adams 1956). Decades of archaeological research, however, had revealed such wide differences in what one influential volume called the "courses towards urban life" (Braidwood and Willey 1962) that it was soon apparent that the rigid unilineal evolutionary schemes of the late nineteenth century could not be easily reconceived to encompass the global diversity in life ways that was now commonly recognized. For a neoevolutionary perspective to work, it would have to be flexible enough to allow for the divergent evolutionary pathways caused by cultural, historical, and environmental variation (e.g., Steward 1955). But could a multilineal approach also help scholars identify more general trends in human history?

In 1960 four young scholars wrote a slender book that tried to address this question. They asked if evolution was "best considered as a succession-of-forms or as a sweeping movement in a certain direction" and then answered their own question by arguing that both considerations of evolution were important if one hoped to understand the full scope of human history (Harding et al. 1960:7). On the one hand, according to the authors, there was *specific* evolution at the level of individual cultures, which diversified by forming new social practices to fill a variety of environmental niches. On the other hand, the authors suggest that there was a *general* evolutionary trend toward successive stages of development that could be deduced by looking for similarities across the spectrum of specific evolutionary sequences.

One of the volume's authors, Elman Service, dedicated much of his academic life to further delineating the stages of development in general evolution. In *Primitive Social Organization* (1962), Service places groups within an ascending typology of bands, tribes, chiefdoms, and states and then attempts to explain why there were periods of relative cultural stasis in the past by showing how each stage of general evolution was grounded in a stable, mutually beneficial social structure that was part of particular environmental and historical settings. Service equates the state stage of development with civilization in *Primitive Social Organization* and probes more thoroughly the emergence of both in *Origins of the State and Civilization* (1975).

In *Origins of the State and Civilization* he compares eight regions of pristine state formation and then attempts to find in each the "stage-stops along the road to civilization" (1975:303). Service suggests that certain environmental and social factors eventually enabled some groups to make an emphatic leap to civilization: "There was a *point* at which some few of the relatively simple hierarchical-bureaucratic chiefdoms grew, under some unusual conditions, into much larger, more bureaucratic empires. There seems to be no particular difficulty in the archaeological discriminations of the original archaic civilizations from previous developments" (1975:305, emphasis added). Fixated on defining the stage-stops of cultural evolution, Service and many of his contemporaries were less concerned with the specific mechanisms that had enabled a group to move from one stage to another at a particular point in time. With cultural evolution seen as "irregular and discontinuous" (Harding et al. 1960:97), they focused instead on how societies could minimize change through the creation of mutually reinforcing institutions.

Yet the Vietnam War, and the cultural upheavals that accompanied the era, led to a questioning of the narrative of human progress in the late 1960s. Civilization had once again lost its luster, and scholars like Lewis Binford (1962) and David Clarke (1973) now sought more detailed explanations for *why* people would take up farming, settle into cities, or become royal subjects instead of taking these actions as givens on the road to civilization (e.g., Hill, ed. 1977; Friedman and Rowlands, eds. 1977; Renfrew 1973). These archaeologists became known as New (or processual) archaeologists.

One approach to studying culture change in the 1970s treated society as made up of articulated subsystems that tended to act in concert for the mutual benefit of all members (e.g., Hill 1977; Rathje 1971). This approach, building off of Elman's Service's model of bands, tribes, chiefdoms, and states, is exemplified by Kent Flannery's "The Cultural Evolution of Civilizations" (1972). Although "civilization" appears in the title of Flannery's article, he follows many authors at the time in dismissing the concept as "vague" and instead favors an emphasis on the state (1972:400). The article argues that shifts in political structure were the results of changes in the way that information was processed and decisions were made. Social and environmental stresses, such as population growth or warfare, triggered these shifts; two of the most important mechanisms were increased segregation (Flannery's term for the differentiation of tasks into a variety of subsystems) and centralization (the degree of linkage between the subsystems and those in power). In a word, he thought that it was increases in *complexity* that precipitated cultural evolution—a theme that would be developed further in connection to Mesopotamia by Gregory Johnson (1978, 1982).

When conducting fieldwork in Oaxaca, Flannery had noted the sudden emergence of the Zapotec state (a topic to which I return in chapter 9). Radiocarbon dating, a routine practice by the early 1970s, allowed him to confirm the rapidity of state expansion, just as scores of radiocarbon dates from other regions were leading other scholars to similarly claim that expansion had been quick in those places. V. Gordon Childe seemed to have been right that there had been an urban revolution, and Flannery therefore suggested in his article that the shift to the state was not an incremental process spread across many centuries. He instead argued for sudden, qualitative change by suggesting that new institutions like the state, "will appear only after some critical threshold in need for information-processing is reached; thus evolution appears *step-like*" (1972:423, emphasis added).

A second approach to studying cultural change during the 1970s found inspiration in Morton Fried's more antagonistic evolutionary model of egalitarian, ranked, and stratified societies, which he presents in *The Evolution of Political Society* (1967). Fried focused more than most on the mechanisms that drove culture change, and he felt that the state arose primarily through the conflict between population growth and differential access to land and other resources. Robert Carneiro's "A Theory of the Origins of the State" (1970) was one of the more influential publications that built off of Fried's work. In the article, Carneiro argues that warfare in regions where agricultural land was circumscribed by mountains, deserts, or other less productive environs was a "prime mover" in the creation of the state; as the population grew, people began to fight over land until a "stage was reached" and defeated villages faced "incorporation into the political unit dominated by the victor" (1970:734, 735). After further battles, these chiefdom-sized political units came together into a single polity, ushering in a "state" stage of cultural evolution.

Conflict-based theories of the origins of the state would predominate by the early 1980s (e.g., Cohen 1984; Haas 1982). Allen Johnson and Timothy Earle's *The Evolution of Human Societies* (1987), one of the more influential books of that decade, for example, emphasizes conflict between groups, and the authors place particular importance on the pivotal roles of well-placed individuals in cultural evolution. Johnson and Earle argue that evolution was an "upward spiral" that was driven by population pressure and resource stress and that was punctuated by changes in "the involvement of leadership" that allowed for better management of the exchange of goods and services (1987:15). The authors suggest that their book does not stress the "gradual, quantitative change" that occurred in a subsistence economy but rather emphasizes the "difficult problem of *qualitative* change in the creation of new social institutions" (1987:21, emphasis added). Johnson and Earle maintain that leaders sought immediate benefit from their newfound positions of power and that therefore shifts in political economy were often abrupt—hence states "come into being" very quickly (1987:21).

Johnson and Earle offer a three-stage model of evolution in their book, with the "archaic state" being the culminating phase of a "regional polity" stage of development. The term "civilization" is nowhere to be seen in their model, but, like Flannery and many others, the authors feel comfortable echoing much of Childe's list of the characteristics that constitute civilizations when they describe the archaic state as being associated with bureaucracies, social stratification, prestige good manufacture, and monumental buildings (1987:246). Johnson and Earle draw on later, better understood, examples like the Inca Empire to model what life must have been like in the world's earliest states (1987:256), while the city itself is obscured behind subsystems—neither "city" nor "urban" appear in the book's index—since society writ large, rather than the individual locales where activities took place, is their primary unit of analysis.

The Evolution of Human Societies culminated an era of comparative research inaugurated by a call to study both specific and general evolution. Marshal Sahlins declared that "any representation of a given cultural stage is inherently as good as any other" (Harding et al. 1960:33), and this mantra was rigorously embraced by a generation of scholars who combed the world seeking to understand the preconditions that drove society from one stage to the next. Yet culture change itself, as Fred Plog notes (1977:39), was implicitly "either forced onto the boundaries" between stages or more rarely "allowed to fall half in one unit and half in another." Decades-long processes were thus left unexamined as they continued to be pressed together into a single giant step, with the result that cities, states, colonies, and cultural horizons seemed to arrive as a package at the dawn of civilization.

The Civilization Concept Today

Concerns about the subjectivity of archaeological interpretations led to a critique of neoevolutionary models during the 1980s (Hodder 1982; Miller and Tilley 1984; Shanks and Tilley 1987). While some scholars sought to refine the 1960s models to address these and other criticisms, many others abandoned attempts to create sweeping narratives of comparative cultural evolution and turned to theories "in which material culture is seen as actively and meaningfully produced, and in which the individual actor, culture, and history are central" (Hodder 1985:1). Gender, class, and factions also became more important in modeling the past (e.g., Brumfiel 1992), and there was an increased emphasis on how places and landscape were experienced (e.g., Bender 1992). This theoretical ferment put into question many of our bedrock conceptions of the past, but I argue that civilization and its steplike transition have remained relatively untouched. How has this come to pass?

Instead of exhaustively tracing the recent fragmentation in theoretical approaches to the past that has occurred in archaeology and related disciplines (see Johnson 2010), this section briefly focus on three trends that have been particularly germane to the ongoing influence of the civilization concept: the return of historical particularism, the rise of Darwinian evolutionary perspectives, and the application of the world-systems approach to the ancient world. I draw on the work of an influential scholar to illustrate each of these trends and then close by discussing the work of two other authors, Norman Yoffee and Timothy Pauketat, who have written well-received books that are critical of many aspects of cultural evolution but that I feel still ultimately fail to question the steplike transition to a civilization stage.

Historical Particularism

A frustration with neoevolutionism has led many scholars to return to the historical particularism that was advocated by Boas at the beginning of the nineteenth century. These scholars have replaced the black boxes of mutually reinforcing institutions that had been pervasive since at least the time of Morgan with models that emphasize a welter of individuals working through conflicting agendas within unique local contexts (e.g., Dobres and Robb 2000). The pivotal role that divinations played in ritual life in early China are now highlighted by these new models (Flad 2008), for example, as are the tensions that played out politically between commoners and elite in places like Cahokia (Emerson 1997).

Rosemary Joyce has been especially influential in the recent reengagement with historical particularism. Joyce works in Honduras, and is interested more generally in the relationships between people and things in Mesoamerica (e.g., "Life with Things: Archaeology and Materiality" [2012]). She suggests that societies are formed through repeated practices that inscribe one's gender, social rank, and other cultural dimensions on to the body. In *Gender and Power in Prehispanic Mesoamerica*, for example, Joyce argues that this process of embodiment led to a distinctive Mesoamerican personhood that can only be understood by carefully unraveling the many threads that connect a region's people to its objects:

> Anyone trying, from the vantage point of the late twentieth century, to recover some of the quality of precolumbian society faces a formidable

> task. If we take as our goal the aim of making precolumbian Mesoamerica more intelligible . . . then we ensure that we will come to understand these societies as different versions of the same thing, lesser or distorted mirror images of Europe. Our alternative could rather be to make precolumbian Mesoamerica *more distinct*, to push at the limits of strangeness from the Europe that absorbed and reformulated it over half a millennium. (2000:1, emphasis added)

The interweaving of practices over thousands of years thus make Mesoamerican groups unique in Joyce's view, and the only way to understand these societies, she argues, is through an exhaustive contextual analysis.

Joyce's research project is anathema to the classic evolutionist's sense of a shared human psyche and fits well with Boaz's more-than-century-old call for a concentration on understanding the rich complexities of local settings. Studies like hers undeniably provide us with a far better understanding of what certain societies were like in the past. There are nonetheless dangers to focusing only on the details of a particular group (Smith and Peregrine 2012). As our horizons narrow, we learn more about how the game of life played out in the palace in eighth-century Palenque or among the copper traders of Bronze Age Crete. Yet, as Robert Drennan argues, this focus on the particular "does not help us 'understand' any better *how* or *why* that game played out in the way that it did—as opposed to the variety of other ways it might have played out" in other places (Drennan 2000:191, my translation, emphasis added).

Joyce also recognizes this problem and argues that research like her own ultimately needs to be placed in a "contextual comparative framework" (2011:182) that juxtaposes the results of historically particular studies, thus allowing us to better understand how certain local mechanisms create cultural diversity (e.g., Meskell and Joyce 2003). Unfortunately, these kinds of comparative studies are rare, and most scholars that have been working on the ancient world during the last three decades have tended to focus on unraveling the complexities of one specific region and time period. Since the chronology and cultural units we use to study these regions have been shaped by evolutionary theory, these researchers tend to do their work on one side or the other of the dividing line between civilization and other types of societies. Much of their scholarship, which

I draw on in this book, can actually be used to critique the idea of a step-like transition to civilization, but the relevance of these data is rarely noted because of the lack of engagement of historical particularists with general models of cultural evolution. By ignoring classic cultural evolutionary theory, one can argue that these scholars have inadvertently made the civilization concept more insidious.

Darwinian Archaeology

In contrast to those who advocate for historical particularism, Darwinian archaeologists have repeatedly engaged with both classic evolutionary theory and its 1960s and 1970s revisionist form. These scholars argue for a general theory of cultural evolution but one that is far more closely linked to processes at work in biological evolution. The Darwinian approach originated with a call to action by Richard Dunnell (1980), who argued that cultures were best seen as sets of traits that were acted on by natural selection. Culture change, according to Dunnell, should therefore be modeled as a directionless adaptation to particular social and natural environments. The evolutionary models of Service, Fried, and others were thus seen by Dunnell as fatally flawed because they were based on classic cultural evolutionary texts that emphasized progress rather than fundamental evolutionary principles—the archaeologists who framed their work around these models were barking up the wrong tree.

Most Darwinian archaeologists have focused on gradual, long-term change. They often emphasize "the reconstruction of artifact lineages" (O'Brien and Lyman 2002:34) and try to understand the differential reproduction of some artifact types as opposed to others (e.g., Bettinger and Eerkens 1999). By emphasizing the many stylistic changes that occur within what was traditionally though to be a unified stage of cultural development, they effectively question the sharp distinctions drawn between societal types by both classic and the neocultural evolutionists. Yet their focus on small, incremental change has tended to work best in hunter-gatherer societies, where shifts in artifact lineages can be traced over hundreds, if not thousands, of years (see many of the chapters in Maschner 1996). Studying the much more rapid rise of cities, states, and the other phenomena traditionally associated with civilization, however, would require a shift in the Darwinian approach trumpeted by Charles Spencer.

In an article entitled, "On the Tempo and Mode of State Formation: Neoevolutionism Re-Considered" (1990), Spencer suggests that Stephen Jay Gould's idea of punctuated equilibrium in biological evolution can be used to develop a "regulatory transformation" model for the shift from chiefdoms to states (1990:10). The jump to a state-level society in his model could occur when "a stressful condition between the demands of the elite, the fundamental needs of the people, and the system's productive base" was created (1990:11). Since states require significant investments in centralized and specialized administration in order to operate, most chiefdoms, according to Spencer, would shrink in size in response to the problems associated with getting too large. When a state did form, it was the result of a burst of innovation that breached the limits of a chiefdom-based society. The transition was therefore most likely "to occur in a transformational or punctuational—not gradual—fashion" (1990:11).

Spencer has continued to refine his punctuated equilibrium position since his 1990 paper. In a 1998 article, for example, he includes a mathematical model derived from predator-prey relations that supports his earlier assertions that territorial expansion went hand in hand with the creation of a state's administrative structure. He argues that

> chiefly political growth . . . will approach a "bifurcation point" in its developmental trajectory, a *point* at which new regulatory strategies must be implemented for the growth trend to be sustained. Among the most effective of such new strategies would be interpolity expansion combined with tributary extraction, which would entail the dispatching of specialized components of administration to the subjugated polities to manage the mobilization and transfer of resources. (1998:17, emphasis added)

The idea of a steplike transition to civilization thus finds an unlikely ally in a model drawn from evolutionary biology that posits a moment of crisis when leaders formed cities, administrative structures, and expansive states in the process of a compulsory bureaucratization (Spencer 2010:7125).

CHAPTER 2

World Systems

The civilization concept has also found support from a perspective first applied to today's global political economy. Immanuel Wallerstein's world-systems approach (1974) divides the modern world into three major zones—a core, semiperiphery, and periphery—and suggests that these zones are tied together through the exchange of goods. He argues that the strong governments and industries in the core use a variety of mechanisms to ensure that peripheral and semiperipheral nations remain dependent on the core for its high-value, finished goods. Without relying on outright coercion, the world system siphons off resources from the poor to make the rich richer. Wallerstein suggests that his model cannot be applied to the precapitalist world both because ancient states had insufficient control over peripheries and because these societies lacked the technologies necessary to produce a significant surplus (1974:15–16). Other scholars, however, have seen value in a world-systems approach to the past and have applied it to earlier interaction spheres, including nonstate ones (e.g., Ekholm and Friedman 1979; Schneider 1977).

Guillermo Algaze thought that a world-systems approach might help him understand how the development of a handful of city-states near the mouth of the Tigris and Euphrates rivers transformed relationships throughout greater Mesopotamia during the fourth millennium BC. Seeking "to delineate the interlocking supply and demand systems feeding the growth of Uruk states" (1993b:124), his *The Uruk World System: The Dynamics of Expansion of Early Mesopotamian Civilization* posits the creation of an Uruk world system formed through the extension of a network of colonial outposts established along primary trade routes. These outposts, founded by the city-states of the southern alluvium, helped to ensure the flow of both raw materials into the cities and of finished goods out to the periphery.

In the same year that he published *The Uruk World System*, Algaze wrote an article suggesting that the creation of an "essentially asymmetrical and exploitative resource procurement strategy" in the periphery was a common practice of the earliest states (1993a:304). The article expands the reach of the state further than Wallerstein suggested was possible in the ancient world by arguing that these early polities could impose their will "well beyond the boundaries of their direct political control" through the assiduous use of their colonial networks (1993a:305). Though stopping short of the term "empire," Algaze likens the creation of these first world systems to "imperial expansions" that could be roughly equated with the boundaries of a civilization (1993a: 324).

Algaze, like many others, has never fully defined what he means by "civilization." Yet he clearly links the term to the creation of cities, and, in his latest book, argues that the "dramatic 'takeoff'" of the Uruk city states occurred when a number of environmental and cultural factors "set the stage for important organizational innovations" in the region (2008:xviii, 5). A "certain threshold" of "critical mass" was reached, and the "dawn of civilization" occurred as cities, states, colonies, and a cultural horizon unfurled across Mesopotamia (2008:145, 146). The city is thus the motor for cultural change in world-systems models like Algaze's, but this change is once again collapsed into a single totalizing moment at the "dawn of civilization."

Attacking Civilization?

Cultural particularism, Darwinian archaeology, and world systems are just three of the wide array of theoretical approaches that have recently been applied to the past (Johnson 2010). Despite the emergence of a diversity of viewpoints over the last three decades, the civilization stage's steplike transition has been routinely ignored, and in fact often reinforced, by today's researchers. Even as other orthodoxies are questioned, the idea of a civilization stage remains so deeply ingrained in our thinking of the past that we shape—both consciously or unconsciously—new theories to fit with long-held ideas about how the first cities, states, colonies, and cultural horizons were created.

Other aspects of the civilization concept, it should be emphasized, *have* been heavily critiqued. Yet the focus of this critique has tended to be on the variability hidden behind the edifice of civilization rather than on the idea itself of a stage of development. Different kinds of chiefdoms and states, for example, have been identified in comparative studies (e.g., Earle 1977, 1987; Claessen and Skalník 1978), and it has even been suggested that civilization could emerge without the state (McIntonsh 2005). There has also been considerable debate about what traits best constitute a "civilization," as well as many efforts made to identify divisions within these traits such as that between attached versus independent specialization (Brumfiel and Earle 1987) or corporate versus network strategies of statecraft (Blanton et al. 1996).

Yet the bundling of traits into a steplike transition to the civilization stage has often been left uncontested by those critical of other aspects of cultural evolutionary theory. The reason for this is likely the by now irrefutable evidence that most of the world's first cities, states, colonies, and cultural horizons came into being over the course of just a few hundred years. This "quick" change—nearly instantaneous in archaeological time—has made us more comfortable with treating civilization as something that arrived through an abrupt and totalizing discontinuity. The writings of Norman Yoffee and Timothy Pauketat provide two examples of the seeming inability of even the staunchest critics of cultural evolution to move past the shortcomings of this aspect of the civilization concept.

Yoffee launched one of the earliest critiques of neoevolutionary typologies in a 1979 article in *American Antiquity*, a journal that had long been the soapbox for cultural evolutionists. Wasting no time in picking a fight, he begins his abstract as follows:

> The typological schemes constructed by many archaeologists to explain the rise and fall of civilization have neither accounted for the processual changes involved in the evolution of social complexity nor contributed to the development of a comparative method for considering regularities and variation in social behavior. (1979:5)

Yoffee goes on to call evolutionism "a teleology without a god" and argues that "the very act of categorization into stages has tended to make researchers ignore the necessity of subsystemic variability within 'stages' and similarities of sociocultural variability across stages" (1979:29, 25–26).

Yoffee's article provoked a fiery back and forth in the pages of *American Antiquity* (Dunnell and Wenke 1980a, 1980b; Peters 1980; Yoffee 1980a, 1980b) and helped spark an ongoing debate about the usefulness of evolutionary stages in archaeological models (e.g., Drennan 1991; Feinman and Marcus 1998; Parkinson 2002). Yet Yoffee was actually quite comfortable thinking in terms of "states" and "civilizations," and in his 1979 article he argues that the state is a centralized authority that uncomfortably drapes itself over a larger civilization:

> The emergence of a [urban] center depends on its ability to express the legitimacy of differentiated social elements, acting through a generalized structure of authority by which it transcends the various societal components and gives an order to the stratification of those components. It is this centralized authority that I wish to designate the "state." The type of differentiated society in which the state is embedded, and for which it symbolizes and institutionalizes social order through its offices of authority, may be usefully denominated a "civilization." *The entities are thus coeval, but they are not coterminous.* (1979:15, emphasis added)

In a fiery article written to dismantle the stages of social evolution, Yoffee thus ends up tying the city, state, and civilization together in a single unified process that he would later describe in his book *Myths of the Archaic State: Evolution of the Earliest Cities, States, and Civilizations* as occurring as a result of "a sharp transition from one state of being to another" that he likens to crystallization or water turning into steam (2005:230).

Yoffee begins *Myths of the Archaic State* by arguing against the perception that states emerged fully formed (2005:22), and in a subsequent review of the literature on ancient cities, he also argues passionately that these settlements had become an "abstract and empty" category that shortchanges the sights, sounds, and smells of city life (2010:282). Yoffee thus recognizes that urbanization, like state formation, is an ongoing, dynamic process—he is well aware that there are inherent problems in thinking in terms of a punctuated shift to a static civilization stage—yet the civilization concept and its steplike transition continues to influence his writings despite this recognition.

Another example of the resiliency of the civilization concept comes from Timothy Pauketat's *Chiefdoms and Other Archaeological Delusions* (2007), a book written with the express purpose of freeing studies of the past from the "conceptual clutter" of evolutionary thinking (2007:4). He echoes Yoffee's concerns about our definitions of state and emphasizes, even more so than Yoffee, the extent to which the process of creating cities, states, and broad cultural horizons was messy and uneven. Pauketat suggests that the "X factor" in the creation of civilization is community building, a "malleable and negotiated field of politics and cultural identity generated from within" (2007:132). He also sees cities as the principal crucibles of change and argues that these communities should be seen as dynamic through time. Pauketat nonetheless shares Yoffee's predilection in practice of treating the emergence of civilization as a discontinuity.

In Pauketat's case study from his own work at Cahokia in the American Bottom region (see chapter 5), he argues that civilization arrived in what he calls a "Big Bang" that began in the city and then swept across a broad region. The original Big Bang created the universe in a fraction of a second through a process known as cosmic inflation (Hawking 1998). Pauketat, of course, does not argue that the Mississippian civilization expanded in an instant. The Mississippian Big Bang was instead an opening salvo that created a city around AD 1050 and then led over the next few hundred years to products, ideas, and people flowing across the American midcontinent (2007:146). There remains nonetheless a sense in his book of a series of near-instantaneous chemical reactions analogous to *the* Big Bang. The first explosion, triggered by people coming together at Cahokia, set off a series of "little bangs" that swept from one region to the next.

As the title in part implies, *Chiefdoms and Other Archaeological Delusions* is especially critical of the idea that chiefdoms are a necessary precursor to the state. Yet for all of Pauketat's concern about the weaknesses of thinking in terms of evolutionary stages, he seems unwilling in the book to break apart the civilization stage in the same ways that he is willing to dismantle the chiefdom stage of development. Pauketat notes in an earlier book that "'civilization' is not a word typically associated" with the American midcontinent (2004:1), although he feels that the region is actually on par with other places like Egypt, Peru, and Mesopotamia that are often associated with the term. To argue for civilization status, he ticks off many of Childe's age-worn boxes. He argues, for example, that Cahokia was a city with monumental architecture, that those who lived there exercised, if briefly, powers associated with a state, and that the actions first taken at Cahokia created a broad Mississippian horizon (2004:170–174).

Pauketat continues to advocate for the civilization status of Cahokia and the Mississippian cultural horizon in *Chiefdoms and Other Archaeological*

Delusions, and this insistence can at times rub uncomfortably against his desire to get rid of the societal labels associated with cultural evolution (2007:163). Like Yoffee before him, Pauketat conflates cities, states, and cultural horizons in his definition of civilization as "a kind of political culture or as a great tradition associated with populated administrative centers and spread across some portion of a continent" (2004:1). He knows that community building across sites, locales, and regions takes time, yet he nonetheless ultimately fails to allow the processes that he associates with civilization to unfold independently and in real time. Arguing for a Big Bang allows Pauketat to argue for the existence of a civilization in the American Bottom. In so doing, however, he reifies the idea of steplike transition that "clutters" our thinking about the past (2007:4).

The purpose of this section has not been to single out Joyce, Spencer, Algaze, Pauketat, and Yoffee for criticism. Rather, my point in analyzing their scholarship is to underline the ongoing difficulties throughout academia in uprooting long-held ideas about a civilization stage and its steplike emergence. Everyone recognizes that processes like urbanization, state formation, colonization, and the spread of cultural horizons unfold across decades, and we also realize that these processes are not necessarily linked together in a single shift to civilization. Yet our models continue to doggedly push these changes to the margins of a stage's time period or flatten these changes out by representing them as part and parcel of a single formative period. In either case, we tend to assume that there was a moment in time when the A, B, C, and D characteristics of "civilization" (or "states" or "social complexity") emerged together and that these characteristics persist across an entire time period. The civilization concept lingers—the golem marches on—as we continue to make the same assumptions about what happened during the hazy chunks of time that brought us the world's first cities, states, colonies, and cultural horizons.

The Revolution Will Not Be Televised

When Lewis Henry Morgan sat down in his library to write *Ancient Society*, the scientific world was aflame with talk of gradualism and the deep history of humanity. This longer chronology allowed for the possibility that society had progressed slowly and incrementally, but Morgan's book instead offered an Enlightenment-era model of long periods of stasis bookended by punctuated changes. Although Morgan acknowledged that gradual change occurred, he thought of it more in terms of a buildup in pressure that eventually culminated in a sudden transition from one stage to the next.

Morgan's hesitance to fully embrace gradualism was well placed. We now know that shifts in social complexity can occur quite rapidly and that most of the world's first cities and states formed over just a few hundred years. These narrow time spans are often difficult for archaeologists to follow, and since we have trouble seeing for ourselves the creation of "civilization," we fill the gaps in our knowledge by both using data from later cultures and borrowing theories from other disciplines. These new theories and data tend to reinforce our deeply held assumptions of what should be happening during the first decades of rapid settlement aggregation associated with the dawn of civilization. But why are we trying to recreate the earliest *civilizations*? Why chase after an Enlightenment construct?

As archaeologists have become more comfortable with the idea of punctuated change, they have also grown more comfortable than Morgan ever was with the idea of cities, states, and colonies, and cultural horizons occurring in lockstep during the first years of a more complex society. We know, of course, that the idea of a steplike transition, strictly conceived, to civilization is wrong. Yet the play-by-play scenarios that we have offered for more than a century tend to conflate urbanization, state formation, colonization, and the creation of cultural horizons into a single unified process.

This often-unconscious conflation, I argue, is a result of the pervasive influence of the civilization concept. Evolutionary stages have proven to be sticky—we expect certain things to occur simultaneously (Drennan and Peterson 2006, 2012)—and we thus tend to keep together those characteristics that we have long associated with civilization even in the light of contradictory evidence. With the transitions to cities, states, and cultural horizons often occurring so quickly, it is understandable that we would treat their arrival as part of a broader phase change. This does not, however, make it right.

In chapter 1, I mentioned that Malcolm Gladwell defines a tipping point as "the moment of critical mass, the threshold, the boiling point" (2000:10). Norman Yoffee uses the same analogy of a boiling point in his discussion of the transition to civilization, and we can trace the idea of a tipping point through more than six generations of archaeologists and ethnographers who have discussed the "moments," "points," and "thresholds" that brought us civilization. I do not object to the idea of tipping points in village life that sometimes led to a cascade of changes that created early cities, states, colonies and cultural horizons, but I *do* object to the idea that this was a tipping point that led to a civilization stage.

Our models, though increasingly sophisticated, continue to be crippled by the civilization golem because the beast's earthy flesh has become confused with the bedrock on which it is safe to build our conceptions of the past. To truly understand life in the first cities, states, colonies, and cultural horizons, we need to rid ourselves of the civilization concept and come up with alternatives that more accurately reflect what really happened. The rest of this book offers one possible alternative that shows how the challenges of living together in large groups could sometimes lead to the many of changes that have often been associated with civilization. By looking first at how urbanization unfolds over time, we can begin to see how the formation of states, colonies, and cultural horizons were possible, but far from necessary, outcomes of the struggles to turn a settlement into a city.

My vision of the past, of course, is just as foggy as that of everyone else—the first urban revolutions, with apologies to Gil Scott-Heron, were not televised. This lack of clarity, however, is no excuse for relying on tidy, abstract scenarios that reinforce the notion of a steplike transition to civilization that even Lewis Henry Morgan and his contemporaries recognized as incorrect. There *are* data available that can help us pierce this fog. We can gain insights from how cities were created in the more recent past, look at early towns that never quite became cities, and look at the variable footprint that different kinds of early cities left on outlying regions. To develop the alternative model to civilization that I briefly introduced in chapter 1, the next chapter considers the frenetic first decades of modern cities like Los Angeles and Abu Dhabi. These contemporary case studies provide us with a range of insights on urbanization. The most important of these insights though is also the most simple: it is profoundly difficult to create a city and countryside from scratch.

3

BECOMING A CITY

THE MUSEUM WHERE I WORK SITS IN THE HEART OF TORONTO, A city with a greater metropolitan population of almost six million people. I live a few minutes walk from a hospital, an elementary school, two sushi restaurants, and three banks. The subway gets me to work in a half hour, and, if I could somehow get tickets, I could watch the Maple Leafs play their hockey games downtown. Two hundred years ago, Toronto had none of these amenities. The settlement that would become the city was "dropped by the hand of government into the midst of a virgin forest" in 1793, and for years few settlers wanted to come to the northwestern shores of Lake Ontario (Glazebrock 1971:3).

Toronto (then called York) was the provincial capital of Upper Canada, and by the beginning of the nineteenth century the founders had already laid an urban grid, built a fort, and constructed a smattering of buildings. Malaria, however, was rampant. The few roads that existed were often impassable and frequently ended at the property line of a truculent owner. Bartenders served as constables, streets were strewn with garbage, and the settlement was utterly reliant on the towns of Niagara and Montreal for such things as paper, carpets, and plates.

There were little more than 700 people in Toronto in 1814, but by 1851 the city boasted 30,000 inhabitants. Trains, gaslights, and piped water soon followed. The population was 208,000 by 1901, and by the time our museum opened its doors in 1914 more than 400,000 people called Toronto home. The museum was constructed on what had been the far outskirts of town until the mid-nineteenth century, but 50 years of urban sprawl had turned the farmland into blocks of houses, as well as university and government buildings. From my office windows there are a few signs of Toronto's century of frenetic growth from 1814 to 1914—the sloped roofs of University College (1859) and the towers of the Ontario Legislative Building (1893). Yet much of this past has been paved over, making way for dozens of new offices and condos.

Toronto's urbanization is not an unusual story. Many, if not most, modern and ancient cities grew very rapidly at certain times in the first centuries of their existence (Tellier 2009:575–592). People throughout history have thus had to finds ways to build both an urban community and a surrounding countryside in the span of only a few decades. In an article describing twenty-first century Hanoi, Robert Kaplan suggests that the Vietnamese city was now in "the ungainly process of becoming"—a fast-changing, "disheveled chaos" of people "prying their way" into the world (2012:56). Kaplan stresses that the future of Hanoi is still unclear and that the city's residents are trying to figure things out on the fly. A sense of everything as (im)possible permeates Hanoi today, as it did Toronto in the late nineteenth century. I argue that the residents of the world's first cities would have experienced that same feeling.

Our models for ancient urbanization lack this sense of a city's disheveled becoming because of the long-standing influence of the idea of a steplike transition that accompanies the civilization concept. Since the beginning of archaeology, the first cities, states, and cultural horizons have tended to be portrayed as either implicitly arriving fully formed at the beginning of a time period or unfurling together in a tidy just-so story. I argue that this tendency to rely on evolutionary stages discourages analysis of what happened decade by decade in those regions where the sweeping changes associated with urbanization were occurring. Seemingly in the blink of an archaeologist's eye, a handful of houses become a teeming metropolis. We therefore often represent the precocious first decades when a city and the surrounding countryside are created as an explosion resulting in a civilization stage of development and commonly use later, better-known cultures to help us reconstruct cities, states, and cultural horizons as they first appeared (i.e., Marcus and Feinman 1998; Marcus and Sabloff 2008).

The problem with this approach is that the people who lived during subsequent periods had already figured many things out. They had built their neighborhoods, knew how to get food on the table, and understood, perhaps bitterly, their position in society. Administrators also had long-standing authority, knew the problems that they faced, and were part of a bureaucracy designed to deal with the problems inherent to urbanized environments. Life, of course, was ever changing, but it played out within more settled economic, political, and social structures. Those living in more established cities today can find it easy to forget about the struggle to create an urban way of life, since routines and outlooks once formed can easily become second nature (e.g., Bourdieu 1977). We recognize that our urban experiences must be quite distinct from those experienced a few generations ago, but we still often essentialize city life. This is especially true when we think about the ancient world: we often push our construct of "the city" to the very beginning of the civilization stage.

Today's Toronto would be a poor stand-in for the city in the mid-nineteenth century. In a similar manner, we should not take the last occupation levels at Copán, Babylon, and Qianyang as representative of what life was like hundreds of years earlier in and around the first cities that were established in these regions. You need to go to a city in the making in order to get a sense of the struggle it takes to make a place. Cities tend to emerge in barely contained fits and starts, and, despite more than 4,000 years of practice in urban living, local and state officials today still often find themselves initially overwhelmed by the avalanche of new migrants. Looking at how modern cities have formed underlines a simple fact that is often overlooked when we think about ancient cities: *urbanization is an unruly process*. The recognition of this fact is the critical first step in creating an alternative to the core assumptions of a steplike transition to civilization.

Growing Pains

The urbanization processes that created cities like Toronto and Hanoi, of course, were in many ways radically different from those that occurred thousands of years ago. The populations of early cities were a tiny fraction of the populations of today's metropolises, and ancient sites were not tied together into a capitalist global system. There is also a long list of transformative technologies, from cars to genetically modified crops and the

Internet, that separate us from even those who lived in the nineteenth century. Books have been written based on the premise that there is a yawning divide between ancient and modern cities (e.g., Robinson 2006).

The litany of differences, however, can blind us to the basic similarities of urban life (Smith 2009, 2010). No matter what the era, there are fundamental challenges that must be overcome when populations rapidly nucleate. Although it is true that the nuances of Toronto's struggle to create a well-functioning sewage system are of little help in understanding hygiene in early third-millennium BC Mohenjo-daro, basic sanitation was a goal of both cities' inhabitants. Malnutrition, overcrowding, crime, wealth disparities, and unemployment are also not distinctly modern problems of urban centers (to focus only on some of the more negative aspects of city life). The scale and complexity of the problems dealt with by administrators in megacities like Tokyo and Cairo would overwhelm those tasked with trying to organize the earliest cities (see, e.g., Sassen 2001). Yet the leaders of these first cities would nonetheless recognize many of today's problems as akin to their own.

It is difficult to overstate the daunting hurdles faced when a city forms for the *first time* (also see Jennings 2011). Urbanization requires fundamental changes in many aspects of a society, and these changes in how people live often go against millennia of tradition. More crops need to be planted, for example, and farmers need to be convinced (or coerced) to contribute their surplus to distant communities. People have to adjust the ways that they build houses, tend animals, and perform bodily functions. They need to figure out when they should trust a stranger and when they should not. These and many other adjustments must be made concurrently in order for a city to be successfully created and sustained.

The just-so story of civilization posits a seamless transition to an era of cities, states, colonies, and cultural horizons. This chapter's case studies on the recent creation of São Paulo, Singapore, Abu Dhabi, and Los Angeles undercut civilization's mythic birth by highlighting common problems of settlement nucleation and the flurry of individual and collective actions that shape urban life when municipal bodies are too nascent, beleaguered, and underfunded to properly function. A consideration of the first decades of these four modern cities thus calls into question those models that both treat cities as somehow emblematic of the early state and consider states as the drivers of colonization and cultural horizons. Powerful states *were* intimately involved in the creation of each of the cities I discuss—Los Angeles and São Paulo were formed within nation states, Singapore began as a British colony, and at its inception Abu Dhabi was a British protectorate. Yet the state and even municipal governments in these case studies initially had only a very limited impact on daily life in the city and the surrounding countryside.

The people of each of the urbanizing settlements described in this chapter solved their growth problems in different ways, and their initial responses to these challenges had an enduring impact on the character of the cities. These case studies provide a decade-by-decade glimpse of the urbanization process that is impossible to achieve in pre- or protohistoric contexts where this degree of chronological precision is unobtainable. The particular struggles that took place in São Paulo, Singapore, Abu Dhabi, and Los Angeles are modern ones, but they nonetheless can be used to underline just how difficult it is to create a well-functioning city. Even today, there is no great and powerful Oz pulling at the social levers of fast-growing settlements. People bumble, fight, and drag their feet toward an urban way of life—why would we think that the world's first cities escaped a similarly ungainly coming of age?

Singapore, 1819–1940

Singapore provides our first example of unplanned, frenetic growth. On January 30, 1819, Sir Stamford Raffles signed a treaty with two local rulers that established a British East India Company trading station on the island of Singapore. The island itself was of little interest to Raffles. It was poorly suited to agriculture, contained no desired natural resources, and boasted only a population of 1,000 people who subsisted by fishing, gathering plants, small-scale trading, and piracy (Turnbull 1989:5). Singapore, however, was located within the Straits of Malacca, a natural shipping passage between British interests in China and India (Wong 1978:52), and Raffles felt that a port on the island could become a "great commercial emporium" if it charged no tariffs for trading (quoted in Cangi 1993:52).

Sir Stamford Raffles had signed the treaty creating the free port of

Singapore without authorization from either the East India Company or the British Crown. The Dutch therefore demanded the settlers remove themselves immediately, as did many British agents (Abshire 2011:40–41). Despite its illegitimacy, the promise of profit attracted people to the port, and Singapore's trade expanded rapidly. By 1821 there were 3,000 Malays living in the town, along with 1,000 Chinese, 500 Bugis, and a smattering of Indians, Arabs, Armenians, Europeans, and other groups (Turnbull 1989:13). The British decided to keep the island.

Raffles wanted to build a city that would "civilize" the people of Southeast Asia (Cangi 1993). Settlement during the first three years was haphazard, but a master plan that created an urban grid with wide streets was drawn up in 1822. Old buildings were torn down, and land was set aside for government buildings, a church, and a school. Raffles then divided up the settlement into different ethnic enclaves that were ranked by their perceived level of civilization. The Europeans got the prime real estate on one side of the river, and other ethnic groups received land on the opposite side. Raffles insisted that each enclave be self-governed by its own leaders (Cangi 1993:176; Turnbull 1989:22), and he argued that the company could save money by leaving the enclaves alone—civilization would trickle down from the Europeans by example.

Over the next four decades, Singapore flourished as an international port of trade. The town's warehouses were filled with pepper, nutmeg, cloves, porcelain, silk, opium, and other goods, while the harbor was dotted with boats from around the world (Frost and Balasingamchow 2009:88). There were 16,634 inhabitants by 1830 and 81,734 by 1860 (Saw 1969:39). Trade volume more than tripled during these three decades. Merchants from across Singapore's ethnic enclaves formed an affluent class that identified closely with their homelands but still mingled easily with European settlers (Frost 2005:35; Turnbull 1989:39).

The municipal government was understaffed, poorly funded, and run by British officials who did not speak the languages of most of Singapore's inhabitants. The resulting administration was "light and lax, providing a semblance of law and order but scarcely touching the lives of the inhabitants" (Turnbull 1989:49). Much of the settlement was a swamp; large parts of the city were crowded, unpoliced slums. Violence, malnutrition, drug use, and prostitution were common (Abshire 2011:51–53), and the city had a rowdy, even lawless, international reputation—pirates openly sold their spoils in Singapore well into the 1850s, and for years European residents lobbied for the construction of a fortress to protect themselves in the case of a revolt by the lower classes (Frost and Balasingamchow 2009:108–113).

The city's biggest problem was that most of the people who were coming to Singapore had no desire to settle there permanently. Malays from the surrounding archipelago had made up most of the population of the town in the 1820s, but by 1850 the majority of people living in the town were Chinese (Saw 1969:41). Most of these immigrants were men from poor villages in southern China who hoped to work in the Malay Peninsula for a few years and then return home. These Chinese immigrants usually entered through Singapore. Some joined the city's vast pool of unskilled laborers, while others labored in the region's tin mines and on gambier-pepper plantations (Wong 1978:55). (The branches and leaves of the gambier tree were used in tanning hides, and it grew well with pepper plants.)

After Raffles left Singapore in 1824, the British East India Company continued to follow his hands-off policy toward the ethnic enclaves that made up almost all of Singapore's inhabitants. This policy of neglect left a vacuum in municipal planning and services that was filled in part by enclave residents. In the Chinese community, for example, rich merchants founded a hospital and sponsored other charitable organizations. The Chinese also relied on family and clan ties for assistance, and secret societies were formed to provide many of the basic social services required by community members (Yen 1981:63; Abshire 2011:53). A similar pattern of mutual support could be found among many of the other enclaves in the city (e.g., Sandhu 1969).

Enclave-based organizations, however, could only provide the most rudimentary of safety nets. The great majority of people in Singapore lived in abject poverty, with most of the poor being transient Chinese and Indian men who came into the port under indentured contracts. These men had little interest in improving a city so far away from home. They crammed into dilapidated housing, slowly starved, and suffered through epidemics of tropical diseases. Most of these men sought a measure of relief from their long hours of backbreaking work in drugs and sex—most of the Chinese and Japanese women who were brought into the port were under contract to serve as prostitutes for transient workers, and the majority of Chinese settlers regularly smoked opium (Abshire 2011:68–69; Warren 1990:361).

The East India Company's disinterest in the well-being of Singapore's residents was also seen in its refusal to invest in the growing city's infrastructure. The water supply remained inadequate almost 40 years after Singapore was founded, and there was still no sewage system, health care, or educational opportunities for the nonelite. The company's neglect was suffocating the city by midcentury, by which point the port's facilities were congested and outdated and the city's streets were jammed with traffic all day long (Turnbull 1989:113–115). To safeguard its interests in the city, the British Crown took over the settlement from the East India Company in 1867.

When British administrators arrived, they were horrified by how the city had been managed—an official commission reporting on Singapore and the other strait settlements exclaimed that "the vast majority of Chinamen who come to work in these settlements return to their country not knowing clearly whether there is a government in them or not" (Frost and Balasingamchow 2009:163). Municipal expenditures in Singapore had been $63,000 annually in the last years of the East India Company, but the crown increased this to $500,000 by 1886 in an effort to extend its tenuous control over the city.

British investment in the city was fueled by the city's increasing importance in the empire. The Suez Canal opened in 1869, and steamships were now making Singapore a regular port of call as a coaling station in the trade networks that connected Europe and East Asia. Rubber and petroleum would also soon join tin as the island's major exports (Huff 1993). The city's trade volume expanded eightfold between 1873 and 1913, and the population surged from 96,087 in 1871 to 303,321 in 1911 (Saw 1969:39; Turnbull 1989:89–91). The British government responded to the city's growth by building a general hospital and central police station in 1882, instituting a professional fire brigade in 1888, and expanding the city's water reservoir in 1904 (Turnbull 1989:111–112). The 1910s and 1920s saw further infrastructural improvements, as the city continued to invest heavily in hospitals, roads, and electricity (Turnbull 1989:128–129).

Efforts to improve city services were assisted by some of the more affluent Asian merchants who had been born in the city. Now citizens of the British Empire, these merchants had a more vested interest in collaborating with the crown. Many began to adopt certain Western customs, take on administrative roles within the municipal government, and reinvest a portion of their money in the city rather than sending it abroad (Aplin and Jong 2002; Frost 2005). The support of these and other community leaders in Singapore was critical as British authorities began to regulate immigration as well as improve education, health care, and public transportation (Frasch 2012; Warren 1990).

Despite these efforts to make over the settlement, early twentieth-century Singapore remained a city composed largely of poor, transient men from China. In 1911 72.4 percent of the city's population was Chinese (Saw 1969:39, 41), and there were eight men for every woman (Turnbull 1989:95). The port continued to live up to its lawless reputation—fights between street gangs were still a daily occurrence in the 1920s—and there was entrenched resistance to any municipal oversight that upset the status quo of enclave independence. Riots greeted the establishment of a post office in Chinatown, for example, and an 1888 decision to clear the sidewalks of retail merchandise caused another outbreak in violence. A British official barely survived an assassination attempt caused by his efforts to curb gambling and break up the secret societies (Frost and Balasingamchow 2009:163–164, 173).

Singapore's population kept growing in the interwar period, reaching 577,745 in 1931 and exceeding 750,000 by 1940 (Saw 1969:39). A restrictive immigration policy in the 1930s, meanwhile, helped to bring the sex ratio to near parity by the time of the Second World War (Saw 1969:42; Turnbull 1989:145). More and more of the people living in Singapore had been born on the island, and a new professional class emerged of lawyers, engineers, doctors, and journalists who had grown up in the settlement and were passionately committed to its development into a world-class city (Frost 2005:30). Though most people still lived in poverty, Singapore was finally beginning to feel more like a city in the 1930s rather than a hardscrabble port where men made money for a few years before going home. The city's "ungainly process of becoming" had taken just over a century—created via a multigenerational struggle that was quite different from our antiseptic, mechanistic models postulated for the rise of early civilization.

São Paulo, 1820–1930

The founders of São Paulo never imagined that the settlement would become a city. In 1554, a small group of Jesuits struggled over a coastal mountain range in southern Brazil in order to establish a religious school among the native population. The school, christened São Paulo do Campo de Piratinigua, became the nucleus of a hilltop village that served as a launching station for those seeking to explore, and later settle, Brazil's vast interior plateau. By 1600, São Paulo had grown into a settlement of more than 2,000 people that included indigenous slaves along with Spanish, Portuguese, German, and Italian colonists (Morse 1974:11). The area in and around São Paulo continued to fill in during the eighteenth century, and by 1765 there were about 6,000 people who called the area home (Morse 1974:16).

Though 20,000 people officially lived in São Paulo and its rural parishes in 1820, it still retained the feel of a much smaller community (Morse 1974:31). The bulk of greater São Paulo's population was comprised of African slaves that were tied to nearby sugar, tea, and coffee plantations. Most free families lived on farms and ranches outside the settlement and only occasionally came to São Paulo. The town itself was made up of only a dozen haphazard streets, a few public buildings, and some residences. Small estates encircled São Paulo proper, and these estates were in turn surrounded by the smaller subsistence holdings of poorer families (Peixoto-Mehrtens 2010:15). Social order was maintained through adherence to a strict patriarchal code of behavior (Morse 1974:43), while the town's religious order, now Franciscans, provided welfare to the less fortunate. There was a municipal authority that ran the town's hospital and prison, but ad hoc committees came together to perform tasks like fighting fires and draining swamps in and around town (Morse 1974:28–30).

São Paulo was an isolated community whose inhabitants were used to providing for themselves. The local population thus expected little from either the Portuguese Crown or city officials, and these expectations did not change in 1822 when Brazil became independent. The town was separated from the coast by an arduous, often dangerous, 45-kilometer climb from the port of Santos. The road to the coast was often washed out in the rainy season, and the mountainous climb was so trying on mule trains that many animals died en route. Traders occasionally carried dried meat, cane alcohol, and especially sugar down from São Paulo in return for salt, glassware, cloth, and other items (Morse 1974:22), but 30 to 50 percent of the profits for São Paulo producers were eaten up by transport-related costs (Mattoon 1977:276). With little to gain from engaging with external markets, inhabitants ended up producing most goods in the home and exchanging them in town (Kuznesof 1980:598).

Change occurred gradually in São Paulo during the mid-nineteenth century. The town became the seat of the new provincial government after independence, and one of the country's two academies of law was founded in the town in 1823 (Morse 1974:51–54). The influx of legislators, professors, and students added a more cosmopolitan feel to the city, as did the immigration into the city of a few hundred Western and Central Europeans that set up restaurants, hotels, and other services. Although these new arrivals were relatively few in number, they tended to settle in town rather than in the surrounding countryside. São Paulo's patchwork infrastructure had worked for a few hundred full-time residents, but it could not handle a few thousand. Drinking water, for example, became scarce, and the existing schools could only accommodate a small fraction of the children (Morse 1974:51–54). There was not even a designated space for burying the dead, since this had traditionally been done on family landholdings outside of the settlement.

The population growth of greater São Paulo reached a plateau in the 1850s and then declined slightly from 31,569 to 31,385 between 1854 and 1874 (Mattoon 1977:278). This decline reflects in part the town's inability to improve basic services, but more importantly the region around São Paulo seemed to have reached its carrying capacity. The soil was poor for intensive agriculture, and São Paulo's links to outside markets were problematic as long as its inhabitants depended on the road to Santos. If nothing had changed during the second half of the nineteenth century, São Paulo would have likely remained an isolated frontier town.

Three developments, however, led to the town's sudden growth. The first development was the completion in 1867 of a British-run railroad between Santos and São Paulo. The completion of this link to the Atlantic Ocean inspired local entrepreneurs to begin a 50-year program of railroad expansion that would lay over 7,000 kilometers of tracks into the area's agricultural and ranch lands. Since all of these railroads funneled into São Paulo, the town could finally realize its full potential as a gateway to Brazil's interior plateau (Mattoon 1977:285–286).

The second change was the increased worldwide demand for coffee. Although its price fluctuated widely, a growing market for coffee led to the crop replacing sugar as the leading export in the region by 1851. By 1860, there were almost 27 million coffee trees on the hills surrounding São Paulo (Mattoon 1977:285–286). Planting trees farther away from town was initially impossible because high transport costs ate up profits, but railways started reaching deeper and deeper into the plateau by the 1870s. Coffee trees could now be grown across hundreds of kilometers at a fraction of the previous cost. The province became the country's largest coffee producer by the turn of the century, and by 1930 it was home to 1.2 billion trees (Font 1990:15; Mattoon 1977:286). All of this coffee flowed through the city of São Paulo on its way to the coast.

The third change was the introduction of free labor: workers were necessary for building railroads and harvesting coffee trees (Stolcke and Hall 1978). The slave trade had been abolished in the 1850s, and railroad and plantation owners knew that the outright end of slavery in Brazil would soon follow. The railways therefore hired European and American workers, and the plantations quickly followed suit (Mattoon 1977:289). Swiss and German sharecroppers were the first groups brought in to meet the coffee plantations' seemingly insatiable need for labor. Wage labor replaced sharecropping by the 1870s, and in 1886 the provincial government used taxes on coffee exports to create a subsidy that paid for the costs of families migrating to the region (Stolcke and Hall 1978:171–176).

More than two million people, many of them Italians, immigrated to the São Paulo region between 1886 and 1930 (Holloway 1978:188). Almost all of these immigrants spent at least a few days in the city of São Paulo. A hostel was constructed in 1887 that provided free food and lodging for as many as 10,000 immigrants at a time as they waited for their assignment to a coffee plantation (Holloway 1978:194). Many immigrants eventually chose to settle in the city, and former slaves also left the plantation to find work in São Paulo. São Paulo's population went from 23,000 in 1872 to 47,000 in 1885, and then to 375,000 in 1910 (Font 1992:33; Greenfield 1980:108; Morse 1974:173).

The city could not handle this influx of settlers. Trash piled up, and some streets were "perpetually covered with mud and filth" (Greenfield 1980:109). Water pipes—at one time made from bitumen-coated cardboard—served only a small percentage of buildings, and only the rudimentary beginning of a public transportation system composed of animal-drawn streetcars was in place (Morse 1974:179–181). Crime skyrocketed throughout the city, corruption was rampant, and officials could only watch as smallpox and cholera epidemics ravaged the population.

The only way for the city to build infrastructure quickly was to grant concessions to entrepreneurs (Peixoto-Mehrtens 2010:22). Major utilities like electricity were taken over by foreign companies, while locals took up less profitable concessions. City officials were incapable of regulating these private enterprises, and the public constantly complained about the quality of service (Greenfield 1980:108). Outsourcing nonetheless worked as a stopgap measure. Gas lighting, telephones, and fire hydrants were installed in the city in the 1880s by contracted businesses, while the city channeled its resources into beautification projects like tree-lined boulevards and a new opera house (Greenfield 1980:114; Morse 1974:179).

The region's light market demands during much of the nineteenth century had been met primarily by family firms working from their homes (Kuznesof 1980), but greater demand led to the first factories being founded in the 1870s. The new railroads, immigrants, and coffee revenues helped support the further industrialization of São Paulo. By 1887 the city already boasted a brick and tile factory, a slaughterhouse, a textile mill, five foundries, and other enterprises (Morse 1974:179). Cheap labor and transportation costs, compounded by favorable municipal and state policies, led to an industrial boom in the 1890s. By 1914 there were at least 1,715 factories in the city, and there were some 3,232 by 1929 (Font 1992:34). The city also filled in—the number of structures within the city limits increased from 33,000 to more than 100,000 in 1930—and the population surged past a million in 1930 (Font 1992:34).

Immigrants owned most of São Paulo's factories, and two-thirds of the city's population was foreign-born in 1920 (Font 1992:34; Owensby 1999:27). Many of these foreigners were Italian, but they were also large numbers of recently arrived Spaniards, Portuguese, Japanese, Germans, and Poles (Font 1992:35). Demand for skilled labor in the factories led to the emergence of a middle class, but that did little to improve the lives of unskilled laborers, who found themselves working for lower and lower pay in unsafe conditions. Afro-Brazilians in particular grew increasingly angry, as racism and limited access to training conspired to shrink their job opportunities to street cleaning and other menial positions (Andrews 1988:505;

Monsma 2006:1143). If this was not enough, the prices of staples like rice, beans, and sugar continued to rise, and during the First World War, the supply of food into the city grew extremely unstable (Owensby 1999:30–32; Wolfe 1991:816).

In the summer of 1917 45,000 workers walked off their jobs in the first of dozens of general strikes that would paralyze São Paulo. Union workers, anarchists, police, and the military fought in the streets, and the mayor moved to fulfill an earlier pledge to cleanse the working-class neighborhoods of their "vicious mixture of scum of all nationalities, all ages, all of them dangerous" (quoted in Wolfe 1991:815). The strikes continued throughout the 1920s, as factories expanded their work forces and embraced standardized, low-cost mass production (Wolfe 1993:41–46). Profits surged despite this unrest, and migrants from other parts of Brazil flooded the city. São Paulo entered the Great Depression as the richest, most industrialized, city in Latin America, but it seemed to convulse from one social upheaval to the next.

Los Angeles, 1850–1930

Los Angeles's chaotic early growth provides another challenge to our assumptions about early urbanism. The 1,610 people living in the isolated settlement hardly noticed when it was admitted to the United States of American in 1850. Los Angeles's economy was based almost exclusively on cattle that were grazed on vast landholdings called ranchos. The rancheros were happy to live off of their animals' products, and they used their excess hides and tallow to acquire a few luxury items from boats that moved up and down the coast (Bowman 1971:141–142; Fogelson 1967:5–12). Everyone in Los Angeles was Catholic, and everyone knew each other. There were no hotels, street signs, or police. Irrigation ditches provided a source of drinking water as well as places to bathe and clean one's animals. Buildings were clustered tightly together around the plaza, and the town's few roads were narrow, haphazard, and often impassable (Fogelson 1967:24–27).

California's admittance into the United States seemed unlikely to change life in Los Angeles. The dry climate precluded extensive agriculture, there were no industries in town to attract newcomers, and the ranchero families were also largely happy with the status quo. Statehood nonetheless brought with it two unanticipated changes that would swiftly break up the ranchos and alter the character of the settlement. Admittance into the union meant that the rancheros would not only need to pay property tax for the first time but also would also need to demonstrate clear title to their land. To pay their bills, many entered the booming cattle market engendered by the gold rush in northern California. When this market collapsed at the same time as a decade-long drought was depressing cattle and agricultural production, many landowners sold portions of their property to cover losses.

European Americans seized the opportunity to purchase land around Los Angeles and began to diversify the economy by creating vineyards, wheat fields, and sheep ranches. More settlers arrived to work at these new enterprises and to establish smaller ones on new subdivisions. By 1880, the amount of farmed land had increased a hundredfold, and some plots had increased 20 times in value. Los Angeles County's population ballooned in size from 4,000 to 34,000 in those three decades, and the population of the town of Los Angeles grew to 11,183 (Fogelson 1967:20).

The city was unprepared for the arrival of these newcomers (Ehrenfeucht 2012). Bandits stole thousands of animals, murders were committed with impunity, and many were aghast when the first shipload of prostitutes arrived from San Francisco in 1853 (Bowman 1974:150–151). There was also no fire company, post office, or public school. Itinerant dentists and doctors served the community sporadically, and other needs were fulfilled by jacks-of-all-trades—Charles L. Ducommun, for example, was a "watchmaker, jeweler, bookseller, stationer, tobacconist, and dealer in paints and glass" (Bowman 1974:158). A welter of hawkers and peddlers fought (sometimes literally) with shopkeepers for customers' business on disorderly streets, and ethnic tensions simmered as groups of Native Americans, Mexicans, Europeans, African Americans, and Chinese settled into different parts of the city (Ehrenfeucht 2012:109).

Newcomers were appalled at the chaotic and unsanitary living conditions of Los Angeles, and this sentiment was echoed by a grand jury that decided unanimously in 1861 that the local government was "a nuisance" that should be "wiped from existence" (Fogelson 1967:28). Residents had such little faith in public officials that they initially refused to pay more in taxes for improvements to the city's infrastructure. Over the next two decades, however, municipal authorities nonetheless managed to gain control over more and more aspects of city life. An administrator was put in control of the water system; inspectors were appointed to monitor butcher shops; regulations were put in place to ease traffic congestion and regulate building activities; and full-time public servants were hired to replace volunteer fire and police officers (Fogelson 1967:28–34). Despite these advances, the city still needed to turn to private investors to build its roads, telephone lines, electric grid, and sewage system (Hise 2009:482).

Unregulated growth was meanwhile clogging the city center with industries and creating a landscape of factories and freight yards "cheek-by jowl with the city's finest hotels and commercial block"—a slaughterhouse and fertilizer plant, for instance, stood a few steps away from Los Angeles's central plaza (Hise 2009:477). Profiting off the desires of newcomers to avoid the unruly city center, land speculators subdivided rural lots and then linked these lots at their own expense to the city's expanding network of basic services (Fogelson 1967:38–42). Los Angeles thus began to sprawl outward in the 1870s toward smaller nearby towns like Pasadena and Anaheim. Despite this growth, the region's population seemed to reach its maximum possible extent by around 1880. To expand further, Los Angeles would need much more water, as well as reliable railroad and shipping access. Somehow it got all three.

City voters first agreed to give $500,000 in 1878 to the Southern Pacific railway in order for the company to lay the first tracks into Los Angeles. The region thus became reliably connected to the rest of the United States, and competition between other railroad companies during the next decade resulted in the linking together of most of the surrounding towns into a system of freight and passenger rail that was anchored in Los Angeles. The city was suddenly no longer difficult to get to, and a fare war in the 1880s dropped the price of a cross-country ticket to the city from $10 to $1 (Bowman 1974:216).

As the railroads were being built, city officials were lobbying Congress for the dredging and creation of a breakwater in San Pedro, the closest harbor to Los Angeles. Since San Pedro was often too shallow for deep-water vessels, ship captains had to routinely anchor far offshore and then use skiffs to laboriously bring their cargo to land. San Diego boasted a far superior harbor, but Los Angelinos somehow managed to convince the federal government that they should invest in their city rather than in their southern rival. In 1899, the Army Corps of Engineers started a project to improve San Pedro that concluded just after the Panama Canal opened in 1914. Once the West Coast was tied to the global shipping economy, the amount of ocean freight moving through Los Angeles skyrocketed, increasing from 200 to 29,106 tons between 1899 and 1929 (Fogelson 1967:119).

Despite its burgeoning rail and sea connections, Los Angeles still faced an acute shortage of water. Artesian wells dug in the 1870s and 1880s had met most early demands, and the city further conserved water by replacing its open canals with pipes for irrigation and sewage (Torres-Rouff 2006). Yet the city's population was approaching 100,000 by 1889, and a more radical solution to its water woes was needed. That year the superintendent of the water department, William Mulholland, began an audacious scheme to siphon off water from the Owens River. The controversial plan plunged the city into debt and required the creation of a 400-kilometer aqueduct through the mountains to the coastal plain (Kahrl 1976). Los Angeles sought to recoup the costs of construction by annexing nearby communities in exchange for water rights. The greatest beneficiaries of the plan were a "syndicate of speculators" who used their political influence to determine where surplus water would be allocated when the aqueduct was completed in 1913 (Kahrl 1976:99). In a few years the city had expanded to four times its original size (Bowman 1974:251).

Migration into southern California during the last decades of the nineteenth century was stimulated in large part by the promotion of the region as a place of leisure. Charles Norhoff, for example, sold three million copies of his *California: For Health, Pleasure, and Residence* (1873), and pamphlet after pamphlet praised Los Angeles's Mediterranean climate, fruit orchards, and clean living (Culver 2010:20–22). Many of the people who came to the region chose to settle in the county's smaller bedroom communities and commute to downtown Los Angeles via the electric railroad system that had been built in the first decade of the twentieth century (Bowman 1974:260).

People kept coming, and by 1920 there were 576,700 people in the city of Los Angeles alone. Many had been lured west by a promised lifestyle that was typified by a single-family bungalow surrounded by a yard and garden (Culver 2010:56). Oil strikes in and around the city added an allure of easy money—Southern California would produce one quarter of the world's oil supply in 1923 (Elkind 2012; Fogelson 1967:126–128)—as did the first generation of Hollywood stars (Bowman 1974:230). The advertised bucolic nature of the city proved difficult to sustain, however, as the numbers of migrants swelled. A hundred thousand people arrived each year during the 1920s, and ethnic and class tensions flared as the gulf between California's promise and reality widened. Strikes periodically paralyzed many industries, and segregation led to the confining of most of the city's African American population to Watts and a few other neighborhoods.

The social disruptions of the 1920s were exacerbated by the strangulation of downtown businesses and industries. Most people came into downtown to work and shop, and they were increasingly deciding to drive into the city, as automobiles became more affordable. The number of cars in Los Angeles increased more than fivefold in the 1920s. Some 770,000 cars were registered in the county by 1929, and the thousands of novice drivers created pandemonium in the narrow streets of the city (Axelrod 2006:7; Foster 1975:464). Business fled downtown, and the public transportation network that shared the roads grew increasingly sluggish.

Los Angeles's notoriously corrupt government was only beginning to deal with the problems of rapid growth. A city planning department was finally put into place in 1925, and soon after the city managed to gain control of water, gas, electricity, and telephone lines that had for decades been held privately by companies that gouged their customers by providing inferior service at an exorbitant price (Fogelson 1967:229, 249). Rather than fighting Los Angeles's low-density sprawl, planners embraced it as a better model for urban living and raced, often unsuccessfully, to regulate land use as the city seemed to grow ever larger. When the Great Depression began in 1930, 1,238,048 individuals made their home in a dispersed, still often dysfunctional, city.

Abu Dhabi, 1950–2010

At first glance, our last case study best fits with models that tout a steplike transition to civilization—a single charismatic leader, Zayed bin Sultan Al-Nahyan, transformed a chiefdom into the capital of one the most prosperous states in the world in little more than a generation. A focus on a sheik raising skyscrapers from the sand, however, misses most of the story and ignores the exuberance, miscalculations, and confusion common to incipient urbanization that prevailed in the three decades that it took to change a village into the metropolis of Abu Dhabi.

In 1950 Abu Dhabi was the temporary home of about 2,000 people (Al Fahim 1995:37). Most people left the island community during the hot summer months, which was when many of the men set out for three months to dive for pearls. The town had been larger 50 years earlier during a period of prosperity, but political instability and a decline in pearl prices had left it depopulated (Commins 2012:86). Most of the people who remained in Abu Dhabi after this period lived in houses made from the leaves of date palms, traveled on the back of camels, and survived on brackish water pulled from the community's wells (Al Fahim 1995:25). Firewood and other necessities came from Bedouin traders or arrived sporadically in boats that called on the villages of the southern Arabian Gulf. Almost everyone was illiterate—the only school was run by "a teacher, poet, barber, marriage counselor, imam of the mosque and the community's healer" who had a smattering of students that read a page each day from the Quran (Al Fahim 1995:58).

Abu Dhabi was the capital of one of the tribal groups in the region that had collectively come to be known as the Trucial States after signing a truce with the British Empire in 1820. The Trucial States were protectorates of the empire but the British played only a very limited role in their internal affairs (Davidson 2009:23–24). The British became more interested in the late 1930s when oil explorations began discovering huge reserves in Abu Dhabi as well as in other places in the Middle East. Oil reserves, at first, had little impact on life in the town. The ruler of Abu Dhabi in 1950, Shakhbut bin Sultan Al-Nahyan, was distrustful of the British and slow to negotiate with the English over landing and oil exploration rights worth millions of dollars. Worried about the corruption of wealth, inflation, and the possibilities of a recession, Sheikh Shakhbut left the money that accumulated in his accounts largely untouched. He banned all new construction, blocked the entry of foreign merchants, and restricted the community largess of his family members (Davidson 2009:32–33; Rabi 2006:43–44).

Despite the sheik's resistance to change, Abu Dhabi began to see limited infrastructural investments by the late 1950s. A six-room schoolhouse was grudgingly built in 1959, and two desalination plants and a hotel were opened by 1962 (Al Fahim 1995:77–79). The community of 3,654 seemed to sit on the cusp of a sweeping transformation—oil companies had paid Shakhbut $2 million in 1962 (El Mallakh 1970:137)—but Abu Dhabi's inhabitants still lived without plumbing, paved roads, and electricity.

Members of the sheik's family, supported by the British, tried to convince Shakhbut to speed up the development of Abu Dhabi and the surrounding region. The sheik refused, and in August 1966 a detachment of British soldiers deposed Shakhbut and set up his brother, Zayed bin Sultan Al-Nahyan, as the seventeenth ruler of Abu Dhabi (Rabi 2006:49–50). Sheik Zayed not only inherited Shakhbut's stockpiled funds but also had at his disposal annual oil revenues that had increased a hundredfold by 1967 to $110.6 million (El Mallakh 1970:137). Zayed immediately created a new government made up of tribal leaders to oversee the development of the region. He further legitimized his rule by removing all taxes in the sheikdom and handing out new homes, land, and agricultural equipment to the region's poorer families (Davidson 2009:51–53).

The sheik encouraged neighboring groups to settle in the city, and these settlers were joined by a stream of foreign oil workers, laborers, and speculators. When Mohammed Al Fahim returned to Abu Dhabi in 1967 after three years abroad, he was amazed at what he saw (1995:136):

> The sleepy fishing village I had left was now a bustling construction site. There were trucks, bulldozers, cars, and people everywhere—they were doing everything from building roads to laying cables—Abu Dhabi was a hive of activity. There were labor camps everywhere to accommodate the large number of workers required for the countless construction projects. Commercial buildings, government building, housing, warehouses, shops—all were going up simultaneously. It was like a scene from the creation of a film set—a whole city was being erected from scratch.

Abu Dhabi, of course, was much more than a movie set. The entire infrastructure of a city—police, urban planning, a judiciary, sanitation—was frenetically being created as well.

Abu Dhabi's anarchic growth in the late 1960s could perhaps be best seen on its beaches. Before a proper port could be constructed, freighters bringing goods to the city were forced to anchor three to four kilometers off the coast and await the arrival of flat barges to bring items to shore (El Mallakh 1970:141). Car and car parts were among the items in highest demand in the city—one merchant went from ordering 200 car tires in 1966 to ordering 10,000 in 1967 (Al Fahim 1995:139). When cars arrived they were purchased immediately with bundles of cash, and there was "no paperwork involved, no documentation or licensing, not even an invoice" (Al Fahim 1995:139).

To build up Abu Dhabi and the surrounding region, Sheik Zayed awarded contracts to local businessmen. They in turn brought in foreign specialists, as well as thousands of workers. There was no place for these people to live, and the settlement's electrical, water, and sewage system were virtually nonexistent. In the rush to create a city, locals were swindled, construction shortcuts were taken, and tribal tensions flared up (Al Fahim 1995:139). The barely contained chaos in Abu Dhabi was mirrored in the surrounding country. The sheik struggled to provide basic services to outlying areas, and he faced setback after setback in his plans to intensify agriculture in the region's oases (Stevens 1970).

In 1968, in the midst of efforts to manage Abu Dhabi's growth, the British announced their intention to withdraw from the region. Sheik Zayed spent the next three years in negotiations to form a confederation among a subset of the Trucial States. The United Arab Emirates (UAE) was formed under a provisional constitution at the end of 1971, but for the next eight years disputes among federation members threatened to tear it apart (Davidson 2009:60–64). As Zayed struggled to create a state, Abu Dhabi continued its frenetic growth. The city's population went from 46,000 in 1968 to almost 128,000 in 1975. The sheik threw money at his problems by continuing to dole out funds to his tribesman to encourage investments in the city, and also by providing financial assistance to foreign leaders in order to help legitimate the UAE (Al Fahim 1995:163–164).

Unfettered growth, however, was unsustainable. In 1976 a recession hit, leaving projects unfinished and many Abu Dhabians in debt. A hidden benefit of the three-year recession was that it allowed time for the government to gain greater control over the city. After taking command of the city's land holdings in 1981, the sheik's government built and then managed thousands of rental properties. The state also began to enforce building codes, encourage the construction of high rises to increase urban density, and demolish hundreds of unsafe structures that had been built before the recession (Al Fahim 1995:155–159). Finally, Sheik Zayed used the recession to encourage the growth of the city's investments firms, heavy industries, and sustainable energy corporations in order to diversify the economy so that it would not be solely dependent on oil production (Davidson 2007:38–39).

With the economy flourishing once again in the 1980s, the city continued to grow. Abu Dhabi's population exceeded 280,000 in 1985, and would near 400,000 by 1995. The city's population growth came largely from an increasing influx of foreign workers. By 2008, the city was home to over a million inhabitants, three-quarters of whom came from abroad. Rather than assimilating foreigners into the state, the UAE denied these individuals the right to become citizens or even permanent residents (Mohammad and Sidaway 2012:608). Most of these visitors were instead issued temporary work visas; a majority of the men on these visas came from South Asia, while the majority of the women were from Southeast Asia. These workers lived in shoddily constructed 1970s apartment buildings in peripheral neighborhoods of the city that were separated from the more recently built glossy malls, luxury hotels, and skyscrapers in the city center (Mohammad and Sidaway 2012:608).

When Sheik Zayed bin Sultan Al-Nahyan died in 2004, Abu Dhabi remained still very much a work in progress. Traffic, for example, was horrendous, and there were no municipal plans for improving public transportation (Abdo 2010:20). One of the most important urban transformations that remained unfinished was the construction of a multicultural society (Bristol-Rhys 2007). By only allowing the leading families of 1960s Abu Dhabi to participate in government, Zayed was able to rely on kinship ties in order to more easily manage the transition to a state government and capitalist economy. Yet the informal structures that have managed the city thus far are increasingly strained as population grows and wealth disparities widen. The reliance on "tribal capitalism" has also caused friction between the emirates that still lingers today (Davidson 2009:110). Zayed's son, Sheik Khalifa bin Zayed Al-Nahyan, recognizes these inadequacies and has initiated limited reforms to create a more inclusive, transparent government.

Ungainly Urbanization and an Alternative to Civilization

For scholars used to understanding ancient history in century-long chunks of time, the formative decades of Singapore, São Paulo, Los Angeles, and Abu Dhabi are humbling examples of incipient urbanization. A hundred years of growth created a Singapore that would be almost wholly unrecognizable to the few dozen families that lived in the settlement in 1811, and a Bedouin trader who got lost in the desert in the 1960s would be overwhelmed by the Abu Dhabi of 1975. The changes that occurred in these four places were not simply cumulative—the Los Angeles of 1880 was not a microcosm of 1930s Los Angeles. These cities were instead transformed over time in radical ways as their inhabitants figured out how to live together. As the cities changed, so did the surrounding countryside. Today's São Paulo cannot therefore be used as a stand-in for what life in and around São Paulo could have been like even a century ago, and, similarly, we should be very weary of using Caesar's Rome or Seti's Thebes to model the dynamics of the world's earliest urbanizations.

It might be tempting to dismiss what could be learned from the urbanization of places like Singapore, São Paulo, Los Angeles, and Abu Dhabi as irrelevant to those of us who are studying the first urban centers. The rise of all four cities, after all, can be tied to recent technological innovations and the expansion of global capitalism. There is nothing quintessentially modern, however, about rapid urbanization. For more than 5,000 years, people have occasionally come together to form cities over the space of a few generations. The mix of reasons why people have come together has changed over time, as have many of the ways in which communities are formed. Yet I suggest that the creation of a well-functioning city is always a struggle, and our four case studies give a sense of "the ungainly process of becoming" that can be difficult to see in earlier eras (Kaplan 2012:56).

If anything, one might expect that contemporary urbanization would be easier to manage. Conceived in an era of strong nation-states and globe-spanning empires, the first city plans of early Singapore, Los Angeles, São Paulo, and Abu Dhabi seem to exude centralized control. Old Los Angeles, for example, was centered on the plaza, the church, and the homes of prominent families. Government offices, a church, and courthouse stood on a prominent hill overlooking Singapore's harbor soon after the colony was founded. A global precedent of centralized control over many aspects of urban life had been set by the time of our four case studies, and there was an expectation in many quarters that a growing city would be administered by a municipal government that was nested within an overarching state structure. Yet administrators were still quickly overwhelmed as population increased dramatically in the space of a few decades. Hundreds of houses needed to be built, thousands of sick needed to be tended, mountains of garbage needed to be picked up, and dozens of poorly lit streets needed to be patrolled. The cities may have looked good on paper, but our four case studies demonstrate that municipality governments—despite the world's 5,000-year history of living in cities—were initially not up to the task of organizing urban life.

The first response of municipal officials to urban growth in all four of our cities was to severely limit their responsibilities. São Paulo's growing pool of laborers was pushed to an outer ring of rural parishes, and in Los Angeles, people were initially encouraged to settle in small, outlying towns. Sir Stamford Raffles decided at the outset that there would be little oversight over the enclaves that made up almost all of Singapore's population; Sheik Zayed bin Sultan Al-Nahyan at first delegated much of the work of creating Abu Dhabi to outside contractors. When local authorities got involved, they tended to rely on traditional mechanisms of oversight and control that had already been long proven ineffective. Vigilante squads, secret societies, religious orders, and a plethora of other organizations stepped in to provide at least some of the basic social services that the municipal governments could not, while local entrepreneurs and foreign companies spearheaded infrastructural developments with little involvement from city officials.

The hurly-burly first decades of these cities should not be surprising. Although citizens recognize that major investments are needed to sustain their settlement, sewer pipes do not grow overnight. Nor do tax codes, public gardens, police forces, and well-functioning bureaucracies. It takes time to build both the physical infrastructure of a city, as well as the myriad of social ties that make urban life possible. A functioning countryside also emerges only in fits and starts, and it is difficult to establish the long-distance diplomatic and exchange relationships that are also necessary to sustain the city. Singapore, São Paulo, Los Angeles, and Abu Dhabi all experienced these kinds of struggles even though many of the administrators in these cities *knew* how to run a city. Many of these technocrats came from more established cities. They could also consult with urban planners, introduce practices and technologies that had worked well in other cities, and read about how other municipalities managed urban growth.

No one knew how to run the world's earliest cities. Although administrative challenges were in some ways less daunting—there were no electrical lines to install, and populations numbered in the tens of thousands rather than the millions—there was no one with ready answers to the pressing concerns of supplying the daily fuel for a thousand hearths or resolving disputes between rival religious factions without bloodshed. The institutions of a well-functioning village could not simply be expanded to fit the needs of a larger population. Mechanical solidarity, as Durkheim noted more than a century ago, had to give way to organic solidarity when people moved into cities and took on more specialized tasks (1984:133–136 [1893]). Political, economic, and social structures needed to be radically reorganized for a city to survive, but there was no blueprint available for creating an urban way of life when populations first aggregated.

It seems obvious that new societies are not formed while people sleep, but the idea of civilization's steplike transition can make it look that way in its tendency to preclude the kinds of disorderly, disheveled, decades-long processes of urbanization that have been typical in the modern world. Cities, states, colonies, and broad cultural horizons have long been tightly bound together in the civilization concept. Recognizing that the world's earliest cities experienced an "ungainly process of becoming" is a critical aspect of my alternative to the concept because an acknowledgment of the messy beginnings of cities calls into questions those models that suggest that a first generation of administrators were capable of creating a well-oiled city and regional polity that could project its power deeper and deeper into the hinterland. If it took time to figure things out, then gaining effective administration over a city and countryside was a difficult, extended process that would succeed only after the initial spread of colonies and cultural horizons. Traits such as the state, bureaucracies, and writing can no longer be seen as hallmarks of civilization in this alternative vision; rather, they should be seen as the occasional, often accidental, by-products of people working—often at cross-purposes—to mitigate the problems of increasing settlement size and density.

Now that our modern case studies have helped emphasize the inherent challenges of urbanization, we turn to the archaeological record from six regions of the world in order to more fully develop an alternative explanation for the creation of the world's earliest cities, states, colonies, and cultural horizons. We begin in an unlikely place: Çatalhöyük. A Neolithic town in central Anatolia that grew to house a few thousand people before its population dissipated, Çatalhöyük is no longer viewed by most scholars as an early city. Yet it is important to our argument because it expanded dramatically in size without forcing residents to make fundamental structural changes to their lives and to the lives of those around them, and it also managed to continue to function at this larger size for more than a thousand years. The frenetic first years of ancient cities like Rome and Huari are largely lost to us—our temporal resolution just isn't good enough to accurately track what was happening during the growth spurts of these settlements. Fortunately, settlements like Çatalhöyük managed to live on the cusp of urbanization long enough for us to see what people did when a settlement first began expanding far beyond the scale of a typical village.

4

ÇATALHÖYÜK AND THE ABORTED CITIES OF THE NEOLITHIC NEAR EAST

THE DESCRIPTION OF SINGAPORE, SÃO PAULO, LOS ANGELES, AND Abu Dhabi's dynamic growth in the previous chapter provides a sense of the range of challenges and opportunities that the residents of any community would face during the first decades of urbanization. A focus on cities, however, can also create a false sense of the inevitability of an urban transition once people began migrating into a village—cities are actually the exception to the rule. For every settlement that becomes a São Paulo, there are dozens of nearby towns that grew quickly early on before plateauing or decreasing in size. These towns might be seen as failures when viewed in hindsight from a well-functioning metropolis. Yet these "failures" were often the result of successful efforts at the time to alleviate the stresses caused by rapid population aggregation. The most obvious solution to too many people coming together too quickly is to stop people from coming, and, as our case studies of recent urbanizations show, the failed settlements could instead be seen as those places that grew into cities after residents were unable to control immigration, arrest wealth disparities, and regulate industry.

Although the modern case studies in the previous chapter provide us with a sense of "the ungainly process of becoming" that accompanied the growth of all cities (Kaplan 2012:56), we must return to the villages of the ancient world in order to better understand the particularities of how urbanism began to unfold for the first time. There are many advantages to city life, but for hundreds, and in some regions thousands, of years humans instead chose to live in villages. When the population of a settlement climbed to more than a few hundred, people left. Only on very rare occasions did a group inadvertently begin the urbanization process by deciding to stay together.

I previously defined cities as permanent settlements that have a large population size, a dense population nucleation, and a high heterogeneity in the social roles of inhabitants and that engage in activities and establish institutions that affect a larger hinterland. Most early cities grew quickly, and a village-to-city transition over the course of a few decades or even of a couple of centuries can be very difficult for archaeologists to track clearly without written records. Fortunately, communities have occasionally managed to arrest the urbanization process midstream for centuries by curtailing the growth of both heterogeneity and hinterland activities. These settlements, with populations in the mid- to high thousands, can be seen as aborted cities and as such offer insights into the social, political, and economic mechanisms at play when the population of a village first started to expand.

As the first part of this chapter attests, many of these village-based mechanisms converged to impede urbanization via an extensive, taut web of preexisting relationships between people, animals, and objects that served to limit societal change (e.g., Hodder 2012). When settlements continued to expand, there were ongoing conflicts and accommodations. Many people fought to maintain the status quo, and no one quite knew how to foster sustainable growth. The second part of this chapter provides an in-depth look into life in the aborted city of Çatalhöyük, a settlement that was occupied during the eighth through sixth millennium BC in Turkey. Although many scholars have used Çatalhöyük as *the* model for early city life ever since James Mellaart's excavations (1965) almost 60 years ago (e.g., Jacobs 1969; Soja 2000; Southall 1998; Taylor 2012), more recent excavation has provided material evidence that compel us to approach this site in a different way. Çatalhöyük *was* huge by the standards of the Neolithic Near East—as many as 8,000 people were crammed into more than 10 hectares of densely packed houses (Cessford 2005:326; Hodder 2004:77). Yet the director of ongoing excavations at the site has called it "just a very very large village" that "pushed the idea of an egalitarian village to its ultimate extreme" (Hodder 2006:98).

Staying Small

The world's first villages were settled about 12,000 years ago in the Near East as the world came out of the last glacial period. Why humans chose to move into villages at this time remains a hotly contested topic among archaeologists (Price and Bar-Yosef 2011). People had previously lived as mobile hunter-gatherers and spent much of their time spread thinly across the landscape in groups of no more than a few dozen individuals. Basic subsistence needs were usually met in these societies by relying on a preferred subset of the broad range of locally available resources (Sahlins 1972; Kaplan 2000), and gift exchanges with those living in other groups likely helped to create a social safety net that stretched for dozens of kilometers (Lee 1984; Wiessner 1996). Life, in short, was often quite good, and it remains unclear why people would have ever decided to settle down in one place (e.g., Rosenberg 1998).

Yet some groups chose to move around less often than others, and the earliest strong evidence of the adoption of agriculture most often appears within these groups (Byrd 2005). Hunter-gatherers already knew that maize, wheat, and other crops could be eaten, but the heavy processing demands of earlier varieties of these staples made these plants lower-value resources relative to the meat, grubs, nuts, and other foods that were available to them as they moved between resource areas (Buckler et al. 1998; Winterhalder and Kennett 2006; Wright 1994). Staying in one place was not typically an option, because easily available wild food resources were often quickly exhausted (e.g., Anderson 2002). Adopting agriculture, along with other resource intensification strategies like herding, was frequently the only way that villagers could remain in the same location for more than a few months. Yet the price for adopting these intensification strategies was often an increased workload and a more monotonous diet.

Sedentism, as Ofer Bar-Yosef has remarked, was "a major 'point of no return' in human evolution" (2011:S175). The appearance of the first villages is cross-culturally associated with a dramatic increase in population growth that is likely due to both a reliance on agriculture (and other resource intensification strategies) and a more sedentary lifestyle (Bandy 2008; Bocquet-Appel 2002, 2008). Infants did not need to be carried as much when the family stayed in one place, and sedentism may have led to weaning at a younger age in early villages (Kohler and Varien 2010:39). Heavy labor was required for crop processing, and a larger family may have also been able to farm more efficiently than a smaller one (Kramer and Boone 2002). Whatever the specific reasons for this initial demographic shift, more and more mouths to feed meant ever-increasing resource intensification. Once people settled down in villages, it was hard to leave.

Village life brings sweeping societal change. Houses create neighbors and walls facilitate the stockpiling of food and wealth. This accumulation in turn makes further status competition, hoarding, and resentment possible (e.g., Banning 2003). The organization of houses within a settlement was also sometimes literally set in stone, and people needed to agree on how and where to perform rituals, bury the dead, and dispose of body waste (e.g., Flannery, ed. 1976). Private property became more of a concern in villages, as residents both invested in their homes as well as in facilities located outside the settlement like irrigation canals, terraces, corrals, and check dams (e.g., Earle 2000). Conflicts could no longer be defused by simply by moving to join friends at the next watering hole, and people needed to find new ways to more routinely obtain items from neighboring groups (Banning 2003; Earle 2000). These and the many other "emergent properties" of early villages quickly led to a widening gulf between the lifestyles of sedentary and mobile groups (Yoffee 2005:201).

Settling down thus seems to create inherent positive feedback loops that should lead to increasing settlement size, economic specialization, political hierarchies, and social differences (Carneiro 1967; Fletcher 1995; Johnson 1982). In almost all cases, however, the stresses of living together short-circuit these feedback loops early on by splitting a village apart when it grows beyond a few dozen households (Bandy 2004). Living in large, dense communities is quite challenging, especially for those accustomed to life within smaller, more mobile groups (Bandy and Fox 2010:13–15). People fight too much, trash piles up, and making decisions becomes more difficult. As villages get bigger they also get noisier, there is more subsistence stress, and there are higher rates of infection and disease. These and other stresses often become overwhelming when a village exceeds a few hundred people, and in most cases a faction breaks off from the village in order to found a new settlement (Alberti 2014; Fletcher 1995).

Yet in rare cases, those living in a village decided to stick it out and take steps to alleviate those problems that are associated with increasing settlement size. In an influential article published in 1982, Gregory Johnson summarizes these problems and suggests that the primary deterrent to further population growth is the amount of information that each person in a settlement must process during the course of his or her daily life both within the village and while engaged in activities outside the village.

For a village to expand, Johnson argues that steps must be taken to reduce the "scalar stress" that comes with increased information processing (also see Alberti 2014). One way he suggests it can be reduced is by elaborating group rituals. Larger, more frequent, and more ornate rituals help formalize actions and relationships, allowing residents to process less information in order to reach a decision. Stress can also be reduced in a village by dividing it into well-defined parts that are spatially and/or socially separated from each other to minimize interactions between them. After compartmentalization, there is less information that needs to be shared between a village's subgroups. Johnson suggests that a third way to reduce scalar stress is to increase the size of the "basal unit." Basal units are the lowest-order organizational group within a community—expanding this unit from the nuclear to the extended family, for example, would reduce the number of decision-makers at a village-wide level and thus the information load that each resident was required to carry would decline. Finally, a greater degree of hierarchization can be introduced into a group to allow a settlement to grow larger. If a subgroup or individual is given the power to make decisions, this can relieve the pressure of information processing on the rest of the community.

The different strategies that Johnson identifies to lower scalar stress would not have been equally palatable to village inhabitants of 12,000 years ago (Birch 2013; Blitz 1993; Hodder 2007; Kuijt 2008; Lewis-Williams 2003). Participating in more ornate group rituals was readily embraced, as were those mechanisms that reduced interactions between the settlement's subgroups through greater spatial or social segregation. These changes, for the most part, required little systematic change—people just did more of what they had already been doing or ignored as best they could those living in other groups. Ritual elaboration and compartmentalization, however, were often insufficient to offset growing tensions between acrimonious factions that were marooned within a shrinking resource base.

Those who were determined to live together often decided to also form larger basal units (e.g., Creese 2012). Increasing the basal unit beyond the extended family frequently meant creating entirely new group identities linked to fictive ancestors and mythic animals. Forging a new sense of belonging to these larger units would have been difficult, but hunter-gatherers and early villagers were used to coming together into larger groups at different times of the year for hunting, trading, rituals, and other activities (e.g., Stanner 1933; Vayda 1967). Increasing the size of one's "family" to unrelated individuals meant acquiescing to both a greater degree of hierarchization within subgroups—important decisions were now made by a smaller group of people—as well as to a greater degree of specialization, as "family" members focused on different activities.

Villagers that chose to stay together as a settlement expanded seem to have been tolerant of these kinds of organizational shifts intended to relieve scalar stress, and many likely recognized that there was an increasing need for the kinds of the horizontal and vertical divisions within populations that are seen in cities (Fletcher 1995:189). Their willingness to elaborate rituals, increase compartmentalization, and expand basal units eroded norms of autonomy and egalitarianism that had long been enforced via storytelling, mockery, ostracism, and other forms of informal social control (Boehm 1999; Cashdan 1990; Wiessner 1996). This erosion, however, would have not gone unchallenged by those in the community seeking to maintain long-standing traditions (Angelbeck and Grier 2012:550; Steadman 2010:30–31; also see Eerkens 2009; Wiessner 2002, 2009).

Overtly introducing greater hierarchization was a bold-faced departure from village traditions and was likely the most odious of the available choices to relieve scalar stress. There have always been individuals with more charisma or more skill than others, and in the earliest villages, these individuals were able to use these attributes to their benefit (Hayden 1995). These "aggrandizers," however, achieved advantages only by working within the system (Angelbeck and Grier 2012:550). The naming of a village-wide leader—an individual with wide-ranging decision-making power over others (Eerkens 2009:88)—would have been a radical departure toward centralization that directly challenged society's core principles (Trigger 2003:669–670). The inhabitants of these growing villages "were not trying to create a town" (Clark et al. 2010:238)—they were just trying to find ways to stay together without sacrificing too much. There was thus often little appetite for shifts in hierarchy that could not be easily couched as increases in basal-unit size.

Settlements that grew beyond the size of a few hundred people usually did so not only via internal population growth but also through the incorporation of outside groups. When aggregation occurred, it tended to happen rapidly instead of over a long period of time (Birch 2013:9). In some cases, these expanding settlements stabilized with a population of a few thousand people, and these are the settlements that I refer to as aborted cities. In other cases, these settlements would continue to expand as shifts in village organization were made in order to relieve scalar stress. Clans might swiftly become the settlement's basal unit, and these clans might later choose to specialize in particular crafts and live in widely separated neighborhoods. Or individuals might eventually appoint a ruler and begin building a temple complex to their ruler's patron gods (i.e., Flannery and Marcus 2012; McIntosh 2005). Why people chose to come together at a site and why certain aggregation sites became cities remains unclear, though I suspect that the answers to both questions relate to a combination of favorable preconditions and historical accidents—a location along trade rounds, a chance military victory, or perhaps a particularly charismatic aggrandizer—that altered the demographic trajectory of a settlement. These accidents rarely resulted in immediate transformations, but they nonetheless sometimes jumpstarted eras of rapid cultural change.

As a settlement quickly grew, the vertical and horizontal divisions within it multiplied and hardened. These divisions could sometimes come together to support the overarching administrative hierarchy of a state, but at other times the result would be more decentralized, consensual, or segmented (Crumley 1995). For example in those locations where scalar stress had been dealt with primarily by segregating units, the result might be a more diffuse settlement composed of largely autonomous neighborhoods linked by highly ritualized exchanges. A ruling council of elders might be the result of those towns that had initially placed greater emphasis on increasing the size of basal units. Reactions to scalar stress, of course, were not the only factors guiding urban development, but my point is that the choices made by residents as a settlement first began to expand helped to dictate the organization of the future city.

The handful of villages that became the world's first cities often did so rapidly enough that few signs remain in the material record of their ungainly becoming. We cannot trace their rise decade by decade without written records, and the leaders that subsequently administered these cities often not only remade history in their favor but also repurposed structures and razed homes in bouts of urban renewal. If we add to this the problems that archaeologists experience both in finding and exposing those deeply buried contexts that date to a city's first years, then it should be no surprise that the first decades of urbanization have been glossed over as a punctuated change from village to urban life. Yet I believe that we *can* tentatively reconstruct the early history of cities despite these difficulties and that we can begin this reconstruction process by turning to those larger settlements that never quite became cities.

Early aborted cities contained a few thousand people who were densely packed together. The inhabitants managed to avoid, sometimes for centuries, much of the heterogeneity in social roles and loss in autonomy that is commonly associated with cities. They lived in relatively stable, very very large villages (Hodder 2006:98), and studying these villages can provide insight into the give-and-takes that were required to relieve scalar stress in settlements of this size. Hundreds of places in different regions of the globe have occupied the liminal space between village and city, and in each of these places, the calculus of living together was different (Birch 2013). Those living in large tell sites in Bronze Age Hungary, for instance, were willing to tolerate limited hereditary inequalities (Duffy et al. 2013), while escalating violence spurred people to embrace new clan identities in the fortified longhouse settlements of sixteenth-century Ontario (Birch and Williamson 2013). Aborted cities like these provide a window into what cities might have looked like just as they were beginning to experience sweeping structural change. Çatalhöyük is one of the best-understood examples of one of these aborted cities.

Çatalhöyük and the Neolithic Near East

The Near Eastern Neolithic period (10,000 to 5000 BC) was marked by an increase in the number, size, and permanence of settlements, a wider subsistence base built on foraging, farming, and herding, a greater frequency and elaboration of group rituals, specialized production of trade goods, and a heightened interaction between settlements (Henry 2004:32–33). Throughout the Neolithic period, settlements tended to get bigger, rituals more complicated, and so forth, but there was nonetheless considerable variation in Neolithic social dynamics across space and time (Kuijt 2005; Simmons 2007) (fig. 4.1).

The first villages were established in the Levant during the preceding Natufian period (13,000–10,000 BC). Made up of only a few houses half-sunken into the ground, these villages sometimes served as base camps for families that lived at least part of the year off-site when they were hunting and gathering (Simmons 2007:67). Status differences between individuals were minimal in these villages, and evidence pertaining to mortuary practices at the end of the Natufian period suggests that they were designed to quell nascent differences while also building group cohesion (Kuijt 1996:331). This emphasis on egalitarianism continued into the Neolithic period even as average settlement size inched higher.

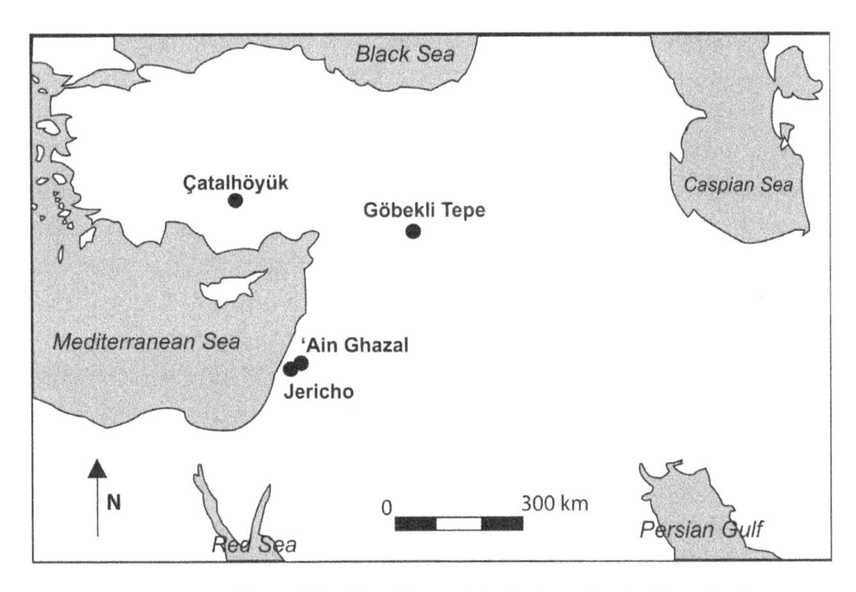

Figure 4.1. Map of the Near East with the location indicated of Neolithic sites discussed in the text (Justin Jennings).

The larger Neolithic sites began to rely more and more on domesticated animals and plants for their subsistence (Kuijt 2000), and scalar stress led to increasing friction between residents. Village fissioning therefore became more common, and ritual practices, manufacturing techniques, and social behaviors started to spread to other parts of the Near East via population movements, intermarriages, and long-distance trade relations (Simmons 2007:164–165). A Neolithic culture thus emerged that was highly variable from one locale to the next but still loosely united across the region by both the long-distance trade of malachite, obsidian, seashells, and other goods, as well as by broad similarities in viewpoints on how to live together and also care for the dead (Asouti 2006; Gebel 2004).

The residents of a few of these larger Neolithic settlements decided to stay together despite growing scalar stress. Although the most effective way to deal with this stress would have been to promote centralization, social stratification, and craft specialization, the residents of Neolithic sites are famous for minimizing these kinds of changes (Hodder 2014a:149–151; Simmons 2007:117). The lack of more urban features suggests that the residents of these settlements found ways to successfully deal with scalar stress while also maintaining a semblance of a village-like social structure. How was this possible? The particular strategies employed to mitigate scalar stress would have varied from settlement to settlement across the Near East, but the people of Çatalhöyük managed to stay together by fixating on their homes.

Çatalhöyük was one of several small villages on the Konya Plain in central Turkey that were first occupied during the ninth millennium BC (Baird 2005:64). The plain's complex mosaic of marshes, seasonal lakes, steppes, and forests would have provided early settlers with a rich variety of resources that were not as easily obtained elsewhere (Roberts et al. 1999; Fairbairn 2005). The artifact assemblages from the earliest levels at Çatalhöyük, and the associated practices that can be inferred from them, suggest that residents not only drew from earlier local traditions (Baird 2007) but also enjoyed a degree of familiarity with other areas in the Near East that had previously supported larger communities (Asouti 2006:114).

The villages on the Konya Plain slowly grew, and by the mid-eighth millennium BC Çatalhöyük was one of six one- to two-hectare communities nestled in or around the alluvial fan of the Çarşamba River (Baird 2005:64).

For still-unknown reasons, those living in the other villages decided to aggregate at Çatalhöyük at around 7400 BC, causing the village's population to surge from a few hundred people to a few thousand. Although the tumult of this transition was likely eased by some knowledge of practices that had reduced scalar stress in other settlements, the people at Çatalhöyük had to find their own unique solution to the challenges of living together in a large group.

Çatalhöyük would grow quickly into a settlement composed of densely packed, superimposed buildings that formed a mound that today rises almost 18 meters above the surrounding plain. Despite years of excavations, remote sensing, and surface survey, the archaeologists working at Çatalhöyük have found "no public spaces, administrative buildings, elite quarters, or really any specialized facilities" (Hodder 2006:95). Çatalhöyük was almost completely made up of houses that served simultaneously as residences, temples, and mausoleums, with the occasional small courtyard nestled among these houses being employed as a garbage dump (fig. 4.2). Since homes often abutted each other, there were no external doorways and very few roadways or footpaths through the site. Instead, people commonly moved through the settlement via its flat-topped roofs and entered their dwelling from above using stairs and ladders (Düring 2007; Hodder 2006).

The main room of a typical house in Çatalhöyük was accessed from a hole in the ceiling and contained an oven and a series of raised platforms. Side rooms in the house were used for storage and for cooking, while other tasks such as flint knapping and hide processing appear to have been undertaken on the roof, where households would have been able to engage in more informal socializing (Hodder 2006:110). Most activities were carried out within the domestic unit (Hodder 2014a:155–156). The mud to make bricks, for example, was likely dug up separately by each family (Matthews 1996), and most families kept their own caches of obsidian that were worked inside the house (Conolly 2003; Carter et al. 2005). Each household also independently stored a wide range of grains, nuts, fruits, and condiments in their side rooms' bins, pots, and baskets. Cooking was done either inside the home or on its rooftop (Atalay and Hastorf 2006; Demirergi et al. 2014). The family thus ate together (Pearson 2013), and house members even sometimes sealed the dead inside the same main-room platforms where they slept at night (Hodder 2006) (fig. 4.3).

Figure 4.2. Layout of Level VIB buildings in a portion of Çatalhöyük (adapted from James Mellaart).

Figure 4.3. A cutaway view of life in Building 1 at Çatalhöyük (Çatalhöyük Research Project and John Swogger).

These kinds of repeated practices created a house-centered society that helped to alleviate the scalar stress caused by the crush of people at Çatalhöyük (e.g., Beck 2007). This stress was relieved not only by restricting the amount of interaction between groups but, just as importantly, by creating habitual ways of acting for all residents. As Ian Hodder and Craig Cessford argue, "the construction of bodily routines that were repeated in daily house practices over days, months, years, decades, centuries, and even millennia" led to the creation of social codes that were often unconsciously followed (2004:22). People doing the same things over and over again *independently* of other households created a community-wide identity without the need to coordinate activities across the settlement.

One of the best illustrations of how the repetition of certain actions served to create a broader identity is seen in the replastering of the main rooms in Çatalhöyük's houses. Although some replastering would have been necessary as surfaces got worn down, the people living in Çatalhöyük seemed to have been obsessed with modifying the appearance of their main rooms. In the case of Building 5, for example, the walls were redone over 450 times. At least 70 of these layers were thick coats of white plaster, and the thick layers were separated by 3 to 9 layers of very thin plaster washes that were often coated in soot (Matthews 2005:367). Since the amount of plastering far exceeded what was necessary for the space—Building 5's side rooms were plastered only 3 to 4 times during its occupation—it is likely that the inhabitants plastered the main room to celebrate the passage of seasons and important life-cycle events like births, marriages, and deaths (Boivin 2000; Matthews 2005:368–369).

Building 5 was more heavily plastered than the other buildings that have been excavated to date at Çatalhöyük, but all main rooms at the site were likely replastered dozens of times in a sequence that differed from one home to the next (Matthews 2005). When and how the walls and floors were resurfaced was therefore a decision that households made independently, but everyone in the community agreed that replastering was necessary and important. The residents of Çatalhöyük thus shared a practice, but they also signaled differences between households by the color they chose to use in the main rooms of their dwellings and the frequency with which they replastered.

Another example of a repetitive practice at Çatalhöyük is the use and placement of bucrania. Bucrania are the plastered skulls of wild animals, and bull, ram, and goat skulls in particular were featured on the walls of many of Çatalhöyük's houses. Around these skulls, in protruding nubs on the wall, residents also placed "the teeth of foxes and weasels, the tusks of wild boars, the claws of bears, and the beaks of vultures" (Hodder and Meskell 2010:43–44) (fig. 4.4). These bucrania were frequently replastered and also painted again and again with geometric designs that were particular to a house.

Interestingly, these sculptural elements were often removed when a house was abandoned and were then likely reused in a subsequent home built directly on top of the abandoned one's foundations (Hodder and Meskell 2010:48). In some cases, people were able to locate bucrania, other types of relief sculptures, and human remains just by digging deep into the fill of abandoned homes years or even decades after their occupation (Hodder and Cessford 2004:33–34). Continuity in practice was thus ensured by the regular engagement of the mound's residents with the material remains buried beneath them.

The focus of Çatalhöyük's residents on domestic life led them to take exquisite care both when they abandoned a house and when they constructed one (Russell et al. 2014). Before a new house was erected, builders cleaned the old house and removed almost all of its contents. They then dismantled the roof, pulled the posts, took the walls down to their foundation, and placed objects like a greenstone axe or an animal scapula on the plastered floor of the abandoned home before finally covering the remains of the building with a layer of carefully selected soil (Cessford 2007:543–547; Hodder 2006:129–133; Russell et al. 2014:118–120). Dedicatory burials were sometimes later placed into this fill, and feasting debris is occasionally found sandwiched between the foundations of homes built directly on top of each other (Hodder and Cessford 2004:32).

When practices like these are carried over from one generation to the next in a settlement, they can gain the force of tradition. The creation of a house-centered society at Çatalhöyük thus led to an atomized, conservative, and inward-looking community that was resistant to social change.

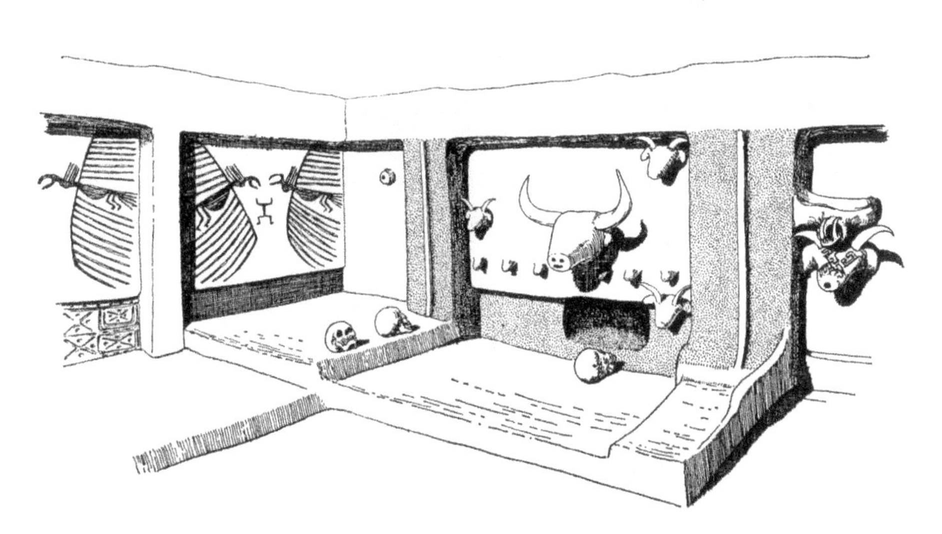

Figure 4.4. Reconstruction of a main room at Çatalhöyük showcasing the plastered walls, paintings, bucrania, and protruding nubs (James Mellaart).

The details of life were tinkered with—someone might paint a new design on a wall or raise the height of a platform—but year after year they slept in the same kinds of houses and remained committed to memorializing each household's specific connections to their past (Hodder and Cessford 2004). Çatalhöyük therefore survived in large part because its residents found a way to live both separately and together.

Yet reducing interactions between the settlement's households was only a partial answer to the scalar stress caused by Çatalhöyük's densely packed population. The high degree of autonomy and redundancy across family groups had helped considerably in relieving much of this stress, but the settlement's house society was by necessity also paired with crosscutting associations between houses that were essential to coordinating the activities of larger groups of people (Düring 2001, 2013; Düring and Marciniak 2006; Hodder 2014a). These associations were especially important in meeting the subsistence demands of the settlement. Villages had been spread thinly across the Konya Plain before aggregation occurred at Çatalhöyük, and families had thus been able to subsist on food that was hunted, gathered, fished, and grown within a few kilometers of home. With everyone now in one place, however, there was a need for people both to walk farther to get their food and also to increase the resource yields that were available closer to Çatalhöyük.

Çatalhöyük's location in an alluvial plain limited the prospects of resource intensification in the immediate vicinity because the spring flooding turned large portions of the surrounding area into marshland for parts of the year (Charles et al. 2014:83; Rosen and Roberts 2005:48). Residents nonetheless took what they could from the local sources. They built a few dams to manage water levels and grew crops like wheat, barley, lentils, and peas on the "ridges and patches of highly productive drier land" that were found interspersed within the wetland environment that surrounded Çatalhöyük (Fairbairn 2005:200; also see Charles et al. 2014). They also penned their sheep and goat herds at the outskirts of the settlement for much of the year, and hunted birds, boars, deer, cattle, and other wild animals a short distance away (Russell and Bogaard 2010:66–67).

Although botanical evidence indicates that Çatalhöyük was occupied year-round, it is clear that the families living there sometimes left for extended periods in order to address their subsistence needs (Baird et al. 2011;

Charles et al. 2014; Fairbairn 2005; Roberts and Rosen 2009). Evidence from phytoliths and carbonized seeds, for example, suggests that residents traveled to grasslands located at least 10 kilometers away in order to grow many of the crops that were consumed in the settlement (Fairbairn et al. 2005; Rosen 2005; but see Charles et al. 2014 for the suggestion that residents also grew crops right outside the mound), and isotopic measurements suggest that many of the animals consumed there were raised or hunted in a variety of distant locations before being brought to the settlement (Pearson et al. 2007).

Those who initially settled at Çatalhöyük may have originally chosen the site partly because it offered a diverse range of food resources (Rosen and Roberts 2005:48–49). As the population increased, however, this zone would have come under increasing strain. Çatalhöyük's shift toward more extensive subsistence practices would have necessitated broad changes in social organization. In smaller settlements, households generally had little need to consult with others regarding their daily subsistence decisions. Those who lived in Çatalhöyük, however, would have been spread too thin across the landscape to effectively perform necessary tasks—a family in the summer months, for instance, could not hope to harvest their dispersed spring crops, herd their sheep in far-off pastures, and collect wood, fruits, and nuts from scattered stands dozens of kilometers away while also replastering their floors, manufacturing mud bricks, and caring for a sick baby (Fairbairn et al. 2005:97). For the settlement to survive, households therefore needed to come together and form larger cooperative groups to coordinate various activities during different parts of the year (Russell and Bogaard 2010:66–67).

Bigger cooperative groups would also have begun to form at Çatalhöyük for other reasons. Long-standing social, economic, and ritual relationships had almost certainly connected local villages to each other prior to aggregation, and it seems likely that people sought to continue these same kinds of relationships within the new settlement. Yet how one treats seldom-seen acquaintances is often different from how one interact with neighbors, and there must have been pressure to both intensify and alter preexisting relationships and create new ones that better fit the changing needs of those living in the abutting houses of Çatalhöyük (Russell and Bogaard 2010:74–75).

The creation of these cooperative groups—probably based in part on preexisting village structures—is perhaps evidenced architecturally in the creation of neighborhood clusters at Çatalhöyük that are defined by the few open spaces that run through the site. Bleda Düring (2007:173) suggests that the settlement's neighborhoods were made up of 150 to 250 people who "were involved in face-to-face interaction and had corporate identities grounded in close personal contacts that took place daily on the neighbourhood roof-scapes." These neighborhoods may have been further divided into groups of households that were linked together by mortuary rituals and other collaborative practices (Düring 2013:31–32; Hodder 2014a:162; Wright 2014:28). The creation of nested cooperative groups beyond the level of the household would have further relieved Çatalhöyük's scalar stress, since neighborhood and household clusters limited interaction between groups. With these clusters in place, a resident would routinely have dealt with only 30 to 200 individuals rather than the up to 8,000 people who lived in the settlement. A collection of 200 people is just below the population levels typically associated with village fission (Bandy and Fox 2010:14–15), and each of Çatalhöyük's neighborhoods could have very well been conceived of by its residents as a largely independent settlement that just happened to abut to the other settlements that collectively composed the mound.

Feasting was likely one of the more important mechanisms for creating cohesion within the neighborhood clusters of Çatalhöyük. Some of the scenes painted on the walls of the settlement's homes show large groups of people hunting and teasing bulls and other wild animals, and these scenes may be related to occasional communal feasts, rituals, and performances that were held outside the settlement (Baird et al. 2011; Hodder 2006:92; Russell and Martin 2005:97). The better-documented feasts that occurred within Çatalhöyük were on a smaller scale and featured meat that was at least partially butchered in the same place where it was consumed. Most of these feasts likely brought together just a few families within a house's main room, but hundreds of people came to some events (Demirergi et al. 2014:105–106). The detritus of one of the biggest feasts found at the site contained the remains of at least five cattle—enough meat to potentially feed the entire settlement—and was located in the fill of an abandoned house (Hodder 2006:173, 198–199). In the interlude between abandonment and construction, a house's footprint was an open space that may have allowed hundreds of people to gather.

Meat sharing is widely practiced among hunter-gatherers (Stanford 2001:155–160). Larger animals are too big for a single family to eat, and, since meat spoils quickly, it is better to share the excess from a kill with other families with the expectation that they will return the favor. Çatalhöyük's residents would have faced a similar dilemma of abundance when they obtained the carcass of a bull, and it appears that sharing meat and other surpluses was an important social practice that encouraged cooperation between households (Bogaard et. al. 2009:665). These links, if they were primarily maintained within neighborhood clusters, would have helped to maintain the cohesion of the subgroups living at Çatalhöyük.

There is some evidence that suggests that Çatalhöyük's neighborhoods also served as the basal units for settlement-wide decision-making. Some of the houses at Çatalhöyük were more elaborate than others in terms of numbers of rooms, posts, painting, platforms, and other features (Düring 2001:9–11). Interspersed across the neighborhoods, these more elaborate buildings also contain more burials, more obsidian, more querns, and likely more figurines (Hodder 2006:151–152; Wright 2014:28). The elaborate houses were not shrines—people slept, worked, and ate in them—but the extra care and reverence dedicated to these buildings might suggest that those living in them exercised a higher degree of authority within Çatalhöyük's clusters and were perhaps occasionally empowered to speak on behalf of their neighbors. These within-neighborhood hierarchical positions, if they existed at all (Hodder 2014c:5), would have also acted to limit scalar stress in the community.

I have thus far said little about change in Çatalhöyük over time. The site's original excavator, James Mellaart, identified 15 occupation levels at the site from the surface (Level 0) to the base of his excavations at Level XIII. (He divided Level VI into A and B sublayers.) Subsequent excavators have maintained this system but added Levels Pre-XII.A to E (Hodder et al. 2007:18). The house societies and neighborhood clusters that I have discussed thus far typify the site's first thousand years of life after aggregation. Although slight changes occurred during this period, the social mechanisms that managed scalar stress helped to ensure remarkable stability at Çatalhöyük until the mid-seventh millennium BC (Level V) (Hodder 2014b, 2014c).

The continuity in house construction, however, began to break down after Level V. Residents changed the footprint of their homes at this time;

they started to add exterior doorways, and they created more courtyards and streets (Düring and Marciniak 2006:180). Those living at Çatalhöyük also moved hearths into the center of main rooms, reduced the number of platform burials, plastered their walls and floors less often, and devoted less time to the creation of elaborate wall art. Some individuals even began building large, multiroomed complexes that dwarfed the houses made during the preceding periods (Hodder 2006:251–253). These and other changes contributed to the erosion of the symbolic and ritual importance of Çatalhöyük's houses and also loosened the tight spatial clustering of neighborhoods (Hodder 2014b:175–179).

Since the practices associated with neighborhood clusters and the house society were essential for maintaining the cohesion of the settlement, it should come as no surprise that Çatalhöyük started to decline when people began to alter and abandon those practices that had successfully alleviated scalar stress for a millennium (Hodder 2006:253–254, 2014:17). The reasons for the social changes after Level V remain unclear, but one possibility is a combination of a shifting resource base, rising inequality, and increasing craft specialization.

Because Çatalhöyük was not ideally located for intensive agriculture owing to its position within a seasonally flooded alluvial fan, the settlement's inhabitants had long cooperated to create an extensive subsistence system of farming, herding, hunting, and gathering that stretched dozens of kilometers away. The region around Çatalhöyük, however, became drier in the last centuries of the seventh millennium BC. Previously waterlogged lands could now be cultivated, and there were therefore fewer reasons for individuals to dedicate themselves to collective action, since more crops could be grown closer to home (Fairbairn 2005:206). Sheep and goats, perhaps previously kept in pooled herds, could also now be managed independently at the family level (Hodder 2014c:12). Families still needed to do many things together, but climate change meant that residents were no longer as dependent on a much broader cooperative group for survival.

The domestication of cattle sometime after Level IV caused another shift in Çatalhöyük's resource base that likely undermined the emphasis on collective action (Hodder 2014b:177; Russell et al. 2005:S104). Once cattle had been domesticated, people no longer had to go on hunts for wild cattle and then laboriously work together to bring the meat back to the settlement.

Owning cattle therefore made people less reliant on others for obtaining meat, but, perhaps more importantly, domestication quickly eroded a religious tradition whose key symbol was the plastered horns and skulls of bulls that had been slain at great risk to life and limb. A significant part of the wild was tamed as a result of domestication, and thus a raison d'être of Çatalhöyük religion was lost (Hodder 2006:255). Herds of cattle meant both a decreased reliance on supra-household groups for meat and also a reconceptualization of group rituals, as hunting feasts turned into potlucks.

Çatalhöyük's residents had long been willing to tolerate a small degree of social inequality in the interests of reducing scalar stress. For most of the settlement's history, the higher status of those living in dominant houses seems to have been based on the more prominent role they played in ritual activities (Hodder 2006:151–152). As group rituals became less important in the last centuries of the seventh millennium BC, those living in these dominant houses may have begun to use obsidian—as well as other exotic objects—to solidify their weakening status positions. Obsidian found in the earliest levels at Çatalhöyük was usually flaked, and these tools were made and stored by each household. In the later levels, however, evidence appears of the specialized manufacture of prismatic blades from nodules that were mined predominantly from the Nenezi Dağ source in central Turkey (Carter et al. 2006, 2008; Conolly 1999). Most of these blades have been found in the dominant houses (Conolly 1999:797).

The change in obsidian production and procurement at Çatalhöyük may have been the result of an increase in cultural interaction across Turkey and the Levant in the second half of the seventh millennium BC. During this period, settlements in Turkey began to participate more fully in the Neolithic interaction sphere by sharing motifs, information technologies, and manufacturing techniques with other regions (Hodder 2014b:182; Özdoğan 2002:255–257). Pressure flaking was one of these shared techniques—it had already been practiced in the northern Levant for 2,000 years (Carter et al. 2008:906)—as were the manufacturing techniques for making very large pots. Although those living at Çatalhöyük had always maintained some connections to outside groups, there were some individuals who sought to intensify these distant connections once the long-standing local practices that bound the members of the settlement together were in decline. With ties across Çatalhöyük weakening, it appears that the dominant households may have tried to position themselves as the most important brokers to the outside world.

The trend of slowly increasing specialization, stratification, and interregional interaction continued for several centuries after Çatalhöyük broke apart. The families that remained there moved to a new location just across the river and created a settlement with an architectural design that departed even more sharply from that of previous traditions (Düring 2001:16). The site shrunk from 13.5 to 8 hectares, but it appears to have served for a couple of centuries as a central place, and the residents may have even exercised a degree of political and economic control over the newly established, much smaller villages located in the surrounding plain (Baird 2005:72–73). There is also evidence for increasing specialization; certain households appear to have focused on ceramic manufacture, while others built large ovens that could serve the needs of multiple families (Hodder 2006:253). These trends toward a more centralized, specialized society persisted until Çatalhöyük was finally abandoned around 6000 BC, at which point the population dispersed and the Konya plain once again became dotted with small villages (Baird 2005:71–73).

Dealing with Scalar Stress in the Neolithic Near East

Not all settlements across the Neolithic Near East relied on Çatalhöyük's mix of social mechanisms to reduce scalar stress. For example, the strain of population aggregation in Jericho, a smaller site in what is now the West Bank, was handled through group rituals that likely encompassed most of the individuals who lived there (Kenyon 1957). The dead at Jericho, as in many other early Neolithic settlements, were generally interred individually under house floors without grave goods. The skulls of adults were later removed after the flesh had decomposed, and then groups of skulls from different locales were reburied together in rituals that brought together multiple households (Kuijt 1996). The focus of Jericho's inhabitants on crosscutting ritual activity is also manifested in its unique 8.5-meter-tall stone tower that was associated with a wide ditch and wall. The steep staircase that provided access to the top of the tower, later used as a burial space for 12 individuals (Cornwall 1981:403–404), may have led to a shrine that was visible to all residents. Although interpretations of the tower's function vary (Kuijt and Goring-Morris 2002:373–374), its construction clearly reflects a community-wide involvement in a single architectural project that has no parallel at Çatalhöyük.

Those living, or perhaps visiting, Göbekli Tepe dealt with scalar stress in a manner slightly different from that seen in Jericho and Çatalhöyük. Göbekli Tepe is a seven-hectare site located in modern-day Turkey that is famous for its large oval structures (approximately 10 by 15 meters) that were decorated with T-shaped monoliths (Schmidt 2000; 2006). The limestone monoliths often weighed more than 5,000 kilograms and were engraved with depictions of snakes, lions, boars, ducks, and other animals (Banning 2011:623; Schmidt 2000, 2001). Interpretations of the site's function vary. Klaus Schmidt, the excavator of the site, suggests that Göbekli Tepe was a meeting place for hunter-gatherers living in the region (2001b:10) and that the oval structures were rival temples that served no domestic function (2001a:46). E. B. Banning has challenged Schmidt's interpretation and suggests instead that the structures were ritually charged homes for households that were organized into different clans (2011:640). In either case, the elaboration of the site's multiple oval structures with seemingly competing imagery reflects a greater emphasis on segmentation into competing subgroups than was seen in Jericho or Çatalhöyük.

Although responses to settlement aggregation varied considerably, there was a consistent preference across Near Eastern settlements during the Neolithic period for options that did not result in a more hierarchical society (Hodder 2014b:149–151; Kuijt 2000:97). As communities got bigger over time, however, it became more difficult to resolve the problems associated with scalar stress without a significant loss in household power and autonomy. Settlements may have reached the breaking point in the Levant during the eighth millennium BC, when populations coalesced into a series of densely packed, 20-acre "mega-sites" that took a terrible toll on the local environment (Simmons 2007). Data from 'Ain Ghazal, for example, suggest that access to wild plants, animals, and firewood had become scarce by the settlement's last years (Rollefson 1996:224). This environmental degradation required decisive action. Yet poised on the brink of a more hierarchically organized society, people decided to walk away from these megasites instead of radically changing relationships between households.

As Ian Kuijt has noted, the large communities of the Neolithic period were ultimately "a failed experiment in balancing antiquated systems of shared power with the need for developing new means of organizing and directing increasingly large urban communities" (2000:98). Faced with rising scalar stress, those living in these settlements were willing to sacrifice only so much in exchange for whatever benefits might accrue from being together in one place. Breaking up into smaller communities shattered the broader Near Eastern interaction sphere that had been anchored by the bigger settlements, but the result was a more sustainable and less stressful way of life (Simmons 2007:226–227).

Çatalhöyük was one of last of the large Neolithic settlements to break apart in the Neolithic Near East. Unlike the Levantine megasites, people likely left Çatalhöyük in part because of *increasing* access to cattle and agricultural land that allowed people to spread out (Hodder 2014b:179). Yet the core issue that led to disaggregation was the same as that found elsewhere. For more than a millennium, a "fierce egalitarianism" had been maintained at Çatalhöyük through the intergenerational adherence to houses and, to a lesser extent, horizontal connections across neighborhoods (Hodder 2014c:5). Changing conditions, however, were leading toward a more hierarchical and specialized society than the majority of residents were unwilling to accept (Wright 2014:29). In midstream, the residents of Çatalhöyük chose to abandon a path that may have led to the creation of a city.

Learning from Aborted Cities

Settlement aggregation ushered in a brave new world. In the space of just a few decades, people in places like Çatalhöyük needed to fundamentally change their way of life. Creating these kinds of communities, as Stephen Kowalewski has noted (2013:215), meant creating "a lot of new culture, from materials on hand" through "extraordinary physical and social work." The material on hand was what had been fine-tuned in villages and pastoral camps over centuries and was thus often ill suited to resolving the challenges of living together in far larger, more densely packed settlements. The best solution to scalar stress in these larger sites may have been to ignore the past—the new settings demanded new ways of thinking—and it is likely that some individuals advocated for sweeping change in the organization of society.

Radical innovation, however, was quite rare in these growing communities (Renfrew 1978). Moving into a new place was risky enough, and people were used to behaving in certain ways. Most of the innovations introduced in these early towns and their surrounding regions therefore amounted to "little more than new ways of doing old things" (Belfer-Cohen and Bar-Yosef 2000:31). People worked hard to create a new kind of settlement, but they also worked hard to make it resemble the places that they had left or outgrown. In order to live together, resident were willing to compartmentalize their dwelling, embellish community rituals, and celebrate communal decision-making. They sometimes became part-time specialists, shifted their subsistence regimes, and engaged in long-distance trade (Kowalewski 2006:117).

They would not, however, be told what to do (Kowalewski 2013:213). There was a tendency over time in longer-lived communities like Çatalhöyük to shift some of the burden of coordination and decision-making away from households and to smaller subsets of people. Residents likely even recognized that a hierarchical, centralized society was a potential solution to the mounting headaches of aggregation. Yet ceding power to a centralized authority would have contradicted long-held commitments to an ethos celebrating egalitarianism and household autonomy (Boehm 1999). Individuals could find ways to become more influential in a community by manipulating the group rituals, hunting expeditions, and the other activities that had been inaugurated to reduce scalar stress. These aggrandizers could work the system to their benefit, but they had to be cautious about community perceptions. Little "l" leaders might have been tolerated if they could justify their actions as benefiting the collective interest of the community, but big "L" leaders would not have been (Eerkens 2009; Weissner 2009).

A good example of the limits placed on centralized hierarchies in these kinds of communities comes from the death of a man on the Pacific Northwest coast (Anglebeck and Grier 2012:567). Slabebtikud was a respected religious leader among the postcontact Upper Skagit peoples. One day he attempted to gain control over the ritual and fishing calendar by demanding the right to perform a single first salmon rite for all households.

Individual families had long conducted this rite, and Slabebtikud's demand was both a striking departure from tradition and a naked grab for power. Slabebtikud religious leadership could not be leveraged into absolute authority, and he was killed by those who had previously followed him.

Çatalhöyük and the aborted cities of the Neolithic Near East add further emphasis to what the early years of the cities of Singapore, São Paulo, Los Angeles, and Abu Dhabi teach us. When people aggregated to form these four cities, they dealt with scalar stress through a welter of tried and true, but often conflicting, strategies that included embellishing group rituals, minimizing interactions between groups, and increasing the size of the basal unit that was used to make decisions. Many were familiar with more centralized, hierarchical structures and would have welcomed their imposition. Yet the official governing bodies of these settlements were often ineffective. Those moving into the world's earliest cities would have been far less comfortable with the idea of overarching hierarchies, and thus more apt to rely on an evolving mix of other mechanisms to deal with the demands of a ballooning population.

Those living in aborted cities like Çatalhöyük were able to catch their breath and create long-lasting mechanisms to keep together communities that numbered in the thousands. The choices made in these settlements during their aggregation periods suggest that settlers in fast-growing sites were not trying to create the high degree of heterogeneity in social roles that typifies cities. On the contrary, residents expended considerable effort to curtail heterogeneity when it began to appear. The layers of plaster on a Çatalhöyük wall and the cowrie shells placed in the eye sockets of a Jericho skull are testaments to a deep commitment to egalitarianism and collective action that was redoubled even as scalar stress made this commitment increasingly untenable (Kuijt 2000; Matthews 2005).

One might wish to argue that life was quite different in those early settlements that, unlike Çatalhöyük, would grow to become cities. Perhaps residents quickly accepted, or even embraced, well-organized centralized hierarchies as part of a punctuated transition to civilization in these places. The chapter that follows demonstrates that this was not the case. As settlements quickly expanded, there were no easy answers to scalar stress, and people still sought to modify their old approaches to problems to solve new ones. Social heterogeneity and long-distance interactions increased by necessity before regional polities had a chance to fully form; the later contours of city and countryside depended in large part on the choices that were made in a settlement during the initial decades of aggregation. Those living at Jericho, Göbekli Tepe, and Çatalhöyük chose various ways to handle scalar stress, and if these sites had continued to grow it is likely that each would have become a different kind of city with different kinds of relationships to the wider world.

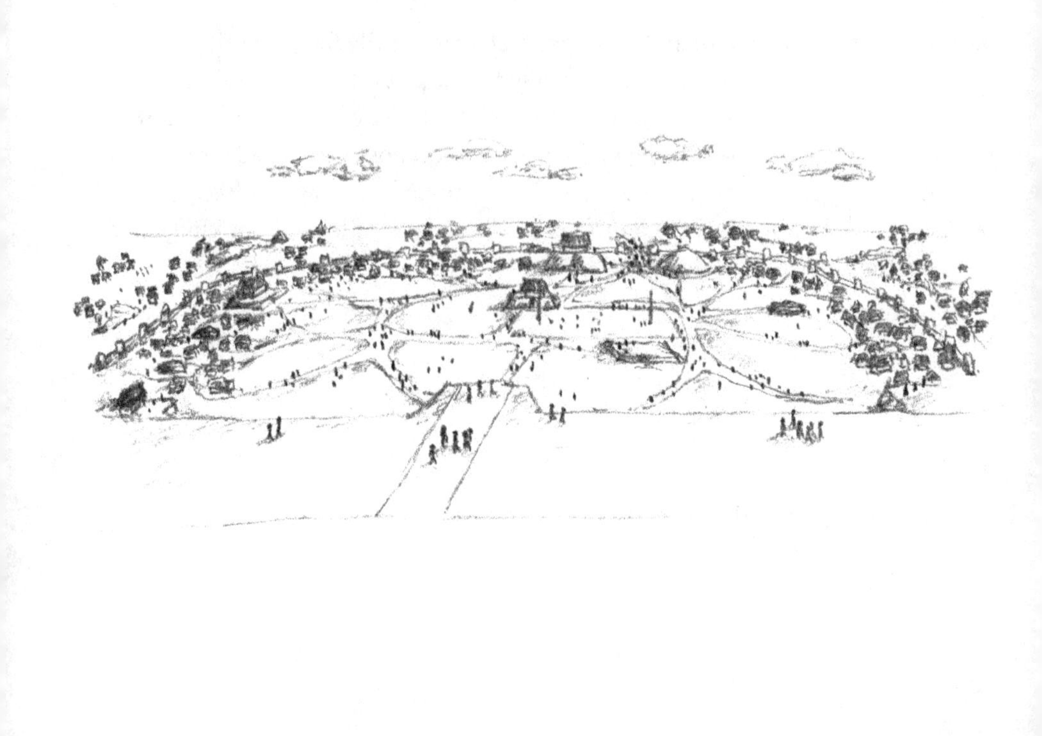

5

CAHOKIA'S FAILURE AND THE CREATION OF THE MISSISSIPPIAN CULTURAL HORIZON

MONKS MOUND, THE LARGEST EARTHEN CONSTRUCTION EVER built north of Mexico, sits just a few kilometers from St. Louis, Missouri (Young and Fowler 2000:3–5). When you climb the mound today, you can count a couple dozen grassy knolls that incongruously dot the surrounding floodplain of the Mississippi River. These knolls are all that remain of the more than 200 other mounds that made up greater Cahokia. The settlement was largely constructed between AD 1050 and 1150, during which time its population ballooned from 2,000 to more than 20,000 people (Pauketat and Lopinot 1997:118). Cahokia became a city by the end of that century, meeting our four criteria of large population size, dense population nucleation, high heterogeneity in the social roles of inhabitants, and participation in activities that affect a larger hinterland, but the settlement did not instantly urbanize when people starting piling together dirt to make Monks Mound.

The residents of aborted cities like Çatalhöyük managed to live for hundreds of years almost as if they had never left their villages behind. They were successful in recreating more familiar neighborhood and household experiences within these proto-urban environments while also restricting the growth of the horizontal and vertical social divisions that are associated with cities. Places like Çatalhöyük bumped up against a ceiling to settlement growth that was formed, at least in part, by the limits of environmental carrying capacity, information processing, and egalitarianism. Residents succeeded in raising this ceiling by tweaking how they lived, but further settlement growth ultimately required fundamental lifestyle changes both on site and in the surrounding region that people were often unwilling or unable to make.

A few early settlements, in contrast, grew quickly and broke through the ceiling of settlement growth to form cities. The creation of cities is often seen as part of the steplike transition to civilization—a "Big Bang" that was "a virtually instantaneous and dramatic shift in political, social, and ideological organization" (Emerson and Hargrave 2000:3). A closer examination of the first years of our earliest cities, however, suggests that there was no deep, totalizing societal rupture. Change *was* fast, but the residents of emerging cities like Cahokia instead initially employed methods similar to those used at Çatalhöyük and other aborted cities to decrease scalar stress. These methods were often adjusted by each generation, as the population expanded and groups settled into an urban life that tended to become more specialized and hierarchical. After a century or two, this tinkering might result in the creation of some kind of stable regional polity. Yet in the interim there were mouths to feed, exotics to acquire, and conflicts to adjudicate. Colonization, the spread of cultural horizons, and the establishments of regional polities were some of the by-products of the struggles to live together in cities that took place in the first years following aggregation.

This chapter and the four that follow discuss the consequences of five early urbanizations from different regions of the world. Our discussion begins with Cahokia, a site that never really flourished as a city. Cahokia's failure to thrive, combined with decades of archaeological work at the site, makes it easier to envision what an early city looked like just as it was coming into being. We can glimpse the off-site strategies that were used to support residents during the first few decades of the settlement's growth and track how Cahokia's rise was related to societal changes across much of the American midcontinent. Since we can *see* more easily the broader impact of incipient urbanization in short-lived places like Cahokia, this case study helps us better understand the initial periods of growth in the longer surviving, but more poorly understood, cities that are described in subsequent chapters.

The Late and Terminal Woodland Periods in the American Bottom

The Mississippi River is one of the largest river systems in the world and has long been an important transportation corridor and resource zone for people living in what is now the central United States (Adovasio and Pedler 2005). The river's watershed provided access to a wide variety of resources to those living in the pre-Columbian world, including the hardwoods of the forests of the Ozark uplift, the seashells of the Gulf Coast, and Lake Superior copper. The river's floodplain also supported creeks, oxbow lakes, marshes, swales, and natural levees that teemed with wildlife and boasted rich soils (Pauketat 2004:28–36). One of the Mississippi's most productive areas was a section of floodplain in southwestern Illinois known as the American Bottom (fig. 5.1).

The America Bottom was home to small, dispersed groups of hunter-gatherers and horticulturalists until the end of the Middle Woodland period (200 BC–AD 400) (Fortier 2001:192). After a brief abandonment at the beginning of the Late Woodland period (AD 400–900), the area was resettled by outside groups that relied more heavily on the cultivation of maygrass, chenopod, sunflower, sumpweed, and other seed plants (McElrath and Fortier 2000:115). These new arrivals lived in a wide variety of settlements. Many continued to move seasonally across the landscape—there are sites made up almost exclusively of food storage pits used for mobile groups who revisited the same locations (Pauketat 2004:55)—while other American Bottom families chose to live permanently in either isolated homesteads or in "dispersed aggregates of dwellings" that often lacked a courtyard or other central feature (Fortier and Jackson 2000:138).

The largest Late Woodland period sites in the region appear to have had a ceremonial function, serving to closely tie those living in the American Bottom with groups in the adjacent upland valleys that overlooked the floodplain. There were a handful of sites in the Silver Creek Valley, for instance, that served as an occasional "meeting ground between the American Bottom inhabitants and those dwellers of the uplands to the distant east, north, and south" (Holley 2006:311). These aggregation locations were pockmarked with storage pits and earth ovens that were dug during visits that likely took place after the harvest. The artifacts from these sites suggest that gatherings featured feasting, gambling, shamanic activities, and mortuary displays (Holley 2006:309–311).

Over the course of the period, population increased and communities appear to have broken apart when scalar stress became too high. Much of the region's prime horticultural land was claimed as a result of this fissioning

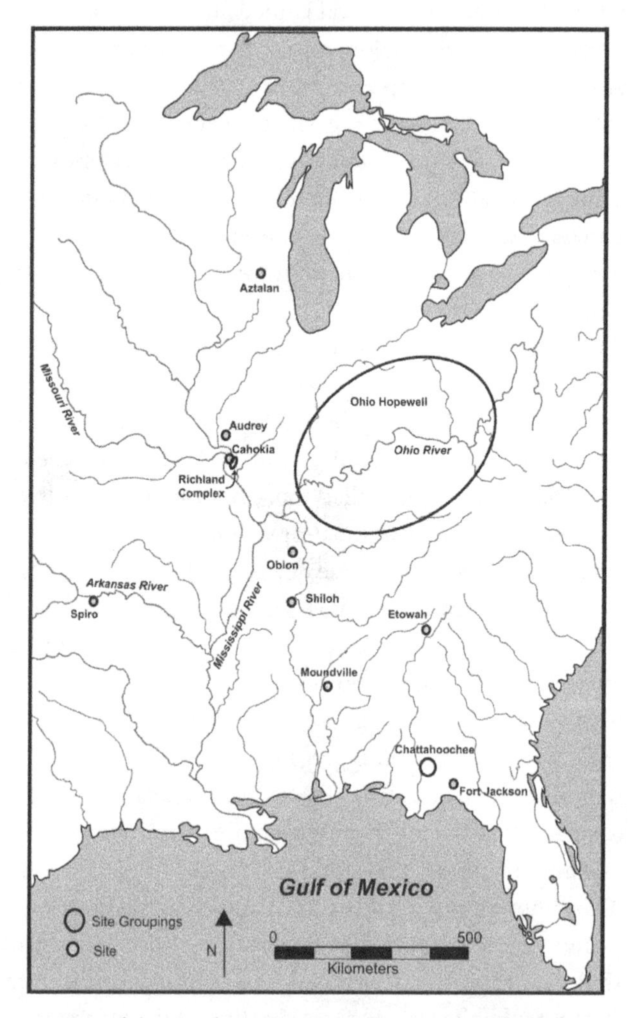

Figure 5.1. Map of the North American midcontinent with the location of sites and site groupings discussed in the text. Note that Emerald and Grossman are both located within the Richland Complex adjacent to Cahokia (Justin Jennings).

process, and after about AD 650, groups began moving into parts of the American Bottom that became available as the water table lowered due to climate change (McElrath and Fortier 2000:115). Maize soon joined the native domesticates in the diet of many groups (Chilton 2005:140–144; Pauketat 2004:7–9), and by about AD 900, residents of some of the American Bottom's larger settlements were dealing with scalar stress via mechanisms that "promoted group solidarity and channeled competition along less disruptive avenues" (McElrath and Fortier 2000:116).

The Terminal Late Woodland period (AD 900–1050) saw new innovations, such as crushed mussel shell for pottery temper, a new type of chipped stone hoe, and a red-slipping technique for vessels, that likely spread into the American Bottom through exchange and migration (Stoltman et al. 2008; Pauketat 2004:8–10). Communities of all sizes appear to have also been more integrated by this time (Kelly 2000:167): some were arranged around courtyards that contained communal storage and a central pole (Kelly 1990a, 1990b), while others were organized around courtyards featuring a pair of pits, one with a square and one with an oval opening (Milner 1984). Excavation does not reveal what exactly occurred in these courtyards, but they were likely used for feasting, sports, rituals, and other activities that brought residents together (Pauketat 2004:62–64).

There was therefore "no cookie-cutter pattern" of Terminal Late Woodland period community organization (Holley 2006:312)—the residents of each community found their own solutions to the problems of living together in permanent villages—but maintaining tradition seems to have been important for everyone. Features like central poles were placed again and again in the same location, and houses were sometimes superimposed on the foundations of older structures (Pauketat 2004:61). A village tended to expand in a modular fashion: a new courtyard might be added, new poles erected, and a new communal building constructed to form the core of an additional subgroup within a larger community that had been previously organized around a single set of these central features (Mehrer 1995:140). Preexisting patterns in villages thus influenced the form they took when some of them grew during the second half of the period.

Even though the number of inhabitants in these bigger settlements remained low during the Terminal Late Woodland period—often just in the high hundreds—residents were already employing scalar stress reduction strategies similar to those that had been used at Çatalhöyük. People in the American Bottom began to elaborate group rituals, compartmentalize living spaces within settlements, and likely increase the size of their basal units. These actions would have decreased the number of decision-makers within growing communities and probably have led to the higher symbolic ranking of certain subgroups over others. Residents, nonetheless, seemed unwilling to accept the existence of overarching, overtly hierarchical, relationships (Kelly 2000:168; Mehrer 1995:140).

Yet social change was accelerating in the American Bottom at the end of the Terminal Late Woodland period. Maize was the staple crop across the region by AD 1000, and the more intensive cultivation of maize likely led to both an increase in the amount of communal and private storage in villages and the creation of routine food surpluses that could be used for feasts and exchange (Mehrer 1995:141). Long-distance contact was also becoming more routine by this time—pottery was regularly coming into the area from 300 kilometers away—and a few of the larger villages were attracting more and more settlers from both inside and outside the American Bottom (Pauketat 2004:60–61).

The mounting scalar stress in the larger settlements in the region was thus compounded by the challenges of managing newfound surpluses, maintaining remote ties, and weaving together settlers from different cultural traditions (Slater et al. 2014:126). In response, communities may have sought to forge new crosscutting identities within and between settlements through the construction of plazas and earthen mounds (Emerson 1997:57; Schroeder 2004a:814; Stoltman et al. 2008:334).

Creating a Ceremonial Center

By the beginning of the eleventh century AD, the largest, and most culturally diverse settlement as measured by the styles found in its ceramic assemblage was Cahokia, with a population of about 2,000 people (Pauketat and Lopinot 1997:119). The site's houses were arranged around small plazas that featured pits, posts, and the occasional special-use structure (Dalan et al. 2003:98). These plaza groups seem to have been the primary organizational unit of the atomized community, but there is some evidence for bigger plazas featuring multiple posts that could have served to tie together various subgroups within the sprawling settlement (Pauketat 1994:120).

Although there is a tendency for Mississippian archaeologists to argue that Cahokia was already a "chiefly center" during the Terminal Woodland period because of its size (Emerson 1991:234; also see Kelly 2000:172; Pauketat 1997a:31), there are no data from this period at Cahokia or elsewhere in the region that would indicate the existence of the kinds of high-status positions or craft specialists that are commonly associated with chiefdoms, nor is there any compelling evidence that can be used to argue that Cahokia controlled the affairs of other villages. This said, Cahokia was undoubtedly a special place—the primus inter pares of villages in the American Bottom—whose residents were likely the most influential players in local affairs.

Cahokia, like the region's other settlements (Kelly 1990a, 1990b, 2000), was likely made up of multiple ranked kin or clan groups. As Cahokia got bigger, aggrandizers within its more powerful subgroups would have sought to find ways to maintain and even strengthen their position vis-à-vis both lower ranked groups and the newcomers who were settling in the community and in the surrounding region. Naked declarations of radical social difference were destined to fail in a society that still valued autonomy and egalitarianism, but one socially acceptable means of accentuating status positions would have been to coordinate the building of monuments to gods and ancestors.

There was already a long history of erecting smaller-scale ceremonial structures in the American Bottom, and the creation of such structures at Cahokia could have been combined with more elaborate group rituals to relieve scalar stress in the growing and ethnically diverse settlement. Post settings, plaza constructions, and other efforts could thus have been couched as a public service rather than as a power grab, and those individuals best positioned to coordinate building efforts would have been those who were seen as having a particularly strong connection to the divine (Emerson 2003). The individuals who began remodeling Cahokia in the first decades of the eleventh century elaborated on ritual practices in use at the time in the American Bottom (Pauketat and Alt 2005), but they also drew inspiration from earlier traditions of mound building in North America (Sherwood and Kidder 2011).

The mounds of the Hopewell tradition may have been particularly relevant to Cahokia's aspiring religious leaders. The American Bottom was on the fringes of this Middle Woodland tradition (Kelly 2002:140–141), and many of the people who had settled in the region's Terminal Woodland period settlements probably knew something about Hopewell mound building through oral traditions. As large as 5.2 meters high and 300 meters in diameter, the construction of the earlier Hopewell mounds had brought together widely dispersed, largely egalitarian groups. The raison d'etre of aggregation was the building of a mound—there is often little evidence for postconstruction activities in and around these locations (Bernardini 2004:350)—that signified the broader group's commitment to a shared set of sacred ideas.

Those who orchestrated Hopewell mound constructions may have been the shamans whose burials inside a few of these monuments were surrounded by caches of seashells, quartz crystals, bear canines, copper celts, and other seemingly nonutilitarian goods. These objects, perhaps assembled together by mourners during mortuary rituals (Brown 2006:480–483), demonstrated the shamans' ability to tap into the power of other worlds. This connection to the divine gave them "the requisite authority to direct . . . earthmoving operations of impressive scale" (Brown 2006:488), but their influence over others was episodic, since it dissipated in large part once villagers left mound building events and returned to their homes.

Cahokia's aggrandizers may have been thinking of those Hopewell shamans when they convinced those living in the village to abandon domestic areas in the middle of the settlement and begin the construction of Monks Mound (Schilling 2012:305). Using only baskets, stone hoes, digging sticks, and their own hands, builders moved about 720,000 cubic meters of earth to form a platform more than 30 meters high that covered 7 hectares at its base (Dalan 1997:98; Schilling 2012:305) (fig. 5.2). The footprint of Monks Mound was established early on, and then its edifice was built upward by the addition of alternating light and dark colored layers of coarse and fine-grained sediments (Schilling 2012:305). Blocks of sods were used to reinforce the face of parts of the mound—the dense rootlets in the sod held the blocks together—and then the mound's sloping surfaces were likely covered repeatedly with a smooth, red clay veneer (Sherwood and Kidder 2011:74–82).

Figure 5.2. Artist's reconstruction of Monks Mound
(Cahokia Mounds State Historic Site, painting by Michael Hampshire).

The 19-hectare Great Plaza was also started soon after construction began on Monks Mound. More houses were razed to build the plaza, and then a single layer of fill was used to both top off the borrow pits where the soil for the mound had been taken and flatten out the floodplain's undulating landscape. A "dense stand" of post pits in the Great Plaza in front of Monks Mound likely reflects the placement of red-ochre painted marker posts that were believed to embody the spirits of the ancestors (Alt et al. 2010:140–142). Cahokia's Great Plaza would have comfortably fit about 30,000 people standing for an event (Dalan et al. 2003:130)—a number exceeding the city's population at its height (Pauketat and Lopinot 2007:121). The builders of mound and plaza had big ambitions.

The scale of Monks Mound and the Great Plaza alone is enough evidence for some scholars to argue that a paramount chief had managed to gain control over the city by the time that these monuments were completed around AD 1050 (Milner 1998:13). The amount of labor required was greater than what had been needed for the Hopewell mounds, yet it is well documented cross-culturally that monumental structures were often built by those living in societies without centralized control or marked status differences (Burger and Rosenwig 2012). The new monumental architecture at Cahokia, often constructed on top of the plazas, central posts, charnel houses, and other features that had previously tied villagers together (Dalan et al. 2003:163; Sullivan and Pauketat 2007:30), was likely portrayed as being beneficial to everyone in the community. Certain individuals undoubtedly orchestrated building efforts, but there may have been a sense that these task-specific leadership roles would have come to an end with the completion of building projects.

Monks Mound and the Great Plaza would soon become the sacred heart of the American Bottom. Most of the houses and mounds subsequently built at Cahokia followed the orientation of Monks Mound, creating a grid pattern that was sometimes also followed by outlying settlements (Dalan et al. 2003:155–157; Pauketat 2013:99–100). This "Cahokia grid" probably reflects an astronomical alignment that coincided with the fall harvest festival, an event that was likely of long-standing importance within the region (Pauketat 2013:100). Circles of wooden post, also known as woodhenges, were also constructed at Cahokia in order to observe equinoxes and other celestial events (Dalan et al. 2003:157), as well as a kilometer-long raised causeway (Baires 2014).

Cahokia's uniformity in orientation was tempered by the modularity in the living arrangements chosen by those moving to the growing city. Homes at Cahokia were arranged around small plazas that contained a central post and one or more storage units. These plaza groups were arranged, in turn, into larger neighborhoods that each clustered around a plaza and mound complex (Pauketat 2004:80). This modularity—a compartmentalization likely employed to mitigate the toll of rising scalar stress—was probably an organic process, albeit one that mapped on to a grid that signaled a set of religious ideas shared by all residents.

Most of Cahokia was built in little more than five decades (fig. 5.3). The frenetic construction efforts, likely powered by religious zeal for the perceived procreative powers of the site (Emerson 1997:223), were organized around social events that brought together large groups of people for work and celebration. Analysis of material dumped into a borrow pit near the Great Plaza suggests that periodic feasts were held in the city's center (Pauketat et al. 2002). The feasting debris in the borrow pit contains the mix of cooking pots, animal bones, and plant remains that one might expect from a party, but there are also tobacco seeds, quartz crystals, human bone, and a broken chunkey stone that hint at a wide array of ritually charged activities that took place at the same time. (Chunkey was a game played by throwing spears at a stone disc rolled along the ground [DeBoer 1993].) This mixture of activities is reminiscent of the events held in the much smaller plazas of household groups during the Late and Terminal Woodland periods (Pauketat et al. 2002:276). The scale was of course different, but people were engaging in the same kinds of community-building actions that they had been for the past few centuries.

The emphasis on scaling-up activities may have reshaped how houses were constructed at Cahokia and throughout the American Bottom. People had previously built structures by digging a few dozen individual postholes for posts; these posts were likely saplings that they then bent and tied together to form a roof. Almost all of the new buildings constructed in the second half of the eleventh century were made instead by digging a wall trench with a stone hoe. Entire wall segments could therefore be put up at once, before, at least for rectangular houses, a hipped, thatch roof was added (Pauketat 2004:80). The newly introduced wall trenches made constructing houses faster and easier: a wall could be made elsewhere, brought to the location, and then raised into place (Alt and Pauketat 2011:108–109). Yet, most importantly for our purposes, this new form of building required cooperation beyond the family level, since multiple adults were required to install the wall segments.

The people who moved into the new neighborhoods at Cahokia came from locations both within and outside the American Bottom (Emerson and Hargrave 2000:4; Pauketat 2003:43; Slater et al. 2014:125). Early ceremonies probably celebrated incipient pan-Cahokian identities, but newcomers from different locales appear to have settled in distinct parts of the mound. There was also a trend both at Cahokia and in its environs toward the localization, segmentation, and specialization of production within neighborhoods (Yerkes 1989, 1991). Those living in the Tract 15A neighborhood of Cahokia, for example, concentrated more on making axe heads and spindle whorls, while residents of the Kunnnemann Tract produced more shell beads and necklaces (Pauketat 2004:84). There is very little evidence for centralized control at this time—groups seem to have been reacting to the economic opportunities created by Cahokia's ascendance by finding a niche and then developing it—and very few of these manufactured items could be classified as goods that could be used to signal elite status (Trubitt 2000:678).

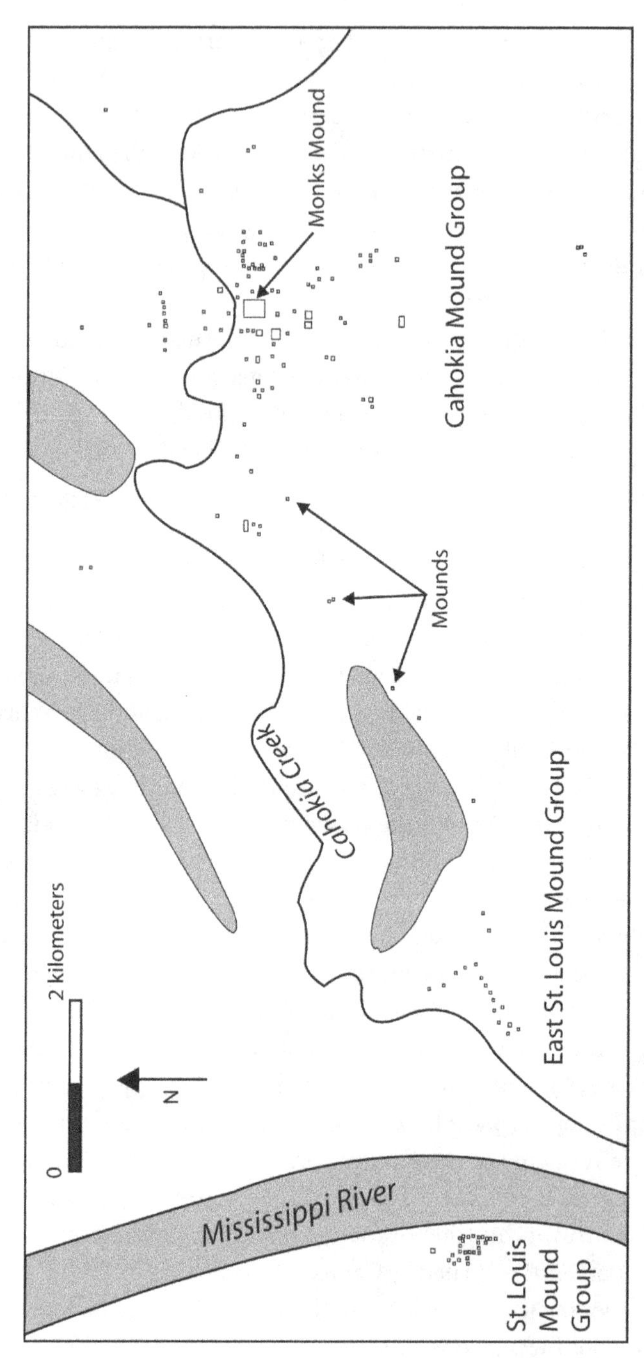

Figure 5.3. Map of greater Cahokia (Justin Jennings).

Despite the monumentality of its architecture, status hierarchies in the mid-eleventh century were initially muted at Cahokia and across the American Bottom, since even the aggrandizing shamans who orchestrated the first mound and plaza constructions were likely seen as facilitating the celebration of commonly held cosmological principles (Emerson 2003; Trubitt 2000; also see Knight 1990). Some of these shamans may have resided on top of a few of the mounds and served as caretakers of Cahokia's sacred spaces, while others presided over rituals in the antechambers of lodges located in different neighborhoods (Pauketat 2013:123–124). They were essential, highly influential individuals, but they were likely viewed at first as occasional, and perhaps even dangerous, conduits to the divine who had little power over everyday affairs.

As Cahokia grew, the authority of these shamans would have become institutionalized (e.g., Rick 2005). The power of Hopewell shamans had been short-lived, in large part because people went back to their communities after a mound was constructed. In contrast, people stayed at Cahokia. Shamans, who would have presided over recurring community events, thus had the opportunity to make status differences permanent. Over time, shamans were able to transform themselves from essential but episodic conduits to the divine into ruling priests who were keepers of sacred laws and the only members of the community authorized to perform certain rituals (Emerson 2003:238). The individuals who had first come together to build Cahokia had not intended to create monuments that would lead to the reification of status differences in the future; they had come together to create a site that celebrated their ancestors, gods, and the cosmos (e.g., R. Joyce 2004). Their ongoing communal building project was nonetheless co-opted over time by an aspiring shamanic elite who effectively added to the meanings of Cahokia's plazas and mounds by turning the structures into symbols of the special connections between certain individuals and the divine.

The best evidence for how status positions were changing during Cahokia's first century comes from the excavations of Mound 72 (Fowler et al. 1999). The area underneath the mound was originally the plaza of a household group that was built soon after the Great Plaza was constructed in the mid-eleventh century. These households were aligned to the Cahokia grid, as were the charnel house and marker post that stood in the plaza

(Pauketat 2004:91). People dismantled the charnel house less than a decade later and then laid out bundles of disarticulated skeletons exhumed from this charnel house on top of where the structure had been. They also removed the adjacent marker post at around the same time, dug a pit in this location for the bodies of 22 youths, and then filled a second pit nearby with the bodies of 19 others (Alt 2008:214–215). Most of the people buried in the pits were women (Thompson 2013:417), and isotopic data from the skeletons suggest that some were likely from poorer communities outside of Cahokia (Ambrose et al. 2003; Slater et al. 2013:125). Finally, a low platform mound was constructed over top of the pits and dismantled charnel house (Fowler 1991:10–14; Pauketat 2004:91, 2010:26).

These early rituals, probably celebrating ancestors and female fertility, did not highlight specific individuals, but the next stage in Mound 72's development placed certain people at the center of communal celebrations. This stage begins when two adult men were buried just to the south of the existing platform mound. The first individual was buried underneath a two-meter-long shell-bead cape, while the second person was laid on top of this cape. The men may have represented mythical hero twins (Baltus and Baires 2011:176). As the mound grew in size over the next few decades, pits were occasionally dug into the mound and filled with recently deceased, sacrificed, and seemingly long dead individuals, as well as with bundles of goods, like mica crystals, copper tubes, projectile points, and shell beads that were both manufactured in Cahokia and obtained from other regions (Rose 1999:68–70) (fig. 5.4). These additions to the mound over time could have had the effect of retelling the hero twin story and thus have contributed to the creation of an "epic narrative" (Brown 2010:49).

The personal items buried with individuals in Mound 72 during its later stages of construction speak to the rising social differences in the community, and isotopic data suggests that the higher status individuals buried there had much greater access than others to animal proteins that would have often been procured from people living elsewhere (Ambrose et al. 2003:223). Yet it is important to stress that the celebration of status positions were always ancillary to the mound burials' more universalizing message of ancestral ties, fertility, cardinal directions, and the coming together of diverse groups and objects into a single place (Baltus and Baires 2012; Goldstein 2000; Pauketat and Alt 2003; Porubcan 2000).

In conclusion, the horizontal and vertical divisions of an urban center were emerging as people settled into life at Cahokia in the second half of the eleventh century. Hierarchical divisions were growing in the settlement *despite* an emphasis on group-oriented ritual, and neighborhoods were starting to diversify their economic production to meet new demands even as residents compartmentalized into smaller units organized around household groups and neighborhoods (Trubitt 2000:672; Watson 2000:231). A civic identity was meanwhile being constructed across these divisions as people played chunkey, reset marker posts, smoked tobacco, and built mounds in similar ways. A century after aggregation began, a city was only beginning to emerge from an urbanization process that was already leading to widespread changes in the American Bottom and beyond.

Figure 5.4. Bundled arrow offerings from Mound 72 at Cahokia (Illinois State Museum Archival Collections).

CHAPTER 5

Creating a Countryside and Colonizing the Midcontinent

Although Cahokia's urbanization occurred in one of the most fertile areas of the American midcontinent, the city's residents were soon dependent on outsiders for a significant portion of the variety of wild and domesticated foods they consumed on site (Buikstra and Milner 1991; Yerkes 2005). The initial population aggregation at Cahokia, however, had led to the decline and often abandonment of the American Bottom villages that would have been best positioned to supply the city. Cahokia's food demands were met instead via isolated farmsteads that emerged in the second half of the eleventh century. The farmsteads that were loosely tied to "rural nodes" that mimicked on a much smaller scale many of the activities that were taking place in the city began to develop (Emerson 1997). These nodes served as barter sites where surplus foods from the farmsteads could be exchanged for the specialized products that were beginning to be produced in the city (Emerson 1997:182–183). Routine visits to these nodes would have reinforced the urban-rural bond that had initially been created through cross-cutting kinship ties and the farmers' participation in mound building, feasting, and other rites in the city.

Those living in the farmsteads may have first opted into relationships with both Cahokia and the rural nodes because they believed in the importance of the city's cosmological project. As the twelfth century unfolded, however, the relationship between farmsteads, nodes, and the city grew more formalized. Elite positions began developing in these nodes, and the flow of high-status items from Cahokia to these rising rural elites hints at deepening relationships with those who were gaining power in the city (Emerson 1997:187). At the same time, fineware ceramics, especially a particular style called Ramey incised, began circulating more widely across the American Bottom, perhaps reflecting an intensification of the rites that bound farmsteads to both the rural nodes and the city (Pauketat and Emerson 1991:934; Wilson 1999:106).

Although American Bottom farmers remained for the large part economically independent (Mehrer 1988:141), they were nonetheless being steadily pulled into a hegemonic relationship with Cahokia under the "guise of communalism" (Emerson 1997:187). Cahokians appear to have been able to cajole, but not yet compel, outside producers to give them the maize, deer, cloth, and other products that were required for the city to function. The settlement nodes were thus a work in progress, the first tentative step in the development of a regional polity. People living at Cahokia, after all, had immediate needs to fulfill—they could not wait for everything to be figured out as they worked to create a well-functioning countryside.

As the city grew, residents tried to draw more distant lands into Cahokia's political and economic orbit. One of these locations was the Richland Complex, an area with great agricultural potential located about 20 kilometers east of the city (Alt 2001, 2002, 2010; Holley 2006; Pauketat 2003). There had been few people living in the Richland Complex during the Terminal Woodland period, but this changed in the mid-eleventh century when several new villages were founded by outside groups—some coming from as far as 300 kilometers away (Alt 2006)—who were attracted to the region by Cahokia's appeal as a sacred center.

The Richland Complex settlers had access to many of the goods produced in the city. In return, they appear to have provided goods that Cahokians desired. There is evidence that the land in the Richland Complex was extensively farmed, and the presence of generous storage facilities scattered throughout the villages suggests that each household likely stockpiled their own agricultural products for shipment to the city (Alt 2010:125). Each village also often specialized in making textiles, shell beads, celts, or other goods that would have been of value to those in Cahokia, as well as to neighboring villagers that were pursuing a different production focus (Alt 2010:126).

Cahokian influence over local affairs in the Richland Complex was initially quite weak. Those living in the area adopted and reconfigured some of the city's ceramic and architectural innovations, but change in general occurred "more slowly and in a more piecemeal" fashion compared to American Bottom groups, as settlers initially rejected those innovations that threatened the more egalitarian, communal ethos that they were accustomed to (Alt 2001:142; also see Alt 2002, 2010; Holley 2006). Their participation in Cahokia's growing interaction network was therefore likely voluntary at first and was probably associated with the construction of a mound and plaza center in the Richland Complex that is known as the Emerald site.

Since ritual spaces were rare in Richland Complex villages, it is likely that Emerald served as the major sacred site of the area. The city loomed large in the imagination of Emerald's builders—the site was linked to Cahokia via an astronomical alignment that celebrated the northern lunar maximum (Pauketat 2013:144)—and the earliest exchanges of goods between the city and the Richland Complex may have occurred during the rituals surrounding its construction. The dearth of debris in and around the Emerald site, however, suggests that it was infrequently visited in subsequent years (Pauketat 2013:138–140). Those living in the Richland Complex, like those living at earlier Hopewell sites, appear to have come together largely to build the mounds. They do not seem to have regularly worshipped in the location.

Emerald's position may have been eclipsed within a generation by the founding of Grossman, a settlement with more formal ties to Cahokia (Alt 2010). Grossman boasted four temples, three sweathouses, and one charnel house; its three lodges with antechambers also probably housed shamans who, like those in nearby Cahokia, were quickly attaining elite status. The site also featured a "very Cahokian" ceramic assemblage, huge storage capacity, and workshop areas where ceremonial items were made (Alt 2010:127). Grossman can perhaps best be seen as a Cahokian colony, though one located just a day's walk away. As Susan Alt has argued, the settlement served both as "a place to come together for ritual and ceremony to celebrate the harvest and the renewal of life" and a "highly politicized place . . . proclaiming and fulfilling the needs of Cahokians" (Alt 2010:129).

Those living in the Richland Complex were, like the farmers of the American Bottom, being brought under increasing hegemonic control through rituals of inclusion that linked settlers to the city. Colonies established farther afield, however, were less successful in controlling local populations. The colony of Audrey, for example, was established less than 100 kilometers from Cahokia in the lower Illinois Valley (Delaney-Rivera 2004) in the mid- to late eleventh century. It was fortified with a palisade and was built following a formalized site plan of wall-trenched structures that mimics contemporaneous American Bottom sites, yet a critical difference between it and these other settlements was that the temple and sweathouse were located at its center (Delaney-Rivera 2004:44). This orientation recalls that used in the Terminal Woodland period across much of this region and likely reflects a more communal, less hierarchical orientation among the Audrey settlers who set off from Cahokia during its first decades of growth.

The artifacts recovered at Audrey can be pointed to as evidence that those living in the colony not only tapped into Cahokia's expanding exchange networks but also maintained far-flung contacts of their own. The Audrey colonists were culturally influential in the lower Illinois Valley—feasts and other events held in the community were likely instrumental in the creation of a new way of life in the area that merged Cahokian and other regional influences with local antecedents (Delaney-Rivera 2004:51)—but they were unable to establish the kind of extractive economy Grossman had. Similar failings are also documented farther north in the Illinois Valley, where small groups of colonists from in or around Cahokia appear to have established only short-lived sites (Conrad 1991; Harn 1991). Their palisades suggest they had been threatened with violence, and Audrey itself may have been burned to the ground.

Classifying colonies like Audrey as unsuccessful, however, tells only part of the story. Robert Hall (1991:31–33) has argued that Cahokia's colonial exchanges of objects most often took place within the context of fictive adoption rituals that enabled strangers to interact peacefully with each other. Following this thinking, we might speculate that symbolically charged objects like Ramey-incised pottery, chunkey stones, shell beads, long-nosed god ornaments, and flint clay figurines from Cahokia could have been exchanged in colonies for a specific set of goods that were desired in the American Bottom (Pauketat 2004:120). Cahokia's more far-flung colonists may therefore have arrived as diplomats rather than would-be conquerors.

Cahokia's rituals, as you may recall, often included objects from other regions—among the goods placed in Mound 72, for example, were bundles of projectile points from Oklahoma, Wisconsin, and Illinois (Fowler 1991:14). These objects were valued because of their exotic origins, which Cahokia's rising shamanic aggrandizers capitalized on, using them to signal their reach into foreign lands. It might thus be argued that the colonists at Audrey and other outposts successfully achieved the twin goals of proselytizing a Cahokian way of life and obtaining a limited number of ritually charged goods for import into the city (but see Emerson and Hughes 2000 regarding more local acquisitions).

The extent of Cahokia colonization remains unclear. The best evidence comes from the north, where colonies dating from the late eleventh and twelfth centuries have been documented in Illinois, Wisconsin, Iowa, Missouri, and South Dakota (Pauketat 2004:124–126). The most well-known of these northern colonies is Aztalan in southern Wisconsin. Settled between AD 1050 and 1100, Aztalan was a palisaded community of some 300 people that was organized around a central ceremonial space that contained two plazas and nine mounds (Birmingham and Goldstein 2005) (fig. 5.5).

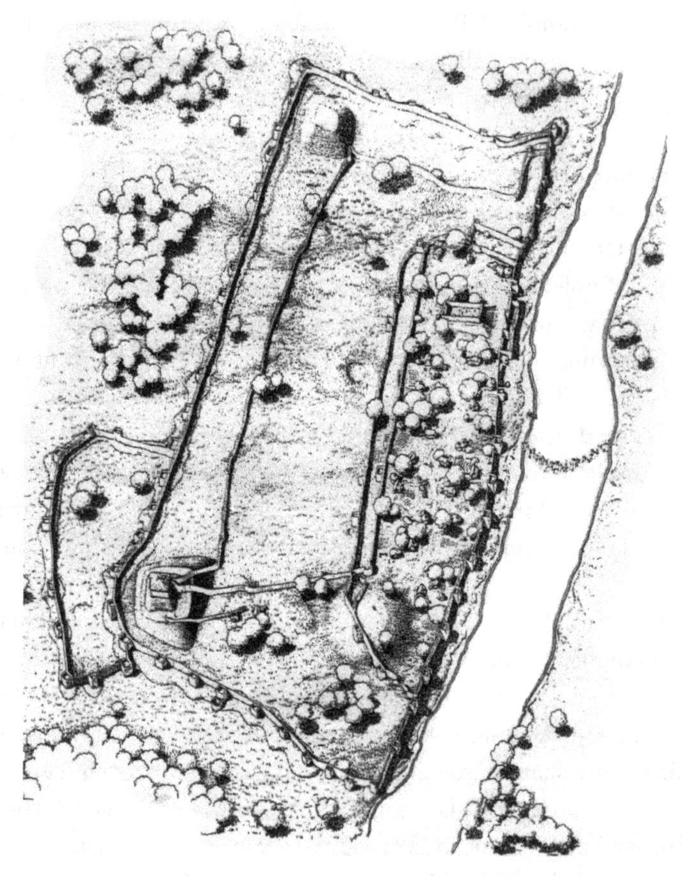

Figure 5.5. Architectural reconstruction of the Aztalan site by E. Palson, 1982 (UWM-ARL image # 1982.0073) (copyright University of Wisconsin–Milwaukee Archaeological Research Laboratory; used with permission).

The site plan, artifacts, and construction techniques at Aztalan closely resemble those of Cahokia, and the strontium isotope ratios of some of the individuals buried there matches that of people from the American Bottom (Price et al. 2007:536). Aztalan was already a sacred place when colonists arrived, and the community of locals that developed around the settlement's palisade was incorporated into aspects of the Cahokian ethos through gift exchanges and shared rituals. As with Audrey, there is no evidence that those living at Aztalan controlled the affairs of local groups (Goldstein 1991:224), but the site was well positioned to access northern exchange networks of native copper from Great Lakes sources (Young and Fowler 2000:294), a much-prized resource in Cahokia and elsewhere in North America.

Colonies were also likely founded to the south of Cahokia in the late eleventh century. The earliest levels of sites like Shiloh and Obion in Tennessee, for example, have artifacts made in the American Bottom, as well as wall-trenched houses and a mound and plaza site plan typical of communities affiliated with Cahokia (Blitz and Lorenz 2002:119; Pauketat 2004:131–137). Like the northern colonies, they were probably sacred sites that were at least in part established to provide a place where Cahokia-made objects could be exchanged for locally available goods that were desired in the city (Kelly 1991a, 1991b). These early colonists were perhaps particularly interested in gaining access to Caddoan-speaking groups in adjacent portions of Texas, Oklahoma, Louisiana, and Arkansas.

Excavations of Caddoan sites have revealed Ramey-style pots, flint clay figurines, and other late tenth- to eleventh-century objects from the American Bottom that are associated with mound burials of incipient local elites who seem to have used connections with Cahokia and other far-off places to support their still-tenuous political positions (Brown 1996; Emerson and Girard 2004; Emerson et al. 2003). These aggrandizers emulated aspects of Cahokian cosmology but also appear to have been interested in repurposing the sacred power that they thought imported exotica possessed. The best evidence for this repurposing comes from a flint clay pipe depicting a kneeling man discovered at the Gahagan site in northwestern Illinois. The flint clay comes from the American Bottom region (Emerson et al. 2003:299), but the pipe was carved or recarved using a more local style (Emerson and Girard 2004:60).

In sum, the aggregation of people in and around Cahokia created a novel environment that presented an array of logistical problems. People, of course, needed to eat, but there were also other pressing concerns, like obtaining the necessary imports for the rituals of inclusion that were being practiced in the settlement and at other nearby locations. As people came into the city, there was a parallel movement of groups outward in the first decades. Some groups began the unenviable task of trying to organize regional production so that a stable subsistence economy could be formed, while others went farther afield pushing up and down the Mississippian River and its tributaries searching for exotica and proselytizing on behalf of the burgeoning sacred center (Pauketat 2013:159).

Cahokian control over colonial settlements located a few days away from the city would have been weak. Elite positions were still forming at Cahokia when most of these colonies were founded, and it is quite possible that many of those who left Cahokia had little interest in propping up city leaders and craft specialists who were only beginning to come into their own when they left the site. Some goods did flow back and forth, but it would have been costly to sustain these long-distance colonial relationships. As time went on, city leaders seem to have given up on the far-flung colonies and instead focused their energies on strengthening and formalizing of relationship with those living in the city, the American Bottom, and the Richland Complex (Pauketat 1997b; see Marcoux 2007 for a similar argument with respect to Moundsville). The faintest outlines of a regionally organized polity could be seen coming together in the environs of Cahokia by the mid-twelfth century, but the city itself was starting to fall apart.

Cahokia's Decline and the Extension of the Mississippian Horizon

Cahokia was the preeminent settlement and ceremonial center of the American midcontinent during the twelfth century AD, and a "Cahokian ethos" pervaded the American Bottom, as people situated their homes, cooked their meals, and tilled their fields in ways that referenced their close relationship to the site (Pauketat 2004:145). This collective ethos had been initially engendered by the religious devotion of settlers that flocked to the center to build a series of monuments honoring their gods and ancestors; taking part in this project together helped combat the scalar stress caused by rapid aggregation.

Despite an emphasis on group ritual and compartmentalization that celebrated egalitarian ideals, horizontal and vertical divisions within and between American Bottom communities began to rise soon after Cahokia was founded. These divisions became more formalized during the twelfth century, when a regionally organized polity started to form around Cahokia based on craft specialization, surplus extraction, and social segmentation. Dissent was by now perhaps being met occasionally with violence—as demonstrated by the discovery of severed limbs at the Grossman site (Alt 2010:129)—and shamans seemed well on their way to becoming rulers.

A Cahokian state, however, never materialized in subsequent decades, and the city's population began a steady decline in the twelfth century (Pauketat 2004:148). Cahokia collapsed for many reasons (Pauketat 2004:151–153), but one of the most important factors in the city's demise may have been the population's resistance to what it rightly perceived as an increasingly hierarchical and centralized society (Pauketat et al. 2013:223). Rising social differences had contributed significantly to the abandonment of Çatalhöyük, and it appears that Cahokia also began breaking apart even as elite positions solidified. The would-be rulers of the settlement could not get along and were scattered across the city's neighborhoods. This decentralization and antagonism seems to have been largely a result of the strategies that these leaders had pursued in order to consolidate their positions.

The first decades of the twelfth century AD was a time of frenetic monument building at Cahokia, but the focus of residents and visitors was already shifting away from the Great Plaza and Monks Mound (Pauketat and Lopinot 1997:121). People were putting most of their energies instead into creating and refurbishing the plaza and pyramid complexes that anchored each of the city's neighborhoods (Mehrer and Collins 1995). Although these complexes began as religious structures that were subsidiary to the central precinct, the fidelity of residents to the Cahokia grid sharply declined, as people began orienting themselves more toward their neighborhood pyramids and the activities that were occurring within the associated plazas.

The group-oriented activities that had initially attracted people into the city center—feasts, rituals, games, and even stimulant use (Crown et al. 2012)—were now occurring more at the neighborhood level. The neighborhood leaders that presided over these activities began a "politicized reorganization of religion" to recast themselves as essential conduits of cosmic forces (Baltus and Baires 2011:187). With each aspiring elite suggesting he had a more privileged connection than others to the divine, Cahokia began breaking up into rival Cahokias. Social tensions rose across the site, and by AD 1150 palisades had been thrown up around the city's ceremonial precinct and other sites in the American Bottom.

In the first decades of the thirteenth century, rising elites took further steps to signal their special status. They co-opted religious symbols, burned and rebuilt temples, and incorporated sacred building material into their homes (Baltus and Baires 2011:184–186; Brown and Kelly 2000; Simon 2002:296–298). They also made their houses bigger, wore more opulent clothes, ate different foods, imported more exotic items, brought together cadres of craft specialists to produce "one-of-a-kind prestige objects," and enforced and extended their power through warfare (Trubitt 2000:682; also see Pauketat 1997b:11, 2004:148; Dalan et al. 2003:179). These status-legitimating activities were costly to maintain, and so neighborhood elites began competing for followers who could provide food and labor to support them. As social complexity increased in the neighborhoods, the city itself began splintering into rival factions.

Most people in and around the American Bottom were likely quite uncomfortable with the rising social inequality. Those living outside of the city had been willing to contribute to communal activities in locales like the Great Plaza, but they were more hesitant to pay what now seemed to be tribute to urban elites who were either unknown to them or had been their social equals just a few generations earlier. With urban-rural ties breaking down, the Richland Complex was abandoned by AD 1150 (Pauketat 2003:58), and population declined throughout the American Bottom over the next two centuries. Those who remained in the area faced rising violence and malnutrition (Hedman 2006:268), and the city's inhabitants started to nucleate around smaller, more dispersed sites presided over by chiefs whose legitimization no longer depended on their relationship with Cahokia. By AD 1300, city was virtually abandoned (Pauketat 1997a:68).

The creation of a cultural horizon across the American midcontinent had begun with the founding of Cahokia (Pauketat 2013:159). A diverse group of settlers streamed into the city in its first decades, and returning pilgrims and embarking colonists from Cahokia propelled the city's new corpus of ideas and objects outward. By the mid-twelfth century, Cahokia-style chunkey stones, arrowheads, long-nosed god ornaments, shell beads, and other objects could be found at sites hundreds of kilometers away. Interregional trade had also increased during this time as a result of the city's escalating demands, and different North American groups began adopting some of Cahokia's ideas such as wall trenching, the use of shell temper, and the organization of public spaces (Bardolph 2014; King, ed. 2007; Lewis and Stout 1998; Rogers and Smith 1995; Scarry 1996).

What began as a Cahokian-centered network in the eleventh century AD, however, quickly became "akin to a cultural mosaic of competing, expanding populations with disparate technological, organizational, and economic patterns" (Blitz and Lorenz 2002:119; also see Anderson 1994; Beck 2003; Blitz 1999; Cobb 2003; Schroeder 2004b). With Cahokia rapidly declining, colonists and the local aggrandizers that were embroiled within the city's exchange network sought to shore up recently won positions of power by demonstrating why they should be in charge regardless of the city's fate (Cobb 2003:78). These leaders poached from the tools that were being developed in the American Bottom—exotica, group rituals, costumes—to create legitimatization strategies that worked best in their local conditions. The priorities of the group won out over these aggrandizers in some places (e.g., Cobb and King 2005), but in the South a series of powerful chiefdoms were created during the thirteenth century.

Many of these chiefdoms flourished between AD 1200 and 1400. The chiefdoms participated in the Southeastern Ceremonial Complex (often called SECC), a religiously charged exchange network defined by a number of related artistic styles found on elite objects (King 2007:250). Some of these SECC styles, like the cross-and-circle motif and paired turkey cocks, allude to a shared set of beliefs regarding the basic organization of the universe (Cobb and King 2005:178–180). Other, often slightly later, motifs were used in burial assemblages to signal an elite's privileged access to the divine.

The rulers of Etowah, for example, were buried in mounds alongside bundles of imported marine shell, copper, projectile points, and other artifacts. As with the burial assemblages at Mound 72 in Cahokia two centuries earlier, the bundles and position of the bodies implicitly linked the dead to supernatural beings (King 2010). These links were, however, made more explicit at Etowah by the depictions of these divine figures on shell gorgets and copper plates that would have been worn by Etowah's rulers. The most popular of these figures was the birdman, a mythic hero with Cahokian roots (Cobb and King 2005:183–185).

The chiefdoms that developed during the thirteenth century depended in part on long-distance interactions to support their right to rule. There were now dozens of mound and plaza centers in the lower Mississippi that were exchanging ideas and competing against each other not only for desired imports but also for followers that could serve as farmers and craft specialists (Anderson 1994, 1996; Beck 2003; Blitz 1999; Cobb 2003; King, ed. 2007; Lewis and Stout 1998; Rogers and Smith 1995; Scarry 1996). Since these intensifying interactions had little to do with a rapidly depopulating Cahokia (Pauketat and Lopinot 1997:114), this cultural horizon is commonly referred to as the Mississippian rather than Cahokian horizon.

Although the roots of the Mississippian era can be traced back to the heady first days of Cahokia (Brown and Kelly 2000), chiefs in later communities like Etowah were far more concerned about their relationships with their peers in places like Moundville, Fort Jackson, and Spiro (Marcoux and Wilson 2010; Rogers 1995; Scarry 2007). Cahokia was by then only a symbol of a shared past, as the cultural horizon reached its peak *without* a city, let alone a state, driving interaction. This second wave of chiefly centers would go into decline at the beginning of the fifteenth century. By the time the Spaniard Hernando De Soto traveled up the Mississippi in AD 1541, most Mississippian towns were already abandoned or populated by squatters. The rest would soon fall in the midst of the mass migrations, epidemics, endemic warfare, and general chaos of the postcontact period.

Cahokia and the Civilization Concept

One of the ways to try to tell Cahokia's story is as the rise of a civilization. By the middle of the twelfth century AD, Cahokia had obtained most, but not all, of the characteristics that V. Gordon Childe associates with civilization

(1950). The city was home to a ruling class, occupational specialists, monumental constructions, and sophisticated art. A knowledge of mathematics and astronomy was visible in the site's woodhenges and grid, and its residents enjoyed regular foreign trade. Yet there is no evidence for taxation, writing, and the state, and thus those who cleave to Childe's list and his notion of civilization would argue that Cahokia was not part of a civilization.

Timothy Pauketat has been a leading voice in arguing for a Cahokian civilization despite these perceived shortcomings (2004:1). Pauketat suggests that Childe's and other classic definitions of civilization are too narrow because they are based largely on studies of Mesopotamia and Egypt. He further argues that Cahokian iconography was the "first steps to proto-writing" and that the city was briefly the capital of a uniquely North American kind of state that developed an economic system featuring elements similar to taxation (2004:169–174). By tweaking Childe's definition, scholars like Pauketat can make an argument that Cahokia should join the list of the world's great civilizations. Yet is Cahokia's story best told by adapting it to fit with our preconceptions of what civilizations should be like?

Shifting the criteria that we use to define civilization addresses long-standing biases against non-Western complex societies (Pauketat and Loren 2005:8–9), but this reshuffling only further reifies the civilization stage and its steplike emergence. The fieldwork that Pauketat and dozens of other Mississippian archaeologists have conducted over the last century has actually unearthed a decidedly *different* tale than the one that we have inherited with the civilization concept. Cahokia's story, as Susan Alt has argued, is instead one of "complexity-in-the-making" (2010:129)—the unfolding of a multigenerational process of overcoming the problems associated with settlement aggregation that has at times been underplayed by Mississippian archaeologists eager to place Cahokia on the civilization stage.

Those who settled at Cahokia near the end of the Terminal Woodland period were not trying to create a civilization. They were struggling to unify a growing village and drew from the midcontinent's long tradition of mound building as a mechanism for uniting the disparate groups that had come together there (Slater et al. 2014:126). Monks Mound and the Great Plaza were perhaps too effective—their construction brought thousands more people into the American Bottom, compounding the problems that the building efforts had originally sought to resolve.

The mass migration into the region increased scalar stress, and Cahokians sought to deal with this stress by adopting a mixture of the same kinds of strategies that had been used in aborted cities like Çatalhöyük. They elaborated group ritual, intensified compartmentalization, enlarged the size of basal units, and, most reluctantly, instituted limited social hierarchies. These mechanisms were effective, but new strategies had to be introduced as more migrants came into the American Bottom. Over the next century, the horizontal and vertical divisions commonly associated with cities began to emerge at Cahokia, as neighborhoods coalesced around a rising, though acrimoniously divided, shamanic elite.

The processes of polity formation and colonization paralleled that of incipient urbanization. There were escalating demands from Cahokians for outside resources. Most of these goods could be obtained locally, but there was also a strong interest in exotica because of the power associated with objects obtained from long distances. American Bottom and Richland Complex farmers initially opted to enter into relationships with Cahokia, perhaps by feeding a sister's family or by bringing offerings to a feast. These tenuous links with the city were reinforced over time through the creation of settlement nodes and eventually the rise of local elites whose grip on power was based on their relationship to Cahokia's leaders. At the same time that the countryside was just beginning to form, colonists were embarking from Cahokia to proselytize and establish new trade relationships. The founding of these colonies spurred the creation of a Mississippian cultural horizon, as Cahokian ideas and objects were adopted and manipulated by a growing number of people.

The process of urbanization, polity formation, colonization, and cultural horizon creation that began in the first decades of the eleventh century AD was short-circuited a century later by the rivalries that developed between Cahokia's emerging elite. With individual leaders seeking their own cadres of specialists and farmers, the city descended into violence and lost its appeal as a ceremonial center. Before a regionally organized polity could form, people began leaving the region, and Cahokia in the thirteenth century reverted back to being just one of a handful of locally important centers in the American Bottom. Cahokia's colonists had to fend for themselves, and the Mississippian horizon was left to develop without its initial catalyst.

Our deep-seated reliance on the civilization concept leads us to assume that urbanization, state formation, colonization, and the creation of cultural horizons came together as a package that arrived in a steplike transformation. We are left with a binary choice—Cahokia thus was or was not a civilization. Since there is no in-between, there is little room for "complexity-in-the-making" that can be evaluated on its own terms. References to Cahokia's "Big Bang" by Mississippian archaeologists reinforce the assumption of a steplike transition (Pauketat 2007:146), even though their own data from this region indicate two centuries of culture change that began with people drawing heavily from previous practices.

There was no societal rupture—Cahokians used their past experiences to fashion an evolving set of solutions to the scalar stress of rapid settlement aggregation in ways that were particular to the American Bottom. Those living in Harappa, our next case study, drew from a different set of experiences when their village began to expand. The result of the actions taken in this South Asian city led to an even more dramatic departure from the standard picture of cultural change that has been ingrained in us by the civilization construct.

6

HARAPPA AND THE WALLED CITIES OF THE INDUS RIVER VALLEY

THE ENGINEERS OF THE BRITISH EAST INDIA COMPANY FACED A stone shortage in the late 1850s. Tasked with building a system of railroads throughout the Indus Valley of present-day Pakistan, they desperately needed track ballast in a fluvial region where rocks were scarce. Some turned to mining the baked mud bricks of the ancient settlements that rose as mounds high above the alluvial plain, and work crews, often in just a few days' times, removed massive walls and decimated entire occupation levels. One of the locales hardest hit by brick robbing was Harappa, a 150-hectare site on the Ravi River that dates from about 3700 to 1700 BC (Wright 2010:6, 315).

Harappa was recognized as an important archaeological site by at least 1826, but the city languished largely unstudied until Rai Bahadur Daya Ram Sahni began excavations there in 1920 (Possehl 1991:6). The early work at both Harappa and at the site of Mohenjo-daro on the Lower Indus River would reveal densely occupied, well-organized cities that contained abundant evidence for craft specialization, long-distance exchange, and a writing system (which remains undeciphered to this day). The similarities in what was being discovered at both sites were so striking that Sir John Marshall declared the existence of a South Asian "Indus civilization" that scholars would later date to between 2600 and 1900 BC (Marshall 1931).

Early excavations at Mohenjo-daro exposed broad swaths of the city—Ernest J. H. Mackay had some 1,200 men working under him during the 1925–1926 field season (Possehl 1999:78–79)—but we focus in this chapter on Harappa, since it is the site that has ultimately provided us with the best evidence for how an Indus Valley city developed over time (e.g., Dales and Kenoyer 1991; Kenoyer and Meadow 2000; Kenoyer 2008a; Meadow 1991; Meadow and Kenoyer 1997, 2005). The inferences about Indus urbanization that can be drawn from Harappa are *not* ones that support the idea of a punctuated, steplike transformation to a civilization stage, but rather ones that suggest ongoing social change over the course of two millennia.

Harappa and other third-millennium BC cities of the Indus differ markedly from Cahokia in that they seemed to have come into being as marketplaces rather than as monuments. Those migrating to Harappa after 2800 BC nonetheless faced the same scalar stress attending aggregation that confronted Cahokians (as well as those living at Çatalhöyük), and thus they too struggled to find the best mixture among those mechanisms available to them—increased compartmentalization, more group rituals, larger basal-unit size, and greater social hierarchy—that would reduce that stress. The shift toward a centralized hierarchy at Cahokia broke that city apart, but Harappans were able over time to find a more sustainable mix of stress-reducing strategies that resulted, by at least 2200 BC, in a city run by groups of competing elites that were drawn from the different neighborhoods of the city (Kenoyer 2011:8).

The residents of Harappa, of course, could not wait 600 years before starting to develop a countryside and reaching out to other groups through new trading relationships, the sharing of ideas, and the establishment of colonies. Harappa's urbanization, like all of our case studies, was a multigenerational process that in conjunction with local, regional, and interregional efforts helped sustain the settlement's growing population. Harappa and its relationship with the outside world was suffused with the tension that comes with trying to resolve the seemingly never-ending challenges of keeping tens of thousands of people together in one place.

The Founding of Harappa

The Indus region is centered on the alluvial plain of the Indus River and its five tributaries—the Jhelum, Chenab, Ravi, Beas, and Sutlej—that flow into the Indian Ocean (fig. 6.1). The Ghaggar-Hakra River, located just to the southwest, was likely a sixth, albeit intermittent, tributary to the Indus River until its course changed about 700 years ago (Giosan et al. 2012:E1691). The Indus region is bordered on the north by the high mountain ranges of the Hindu Kush, Karakorum, and Himalayas and by the smaller mountain chains of Baluchistan and Suleiman on the west. The region is further bracketed in the east by the Thar Desert (Wright 2010:28).

Paleoclimatic reconstructions suggest that weather in the Indus region was wetter and more highly variable until about 5000 BC (Courty 1995; Giosan et al. 2012; Madella and Fuller 2006; Prasad et al. 2014). People entered the heart of the river basin during this wetter era—basal finds at Harappa and other sites suggest that individuals were at least foraging in these locations—but unpredictable inundations of the alluvial plain made life there difficult. Most people lived instead in the mountains or along the edges of the Indus River drainage (Possehl 1999:470–472). Our best understanding of life during this preurban era comes from one of these fringe sites, Mehrgarh, a community in Baluchistan.

Mehrgarh's millennia-long occupation sequence reveals not only the domestication of plants and animals but also the beginnings of the Indus region's enduring focus on long-distance trade and craft specialization (J. Jarrige 1993; C. Jarrige et al. 1995; J. F. Jarrige et al. 2005). Mehrgarh's initial occupation levels, dating to as early as 7000 BC, already contain evidence of a mixture of domesticated and wild varieties of wheat and barley (Constantini 1984:29). The animal remains, in contrast, seem to have all been wild; the local domestication of goats, cattle, and perhaps sheep occurred only gradually over the next 2,000 years (Meadows 1998; Meadows and Patel 2003).

At least a subset of Mehrgarh's population lived on site year round, and by at least 4000 BC the settlement had become a regionally important production and trading center. Residents used their homes as workshops for making pottery, textiles, wooden objects, and hides that were likely exchanged for other goods (J. F. Jarrige et al. 2005). Craft specialization increased throughout the fourth millennium, as the artists of Mehrgarh produced a widening variety of objects from local sources as well as from exotic material that was obtained from pastoralists and other mobile groups who routinely moved back and forth between the highlands of western Baluchistan and the lowlands leading into the Indus Valley (Jarrige 1995).

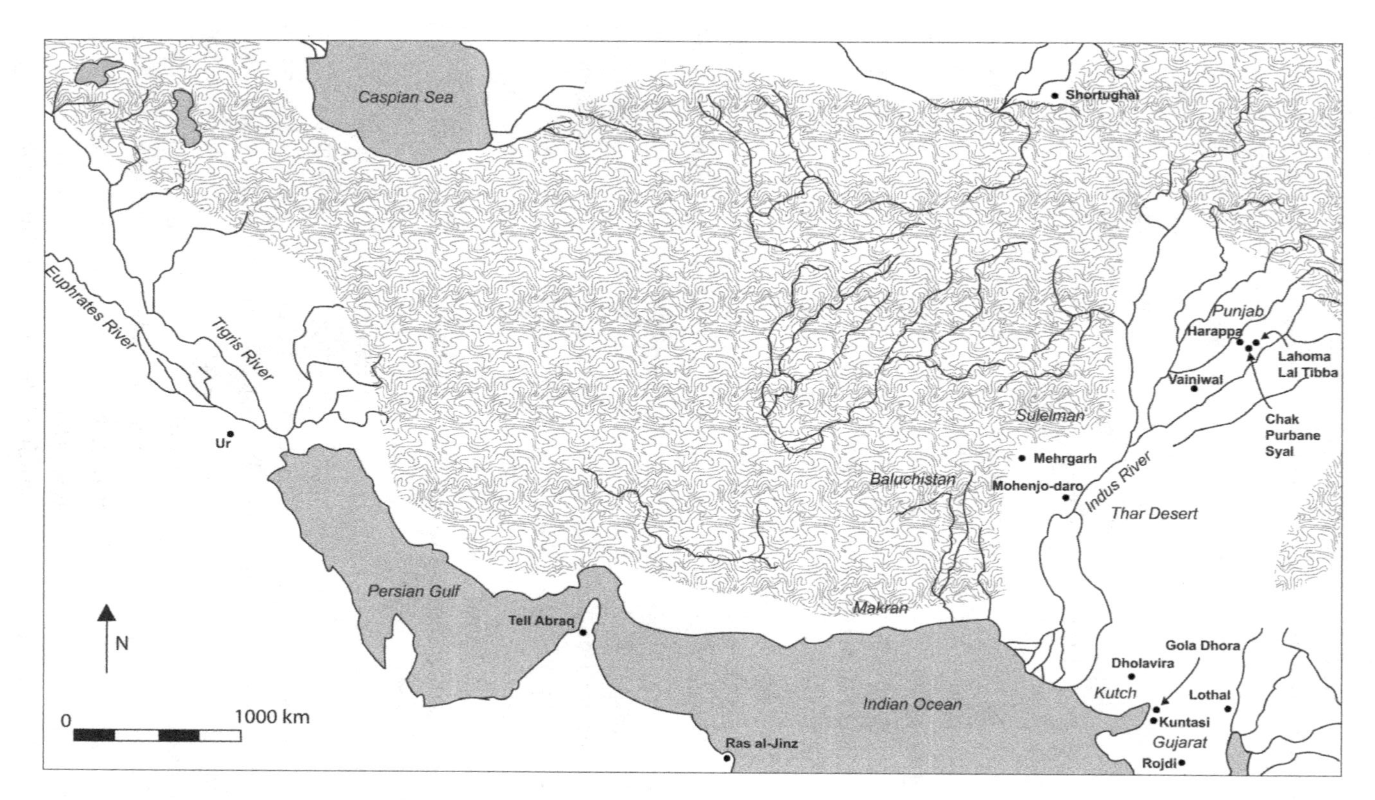

Figure 6.1. Map of Middle Asia showing sites mentioned in the text (Justin Jennings).

Exotics and objects that require considerable amounts of labor, skill, or knowledge to produce are inherently prone to becoming wealth items (Kenoyer 2000:90–91). This potential was likely realized in Mehrgarh and elsewhere by the beginning of the third millennium BC, when there was a "veritable explosion in the diversity of coiffure styles and body ornaments for both male and female figurines" that was paralleled by the production of an increasing variety of ornaments in the settlement (Kenoyer 2000:92). What people wore now signaled who they were in the Indus region—the race was on to provide people with beads, bangles, and other ornaments that could be used to symbolize social status.

The rise in craft specialization and long-distance exchange toward the end of the fourth millennium BC occurred just as the Indus Valley proper was opening up to permanent settlement. The weakening of the spring monsoon rains sometime before 5000 BC had led to decreasing sediment load and the incising and stabilizing of the valley's river channels (Giosan 2012:E1692; Schuldenrein et al. 2004:795; Wright et al. 2008:43), and these climate changes made the Indus River Valley a more desirable place for permanent agropastoral settlements whose residents could profit by becoming nodes in the trade networks that were beginning to crisscross the region. Harappa with its "extensive tracts of productive land for cultivation and pasturage" was one of the first places settled in the river basin (Wright 2010:34).

When the first families moved to Harappa as early as 3700 BC, they lived in two discrete clusters of houses separated by a few hundred meters (Kenoyer 2011:5; Kenoyer and Meadow 2000:56). Harappa's earliest homes were built from wood and had wattle-and-daub walls. They were laid out to follow the cardinal directions, a practice likely linked to widely shared cosmological principles that would continue to be followed for as long as the settlement was occupied. Residents ate a wide variety of food, with their subsistence based primarily on the cultivation of wheat and barley and the herding of cattle, sheep, and goats (Kenoyer and Meadow 2008:125–126). Since this architectural and subsistence pattern is similar to that found in Mehrgarh and other contemporary villages in Baluchistan, it is likely that Harappa's founding families budded off from an established village in that region to create a new village within the river basin.

We know that the families that arrived in Harappa brought with them knowledge of a wide range of craft specialties because the detritus of terracotta, shell, stone, and possibly copper production is found in the earliest contexts there (Kenoyer and Meadow 2000:65–68). Harappa quickly became an important trading center in its own right, a location where exotic raw materials were transformed into coveted finished products by specialists working out of their homes (Kenoyer 2005:163). Highly complex work can be documented in the earliest levels of the site—some artists, for example, were soon producing longer steatite beads by arduously drilling the stone with copper drills and then firing the beads at 940° C with a clear or blue-green glaze (Kenoyer 1997:257, 2005:162). Such "technical virtuosity" would only continue to increase over the next 2,000 years (Vidale and Miller 2000:115).

Harappa's prosperity hinged on its connections to outsiders. With the exception of clay, the necessary raw materials to create the products made in the settlement were only available dozens or even hundreds of kilometers away (Kenoyer 2005:162; Law 2005a:187). Harappans therefore relied, at least in part, on more mobile pastoralists and hunter-gatherers, who likely obtained shells, stone, and other materials from the mountains or coast via down-the-line trading. These mobile groups came to Harappa for its finished products, as did farmers from other early settlements that were located a day or two's walk away (Wright et al. 2005a; Mughal 1997a, 1997b). A seal found in the first occupation levels at Harappa may reflect a desire to better document the flow of goods coming in and out of the village (Kenoyer and Meadow 2008:127), while the remains of a model cart suggest that carts may have already been in use to facilitate transport over longer distances (Kenoyer 2004:90).

Harappa slowly grew over the next 900 years, reaching a size of 7 hectares by 2800 BC. Mud brick was replacing waddle and daub in houses by this time, and more and more pottery was wheel thrown. Harappans were now increasingly trading with groups across the entire Upper Indus Valley, and a few pieces of imported pottery and a chert arrowhead in the excavation levels from this period also suggest a deepening of relations with those still living in Baluchistan (Meadow and Kenoyer 2005). Further efforts were also being made to track the flow of goods, as marks began appearing on more ceramic vessels. These inscriptions, created using a proto-Indus script, likely identified the maker, trader, or recipient of the vessel (Kenoyer and Meadow 2000:68–70).

The Urbanization of Harappa

Like Cahokia, Harappa had a sudden growth spurt, almost quadrupling in size between 2800 and 2600 BC (Kenoyer 1991:47; 2008a:192). The site's rapid expansion from 7 to more than 25 hectares was part of a broader trend of settlement aggregation that was occurring during this time in other areas of the Indus (Mughal 1997a; Wright et al. 2005). Why people were congregating into smaller number of settlements remains unclear, but farmers—as well as an array of previously mobile pastoralists, hunter-gatherers, and fisherfolk—chose to live in those places that boasted already established craft specialists, merchants, and long-distance traders (Mughal 1994:61–64; Wright 2010:94). The influx of new families into Harappa after 2800 BC correlated with a dramatic increase in the number and variety of bangles, beads, pottery motifs, and seals being produced there (Kenoyer 2000:95). More people in one place meant an even greater need for social distinctions, as well as more work for those supplying the ornaments and other paraphernalia that signaled these distinctions.

Twenty-five hectares was just the beginning for Harappa. More and more people continued to move into the settlement—by the end of the third millennium BC, there would be some 40,000 residents living in a city that sprawled across 150 hectares (fig. 6.2). Another 40,000 likely crowded into the city during the trading seasons after the end of the monsoons (Kenoyer 2003:71). The dietary needs of this crush of people were dealt with in part by tweaking subsistence regimes. Most of those who moved to Harappa would have continued to farm, herd, and fish off-site, but the percentage of hunted and gathered foods in the diet in Harappa decreased after 2800 BC, and a greater diversity of domesticated plants was exploited as farmers sought to squeeze as much food as possible from the land surrounding the city (Weber 2003:18).

The botanical data suggest that Harappans "continued efforts at broadening and intensifying agricultural strategies" as the city grew (Weber 1999:824). Residents had initially farmed largely in the wintertime, but the increasing presence of gram, rice, linseed, and millet in assemblages—crops usually grown in the summer months—demonstrates that a year-round cropping system was in place by at least 2600 BC (Weber 1999:820, 2003:180; Wright 2010:89). A similar trend toward intensification is seen in the faunal data that demonstrate the use of "a broader spectrum of faunal resources" over time (Meadow 1989:68; also see Meadow 1993, 1998). Finally, cattle were getting bigger and were being slaughtered later in life. These trends, combined with evidence for bone pathologies associated with traction, suggest that more cattle were being milked and used to pull carts before being eaten (L. Miller 2003, 2004).

This resource intensification was made possible by a further wave of specialization: some individuals began farming year round, for example, while others pursued innovative fishing techniques. Animal traction also led to cart drivers, and milking to dairy farmers. These specialists lived next door to potters, merchants, and street sweepers, as people took up occupations in a diversifying community (Kenoyer and Meadow 2000; Meadow and Kenoyer 2005). The rapid increase in both the size and heterogeneity of

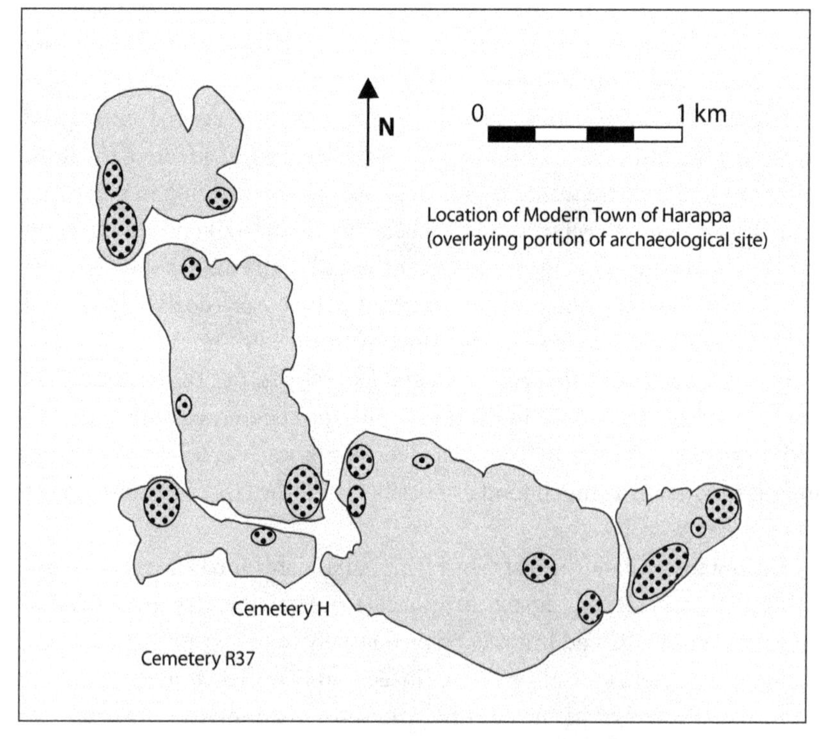

Figure 6.2. Site plan of Harappa—the stippled areas of the mounds were centers of craft production (Justin Jennings).

Harappa—a trend following aggregation that is seen in all of our case studies—undoubtedly led to scalar stress that was relieved in a number of ways.

Compartmentalization was perhaps the earliest strategy pursued to reduce scalar stress. Soon after Harappa began to urbanize, residents constructed a pair of mud-brick enclosure walls that maintained the original division of the site into two occupation areas (Kenoyer 2008a:192). These walls, and the spaces that were left open between the occupation areas, served not only to delineate two distinct neighborhoods but also to separate city dwellers from outside groups (Wright 2010:241). This compartmentalization reduced scalar stress by limiting the number of people who commonly interacted together, and Harappans achieved further compartmentalization in each neighborhood by forming blocks of households defined by north–south and east–west trending streets. Mud-brick platforms and other features may have also vertically separated areas across the city (Meadow 1991).

Harappa's residents would continue to compartmentalize the settlement over the next 800 years (Kenoyer 2008a:195). New neighborhoods were added over time, and by the mid-third millennium BC there were as many as seven discrete neighborhoods there. Each of these neighborhoods was walled, and they also had gates that restricted the flow of people from one area of the city to the other (Wright 2010:241). The neighborhoods, in turn, were divided into blocks of houses (Kenoyer 1998:55). The houses were usually composed of an enclosed courtyard facing one or two sleeping rooms (Wright 2010:117) and served as self-contained units that limited the intrusions of other families into the domestic sphere.

The layout of the city, of course, reflected more than just an effort to reduce interpersonal interactions across the site. A "unifying ideology" also likely helped guide how the city was organized, and this ideology was perhaps exemplified by the swastika, a symbol found on one of the earliest seals used in Harappa (Kenoyer 2010:120; also see D. Miller 1985). The swastika in historic periods symbolized the triumph of order over chaos, with the idea being that the entire community benefited by each person behaving in a proper manner (Kenoyer and Meadows 2008:127). If the construction of Harappa's streets, homes, walls, and platforms were guided by a similar unifying ideology—a very big if—then those contributing to the building of these structures can be seen at least in part as engaging in a group ritual akin to the house society of Çatalhöyük. In making Harappa, they were carving out a place of order in what was naturally a chaotic world.

The ritualized nature of construction in Harappa can perhaps best be seen in the investment made in water- and waste-management systems. Indus settlements are famous for their "Wasserluxus"—a fixation on the splendor of water (Possehl 2002:57–58)—that resulted in the construction of drains, toilets, wells, and baths across a community. This water fixation was probably tied to a concern for hygiene that dictated "the proper places to conduct bodily functions" and dispose of waste (Wright 2010:245). Cities were seen as civilizing places in the old sense of the word because of these investments in *Wasserluxus*, and as time went on the residents of Harappa developed more and more sophisticated construction methods to mark themselves as distinct from those living outside the city who were living closer to a state of nature.

This sense of a proper way of doing things extended beyond the built environment, helping to relieve scalar stress by making it easier to make many other decisions like how to exchange goods, flaunt jewelry, and style hair (Kenoyer 2010; H. Miller 2007). This is not to suggest that everyone acted and looked the same. The vertical and horizontal divisions between people were widening in response to the scalar stress of settlement expansion, and personal ornamentation was a critical means through which these new divisions were expressed (Cork 2011:197–198; Kenoyer 2000:104). Yet this expanding diversity in ornamentation took place within a limited stylistic range. The dozens of subtlety different bangles, for example, were all variations on an Indus Valley theme, but everyone would have recognized the value of a gold over a terracotta bangle (Kenoyer 2000:104).

The status differences that were already present throughout the Indus region widened as Harappa grew. Craftspeople and traders engaged in an ever-escalating race to create new kinds of prestige items, experimenting with new materials like gold, copper, and faience, while others competed to perfect more complex techniques that used even higher firing temperatures to transform the essence of raw materials already in use (Vidale and Miller 2000:122). Traders at the same time sought exotics from farther and farther afield: they obtained a widening variety of marine shell from coastal settlements located 800 kilometers away, for instance, and acquired stone and ores from a broadening range of more distant sources (Kenoyer 2008a:192; Kenoyer and Miller 1999:117–118; Law 2005a:188, 2005b:119).

Status displays were not limited to bracelets and hair ornaments: the well-off also lived in bigger houses (Cork 2011:80). Although the brick robbing of Harappa has left few neighborhoods intact, the much-better preserved houses of Mohenjo-daro reveal striking differences between residences (Jansen 1993). One of the biggest houses in Mohenjo-daro is House VII in the HR-A area (fig. 6.3). In its time, the six-room, two-storied house featured interior courtyards, a well, a bathing platform, and a terracotta drain that passed into the street (Jansen 1993:246). The house appears to have been much more embellished than others found at the site, and with an overall footprint of 400 square meters, it was also substantially

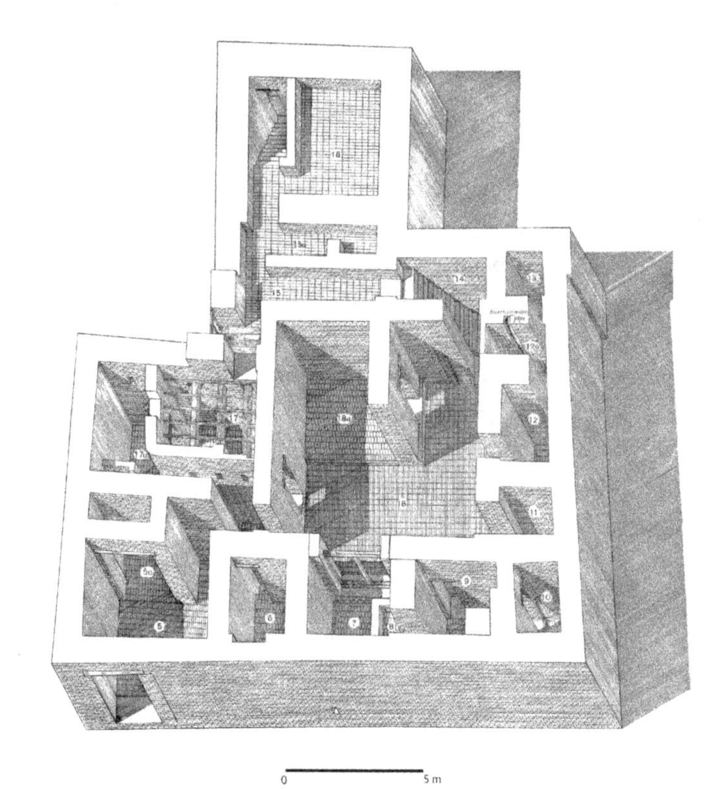

Figure 6.3. Oblique view of House VII (Block 3, HR-A) at Mohenjo-daro (Sir John Marshall).

larger (Cork 2011:76–81). The size and number of larger houses, each often associated with a greater number of copper, stone statues, and other prestige items (Wright 2010:257), grew over time at Mohenjo-daro as status differences widened in the settlement (Vidale 2010:62–63).

The rising social differences in Mohenjo-daro, Harappa, and other Indus Valley cities seem to have been accepted, but there appears to have been a pushback on more ostentatious displays of wealth because these displays threatened to exacerbate tensions between groups (Coningham and Manuel 2009; Rissman 1988). Elite funerary feasts, for example, may have become smaller and less extravagant over time (Jenkins 2000:38; Wright 2010:265), and the wealthy likely hid sumptuary items in the recesses of their homes (Wright 2010:248–256). Indeed, the use of a swastika on one of the earliest seals found at Harappa might reflect an attempt to assuage discontent just as life was beginning to change in the larger Indus Valley settlements (Kenoyer 2010:120). Inscribing this symbol on a seal whose purpose was to restrict access to a jar or storeroom suggests perhaps a need to justify such restriction of access by appealing to a shared principle that suggested that unequal access was ultimately beneficial to all members of society.

The corrosive effects of widening status differences were also likely mitigated through the ways people lived and worked at Harappa. Indus Valley sites appear to have been organized primarily around occupation and kinship rather than status positions. There were no elite neighborhoods in Mohenjo-daro, and the scatter of prestige goods across Harappa suggests a similar intermixing of status groups in each neighborhood (Jansen 1993; H. Miller 1999; Vidale 2010). Occupational groupings are most clearly seen in the spatial segregation of craft production areas, at least at Harappa. Stone and shell workshops, for example, are often found grouped together in one portion of the site, while metal and pottery production are grouped elsewhere (H. Miller 2007:44) (see fig. 6.2).

Craft specializations, along with other activities, were likely organized around blood relationships. Bioarchaeological and isotopic analysis of individuals buried in the R37 cemetery at Harappa, for example, demonstrate that the women in the cemetery were closely related to each other as well as to women buried in cemeteries that pre- and postdate the use of R37 (Hemphill et al. 1991:172–174; Kennedy 2000:306). The men, however, had a more varied genetic makeup, suggesting that many had migrated into the city from areas outside of Harappa (Kennedy 2000:306; Kenoyer et al. 2013:2296). This pattern not only suggests matrilocality—a system wherein a husband resides with his wife's kin group—but also that women from some of the oldest families of Harappa likely played a significant role in organizing activities within the city's neighborhoods (Wright 2010:264).

Kinship, at least initially, appears to have been influential in the governance of Harappa. When the city first started to expand, there was a proliferation of various animal motifs on seals—including unicorns!—with each animal perhaps representing one of the various kin groups that constituted the growing community (Kenoyer and Meadow 2008:128) (fig. 6.4). The writing on these seals would have flummoxed most people in Harappa's largely illiterate population, but they would have been at least able to relate an animal symbol to the particular kin group involved in an exchange of goods (Kenoyer 1998:74).

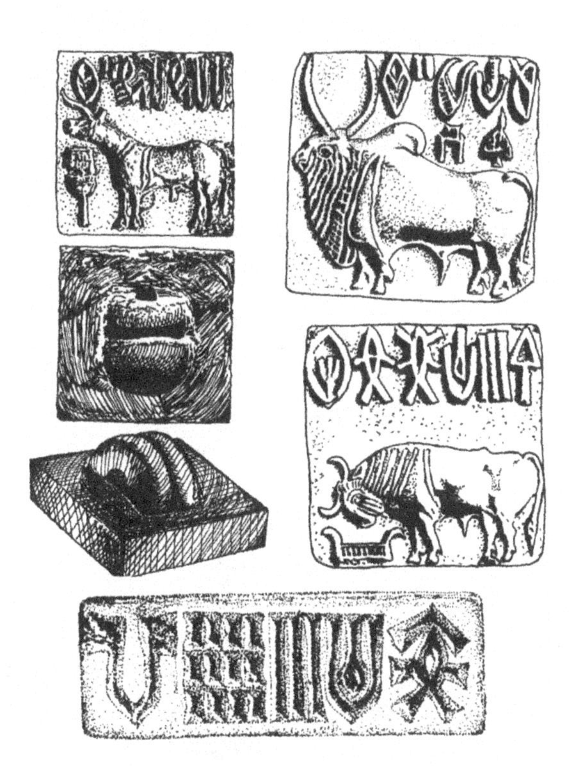

Figure 6.4. Examples of Indus Valley seals (courtesy of Penn Museum).

The practice of inscribing such symbols on seals was long-lived, and its longevity, paired with genetic studies and the multigenerational occupation of many houses, suggests a city wherein lineage heads organized many of the activities that occurred within neighborhoods or household blocks (Wright 2010:270). The additive nature of this system would have contributed to reducing scalar stress by making it easier to introduce new kin groups into Harappa without upsetting the status quo—an additional household block could have easily been nested inside the larger modal unit of a neighborhood that was composed, at least nominally, of blood relations that all reported to a lineage head.

Yet craft specialists, merchants, traders, and other higher status individuals may have started pushing by the mid-third millennium BC for a system of class-based governance that would bridge Harappa's neighborhood divides. Whereas the leaders of Cahokia had moved quickly toward this goal—blowing the city apart in the process—the approach taken by Harappa's leaders was much more extenuated and far subtler. Status for the most part was linked to the growing network of long-distance connections that brought together raw materials and exchange partners from an area stretching more than 12,000 kilometers. As status differences grew, these long-distance interactions became ever more crucial, and thus key individuals pushed advances such as refinements in the Indus valley script and the standardized system of weights (Kenoyer 2003:70, 2010:115; Kenoyer and Meadow 2008:128; H. Miller 2013:173). Yet the creation of a truly class-based society—the defining feature of Bruce Trigger's concept of civilization (2003:46)—would also require a stable urban environment, since trading operations routinely crosscut the deep internal divisions in the community.

Creating an overarching administrative structure would prove challenging. Harappa was ever changing, experiencing "numerous episodes of growth, decay, and renewal" across different sectors (Meadow and Kenoyer 2008a:106). This instability, perhaps linked to the lack of significant coordination between neighborhoods, may have led to a breakdown around 2450 BC, when at least a portion of the city appears to been subject to neglect: sewers overflowed, gateways broke down, and animal carcasses were left lying in the street (Kenoyer 1991:55). Crises like this one, of course, were bad for business and may have compelled Harappa's mercantile elites to take a more active role in managing aspects of city life.

The gateways into the city were refurbished and expanded after 2450 BC, creating monumental entrances into each of Harappa's neighborhoods that stood as the "hallmark" of the city for visitors (fig. 6.5) (Wright 2010:241). Although craft specialists would continue to work independently during the late third millennium BC, the producers of high-status items such as steatite beads, inlaid furniture, and gold ornaments became increasingly clustered in the interior plazas of the city's refurbished gateways (Meadow and Kenoyer 1997:57; H. Miller 2008:147). The one exception to craft specialist independence may have been for those manufacturing newly developed stoneware bangles. The producers of these objects worked inside gated enclosures, etching the bangles with writing before placing them in a jar that was sealed before firing (H. Miller 2008:146; Vidale 1989:178).

The movement of craft specialists to the gateway plazas was likely welcomed by many, since it brought these producers closer to customers who were moving in and out of the city (Meadow and Kenoyer 1997:57; H. Miller 2008:147). Yet the higher concentration of tablets and seals in these spaces relative to other parts of Harappa suggests that the trade in

Figure 6.5. Artist's reconstruction of one of Harappa's gateways (copyright Chris Sloan/Harappa.com; courtesy of J. M. Kenoyer).

these higher-status items was also being more closely monitored after 2450 BC (Kenoyer 2000:99). Many of the seals and tablets found in these plazas now featured only the Indus script (Kenoyer and Meadow 2008:129). Instead of being inscribed with pictures that everyone could read as was often the case with earlier seals, this next generation of seals was marked with script that could only be read by a select few who were likely involved in the production and trade of prestige objects across the Indus Valley and beyond.

An attempt to further regulate high-end trade may have occurred after 2200 BC with the circulation of mold-made tablets of steatite, faience, and copper. Each of the tablets has an identical inscription on one side and possibly a number on its other side. The production of these tablets in large quantities suggests an effort by an at least nominally centralized authority to introduce standardization. Although the exact function of the tablets remains unclear, they may have served as credit tokens or even as local coinage that was accepted across neighborhoods (Kenoyer 2008b:23).

An association with gateways made certain specialists, merchants, and traders de facto gatekeepers of Harappa and perhaps put them on a more equal footing with the lineage heads that organized most other neighborhood activities (Miller 2008:147). Powerful factions within both of these groups would have likely seen a need for creating institutions that bridged the city's internal divisions. Efforts to unify Harappa may have been behind the construction of what is known as the Great Granary or Great Hall soon after 2450 BC. Only the foundations of the original hall remain, since it was razed 200 years later to make room for the massive mud-brick platform that was built underneath the Great Hall's second itineration (Meadow and Kenoyer 2008:101).

The new Great Hall was a highly visible structure that towered over the rest of Harappa (Meadow and Kenoyer 2008:101; Vidale 2010:60). The hall measured 50 by 40 meters and was composed of 12 rooms reached via a central corridor (Meadow and Kenoyer 2008:99). The function of the Great Hall is unknown, but it was likely constructed as part of a civic architecture program similar to one that was more fully developed in Mohenjo-daro, where a high mound became home at around this same time to a cluster of three buildings today known as the College, Great Bath, and Warehouse (Possehl 2002:185–196). The functions of the College and Warehouse also remain unclear—the buildings, like Harappa's Great Hall, were neither living spaces nor storage facilities, and they were not found to contain high percentages of sumptuary items—but some scholars suggest that the structures likely served as meeting places for the leaders of Mohenjo-daro (Kenoyer 1998:65; Possehl 2002:193). This same group may have also come together for rituals of purification and renewal in the Great Bath (Kenoyer 1998:64). Harappans chose to invest in individual gateways instead of in corporate architecture that would have joined their houses to the Great Hall, suggesting that many were not particularly concerned about transcending divisions between neighborhoods.

In sum, Harappa began as a small collection of households that specialized in obtaining raw materials from distant sources and then converting these raw materials into personal ornaments and other finished products. When the village began to urbanize after 2800 BC, these independent craft specialists became part of a higher-status group associated with the production and exchange of prestige goods for local, regional, and foreign markets. Some of these craft specialists, along with merchants and traders, grew wealthy, but most activities in the city were likely run through clan or lineage heads who were charged with organizing the affairs of particular neighborhoods within Harappa. Periods of unrest and neglect in the city eventually led to more centralized control of the market for high-status goods after 2450 BC and also stimulated the construction of the Great Hall, a building that may have been used as a meeting place for the lineage heads and mercantile elites from each neighborhood.

The Harappa Countryside

Urbanization in Harappa was paralleled by a process of regional polity formation, colonization, and the creation of a cultural horizon. In terms of regional polity formation, Harappa had been a fairly typical Indus Valley village before 2800 BC. Most people in the region at this time had stayed mobile, while those few that chose to settle down in this part of the valley moved to river floodplains. They established independent, self-sufficient agropastoral communities like Harappa that also tended to specialize in creating personal ornaments and other items from imported stone, shell, and copper (Mughal 1997a:248; 1997b:68).

The rapid growth of Harappa after 2800 BC necessitated fundamental changes in the its relationships with other locales. The resource intensification strategies it adopted, such as exploiting summer crops and secondary animal products, would have made it possible for the settlement to have doubled or perhaps even tripled in size. Yet urban growth would have swiftly outpaced the ability of residents to produce their own food—with 40,000 residents, the city required considerable help from those living elsewhere in order to function.

There are hints in the botanical and faunal data recovered from Harappa of outside providers. Wheat, for example, replaced barley as the dominant crop at Harappa from 2600 to 2000 BC (Weber 1999). Wheat is preferred in South Asia today, but barley makes more sense to produce, since it is more drought-resistant, takes less time to grow, and tolerates more saline soil. If Harappans grew most of their own food, then they would have been forced into eating barley as the city expanded—the switch to wheat therefore likely reflects the ability of Harappans to draw on wheat harvested by farmers living a few days away (Weber 1999:823). Outside providers of grains are also hinted at by the dearth of on-site seed processing by-products like hulls and chaff (Weber 2003:81). These data suggest that people living elsewhere often threshed, winnowed, and ground the grains that were consumed in the city.

The faunal data also suggest that food was being brought into Harappa. The number of gazelle, deer, boar and other wild animals available around the city would have been in steep decline as the city grew, but evidence from after 2600 BC indicates their presence, so hunters must have brought this game in (Meadow 1989:68; Weber 1999:823). Bone assemblages also suggest that most Harappan households were getting more of their fish indirectly in the second half of the third millennium BC—residents were seldom out fishing for themselves—and a trade in dried and salted marine fish also began at this time that connected the site to producers living on the coast, more than 700 kilometers away (Belcher 2003:161).

The concomitant creation of a countryside can also be seen in the settlement data. The aggregation of people in Harappa after 2800 BC was part of a region-wide aggregation that occurred across the southern Punjab, resulting in an eightfold increase in the number of permanent settlements (Mughal 1997a:241). There was initially little difference in the size of settlements, but over time many people choose to move into those places that had a slight edge over other villages in terms of service and subsistence opportunities. This trend would lead to the creation of hierarchically organized settlement clusters sometime after 2600 BC (or perhaps earlier; see Mughal 1990). These clusters consisted of a handful of key southern Punjab communities that were surrounded by a smattering of larger settlements and a plethora of villages (Cork 2011:185; Possehl 2002:46). Although the settlement data for Harappa is poorer than that for most other parts of the southern Punjab, it is nonetheless clear that the city was the largest of the key communities in its part of the Indus Valley.

Our best understanding of how life changed after 2800 BC for those living near Harappa comes from surveys and excavations of sites located just to the south of Harappa along the now-dry bed of the Beas River (Wright 2010; Wright et al. 2005a, 2005b) (see fig. 6.1). Two of these well-studied villages, Lahoma Lal Tibba and Chak Purbane Syal, are located less than 25 kilometers from Harappa. Lahoma Lal Tibba was founded between 2800 and 2600 BC as Harappa first began to urbanize, and Chak Purbane Syal was settled after 2600 BC, a time both when Lahoma Lal Tibba was expanding in size and when most of the rural settlements on the Beas River sites were being created (Wright et al. 2005a:329).

The two communities were closely linked economically to Harappa. The range of activities conducted at Lahoma Lal Tibba and Chak Purbane was restricted relative to Harappa—residents of these villages seem to have depended on city manufacturers to meet many of their needs—and the immense storage jars found at Lahoma Lal Tibba could have been used to stockpile food for export to Harappa (Wright et al. 2005a:330–332; Wright 2010:129). The reasons why people living in rural communities like these would have produced food for the city likely changed over time. At first, most of the plants and animals that came into Harappa were perhaps offered in exchange for beads, tools, and other desired items being produced by the city's craft specialists.

The vagaries of a market economy, however, would have made the crucial relationships linking the city to the countryside unstable. The production of pointed-based goblets after 2200 BC may represent an attempt to further regulate affairs with a fickle countryside. These goblets were manufactured by the thousands in Harappa and most seem to have been thrown out after a single use (Kenoyer 1998:155). Since many of the vessels were seal impressed—they were inscribed before they were fired—it can be argued that they were designed to be used at festivals that honored specific deities or individuals (Kenoyer 1998:120). The presence of these goblets in Lahoma Lal Tibba and Chak Purbane Syal may suggest that Harappans had sought to form a more stable regional polity by better integrating villagers into events that were taking place in the city (Wright et al. 2005:331).

Settlements more than a few days' walk from Harappa, however, likely remained beyond the city's reach. Evidence from Vainiwal, a village on the Beas River more than 100 kilometers away from Harappa, suggests it remained largely independent throughout the third millennium BC (Wright et al. 2005b:329). Vainiwal's residents probably met some of the needs of Harappans as a trading partner—large storage jars and the remains of a few pointed-based goblets have been found at the site, and there is an "overall similarity of ceramics and small finds" between the two places—but the much smaller Vainiwal was home to a group of craft specialists who largely filled the needs of their community and enjoyed their own independent ties to distant regions (Wright et al. 2005a:329).

Although much work still needs to be done in detailing the regional polity that formed around Harappa in the second half of the third millennium BC, the data suggest a centuries-long process of shifting subsistence strategies and the gradual integration of surrounding settlements into more formalized relationships with the merchant elites and lineage heads who were exerting increasing control over Harappa's affairs. As in Cahokia, polity formation was a *reaction* to the myriad of challenges that were incumbent to urbanization. Another reaction to the needs of a rapidly urbanizing Harappa was a further extension of trade networks.

Randall W. Law's study of the "marked increase" in the variety of stone coming into the settlement after 2600 BC provides us with the best sense of how traders were meeting Harappa's escalating demands for imports (2005b:119; also see 2005a, 2006). Traders started importing higher-quality chert and grinding stones from farther away, for example, and, in a race to find more exotic material for their customers, began dealing with those groups who had access to stone sources to the east in the Himalayan foothills and to the southwest in southern Baluchistan (Law 2005b:116, 119).

The longer distances that stones and other goods traveled were impressive, but the trade required little infrastructural development, since the city's exchange network was "extensive but not necessarily labour intensive" (Law 2006:309). Stones are heavy, but in this case they were transported in very small quantities that were destined to become personal ornaments or other kinds of portable objects. Traders could therefore make arrangements for a bag of stones to be brought back with someone returning with their animals from high pasturage, hire a couple of porters, or even do the job themselves by taking their families on an extended trip. Other widely traded goods, like silk (Good et al. 2009), were considerably lighter and could be easily added to the loads of imports that were coming into Harappa (Smith 2013:146).

The Harappan traders, of course, were not the lone Indus group in pursuit of far-flung material. After families began aggregating into a handful of larger settlements, import demands rose throughout the region. Harappa was founded in the fourth millennium BC at least in part as a gateway center that could provide people living in the upper Indus Valley with access to desired raw materials from highland sources to the north and west of the city (Kenoyer 2011:5; Ratnagar 1993:262; Uesugi 2012:367). Major settlements elsewhere in the Indus Valley enjoyed access to sources from other regions. The geographic, cultural, and perhaps technological barriers that had limited interaction between subregions began breaking down as goods, as well as people and ideas, began traveling more extensively throughout the Indus Valley and beyond via boats and oxcarts and on foot (Chase et al. 2014:75; Park and Shinde 2014:137; Uesugi 2012:372).

The Creation of a Cultural Horizon

The Indus Valley cultural horizon that emerged by the mid-third millennium BC was thus a product of the extension and intermeshing of smaller exchange networks that had previously developed around Harappa and other settlements. Although the horizon was far from homogeneous—regional variation is well recognized (e.g., Ameri 2013:370 and Possehl 1993:20, 1997:435)—there was nonetheless a "marked uniformity" in the use of seals, a written script, standardized measurements, and particular styles of pottery and figurines, as well as striking similarities in site layout, waterworks, and cuisine (Wright 2010:23; also see Gouin 1990; Kenoyer 2011; Miller 2013). Some of these shared practices reflect pragmatic efforts to better organize long-distance trade, while others suggest that people across the Indus Valley had related ideas about how the world should work (Kenoyer 2010:120; also see Miller 1985). The kinds of "unifying ideology" that had first guided Harappa's construction were now being shared across the Indus Valley and creating a proper way of doing things that was recognized by all (Kenoyer 2010:120).

The increasing appetite for exotic material after 2600 BC pushed the boundaries of this cultural horizon outward, and thus it ended up touching the lives of many who lived elsewhere in Middle Asia (Possehl 2007). Preexisting trading practices soon proved insufficient to meet rising demands—down-the-line trading partners were too unreliable and trading expeditions into distant regions could be dangerous—and to ensure access to distant resources entrepreneurial colonists began building settlements along trading routes and in source areas (Ratnager 2004:88–94). Outposts, for example, were established in the Quetta and Gomal valleys; two of the most important routes used today to travel across the mountains of Baluchistan and Suleiman run through these valleys (Ratnager 2004:92). Colonists also founded settlements along the coast in Makran, Kutch, and Gujarat and pushed eastward into what is now northwestern India (Kenoyer 1998:91) (see fig. 6.1).

One of the furthest-flung colonies was Shortughaï, which was located near the confluence of the Kotcha and Oxus rivers in present-day northeastern Afghanistan (Francfort 1984, 1989). A small group of Indus Valley colonists settled at Shortughaï in order to directly exploit nearby lapis lazuli sources, as well as to gain more reliable access to the metals being moved along this important trade route. The site's architecture, as well as its artifact assemblage, demonstrates both that the settlers "clearly originated in the Indus Valley" and that these colonists were able to retain access to a wide range of artifacts and raw materials from their homeland for hundreds of years (Francfort 1984:808). Some of these Indus Valley imports, such as carnelian beads, square seals, and bronze figurines, were likely coveted locally since they are occasionally found in tombs from this region.

In contrast to Cahokians, the Indus Valley colonists seem to have seen themselves as traders and craft specialists rather than as cultural or religious ambassadors (e.g., Dhavalikar 1992). Sites adjacent to colonies were often devoid of Indus Valley imports (Chase 2010:531; Wright 2010:226), and there seem to have been few efforts made to incorporate local groups through feasting or other inclusionary events held inside colonial outposts. Although their lack of missionary zeal restricted the spread of the Indus global culture, the culture's influence can still often be seen in local assemblages, especially in those artifact classes like seals that would have facilitated exchange between unrelated groups (Jarrige and Quivron 2008). Indus Valley material can also be found hundreds of kilometers from any known colony, but these chance finds likely reflect "sporadic trade contacts, individual trips or marriages rather than systematic, specialized forms of long-distance trade" (Cortesi et al. 2008:29).

The overland colonial expansion orchestrated by Harappa and the other cities of the Indus Valley was paralleled by a pioneering of sea routes that likely stretched to as far as Mesopotamia (Kenoyer et al. 2013). Some of the first colonies established were seaports like Lothal and Dholavira that allowed access by 2500 BC into the Indian Ocean (Dhavalikar 1992:75). Ships launching from these ports could hug the coastline, enter the Persian Gulf, and make their way into Mesopotamia. These ships were likely responsible for the Indus imports that can be found at many sites along the gulf's coastline (During Caspers 1992), and a few settlements, such as Ras al-Jinz and Tell Abraq, may have been built as way stations for Indus Valley sailors (Cleuziou and Tozi 1994; Potts 1993a) (see fig. 6.1).

One of the most common Indus Valley imports found in the gulf by the end of the third millennium BC were standardized large black storage jars that were often stamped or incised with the Indus script. These vessels, produced in the Indus Valley, perhaps originally contained indigo, clarified butter, honey, or wine (Kenoyer 1998:97), but then they were reused by other groups in the gulf as containers for a wider range of goods (Cleuziou and Tosi 2000:52; Mery and Blackman 2005:233)

The earliest evidence for Indus Valley imports into Mesopotamia are carnelian and amazonite beads from the Royal Cemetery at Ur that dates to sometime between 2550 and 2450 BC (Kenoyer 2008b:23). The raw material used to make the beads came from sources available to Indus Valley settlements, and the beads were made using techniques known only to Indus Valley craft specialists. Some of the forms, however, are unique adaptations designed specifically for the Mesopotamian marketplace (Kenoyer 1998:97). These data suggest that Indus Valley craft specialists were likely established by this time in Mesopotamia, an idea buttressed by textual references beginning in 2300 BC to Indus Valley ships and settlers coming into the region (Parpola et al. 1977:130).

The first textual references in Mesopotamia to contact with the Indus Valley appear when Mesopotamia's overland routes were being disrupted by hostilities (Potts 1993b:394–395). A surge in Mesopotamian demand for both Indus Valley products and the raw materials that could be obtained through the valley's trade network followed (Parpola et al. 1977). This demand appears to have been met by Indus Valley merchant elites, who asserted greater control over the ports and maritime routes that were engaged in the Mesopotamian trade. The increasing use of standardized, stamped jars in maritime trade was likely part of an attempt to regulate trade. At the same time, a formalization of architecture in some places may suggest the creation of a more tightly integrated trading network that connected Indus Valley cities more closely to sailors, merchants, and craft specialists who had hitherto operated independently out of coastal outposts (Chase et al. 2014:3).

Many coastal settlements that were involved in long-distance trade were walled after 2200 BC, which meant that people and goods were being funneled through gateways that could be more closely monitored. Each settlement thus now functioned like an "ancient Hudson's Bay Trading Post" rather than as a largely subsistence-based community that only dabbled in craft production and long-distance exchange (Possehl and Raval 1989:16; also see Dhavalikar 1992:73).

Ghola Dhora, a small settlement in Gujarat, provides insight into how some of these independent, often sleepy, colonial settlements were transformed into trading and manufacturing centers by the end of the third millennium BC (Bhan et al. 2005; Chase 2010). Ghola Dhora was first occupied as early as 2500 BC by a small group of Indus Valley colonists and functioned largely as an agropastoral village for some 200 years until an enclosure wall was built around a portion of the settlement (Chase 2010:531, 534). A series of workshops were then set up within the walls of the settlement to manufacture objects made from semiprecious stones, faience, copper, and especially marine shell (Bhan et al. 2005:1). Ghola Dhora's shell bangle workshop, "the largest and most significant ever discovered" (Chase 2011:531), received shipments of shells from coastal settlements that were as far as 100 kilometers away. Some of these shell bangles likely returned to these settlements for local consumption, while others were shipped to the Gulf region and Mesopotamia (Kenoyer 2008b:24). The seals and sealing found inside the compound walls suggest that many of the objects made in Ghola Dhora were also imported to Indus Valley cities in closely monitored exchanges (Bhan et al. 2005:3).

A global culture was being created just as processes of urbanization, colonization, and polity formation unfolded. Harappa, like many other Indus Valley settlements, was founded by a small group of people as a trading and production center. To survive, such settlements initially relied on pastoralists, itinerant traders, and other mobile groups to provide them with distant raw materials and transport their finished products to far-off clients. These relationships worked well for villages of a few hundred people, but they would have soon become inadequate once aggregation began. Colonization, seafaring, and almost certainly caravanning provided a modicum of control by directly placing people from the Indus Valley along the overland and maritime trading routes that fed into the cities (Wright 2010:230–232).

This outmigration was initially composed of independent entrepreneurs rather than state-sponsored agents—Harappa and the other Indus Valley cities were still very much inchoate when the first peripheral settlements were founded—yet over time there would have been increasing efforts to formalize and monitor the relationships between far-flung Indus groups through the use of seals, writing, and weights (Kenoyer 1995; Miller 2013). These and other innovations spread outward through colonists and their immediate trading contacts and soon went far beyond the hands of Indus Valley settlers, helping create a cultural horizon that impacted the lives of people living throughout much of Middle Asia (Possehl 2007).

Harappa's Decline

Although nineteenth-century brick robbers destroyed most of the strata dating to Harappa's final occupation levels (Kenoyer 1991:56), it is clear that the site began declining after 1900 BC. People began leaving the site around this time—Harappa would shrink from 150 hectares to 30 hectares by 1700 BC (Wright 2012:102)—and there was a "general disruption of orderliness" across the settlement as surviving neighborhoods became overcrowded and houses were built into streets and on plazas (Wright 2010:315; also see Meadow and Kenoyer 2008:105). No one attempted to create public architecture like the Great Hall. Violence, especially toward women and children, became "much more prevalent" in the shrinking settlement (Schug et al. 2012:144).

Perhaps most importantly, the seals, writing, and weights that had helped to organized the city's economy largely disappeared, as long-distance trading broke down (Kenoyer and Meadow 2008:130). The raison d'être of Harappa's rise—the manufacture and exchange of prestige goods from exotic raw materials—was thus gone and with it went the lifeblood of the mercantile elite who had sought to organize the city's affairs. With little binding Harappa's residents together, it is perhaps surprising that some families lingered as long as they did. Neighborhood after neighborhood was depopulated until the city was completely abandoned, sometime after 1700 BC (Kennedy 2000:306; Meadow and Kenoyer 2008:105; Wright 2012:102).

Those who remained in the collapsing city attempted to carry on as best they could. Craft specialists continued to make technological innovations with whatever materials they could obtain, and traders struggled to maintain a semblance of the long-distance trade networks of the previous era (Meadow and Kenoyer 2008:104–105). Yet these efforts could not compensate for a swiftly dissolving countryside. Many of the sites that surrounded Harappa were abandoned after 1900 BC, and the few that remained were greatly diminished in size and had little to no ties with the city. In response to the loss of their breadbasket, Harappans began fending for themselves by processing more of their own grains (Weber 2003:181) and bringing back the more sustainable, less risky, mix of sheep, goats, and cattle that had typified the region before Harappa's urbanization (Miller 2004:618). Yet more time spent fulfilling subsistence needs meant less time for trade and craft production.

The residents of Harappa actually stayed together longer than those in most of the other cities in the region. After 1900 BC, there was a trend across the Indus Valley toward "deurbanization," as the population moved into smaller, more self-sufficient, communities (Possehl 1997:450). There were many reasons for the decline and eventual abandonment of the Indus

Valley cities (Wright 2010:309–324). Climate change may have been a factor—the volume of water in the Upper Indus rivers, for example, was likely decreasing at the beginning of the second millennium BC (Wright et al. 2008:42; also see Prasad et al. 2014)—and societal upheavals in Mesopotamia and central Asia undoubtedly disrupted long-distance trade routes. Another factor was the introduction of new crops and animals—horses, donkeys, and camel, for instance, arrived in the Indus Valley at this time (Meadows and Patel 2003:82)—that offered farmers and pastoralists greater independence from urban merchants, who by this time were starting to flounder as their trade networks declined (Kohl 2007:231). Unmoored from the cities, people dispersed into locations with an eye toward their own subsistence needs.

Yet the most important reason for the decline of the Indus Valley cities might lie in their failure to sustain the public institutions that crosscut the internal divisions found within each metropolis (Possehl 1997:458). Short-lived civic institutions like Harappa's Great Hall and Mohenjo-daro's Great Bath are likely vestiges of a late third-millennium BC attempt to create a more formal governing structure not only for Indus Valley cities but also for the budding regional polities that surrounded them. Their abandonment, a few centuries before the cities themselves were deserted, perhaps suggests the inability of merchant elites and lineage heads to move away from a neighborhood-based political economy that depended on kinship ties and particular craft specialties. When this millennia-old political economy was short-circuited by disruptions in long-distance trading routes, there was little left to keep people in town (Wright 2012:105).

Many of the Indus Valley colonies were abandoned or reduced to squatter's settlements as trade volume rapidly decreased (Possehl 1997:455–457). The few colonies that survived, like Shortughaï and Rojdi, were repositioned by their residents as important local trade brokers, who formed regional exchange partnerships beyond those that had existed previously (Francfort 1989; Possehl and Raval 1989). The surviving colonies thus turned their back on their homelands as the Indus global culture splintered in the wake of the decline of long-distance interaction, and the valley's broad cultural horizon was replaced by more circumscribed regional cultures defined by shared artifact styles and burial customs (Jarrige and Quivron 2008:62; Kenoyer 1998:174). With an overarching Indus Valley identity no longer desired, some people began turning to newly introduced ideologies for guidance, especially those developed out of the Bactria-Margiana Archaeological Complex of central Asia (Kohl and Lyonnett 2008:38).

Civilization in the Indus Valley

By advancing the idea of an Indus civilization, Sir John Marshall placed the region on equal footing with the great Old World centers of Egypt, Mesopotamia, and China. Archaeological investigations in the Indus Valley were just beginning at the time of Marshall's pronouncement in 1931, and so he and his contemporaries filled in the blanks in their knowledge with data from better-known cultures to paint a picture of an Indus society that fit with the expectations for what civilizations should be like. These early researchers therefore ticked off each box in the early twentieth century's various trait lists for civilization. Some traits, like writing and craft production, were well demonstrated by existing data, while others, like the state and military force, were simply marked as present because they had to be found in all civilizations.

Subsequent researchers have found it more difficult to argue that the Indus Valley settlements fit within the classic definition of civilization. Yet they have also been loath to give up the Indus Valley's designation as a cradle of civilization, especially since research has demonstrated that writing, the use of seals, craft specialization, urbanism, and other classic aspects of civilization have proved to be largely, if not fully, indigenous developments (Kenoyer 1998; Wright 2010; Possehl 2002). The Indus civilization is instead offered as an example, in the words of Gregory Possehl, of "sociocultural complexity without the state"—an "experiment in urbanization" that can be used to demonstrate that "ancient civilizations . . . are far more variable in their form and organization than the typological schemes of traditional, unilineal evolution can accommodate" (1998:291).

That the Indus civilization fails to meet the criteria classically listed for civilization (e.g., Childe 1950) is thus seen as a deficiency in these lists rather than as the failure of Indus Valley settlements to reach the civilization stage of development. Just as Timothy Pauketat argues with respect to Cahokia, many archaeologists working in the Indus Valley region today maintain that the civilization stage as delineated along the lines of Lewis Henry Morgan is far too constricting of a strait jacket to allow for the rich diversity in social complexity that is found in the archaeological record (Kenoyer 1998; Possehl 2002; Wright 2010). Rather than getting rid of the concept, these scholars are instead striving to save it: they insist on an Indus (as well as a Cahokian) *civilization*.

Claiming the Indus as a civilization or even as a peculiar form of sociocultural complexity, however, also preserves the idea of an abrupt, steplike emergence of a stage of cultural development. The package of traits associated with this stage is laudably broadened by including cities like Harappa, but our embrace of the concept still leads us—albeit often unconsciously—to think in terms of the sudden arrival of mutually reinforcing institutions that breaks a society free from a previous way of living. The golem, to return to my personal metaphor for the civilization concept, walks through our excavations of the ancient settlements of Pakistan, twisting our interpretations, even as data from Harappa and other sites clearly demonstrate processes of social change that lasted hundreds of years.

The path taken during Harappa's urbanization can be traced back to the settlement's founding around 3700 BC. The first families that lived at the site settled into two distinct household clusters and were involved in long-distance trade and craft specialization. When the settlement began to rapidly grow in size after 2800 BC, the scalar stress that accompanied aggregation was initially managed by increasing compartmentalization, group ritual, basal-unit size, and social hierarchy. Harappans probably only reluctantly accepted a shift to a more hierarchical society—at least there was a reaction against displays of wealth later in the city's history—and the hierarchal positions that did develop were limited by kinship/neighborhood ties, craft specializations, and a shared suite of acceptable behaviors.

Harappa would soon grow to at least 150 hectares. Each of the city's neighborhoods was probably organized independently and run by a fluctuating group of lineage heads and mercantile elites whose agendas conflicted at times. This independence, though it helped to alleviate scalar stress, led to instability as the fortunes of individual neighborhoods waxed and waned over time. Certain merchants, traders, and craft specialists would eventually come together to regulate at least high-end trade at Harappa, and the construction of the Great Hall around 2450 BC was likely part of what was ultimately an unsuccessful attempt to create an overarching governing structure for the city.

Harappa was thus a work in progress throughout the mid-third millennium BC. Yet as Harappans were still sorting out city life, they also needed to scramble to build a countryside and extend their trade connections across the land and sea. Thus colonization got under way, a regional polity started to form, and a cultural horizon began to spread just as the settlement started to grow. This expansion outward was not orchestrated by bureaucrats—those who held a tenuous grip on power at Harappa had their arms full just trying to organize affairs in each of the swiftly growing neighborhoods—but rather by entrepreneurial individuals who sought to fill the needs of a growing metropolis. The satellite sites around Harappa eventually became part of a well-functioning regional polity, and some colonies were ultimately run like Hudson's Bay trading posts, but this was the culmination of processes that started some two hundred years earlier when people first began aggregating at Harappa and a handful of other settlements in the Indus Valley.

Harappa is therefore another example of "complexity-in-the-making" (Alt 2010:129), a site whose "ungainly process of becoming" fits well with what we have learned already about how modern and ancient cities grow (Kaplan 2012:56). The Harappa of 2600 BC was not the Harappa of 2400 or 2200 BC. An array of decade- and century-long processes unleashed by urbanization meant that ways of life across the Indus Valley and beyond were always changing. Thinking in terms of an Indus civilization tends to lead scholars to reduce these ongoing changes to a single transformative moment at the beginning of a stage of development. The data from Harappa tells a story decidedly different that the one that we have inherited through the civilization concept, as do the data presented in our next chapter from Jenne-jeno and the clustered cities of the Middle Niger.

7

JENNE-JENO AND THE CLUSTERED CITIES OF THE INLAND NIGER DELTA

LEFT LARGELY "HIDDEN AND UNNOTICED" BY A WORLD FOCUSED on the achievements of ancient Egypt, the rest of Africa has often been neglected in discussions of early urbanization (R. McIntosh and S. McIntosh 1988:141). Explorers have been documenting large settlements in sub-Saharan Africa since the 1930s, but before the 1980s, most scholars assumed these sites were derivative products of largely Islamic, and later European colonial, influence during the second millennium AD (Fourchard 2011:228; LaViolette and Fleisher 2004:327; R. McIntosh and S. McIntosh 2003:105). We now know that cities emerged independently in sub-Saharan Africa hundreds of years earlier. One of the digs that helped change our perceptions of this vast region began in 1977 at the site of Jenne-jeno in the Inland Niger Delta of present-day Mali (S. McIntosh and R. McIntosh 1980; S. McIntosh, ed. 1995).

Like that of much of sub-Saharan Africa (see LaViolette and Fleisher 2004 and Stahl 2004), Mali's history over the last few thousand years remains poorly understood because of a lack of fieldwork. In 1959 George Peter Murdock noted that "the spade of archaeology . . . has thus far lifted perhaps an ounce of earth on the Niger for every ton carefully sifted on the Nile" (1959:73), and little had changed by the time Susan Keetch McIntosh and Roderick McIntosh began their work at Jenne-jeno. Subsequent survey and excavations by these and other scholars in the Inland Niger Delta have succeeded—despite pervasive looting (Brent 1996)—in reconstructing the history of this region's "clustered cities" (R. McIntosh and S. McIntosh 2003). Though this reconstruction often remains tentative, if not occasionally speculative, in its details, Jenne-jeno tells a story of early urbanization that differs markedly from that of Cahokia and Harappa (see Smith 2006 for a critique of Jenne-jeno's reconstruction).

At its height during the latter half of the first millennium AD, Jenne-jeno was a "rabbit's warren of weaving alleys between tightly packed compounds linked by walls" (S. McIntosh and R. McIntosh 1993:632). The only public architecture was a late-addition mud-brick wall that surrounded the settlement and possibly an open-air marketplace. Although Jenne-jeno was occupied for 1,500 years, there is no evidence for temples, palaces, or military barracks until after it was well into its decline, and thus it appears there was no high priest, king, general, or even cohort of elites that held sway over the settlement when it reached its greatest extent (R. McIntosh 2005:10). Even though many of the buildings and social arrangements that we commonly associate with urban centers did not exist in the community, there were 27,000 people living on the Jenne-jeno main mound or in one of the 25 satellite settlements that were found within a one-kilometer radius (S. McIntosh 1995a:374). How did all of these people get along with each other for hundreds of years?

As in all of our case studies, the Inland Niger Delta's response to scalar stress was unique—a product of a particular mix of regional climate change, local environmental conditions, human migrations, and deep-seated cultural and religious traditions. Jenne-jeno, Dia, Timbuktu, and the other large sites from the region clearly meet all of our criteria for a city, but they confound our expectations of what the transition to civilization *should* be like in ways that are even more radical than those evidenced in Cahokia and Harappa. The residents of Inland Niger Delta cities successfully, perhaps one could even say *defiantly*, managed to live together for centuries without a ruling class, taxation, writing, monumental constructions, and state-level political organization—characteristics long seen as essential parts of a civilization package that arrived together at the inception of urban life.

For those who adhere to the civilization concept, Jenne-jeno should not exist because cities are impossible outside of the confines of a class-based society (i.e., Trigger 2003, 2008). Yet the people of the Inland Niger Delta found a way to live together for centuries in stable urban clusters. They did so, in the words of Roderick McIntosh, by creating a "distinctive heterarchical grid of authority" across the region (2005:206). The creation of this grid—the concept of which I explain in this chapter—was a work in progress, the backbone of a regional polity derived from past practices that was still forming when it was overwhelmed by intensifying interregional interaction between North and West Africa that disrupted the relationships between groups in the Middle Niger.

The Inland Niger Delta and the Founding of Jenne-jeno

The Inland Niger Delta lies within the Sahel, a biogeograhic zone of transition between the Sahara Desert to the north and the Sudanian Savanna to the south (fig. 7.1). The Sahel's grassland and savanna environment gives way in the delta to a vast 30,000-square-kilometer floodplain crisscrossed by lakes, swamps, and water channels. Parts of the delta are flooded for several months each year, though the level of flooding varies with the amount of rainfall in the upper courses of the Niger and Bani rivers. This dynamism in precipitation makes the Inland Niger Delta an active hydrological system: channels migrate, sand dunes shift, and the rivers braid (R. McIntosh 1983; S. McIntosh and R. McIntosh 1995:2–9).

The delta is an incredibly rich ecological mosaic (R. McIntosh 2005:93–95). There is a wide array of wild plants that remain important today as food, construction material, fuel, and ritual items. Hundreds of thousands of birds either live or migrate into the delta, and 100,000 tons of fish are pulled out of the Niger River each year. Although most other wild fauna is now severely depleted, the remains of antelopes, hippopotamuses, crocodiles, turtles, warthogs, and other animals have been recovered archaeologically at sites in the Inland Niger Delta (e.g., MacDonald 1995:291–315). The region was thus "a table groaning in diversity" even without domesticated plants and animals (R. McIntosh 2005:95). Cattle, sheep, and goats nonetheless arrived in the area by as early as 5,000 years ago (MacDonald and MacDonald 2000), and rice—likely first domesticated in the delta (Sweeney and McCouch 2007:952)—millet, and sorghum were harvested in the region by at least the first millennium BC (S. McIntosh 1995a:379).

The environmental conditions of the Inland Niger Delta have changed drastically over the last few thousand years. Until the end of the first millennium BC, the delta was covered in water for most of the year and thus only accessed occasionally by groups living around the Sahara lakes to the north. Precipitation, however, began to decline in the first millennium AD, which had the effect of slowly pushing people southward toward the delta as the northern lakes dried up (R. McIntosh 2000:153). The drier conditions were turning the Inland Niger Delta into an important resource zone, but it remained a difficult place to live year round. The heavy soils of the floodplain were likely a deterrent to agriculturists working largely with stone tools, and waterborne diseases as well as hoof rot were a likely concern for those caring for animal herds (MacDonald 1999:337).

A very dry period from 300 BC to AD 300 transformed the delta into one of only a handful of viable locations in the region for more sedentary populations (Mayor et al. 2005:51; R. McIntosh 2000:155; S. McIntosh and R. McIntosh 1995:10). Decreasing precipitation likely mitigated the disease risks over time, and the introduction of iron technology around 500 BC would have made the prospect of breaking up the delta's soils less daunting (S. McIntosh 1999:67). With few other options, more and more people began migrating into the Inland Niger Delta.

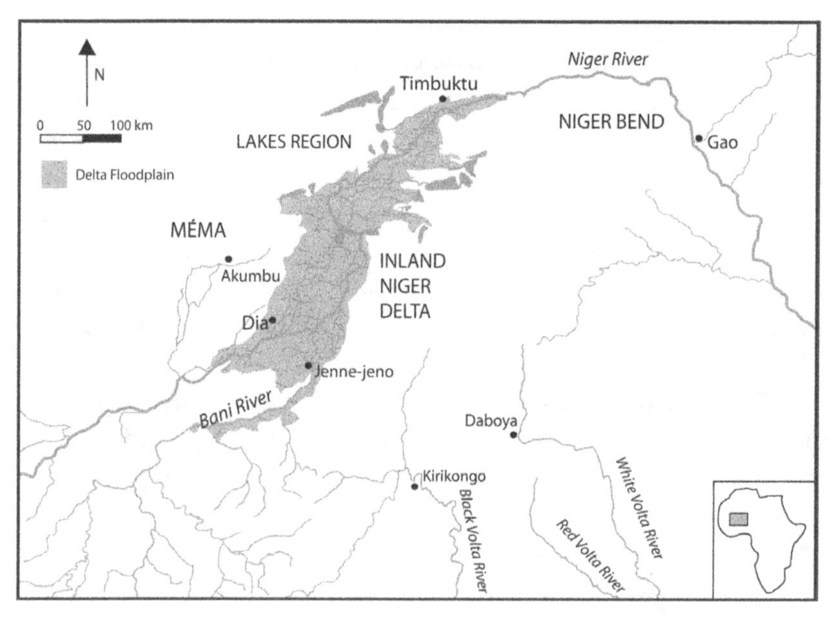

Figure 7.1. Map of portion of West Africa with sites mentioned in the text (Justin Jennings).

Like most people living at that time in Central and West Africa, those who first settled year round in the region came from "small, scattered, and ephemeral" groups used to moving seasonally across the landscape (MacDonald 1997:195). These groups often had contrasting subsistence strategies that focused on distinct food resources. Given that many of the migrants who settled in the area likely were from groups living in the Méma region just to the north of the delta in the early first millennium BC, we can look at the lifestyles of two of these groups to get a sense of how varied the lifestyles of the delta's earliest settlers would have been. Those Méma who followed the Ndondi Tossokel cultural tradition herded cattle and grew millet, while those of the Kobadi tradition hunted, gathered, and fished. Although the Kobadi had preceded the Ndondi Tossokel groups into the Méma region, the groups would routinely come together at aggregation sites for at least a portion of the year to trade, conduct group rituals, and engage in other activities (MacDonald 1999:337–342).

Those who moved into the Inland Niger Delta would have already been familiar with the wild resources available across the Middle Niger. Some of these settlers also brought rice, millet, and sorghum with them, while others came with cattle, goats, and sheep (S. McIntosh 1995a:377). Each group would have likely focused for their subsistence on the subset of the region's available wild and domesticated resources that was most familiar to them. Despite these different foci, new arrivals would still have been looking in broad stroke for zones that not only could provide easy, nearby access to the kinds of resources they had traditionally relied on but that also had good soils and a mix of raised and floodplain lands for pasture (S. McIntosh 1999:68). Population density quickly rose in Jenne-jeno and the other few places in the delta that best met these criteria.

The delta's more risky, ever-changing landscape required that these groups aggregate more regularly to pool their resources. Roderick McIntosh uses this aspect of delta life to develop what he calls a "pulse model" to explain how cities emerged in the Inland Niger Delta (1993). He suggests that Jenne-jeno and the other cities in the delta may have begun as seasonal aggregation sites that were modeled after the same kinds of sites that many settlers had left behind. As more and more people came into prime areas within the delta, environmental stress rose and conflicts escalated between groups. Increasing specialization helped relieve this stress—a dedicated rice farmer produced more rice and did not get in the way of millet farmers—and also made aggregation even more important, as the self-sufficiency of families declined. Some groups eventually settled permanently at these aggregation sites, and other kinds of specialists like potters and blacksmiths emerged to serve the needs of the subsistence specialists who regularly visited the site.

A critical aspect of the pulse model is that the permanent villages that were established were clustered communities composed of different groups that came together voluntarily to take advantage of the products and services offered by others. These groups formed a collective unit of production but nonetheless went to considerable effort to maintain their separate identities. They lived in spatially discrete locations within the cluster and likely used cuisine, clothing, and body modifications to mark their separate identities (R. McIntosh and S. McIntosh 2003:111). Like those living in the American Bottom and Indus Valley, those living in the Inland Niger Delta were especially resistant to any vertical mechanism of integration that would have created an overarching hierarchical structure across the clustered communities.

The pulse model meshes well with both oral histories that describe how the region's cities were founded and with the ethnographically observed tradition of dispersed distributions of power in West Africa (Fortes and Evans-Pritchard 1940; R. McIntosh 2005:112–114). Yet the archaeological data from the Inland Niger Delta are too sparse to reconstruct what these clustered villages may have been like during their earliest years. Luckily, Stephen Dueppen's recent excavations of the Iron Age site of Kirikongo in Burkina Faso (AD 100–1450) provide us with a sense of how a contemporaneous West African village developed over time. His findings, broadly taken, dovetail well with Roderick McIntosh's pulse model for the origins of the clustered cities of the Middle Niger (2012a, 2012b).

Kirikongo is located in a bend of the Black Volta River, an area 200 kilometers south of the Inland Niger Delta. Though less fertile than the delta, this river bend was still an attractive location for settlement because it boasts the most rainfall for its latitude in Africa (Dueppen 2012a:70). An extended family founded the settlement of Kirikongo around AD 100. This family and their descendants were self-sufficient for 400 years—they smelted their own iron, made their own pots, and herded their own cattle—until two other families moved into the settlement. These new families moved on to their own discrete mounds, and there is evidence from each of the mounds for both increasing specialization and the use of identity markers (Dueppen 2012a:283–289; 2015:38).

How economic activities were coordinated across village clusters like Kirikongo remains unclear. Susan Keetch McIntosh and Roderick McIntosh have at times likely underemphasized the efforts that aggrandizers made to control the affairs of growing communities (e.g., S. McIntosh and R. McIntosh 1993), but they nonetheless note that the founding families of a settlement would have had greater authority within settlements because their residence would have been built in a privileged location within the ritual landscape that granted them stronger connections to spirits and ancestors (R. McIntosh and S. McIntosh 2003:111). In the case of Kirikongo, the site's founders appear to have exploited this spiritual advantage by slowly extending their control over the rest of the settlement. This control is evidenced by the beginning of the second millennium AD, when iron production was in the hands of the founding families and their children were being buried in ways that had been previously reserved only for honored adults (Dueppen 2012a:287).

Maintaining hierarchical positions by appealing to ritual knowledge, however, may have proved difficult for Kirikongo's founders. The people of the Middle Niger today believe in a cosmic force called *nyama* that flows through the universe (R. McIntosh 2000:161). Both animate and inanimate objects possess nyama, and everyone needs to cooperate in order to harvest as much of it as possible for the benefit of the entire community. If this concept existed during the Iron Age—another big *if* (see Henige 1974, 2005)—then community leaders may have "had much ritual authority, but relatively little power," since cosmic power would have been equally accrued by each family through the specialized tasks that they performed (S. McIntosh 1999:76). The diffuse nature of power would have made hierarchical relationships difficult to establish and sustain, and indeed Kirikongo witnessed a "drastic and rapid egalitarian revolution" after AD 1100 (Dueppen 2012a:289). Ironwork—the basis of the founding family's power—was no longer done in the village but instead at a remote location, and bride service and communal hunting were introduced as site-wide activities to bring households closer together while leveling social differences.

To return to Jenne-jeno, excavation and survey data suggest that the site was founded around 250 BC by a variety of herders, farmers, hunter-gatherers, fisherfolk, and metal workers. The very limited available data suggest that the site grew over the next 650 years, reaching 12 hectares in AD 100 and 25 hectares by AD 400 (S. McIntosh 1999:70) (fig. 7.2). There is some evidence for clustering of smaller sites in these earlier phases around the Jenne-jeno mound (R. McIntosh 2003:175), and survey data from elsewhere in the Middle Niger has also documented the existence of the clustered early villages as predicted for the delta by Roderick McIntosh's model and documented in the Black Volta River bend by Stephen Dueppen (Clark 2003; R. McIntosh and S. McIntosh 1988; Park 2010, 2011; Togola 2008).

By AD 400, the population in and around Jenne-jeno's central mound was likely in the low thousands and continuing to grow. The spread of households across the satellite settlements in the Jenne-jeno cluster served as a form of compartmentalization that helped mitigate rising scalar stress, and specialization also helped decrease the information load borne by each resident. The site, however, was creeping toward the same ceiling of settlement growth that had eventually led to the abandonment of Çatalhöyük.

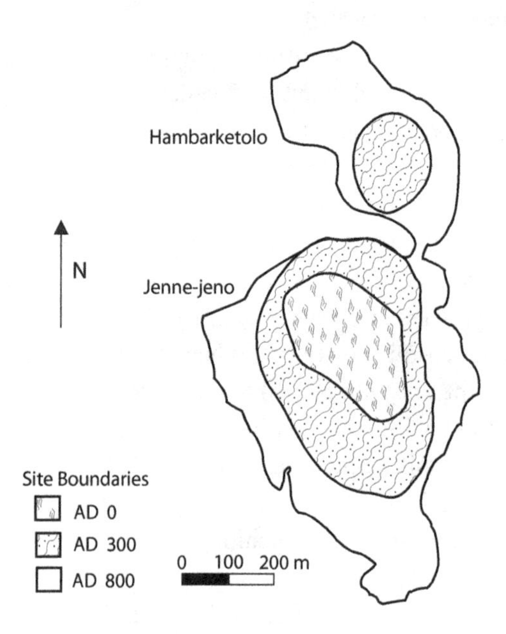

Figure 7.2. Growth of the Jenne-jeno mound over time (Justin Jennings).

At Çatalhöyük, the families had balked at the increasingly hierarchical relationships that were developing there. Many Cahokians walked away from the city after their shamans began behaving like chiefs. Harappa flourished in part because its residents embraced a shared ideology that obscured the rising social differences that became integral to the functioning of the settlement. Yet Jenne-jeno seemingly managed to prosper for centuries as a much larger site with relatively minor differences in wealth and status. How was this possible?

The Urbanization of Jenne-jeno

Jenne-jeno's growth rapidly accelerated after AD 400. The main mound of Jenne-jeno grew from 25 hectares to 42 hectares between AD 400 and 800 (S. McIntosh 1995a:375; S. McIntosh and R. McIntosh 1993:631; R. McIntosh 2005:175) (the 42-hectare figure includes the adjacent mound of Hambarketolo, since it was "physically linked and functionally integrated with Jenne-jeno" by the end of the eighth century [S. McIntosh and R. McIntosh 1993:631]). The village did not just get physically larger but also became more densely occupied, as an increasing number of houses were crammed onto its surface.

Yet only a small portion of the people moving to Jenne-jeno settled at the main mound. There were 24 other sites within a one-kilometer radius of the Jenne-jeno and Hambarketolo mounds by AD 800, and oral traditions suggest that all of these mounds were considered part of a single community (fig. 7.3). If the occupied areas of each of these settlements are included, then the Jenne-jeno cluster would have, on a conservative estimate, covered 69 hectares and been home to as many as 27,000 people (S. McIntosh 1995a:374–375). Archaeologists, moreover, have documented 44 additional sites within a 4-kilometer radius of the Jenne-jeno mound. At least 50,000 people were thus living within an afternoon's walk of each other (R. McIntosh 1998:200; R. McIntosh and S. McIntosh 2003:110). Discrete neighborhoods had helped those living in in Çatalhöyük, Cahokia, and Harappa manage scalar stress. Those living in the scattering of sites around Jenne-jeno took this idea to its logical extreme by creating even further spatial separation between what were essentially neighborhoods of a diffuse urban complex.

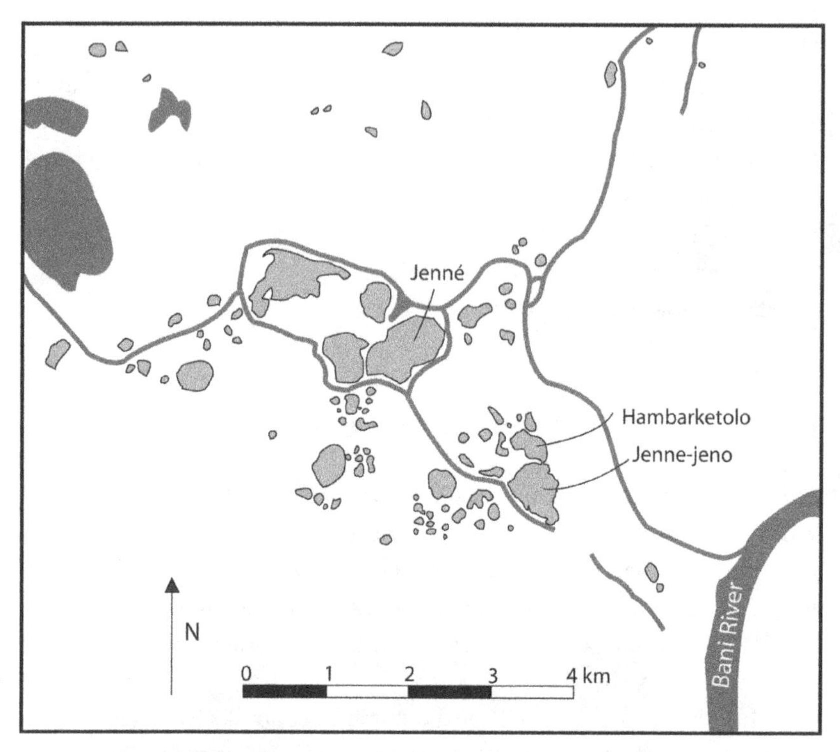

Figure 7.3. Jenne-jeno settlement cluster—note that the largest extent of all sites regardless of time period is indicated on the map. Jenné, for example, was a smaller site when the Jenne-jeno mound reached its greatest extent (Justin Jennings).

We lack the means to precisely track the growth of the Jenne-jeno cluster from AD 400 to 800, but almost all of the satellite sites located around the main mounds appear to have been founded during these four centuries of frenetic growth (R. McIntosh 1991:203–204). This suggests that new arrivals either usually avoided or were pushed away from the main mound and looked instead for desirable land in the vicinity on which they could found their own spatially discrete settlement. Each of these new locales was organized into extended household compounds that were defined by low-lying walls (S. McIntosh and R. McIntosh 1993:631).

This basic organization of households units in Jenne-jeno appears to have been maintained throughout the life of the site, but building materials changed after the post–AD 400 population influx. People had used waddle and daub to construct their houses during earlier periods, but they increasingly switched over to solid coursed mud (called *tauf*) as the Jenne-jeno cluster grew (R. McIntosh and S. McIntosh 1995:64–65). The use of a longer-lasting, more laborious to produce building material perhaps reflects an ossification of social arrangements that had previously been more fluid, as families moved in and out of the community (see Park's 2011 description of temporary settlements in the Timbuktu cluster). Switching to tauf meant that people in Jenne-jeno were committing not only to the site but also to their particular place within one of the various settlements in the cluster.

The centuries after AD 400 were a period of rapid social change at Jenne-jeno that resulted, as Roderick McIntosh has noted (1998:200), in "the most generous yield of exotic items, diversity of local manufacture, and ceramic heterogeneity" in the city's history. Many of these changes can be seen largely as accelerations of the trends identified in the pulse model. More people coming into the area meant additional clustering around the Jenne-jeno mound, increasing specialization of these clusters, and more concentrated efforts to distinguish between the subgroups living across the urban complex (S. McIntosh ed. 1995; R. McIntosh 2003). The cluster's smaller sites of 0.5 to 1.5 hectares tended to be home to just one of these subgroups—a group of potters, perhaps—while sites larger than 1.5 hectares were amalgamations of a few subgroups. The intensity of household specialization increased as one moved closer to Jenne-jeno's main mound (R. McIntosh 1993:204–206).

The emphasis on spatial compartmentalization and specialization made it possible for each of the communities in the Inland Niger Delta clusters to "exploit proximity to clients and suppliers of other services without surrendering their identity to a single urban identity" (R. McIntosh 1993:204). Clustering not only minimized scalar stress as population climbed but also allowed for the creation of a resilient economic system based on reciprocal relationships that was well suited to the region's patchy, often unpredictable, environment (R. McIntosh 1998:175; see Fletcher 2009 and Scarborough and Lucero 2010 for a broader discussion of these kinds of systems). The sustainable, horizontally organized political system of mutual dependency that was cobbled together was perhaps reinforced by a belief in a nyama-like cosmic force that flowed through the universe. The system worked because you needed your neighbors not only for the food you ate and the clothes you wore but also for their contribution to the general production of the cosmic energy that ensured that the universe was properly balanced.

A description like this one of Inland Niger Delta urbanism might make it seem that the region deserved pride of place at the First International—"from each according to his ability, to each according to his needs" (Marx 1977:569 [1875])! Yet it is important to emphasize that the region's overarching egalitarianism was made possible by networks of competing hierarchical relationships that served to minimize political centralization (McIntosh 2005:1987). The heads of the first settlers of a new community in a cluster, for example, may have made many of the subsistence and ritual decisions for that community, while the leaders of secret craft specialist societies likely shaped how their society's members worked throughout the multiple settlements of a clustered city (R. McIntosh 2000:160–162; R. McIntosh and S. McIntosh 2003:111).

The relative equality of all families within the cluster was therefore not a given. The sheer act of clustering around a particular place gave that location primacy, and, as Susan Keetch McIntosh has argued, the ritual authority of Jenne-jeno's "founding families who controlled the spirits of both the land and the water must not be underestimated" (1999:76). Some of those living on the central mound were thus, at the very least, treated as firsts among equals, and these individuals no doubt used this authority to coordinate activities across Jenne-jeno and other clustered cities. The scope of their influence was nonetheless held in check by both a belief in a unifying cosmic force and their dependency on multiple, dispersed producers within the cluster who could easily have left for other Middle Niger settlements if they grew unhappy.

Blacksmiths, as Roderick McIntosh (1998:176–179) and Randi Håland (1980:44–46) suggest, may have been the greatest threat to the relatively egalitarian status quo in the Inland Niger Delta during the mid-first millennium AD. Often concentrated in or around the main mounds of clusters, the blacksmith's work required imported ores—from at least 75 kilometers away in the case of Jenne-jeno (R. McIntosh and S. McIntosh 1988:151)—and they demanded prodigious amounts of fuel to feed their furnaces, a resource that would have become more difficult to obtain as population densities rose. Their social networks alone may have been the envy of many, but in addition they also could have been seen as magicians who tapped into extraordinary reservoirs of cosmic energy by turning earth into iron (R. McIntosh 2000:168). Their access to more of this energy likely translated into a stronger voice in village affairs. To paraphrase George Orwell, they were becoming more equal than others.

Sometime after AD 400, the blacksmiths in Jenne-jeno started experimenting with copper and copper alloys, which may have meant that they came to be seen as accruing even more cosmic energy (S. McIntosh 1995c:264). The growing imbalance in cosmic energy caused by the blacksmiths would have been a concern for everyone in the settlement, and this concern may have been addressed by the reorganization of metals production around this time. Smelting and smithing had been done together on the central mound for centuries, but after this time more smelting was done in peripheral clusters (S. McIntosh 1995c:278). This spatial separation follows the trend of greater compartmentalization and specialization over time in the Inland Niger Delta (R. McIntosh 1998:178), but is also reminiscent of how the residents of Kirikongo reasserted egalitarianism by shifting ironworking off-site (Dueppen 2012a:289). Perhaps the relocation of smelting activities to the periphery of the Jenne-jeno cluster was also an attempt to reassert the proper balance between subgroups?

The growth of long-distance trade posed an additional threat to Jenne-jeno's horizontally integrated political economy. There was much more iron ore flowing into the city by AD 800, and more copper, decorative stones, salt, and perhaps gold was now coming into the delta from hundreds of kilometers away. In return for these imports, people in the Inland Niger Delta were likely shipping out dried fish, rice, and other staple goods with a long shelf life (Dueppen 2012c:99; S. McIntosh and R. McIntosh 1993:641). Trade, of course, was essential to the prosperity of everyone in the clustered cities, but certain subgroups would have been far more involved than others in these transactions.

Those living in and around Jenne-jeno were likely acutely aware of how differential access to highly valued exotica threatened egalitarianism, since rising social differences linked to trade are documented elsewhere in the Middle Niger region. Tereba Togola's Akumbu Mound Complex excavations in the Méma region, for example, uncovered an extended burial from this period that was accompanied by 2 copper bracelets, 13 cowrie beads, and 13 white and coral quartzite beads (2008:31), and slightly earlier burials found in Timbuktu featured necklaces with glass and decorative stone beads that were only available from sources hundreds of kilometers away (Park 2011:159). These burials, although they contain just a few imported items, are more ostentatious than any burial recovered to date in the Jenne-jeno cluster (R. McIntosh and S. McIntosh 1995:66). Status differences were likely most pronounced in the Lakes Region, where poorly known funerary tumuli may date to as early as the seventh century AD (R. McIntosh 1998:223). The excavations of tumuli that date to a slightly later period contain the burial of two individuals who were interred with ceramic vessels, copper and iron objects, glass and semiprecious stone beads, and projectile points (R. McIntosh 1998:225–226).

Since funerary customs are often used as a hedge against rising inequality (e.g., Kuijt 1996; Yépez Álvarez and Jennings 2012), it is possible that the simple graves of Jenne-jeno reflect residents' attempts to enforce their traditional egalitarian ethos and curb the growing power of traders. Those living there had access to the same kinds of imports that were used as status markers elsewhere in the Middle Niger. For example, iron was often used to make bracelets and rings, as were copper and bronze at a later time (S. McIntosh 1995c:264–272). A glass bead chemically sourced to south Asia was recovered from the earliest levels of the settlement (Brill 1995:254). Yet Jenne-jeno's dwellers largely eschewed these items as grave goods and chose instead to bury their dead in the same way their ancestors had done for centuries.

Although the pace of Jenne-jeno's growth from AD 400 to 800 eludes us, it appears that its residents overcame the scalar stress of aggregation by increasing compartmentalization and specialization, as well as by drawing on the abundant, if often unpredictable, food resources in the Inland Niger Delta. A network of mutually reinforcing economic interactions developed across the region's clustered cities, while a belief in a nyama-like cosmic force likely limited the trends toward centralization and social stratification that seem to be inherent in the urbanization process. Mutual respect and interdependence—leavened by giving people the space to pursue their own activities—resulted in the creation of an acephalous, more bottom-up regional polity composed of dozens of smaller settlements surrounding a central mound.

Countryside, Colonies, and the Creation of a Middle Niger Cultural Horizon

In most cases, urbanization results in population nucleation. The region surrounding a growing city is sometimes nearly depopulated, and new settlements need to be founded in order to meet the subsistence needs of the urbanized population that can no longer feed itself. The creation of these new communities, often accompanied by the development of wide-ranging programs to increase the yields of domesticated and wild animals, is part of ruralization—the creation of a countryside (Yoffee 2005:214). In the case of the Inland Niger Delta, however, clustering *was* equivalent to the creation of a countryside. Spreading the population out across a broader region lessened the strain on the environment. The existence of such clusters also allowed specialists to choose locations that were more conducive to performing their particular activities. Farmers, for example, could settle next to patches of fertile lands a few kilometers from the main mound, while herders and fisherfolk could settle in other nearby places that worked better for what they did (Clark 2003; McIntosh 1993).

The greater environmental sustainability of clustered versus nucleated cities can perhaps be seen in the subsistence data. While diet breadth often declines after urbanization (e.g., Storey 2006), this was not the case in the Upper Niger Delta. Throughout the occupation sequence, households consumed a broadly similar mix of farmed, herded, hunted, gathered, and fished resources (R. McIntosh and S. McIntosh 2003:108). With this said, an emphasis on the "remarkably stable subsistence system of the Middle Niger" (R. McIntosh 2005:119) can obscure the evidence for environmental stress and the adoption of resource intensification strategies that enabled the growth of the region's clustered cities. People were eating the same kinds of foods in different ways after urbanization.

Overfishing was never a problem at Jenne-jeno (Van Neer 1995:341), but overhunting reduced the number of antelope and other large mammals in the region by the second half of the first millennium AD (MacDonald 1995:313). The decline in wild sources of meat meant an increasing reliance on dwarf varieties of sheep, goats, and cattle. The use of these varieties is telling because these smaller animals yielded less meat and milk relative to their larger counterparts in North Africa, and transhumance was also limited because dwarf sheep and goats traveled poorly over long distances (MacDonald 1995:313–314). Dwarf varieties, however, are "renowned for their ability to survive in tsetse-invested zones," and thus the breeding of these animals in the Inland Niger Delta likely reflects herders' ongoing concerns about tropical diseases (Gifford-Gonzales 2000:12; also see Dueppen 2012c): with wild meat disappearing, the cities' prosperity became increasingly tied to the health of its flocks.

Urbanization at Jenne-jeno is also associated with shifts in how food was prepared. There was a 40 percent increase in the average rim diameter of vessels after AD 400, and platters were introduced at this time as well. There are also higher concentrations of ash and burnt earth in earlier deposits, while later levels have fewer grinding stones (S. McIntosh 1995b157–162). Susan Keetch McIntosh (1995c:160–162) argues that these and other trends in the excavation data can be used to suggest that the earliest inhabitants of Jenne-jeno ate their grains in the form of unleavened bread pancakes and also grilled, roasted, or smoked their meat and fish. The small vessel size during these first centuries reflects limited storage needs and/or small family size. McIntosh sees a shift after AD 400 toward a diet that included more vegetable stews and boiled whole grains. Families were likely larger by this time, and so storage would have become a greater concern.

These changes in cuisine appear to reflect a desire to increase caloric yields from farming and to better manage food shortfalls. Less bread consumption, for example, meant less time milling flour; more storage meant that one could save a bit more smoked fish for the leaner months of the year. Specialization, which both expanded over time and was more pervasive the closer a cluster was to the central mound, would have increased productivity through changes in technology and shifts in labor organization, putting more food on everyone's plate in those locations where population densities were highest (R. McIntosh 1993:204–206; Morrison 1994). Localized efforts to tweak the landscape by building check dams and cleaning channels would have added another measure of stability in an ever-changing landscape (Scarborough and Lucero 2010:198).

Yet clustering and specialization could squeeze out of the Inland Niger Delta only those resources that were available in an alluvial plain. The cities in the delta lacked salt, iron ore, stone, and other critical resources, and evidence for long-distance trade in these items is found in the earliest levels of sites (Bedaux et al. 2001:843; S. McIntosh 1995a:390; Park 2010:1080). In the case of Jenne-jeno, residents likely obtained iron ore from Bénédougou, located 75 kilometers away, and most stone would have come from a variety of places along the fringes of the delta (R. McIntosh 2005:145–147). Salt was acquired from Berber traders who crossed the Sahara desert (S. McIntosh 1995a:391), and food was likely exchanged with groups living in adjacent regions within the Middle Niger (S. McIntosh and R. McIntosh 1988:123). How long-distance trade was regulated remains unclear. Yet the hundreds of grinding stones found in the earlier levels Jenne-jeno were made in only 11 forms, suggesting that trade, at least in this particular item, was "somewhat organized" by the beginning of the first millennium AD (R. McIntosh 2005:146).

The Middle Niger, a vast region containing the Inland River Delta, Memá, the Lakes Region, and Niger Bend, was bound together through trade and other kinds of interactions into a series of closely related cultural areas by the last centuries of the first millennium AD (Dueppen 2012c:99; Mayor et al. 2014:19; S. McIntosh 1995a:360–372). The existence of these affiliated culture areas, defined largely by similarities in surface ceramic assemblages, suggests close interactions between these groups: potters in the different areas seem to have chosen from among the forms and decorations that were in wide circulation at that time (Togola 2008:81). These interconnections would be later exemplified by the distribution of Tellem Footed Bowls, a distinctive vessel form found from one end of the Niger to the other (Bedaux 1980; Mayor et al. 2005:52) (fig. 7.4).

This Middle Niger cultural horizon was likely spurred by developments occurring within the Inland Niger Delta, where the largest and earliest clustered cities appear to have been located (Bedaux et al. 2001; Park 2010; S. McIntosh ed. 1995). As population and specialization increased in these locales, demand for imports throughout the delta escalated. Akumbu and Gao exemplify the impact of the delta's urbanization on adjacent resource zones (see fig. 7.1). Akumbu was one of a number of small settlements that "exploded" in size in the iron-producing Méma region during the seventh century AD (Togola 2008:79). Many of these settlements, clustered like those in the delta, contained groups of furnaces and heaps of slag suggesting that "industrial scale" smelting occurred in these locales that far exceeded local demand (Togola 2008:79; also see Håland 1980). The Méma ironworkers were perhaps producing blooms or ingots that were exported to the blacksmiths in the Inland Niger Delta who did not have access to locally available ores (S. McIntosh 1995a:384). In return, ironworkers could have received foodstuffs from the delta settlements, as well as access to the exotic goods—copper pins, cowrie shells, stone beads—that were being obtained by traders living in the larger settlements (Togola 2008:80).

Although imports came into the delta from all directions (S. McIntosh and R. McIntosh 1993:639), the trade routes that connected the Inland Niger Delta to northwest Africa and the Middle East were particularly important for beads and other kinds of personal ornaments (Mayor et al. 2014).

Figure 7.4. Tellem-footed bowl from thirteenth-century Mali (Metropolitan Museum of Art, Gift of Lester Wunderman, 1977, www.metmuseum.org).

The desire for such items may have led to the rapid expansion of Gao in the eighth century AD (Insoll 2000:150; Cisse 2010:257). Located in the Niger Bend, Gao was a large, densely occupied trading site whose settlers processed imported copper from places like Tunisia and glass beads from as far off as the Middle East (Cisse 2010:268, 272). Gao's polychrome pottery assemblage hints at a multiethnic community made up of local people from the Middle Niger who lived alongside enclaves of North Africans who were involved in long-distance trading (Insoll 1996:83; Cisse 2010:275–277). Many of the imports processed in Gao were likely sent along to Timbuktu and the other Inland Niger Delta cities (Brill 1995:256; Park 2010:1081; Roy 2000:100).

Gao and Akumbu were undeniably local responses to the new demands of Inland Niger Delta urbanization, but it is also possible that small groups of people from Jenne-jeno and the other clustered cities of the delta were moving into other parts of the Middle Niger during the last centuries of the first millennium AD. Roderick McIntosh argues that Jenne-jeno had grown into a city by creating "bonds of fictive kinship" that served to link arriving ethnic groups from the region to the more established groups living on the its central mound (2005:113). The mixture of designs on Jenne-jeno pots may be a reflection of this ethnic diversity, and the conservatism in design syntax on pots found at the site might be an indication of efforts to find common ground in a rapidly diversifying settlement (S. McIntosh 1995c:162–163). If Roderick McIntosh's interpretation is correct, then a mix of people from across the Middle Niger may have also settled in Gao, as well as in other locations in the region where greater ceramic heterogeneity has been noted (S. McIntosh 1995a:364–368).

Groups from the Middle Niger may have moved into other locations as well. The best evidence for a more distant trading enclave comes from the site of Daboya in northern Ghana (Shinnie and Kense 1989) (see fig. 7.1). Long-distance trade networks had deepened the relationship between the Inland Niger Delta and the West African rain forests to the southwest, and Daboya's position along the White Volta River allowed its residents to begin profiting off of these interregional interactions during the last centuries of the first millennium AD (Casey 2010:84–87). Daboya's ceramic assemblage from this period reflects mounting influence from the Middle Niger and North Africa (Shinnie and Kense 1989:244), and the variety of ceramics found in different parts of the site has led the excavators to argue that several ethnic groups of traders may have lived there alongside locals (Shinnie and Kense 1989:239, 245).

In sum, the rise of Jenne-jeno and the other clustered cities of the Inland River Delta had broad consequences across the Middle Niger and beyond. Though data remain quite sparse, it appears that residents of the region managed population growth in the delta by spreading themselves out across the landscape, specializing economically within clusters, and obtaining desired nonlocal resources from other delta settlements and adjacent regions. Clustering, specialization, and trade increased over time, and by the eighth century a cultural horizon had developed across the Middle Niger. All of these developments had occurred without the rise of an elite, the formation of states, or the elaboration of monumental architecture, but this was about to change with the introduction of Islam into North Africa.

Trans-Saharan Trade and the Fall of the Clustered Cities

The Arab conquest of North Africa began in AD 670 with the founding of Qayrawān in present-day Tunisia. By the beginning of the eighth century, the Umayyad Caliphate had control of a 200-kilometer strip of land running along the Mediterranean Sea from Egypt to the Atlantic Ocean. The invaders initially had little interest in establishing a government over this enormous territory and instead raided towns, exacted tribute, and—most importantly for the history of West Africa—converted nomadic Berbers to their faith and cause (Austen 2010:19).

The Berbers had experience crossing the Sahara Desert and were very active in the trade routes connecting West and North Africa. Berber know-how, perhaps combined with the Arabs' deeper appreciation of the camel's value for carrying loads across the desert (Connah 2004:108–109), led to a surge in trans-Saharan caravan trade that began in the ninth century AD and ended only with the completion of European colonial railroads in the early twentieth century. Slaves, gold, and the highly caffeinated kola nut were the primary goods sent from the south, while salt, glass beads, cowrie shells, and paper were among the main items received from the north.

The clustered cities of the Inland Niger Delta were well positioned to serve as intermediaries in this trade with the caliphate, but data suggest that although trade volume increased in the ninth and tenth centuries AD, the delta's inhabitants remained concerned about the corrosive influence of engaging in long-distance interaction. Mamadou Cisse (2010:275) provides us with the best evidence for this worry when he notes a marked difference in the amounts of trade goods recovered in domestic contexts to the east and west of the Niger Bend. Glass beads are "seemingly ubiquitous" east of the bend, and there are "substantial quantities" of copper, but both are "much less frequent" at sites to the west of the bend—the heart of the Middle Niger that includes the Inland Niger Delta—and have most often only been found in burial contexts.

The cities in the delta had survived for centuries by virtue of a "heterarchical grid of authority" that stretched across much of the Middle Niger (R. McIntosh 2005:206). This heterarchical grid—a mutually reinforcing network of overlapping political, economic, and social relationships—had grown organically with the development of the clustered cities. Status aspirations were held in check by both the competing desires of other subgroups and the belief in a cosmic force that demanded cooperation and respect. When a subgroup's rising power threatened this heterarchical grid, other groups sought to maintain the status quo through such strategies as the reorganization of metals production.

Yet differential access to exotica had begun to create a wedge between families by the eighth century AD, exacerbating the subtle status differences already in place in the Middle Niger. Many residents of the region's clustered cities likely recognized that escalating long-distance trade would further corrode their way of life. The spiraling demand from North Africa for delta products, however, would prove impossible for some to resist, leading to an ever-escalating flood of imports that presented individuals with tantalizing opportunities to secure greater wealth and status.

Those leery of increased interaction proved prescient, since the post–AD 800 surge in trading brought more than just goods across the desert. The Inland Niger Delta was also exposed to pandemic diseases from the Mediterranean—oral histories speak of the abandonment of Jenne-jeno following an infection that killed all male children, and some statues from the beginning of the second millennium AD depict people with buboes and pustules (R. McIntosh 1998:248–249). Another import, Islam, likely eroded adherence in some quarters to traditional beliefs, and the introduction of horses, as well as more warfare-oriented migrant groups, likely contributed to the instability of the delta's political economy (R. McIntosh 2005:176–177). To make matters worse, a drier, more unpredictable, environment placed additional pressure on the delta's population after AD 1100 (Mayor et al. 2005:52–53; R. McIntosh 1998:77).

The construction of a wall around Jenne-jeno at the beginning of the ninth century AD was one of the first signs of the decline of the political, economic, and social structures that had made clustered cities possible. The 3.7-meter-wide "mass of grayish, cylindrical bricks" can be traced around much of the site and may have been built to protect the site more from floods rather than from military attack (R. McIntosh and S. McIntosh 1995:55; also see S. McIntosh and R. McIntosh 1993:632). Whatever its functions, the wall became the mound's most prominent architectural feature. Walls, at least later in West African history, were symbols of urbanism, status, and power (Haour 2005:153–155)—ideas that seem antithetical to the guiding principles of Middle Niger communities. The central mound at Jenne-jeno had always been the heart of the settlement, but the wall likely crystallized the locale's prominence in a way that made those living nearby uneasy.

Trans-Saharan trading altered the delta's political economy, and as a result, the social contract underlying the clustered cities unraveled. Two-thirds of the settlements around the Jenne-jeno mound were abandoned by the very beginning of the first millennium AD (R. McIntosh 1998:246). Some people may have moved behind the walls—Jenne-jeno's mound would reach its greatest extent from AD 1100 to 1200 (R. McIntosh 2005:177)—but most left the area to live in nonspecialized, more self-sufficient, villages. A "flurry of building" on the central mound during the twelfth century created a new urban landscape that, according to historical documents, was now heavily invested in its relationship with outsiders and centered on a chief and his palace (R. McIntosh 1998:245; also see S. McIntosh 1995a:392). When Jenne-jeno's chief converted to Islam in AD 1180, he moved his palace, and likely by now his mosque, to the nearby site of Jenné. This move appears to have precipitated a two-century decline in the Jenne-jeno mound's population that ended with the settlement's abandonment around AD 1400 (S. McIntosh 1995a:392–393).

Civilization and the Clustered Cities of the Inland Niger Delta

In Roderick McIntosh's words, Jenne-jeno lacks the "expected purple-prose manifestations of power" that we have come to associate with urbanization (2005:13). Even more than Cahokia and Harappa, Jenne-jeno defies V. Gordon Childe's classic conception of a civilization (1950). Jenne-jeno and the other clustered cities of the Inland Niger Delta prospered for centuries without the imposition of a vertical, centralized hierarchy. There were no palaces, citadels, military barracks, great temples, or audience halls in these cities; taxation, writing, and bureaucracies were seemingly not needed. The first monumental constructions—city walls—marked the end rather the beginning of the horizontal, heterarchical political economies that developed in the delta during the first millennium AD.

Inland Niger Delta urbanism, like that of Cahokia and Harappa, rebels against our attempts to enumerate civilization criteria that work around the world. A trait like monumental architecture that one might associate with the arrival of civilization in one place could appear too early in another place or not show up at all. As others have noted (Drennan and Peterson 2006, 2012), critically comparing data from different regions of the world clearly demonstrates that thinking in terms of stages of cultural development does not work. Cultural developments in places like the North American midcontinent, Indus Valley, and Middle Niger Delta can no longer be dismissed as extreme outliers to the typical steplike transition to civilization (e.g., R. McIntosh 1991, 2005:227–228). As this book continues to demonstrate, there was *no* punctuated phase change to a civilization stage both because change was not punctuated and, more importantly, because there is no common, crosscutting civilization stage.

What unites our case studies is instead the challenge of aggregation. Jenne-jeno's residents had the same basic concerns that everyone would have in a rapidly urbanizing settlement: they needed to find a way to create a city from a collection of people. Urbanization in the delta led to a series of by-products that are by now familiar to us—ruralization, colonization, polity formation, and creation of a cultural horizon—but the distinct people, history, and environment of the Middle Niger led to results that were often quite distinct from those seen at Cahokia and Harappa. In this case residents used the tools at their disposal to create a resilient "civil society" that was opposed to the "arrogance of power hierarchies" (R. McIntosh 1998:302–303).

Drier conditions in North and West Africa during the second millennium BC drove groups out of the Sahara and into the Inland Niger Delta. These groups came into the delta following different subsistence regimes, and they settled into disparate routines within the delta's patchy and highly variable environment. The fickle nature of the delta's environment encouraged periodic aggregation whereby goods could be exchanged between families that were exploiting different ecological niches. Over time, some individuals chose to live permanently in those places where aggregation routinely occurred (R. McIntosh 1993).

Aggregation, and later permanent settlement, was particularly intense in those locations like Jenne-jeno that boasted a nearby assortment of good farming, herding, and fishing lands. The central mound in Jenne-jeno was likely a ritually charged location—perhaps associated with water spirits—and the first families to move to the spot would have been instrumental in coordinating the growth of both the mound and the handful of settlements that began to cluster around it by the beginning of the first millennium BC. The cluster slowly grew larger and more internally specialized over the next four centuries (S. McIntosh, ed. 1995; R. McIntosh 2005).

Chronological control throughout the Middle Niger is poor before the introduction of writing, but it appears that scalar stress was intensifying among the population of Jenne-jeno by around AD 400. The area's increasing population density was straining the natural environment, and the rising power of blacksmiths was threatening to upend the reciprocal relationships that bound the settlement together. Reducing scalar stress meant both the acceptance of significant changes—a shift in cuisine and the separation of smithing and smelting—as well as a redoubling of the specialization and spatial compartmentalization that was part and parcel of the settlement clustering already occurring (S. McIntosh, ed. 1995; R. McIntosh 2005).

The growth of clustered cities within the Inland Niger Delta escalated demands for products that were unavailable in an alluvial floodplain. Traders, if not colonists, traveled to neighboring resource zones and triggered a flow of objects and ideas across the entire Middle Niger region. A cultural horizon formed that not only linked together Middle Niger groups but also brought people into contact with outsiders whose beliefs were antithetical to the heterarchical ideals that structured relationships in Jenne-jeno and the other cities in the delta (S. McIntosh, ed. 1995; Park 2011; Togola 2008). The mutually reinforcing relationships that crisscrossed the clustered cities were resilient to change—immune to a stray conversation on enlightened despotism or the arrival of a few glass beads. Yet the unimaginable riches of the trans-Saharan trade, combined with a changing climate and other factors, led to the decline of clustered cities beginning in the first millennium AD.

Jenne-jeno is yet another example of "complexity-in-the-making" (Alt 2010:129). Rather than an abrupt, steplike transition to a civilization stage, there was a cascading series of related processes that began with the scalar stress caused by the aggregation of people in and around the settlement sometime after AD 400. The multigenerational struggle to create functioning cities in the Inland Niger Delta had the unintended consequence of stimulating a surge in interregional interaction that transformed a broad region through the circulation of a wide array of ideas, objects, and individuals. The growth of Tiahuanaco, a city in the Bolivian Altiplano, had a similar impact on people living in the south-central Andes.

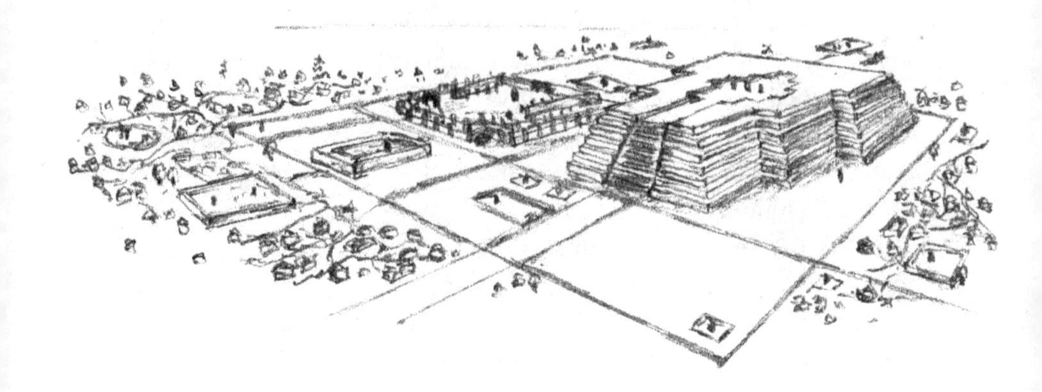

8

TIAHUANACO AND THE CREATION OF THE ANDEAN MIDDLE HORIZON

WHEN EPHRAIM G. SQUIER VISITED TIAHUANACO DURING A diplomatic mission to the central Andes in 1864, he wandered through a site "in such an absolute condition of ruin as almost to defy inquiry or generalization" (1877:299). The American consul general thought that the handful of "shapeless" mounds of earth with "impressive" traces of architecture and remarkable sculptures formed the heart of an empty ceremonial center in a land far too "cold," "arid," and "barren" to support a city (1877:299–300). Tiahuanaco in his eyes was a "sacred spot" plunked down in the middle of nowhere "by an accident, an augury, or a dream" (1877:300).

Tiahuanaco's seemingly formidable location in the highlands of northern Bolivia—the site sits in a nearly treeless valley some 3,840 meters above sea level—led subsequent scholars to echo Squier's empty ceremonial center model even as they came to define a vast Tiahuanaco-influenced Middle Horizon period that transformed the lives of many Andean people between AD 500 and 1150 (Janusek 2008:5–12). This view predominated until 1966, when Jeffrey Parsons mapped the surface artifact scatter extending outward from the site's mounds. He discovered that this "empty" ceremonial center had covered an area of at least 2.4 square kilometers (1968:244). Tiahuanaco had in fact been a city with a population now estimated at 30,000 to 40,000 people (Kolata 1993:174).

Tiahuanaco is commonly considered by scholars today to have been the capital of a state that controlled much of the Lake Titicaca Basin (e.g., Janusek 2008; Kolata 1993; Stanish 2003; Young-Sánchez 2004). This eponymously named state, which I spell as Tiwanaku to distinguish the state from the city, is known for founding colonies in distant resource zones and pioneering exchange relationships that resulted in the wide dispersal of objects created in a Tiwanaku region-wide style. Yet a state matching our definition of the term—a regionally organized society with a professional ruling class, commoner class, and a highly centralized and internally specialized government—was a late development in a centuries-long process of development that began with urbanization, colonization, and the formation of a cultural horizon that began at Tiahuanaco. State governance, when it finally occurred midway through the Middle Horizon, only lasted for a few generations. The state thus emerged near the end rather than the beginning of Tiahuanaco's story.

There was thus no punctuated, steplike transformation to a civilization stage in the Lake Titicaca Basin. Tiahuanaco, like the other settlements explored in this book, did not emerge as part of a bundled suite of novel characteristics. The origins of the city's massive temples, broad plazas, and scores of housing compounds can be traced back across a millennium of community building in the basin. Some of the traits that one commonly associates with civilization—monumental construction, sophisticated art, regular long-distance trade—appeared much earlier during this thousand years of experimentation. Others emerged generations after thousands of people had moved into Tiahuanaco. A few traits never showed up at all. Those working in the basin know this, but that same nagging, often unconscious, desire for a single moment of sweeping cultural change that impacts our interpretations of other regions also subtly shapes their work.

The particular trajectory of Tiahuanaco's development and its broader impact was a unique product of the Lake Titicaca Basin's historical, cultural, and environmental context. The story of the city's rise and fall is nonetheless similar to those already told in this volume. Tiahuanaco dwellers dealt with the scalar stress caused by rapid population aggregation by drawing on the same mechanisms the other cities in the making we have examined drew on: ritual elaboration, compartmentalization, larger basal-unit size, and, more reluctantly, social hierarchization. In addressing the problems of living together, the residents of Tiahuanaco created a countryside and transformed a region.

The Lake Titicaca Basin and the Formative Period

Sandwiched between the Pacific Ocean and the Amazon jungle, the Andean world is composed of an arid coastal plain, high sierra, and humid eastern flank (fig. 8.1). The highlands are home to two parallel mountain ranges that part in far southern Peru to form the boundaries of a wide plain that stretches southward for more than 800 kilometers. This high, semiarid plain, called the Altiplano, has an average elevation of 3,750 meters above sea level. With vegetation restricted primarily to a variety of alpine grasses, the population has always been sparse throughout much of the Altiplano, and most of the land has typically been used only for the herding of llamas and alpacas (Binford and Kolata 1996).

The resource potential of the northernmost portion of the Altiplano is different because of Lake Titicaca. The vast lake, which is 8,600 square kilometers and more than 200 meters deep, provides a wealth of aquatic resources. People have long pulled a variety of catfish and pupfish out of the lake's frigid waters and have hunted many of the 50 species of birds that frequent its shores. The lake's "extraordinarily high levels" of aquatic plants can also be used for building material, animal feed, and food (Binford and Kolata 1996:41–42; also see Orlove 2002). Perhaps more importantly, the lake moderates temperatures in its vicinity, leading to more abundant and predictable rainfall. These lake effects make it possible to grow a variety of high-elevation food crops like potatoes, quinoa, and tarwi that are difficult, if not impossible, to grow elsewhere on the Altiplano (Kolata 1993:45).

When the climate became progressively wetter at the end of the third millennium BC, people began settling down into small, dispersed villages along the shores of Lake Titicaca (Hastorf 2005:66). Inhabitants of these villages subsisted on a wide range of wild and domesticated plants and animals and engaged in a "brisk trade" of stone tools, salt, and other items that crisscrossed the region (Stanish 2003:109). Village cohesion appears to have been initially quite weak, since each household boasted its own ritual structure and conducted its own ceremonies to honor both the earth's fecundity and the recently deceased (Janusek 2008:70–71). As population grew in the region during the second millennium BC, these weakly consolidated villages would break apart when the number of people living in them exceeded 200 (Bandy 2004:330). Departing households would move into untapped areas or,

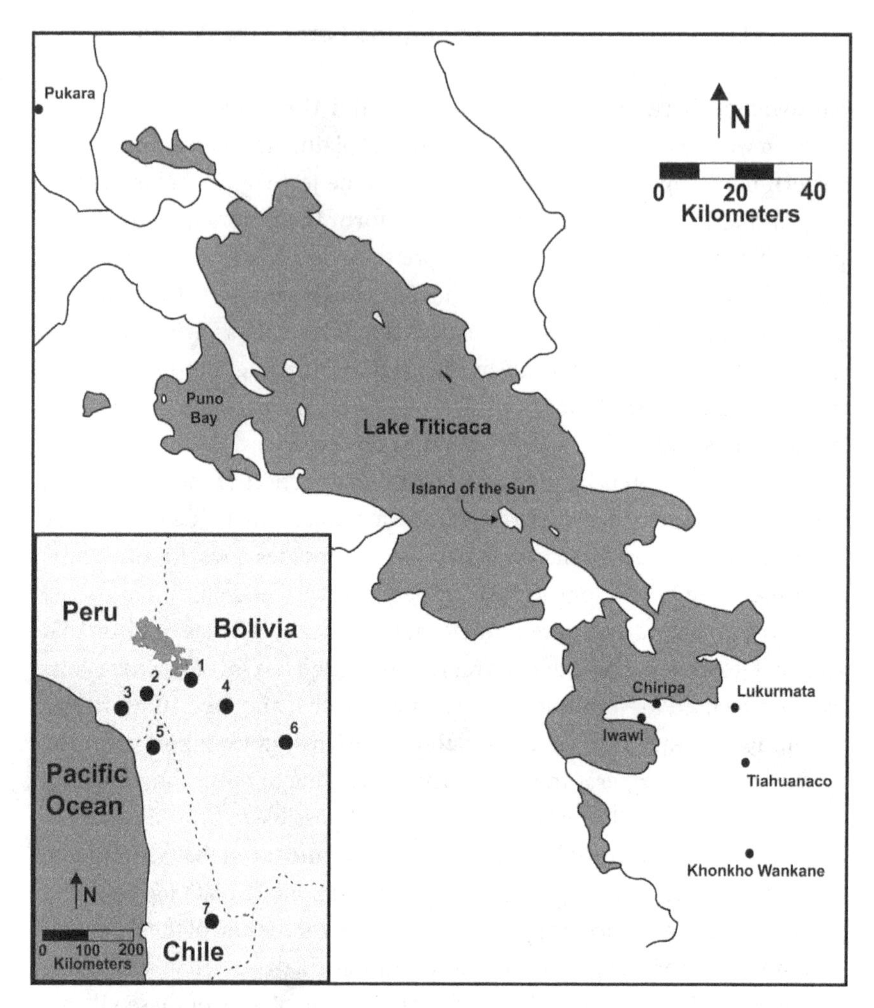

Figure 8.1. Map of the Lake Titicaca Basin with sites discussed in the text. The inset map shows the city in relation to more distant locations. The number 1 corresponds to Tiahuanaco, 2 to Suches, 3 to Moquegua, 4 to central Altiplano, 5 to Azapa, 6 to Cochabamaba, and 7 to San Pedro de Atacama (Justin Jennings).

more rarely, settle nearby by converting hillsides into agricultural terracing and marshes into raised fields (elevated growing areas surrounded by water canals) (Bruno 2014:140; Stanish 2003:135).

Efforts to find common ground among those living together in the basin appear to have led to the creation of ritually charged sites by as early as 1350 BC. These sites usually contained stone monoliths, a sunken enclosure, and a raised platform mound on which small structures were placed. Feasting debris litters these sites, as do the remains of braziers, trumpets, and serving vessels (Hastorf 2005:69). The rituals that were performed at these sites appear to have been drawn from a household-based tradition of ancestor worship that enabled practitioners to metaphorically embrace larger and larger groups of people as members of the same family (Hastorf 2003:327). As time went on, these and other efforts to build a larger sense of community led to the emergence of a broadly shared ritual and stylistic practice throughout the Lake Titicaca Basin (Cohen 2010:343; Levine et al. 2013:145; Roddick 2013:287; Roddick and Hastorf 2010:173).

Competition between the basin's various ritual centers during the first millennium BC led to their elaboration and eventually to the expansion of those that were particularly successful. Chiripa, located on the southern shore of Lake Titicaca, provides an early example of how ritual centers alleviated the scalar stress of settlement aggregation (Hastorf 1999). When Chiripa began growing slowly at the beginning of the first millennium BC, residents added at least two sunken courts that may have served different parts of the community. This was then followed in 800 BC by the addition of a platform mound topped by a set of small buildings arranged around a central sunken court. The buildings, used for burnt offerings and the storage of ritual objects, were each likely tended by a different subset of the community, since they "were not in the same style nor were they all rebuilt simultaneously" (Hastorf 2003:322).

Ritual activities in Chiripa would have alleviated stress in a settlement that had grown to more than 7.5 hectares (Bandy 2001:118). At least some of this growth was fueled by immigrants from surrounding villages, who sought to continue to worship their particular set of ancestors in a new home (Beck 2004:341). The 800 BC platform mound created a ritual focus for this diverse population, even if each group chose to worship independently.

Yet adding more and more buildings atop the existing platform would prove difficult as Chiripa's population increased, and so in 400 BC the top of the platform was instead buried under a fill that was used to make a more prominent platform featuring 14 larger structures overlooking a more ample sunken court. The stylistically similar buildings in Chiripa's new platform—conceived of and manufactured as a single unit—created a ritual space that would have more closely unified the various subgroups now living in and around Chiripa (Hastorf 2003:327).

As impressive as Chiripa's architecture was, it was only one of dozens of locally important ritual sites in the Lake Titicaca Basin at that time (Bandy 2006:229; Levine et al. 2013:292; Roddick et al. 2014:143–144; Stanish 2003:110–123). The recurring ritual elaborations in settlements like Chiripa created and maintained a sense of community that stretched beyond particular kin groups, and in coordinating rites at these centers, lineage leaders could strengthen their higher status positions. Some of those who organized the last events that took place at Chiripa, for example, were buried on top of the platform with gold, copper, stone beads, polychrome pots and other high-status goods (Hastorf 2003:324). These difficult to make or acquire goods were honest signals of a leader's connections and knowledge (Plourde 2006), and the acquisition of prestige goods, along with raiding and feast sponsoring, would be used in subsequent centuries to further buttress status positions and to broker alliances between kin groups (Levine et al. 2013; Stanish and Levine 2011).

The second half of the first millennium BC saw the creation of a second generation of ritual centers that served increasing numbers of communities (Levine 2012:144). The most important of these regional centers was almost certainly Pukara, a site located about 80 kilometers north of Lake Titicaca (Klarich 2005, 2009, 2012; Klarich and Román Bustinza 2012). The site was dominated by a 32-meter-tall terraced platform topped with three sunken courts, the largest of which was surrounded on three sides by small buildings. The platform—built on top of what had likely been the earliest ritually charged location at the site—was the end result of a thousand years of constructions (Klarich 2005:64–66). Most of the building at Pukara occurred near the end of the first millennium BC, when many smaller platforms and sunken courts were created around the main platform. These new ritual spaces, all unique in style and orientation, appear to have been built by different communities that came to Pukara and created their own temples there (Janusek 2008:88).

Pukara was much bigger than Chiripa—people visiting or living there would leave behind an artifact scatter that sprawled across 2.2 square kilometers by AD 100 (Klarich and Román Bustinza 2012:118)—but the settlement was as sharply divided into distinct lineages and other subgroups as the earlier ceremonial centers in the basin. As distinct groups came into the site, Pukara's leaders first chose a more inclusive, public-facing strategy that encouraged people to participate in rites and feasts. The leaders abandoned this strategy as the site grew. Rituals on the main platform became more exclusive and greater effort was expended to control the production and circulation of highly valued goods like obsidian, stone sculptures, and polychrome pottery (Klarich 2009:298–300). In later years, groups may have also waged war in an attempt to bring Pukara's disparate groups together into an overarching polity (Stanish and Levine 2011; Tantaleán et al. 2012).

Pukara, especially outside of its ceremonial core, remains poorly known. The settlement may have been the first city in the Lake Titicaca Basin, but if so it was never quite able to bridge the internal divisions of the migrants and pilgrims that came to it. Pukara was rapidly abandoned after AD 100 (Klarich 2005:67), and other, far smaller, ritual centers gained prominence in the region (Stanish 2003:159). For the next 300 years, there was an ever-shifting landscape of ritual centers across the Lake Titicaca Basin that fleetingly brought communities under their influence (Janusek 2008:95). Groups diversified their strategies of incorporation, with some centers like Khonkho Wankane experimenting with new ritual spaces and practices that attracted more mobile populations attached to llama caravans (Janusek 2012:113–118; Gasco and Marsh 2013; Smith and Pérez Arias 2015:117–118). Yet none of these would come close to rivaling Pukara in size, until Tiahuanaco began its rapid expansion toward the end of the fifth century AD.

The Rise of Tiahuanaco

At the beginning of the first millennium AD, Tiahuanaco was a small, local center organized around a sunken temple and monolith (Marsh 2012a:183) (fig. 8.2). The first years of the site are obscured by the detritus of centuries of subsequent occupation, but we know that Tiahuanaco began to grow in size sometime after AD 250. Like the other ritual centers of the basin, the settlement got bigger by attracting people from outlying regions. Much of this initial growth was ephemeral, since many of those who came to Tiahuanaco stayed for only a few days to conduct ceremonies and then return to their communities (Bandy 2001:197; Marsh 2012b:454, 2012c:214–215). Yet more and more people were also moving permanently to the settlement.

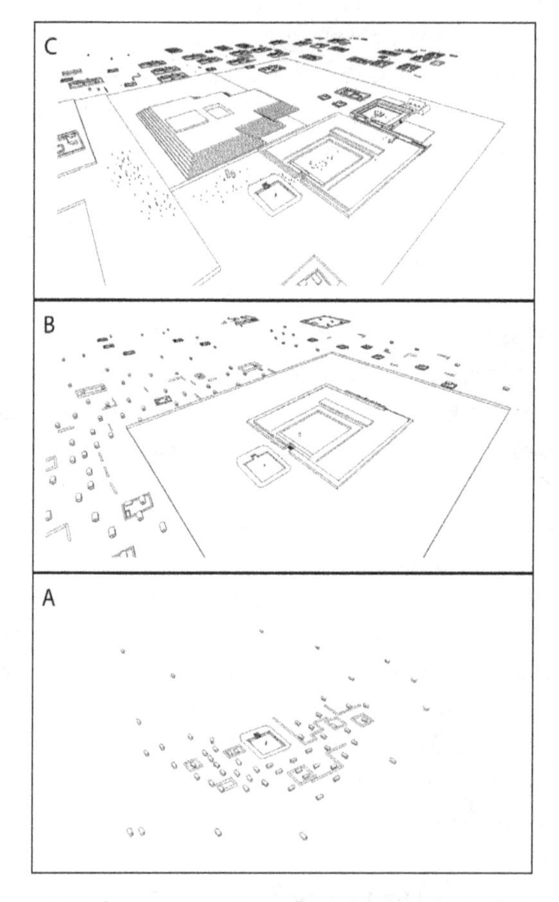

Figure 8.2. Artist's reconstruction of the development of Tiahuanaco's monumental core at three moments of time: as a small settlement surrounding a sunken temple, soon after the construction of the Kalasasaya next to the sunken temple, and after the creation of the Akapana and other monuments (Alexci Vranich).

Those who chose to live in Tiahuanaco brought with them their particular gods and ancestor cults and began building their own rectangular walled compounds and ritual spaces (Marsh 2012b:424–425; Janusek 2008:97). These first groups that moved into Tiahuanaco kept their distance from each other, and the result was a sprawling but lightly occupied settlement. The immediate area around the site's original sunken temple, for example, was mostly unoccupied (there was one residential compound that may have housed the founders of the site [Couture 2002:315–316]). The scalar stress of aggregation was thus dealt with largely through compartmentalization, as it had been in Harappa and especially Jenne-jeno, as each group migrating to Tiahuanaco turned inward on arrival.

Compartmentalization alone, of course, is not an effective means of creating a stable urban environment, and tensions would have inevitably grown as Tiahuanaco's permanent population climbed into the low thousands (Marsh 2012b:454). Ritual elaborations in and around the sunken temple were therefore used to strengthen relationships between families that were both living and visiting the site. The walls of the temple were decorated with more than 200 sculpted stone tenon heads. Each of these unique architectural elements may have depicted an honored ancestor of one of the different groups coming into the city. The placement of these sculptures in one location, set alongside centuries-old sculptures celebrating the earth's fertility, likely symbolized the deeply rooted power of collective action that had been celebrated in earlier centers like Chiripa and Pukara (Couture 2004:129–130; Janusek 2012:120).

Greater investment in crosscutting ritual activities, however, was required as the needs of the population outgrew the confines of the original sunken temple during the fifth century AD. Like in Cahokia, the leaders of Tiahuanaco's various communities may have therefore sought to unite the city's constituents through the construction of a larger monument. Such a monument, a 128- by 119-meter platform known today as the Kalasasaya, was built on top of the founding families' compound located just to the west of the sunken temple (see fig. 8.2). The walls of the Kalasasaya were made of massive stone blocks, and in its center was a sunken courtyard that was surrounded by a series of small rooms (Couture 2002:314–315; Kolata 1993:143–145; Koons 2013:163; Vranich 2009:21).

The Kalasasaya, like previously built monuments in the Lake Titicaca Basin, would remain a work in progress throughout its use life (Vranich 2009:26). The act of building and renovating the monument brought disparate groups together on a regular basis, as did the ceremonies that collectively celebrated the earth gods and local ancestor cults. Yet if this was all that was done at Tiahuanaco, then it is likely that the settlement would have been as short-lived as previous centers in the basin. The innovation at the Kalasasaya—one shared with nearby Khonkho Wankane (Janusek 2012:123)—was the joining of the basin's long-established ritual practices with new ones that linked worshipers to distant mountains and, perhaps more importantly, the sky (Benitez 2009; Janusek 2006; Kolata 1993). The Kalasasaya, like Cahokia's Monks Mound, was thus both intelligible to visitors and also radically distinct.

Earlier religious centers in the Lake Titicaca Basin had been visually orientated toward local mountain ranges and thus appealed to only a subset of the basin's population. The creation of the Kalasasaya, however, marked the beginning of a reorientation of Tiahuanaco to an east–west axis that made reference to cyclical solar movements (Janusek 2006:477). This reorientation toward the sun was furthered a few decades later, when a solar observatory was added to the west side of the Kalasasaya (Benitez 2009:55–57). The many people who climbed the Kalasasaya's "wide and well-trodden" staircases therefore did so not only to propitiate their particular sets of ancestors but also to take part in "an emergent cult orientated to the sun and sky" (Janusek 2006:477,479).

The construction of the Kalasasaya was followed by a frenetic century of urbanization that would culminate soon after AD 600 with the building of the Akapana—a seven-tiered platform pierced by a deeply sunken court (Manzanilla 1992; Vranich 2009:25–26) (see fig. 8.2). The creation and never-ending renovations of Tiahuanaco's platforms, plazas, and courts were festive events that reaffirmed and strengthened social ties (e.g., Golden and Scherer 2013:405); people built a community not only through work but also through feasting, worship, and sacrifice. Tiahuanaco's ritual structures were meant to be experienced through movement: pilgrims walked together up stairwells, through portals, and into open spaces. Along this journey, care was taken to create sight lines that linked the architecture to distant peaks and the horizon (Conklin 1991).

There is "a tension of order and heterogeneity" evident at the site (Janusek 2008:132). Tiahuanaco's various monuments share both a basic east–west orientation and a recognizable architecture style, but each monument significantly differs in form and, likely, religious intent. There is also no discernable master plan in the layout of the city, even though households and plazas loosely mimic the orientation of the city's main monuments (Janusek 2002:41, 2004:135, 2008:133; Protzen and Nair 2013:16). Seen from above, the organization of the settlement suggests those moving to the settlement managed to embrace a Tiahuanaco way of doing things without sacrificing their distinct group identities. This impression is confirmed by excavations (Couture 2003, 2004; Couture and Sampek 2003; Janusek 2002, 2003, 2004, 2008; Marsh 2012b; Rivera Casanovas 2003).

As Tiahuanaco grew rapidly after AD 500, arriving families built largely self-sufficient compounds that were bound to the rest of the community by roads and canals. Each household in a compound had its own storage bins, animal pens, kitchens, and refuse dumps, and family members produced most of the food, textiles, and tools that they used on a daily basis (fig. 8.3).

Figure 8.3. Artist's reconstruction of a residential compound in La K'araña, a neighborhood at Tiahuanaco (courtesy of Alan L. Kolata, Proyecto Wila Jawira Archive).

The compounds also served as ritual spaces where people made sacrifices and buried their dead (Janusek 2008:155–156, 2009:167–169). Compounds were often clustered together into loosely organized neighborhoods that may have been formed by groups of migrants who settled in the city from various parts of the basin and beyond (Janusek 2012:135).

The high walls of the similarly orientated compounds would have created a certain visual symmetry across the settlement (Kolata 1993:165), and this architectural symmetry is mimicked in aspects of the artifact assemblage. There was, for example, a "striking uniformity" in the form and style of certain ceramic vessels after AD 500 (Janusek 2002:41). Everyone seemed to have had access to red-slipped, often highly decorated, bowls, cups, and pitchers that depicted stylized animal, human, mountain, and water motifs. Ceremonial wares, such as large basins and incense burners, were more rare but also found in most compounds across Tiahuanaco (Janusek 2002:43, table 1). One of the most common figures found on the new ceramic assemblage is a front-facing figure that may have been seen as a deity ancestral to all of the communities that lived in or visited the growing city (Janusek 2008:144).

A closer inspection of life in Tiahuanaco's compounds and neighborhoods nonetheless reveals a kaleidoscope of art styles, specialties, cuisines, social networks, and ethnicities lying beneath its surface uniformities (Glascock and Giesso 2012; Janusek 2002, 2004a, 2008). The residents of the Ch'iji Jawa neighborhood, for example, specialized in making large storage jars and serving vessels (Rivera Casanovas 2003:310). They also enjoyed wider access to maize than other neighborhoods (Wright et al. 2003:397) and maintained strong ties—at least stylistically—to Cochabamba and other valleys of southern Bolivia (Rivera Casanovas 2003:313). In contrast, those living in Mollo Kontu, another neighborhood in Tiahuanaco, favored meat over maize in their diet and also practiced a particular form of cranial modification (annular) that likely set them apart from their immediate neighbors (Valliéres 2012:172, 318). Behind compound walls, there thus seems to have been limited effort to assimilate, and the result was a bewildering heterogeneity in sights, sounds, and smells that would have rivaled those found in today's cities.

One of the most significant variations between compounds was in social status, a difference that widened as the city expanded. By the last decades of the seventh century AD, there were high-status groups living close to Tiahuanaco's main monuments—an area that had remained almost completely free of domestic compounds in the decades after the construction of the Kalasasaya (Couture and Sampeck 2003:263n6; Janusek 2012:135). The families that had moved into the monumental core of the site lived in bigger houses with paved plazas and extensive drainage networks. They consumed a greater range of both exotica and high-end local products, and at least some of their food was likely supplied by outside producers (Berryman 2010:236; Janusek 2004:153–157; Wright et. al. 2003:402).

These high-status families made efforts to play down Tiahuanaco's widening economic disparities. Those who settled in the Putuni area next to the Kalasasaya, for instance, were among the richest and most powerful individuals living at that time in the city. Yet massive exterior walls shielded their wealth from view, and the residential plan of the area's two compounds was "not readily distinguishable from that of non-elites" (Couture 2004:134). Certain artifacts and architectural embellishments found in the excavations would have served as status markers, but these objects were "subtle" in the way they distinguished Putuni residents "materially and symbolically" from other residents (Couture 2004:134; also see Couture and Sampek 2003:233–238). These data suggest that status differences, though readily apparent to everyone in the city, were not flaunted.

The glue that held Tiahuanaco together was the ceremonies conducted in and around its great monuments. Higher-status positions were in large part achieved, as they had long been in the Titicaca Basin, by organizing these ceremonies and then using them to assert a more privileged relationship to the sacred. Hundreds, if not thousands, gathered together to participate in building projects and witness "spectacular rites" replete with gifts, feasts, and, on rare occasion, human sacrifices (Blom and Janusek 2004:137). The participation of the heads of the various groups in these and other activities led to an "ever-tightening spiral of factional competition" among them (Goldstein 2003:166). Group heads slowly made themselves more central to worship, and eventually a subset of these leaders became comfortable enough in their positions to move into the monumental sectors of the settlement during the seventh and eighth centuries AD.

The heads of the various factions that composed the city took a hand in shaping Tiahuanaco's art and architecture to emphasize their increasingly essential role in Tiahuanaco religion (Janusek 2012:128–135). One glaring example of this tinkering was the placement of massive stone monoliths depicting high-status individuals in ceremonial garb in the Kalasasaya, sunken temple, and other monuments (Couture 2004:130). The statues became new focal points in these structures, and in their stone hands were often placed the two objects—a cup and snuff tablet—used to legitimate the elevated positions of those who organized activities (Janusek 2008:138; Kolata 1993:135–141; Torres 2002) (fig. 8.4).

The cups and snuff tablets depicted in the sculptures likely refer to the "competitive hospitality" of the leading families of Tiahuanaco, who sought to attract followers and repay debts by sponsoring events that featured copious amounts of food and drink (Goldstein 2003:166). The featured item at these events was almost certainly maize beer, and Paul Goldstein has argued that there was a significant shift in Tiahuanaco culinary practices after AD 500 toward increased beer production (Goldstein 2003). Although maize beer had been used in Lake Titicaca Basin ceremonial contexts since at least the time of Chiripa (Logan et al. 2012:248), the amount of maize consumed at Tiahuanaco skyrocketed during the sixth century AD. Of the crop remains found across the site, 25 percent were from maize—a startling percentage when one remembers that the plant grows poorly at this elevation (Wright et al. 2003:393).

The people who stumbled back to their compounds or villages after these events—perhaps gingerly carrying keros and other Tiwanaku-style gifts—were perhaps both drunk and high (Janusek 2008:167). Psychotropic plants had been in use in the Lake Titicaca Basin since the end of the first millennium BC (Hastorf 2005:89; Janusek 2008:222), but the residents of Tiahuanaco took this to new levels. Snuff tubes, spoons, and trays have been found throughout the settlement, and were likely associated with ceremonies honoring each household's ancestors (Janusek 2008:161). Yet the monoliths placed in the city's monuments suggest that higher-status individuals may have been conceived of as powerful shamans with a special connection to the divine world (Arnold and Hastorf 2008:192). Their status was perhaps affirmed by their greater access to *Anadenanthera* and other psychotropic plants that grew in the Amazon jungle and the eastern slopes of the Andes, as well as by their possession more generally of exotica that signaled links to far-off worlds (e.g., Helms 1993).

Figure 8.4. The Ponce Monolith depicting an elite holding a cup and snuff tablet (courtesy of Andrew Roddick).

The social hierarchy that emerged within the city's various communities from the sixth through the eighth centuries was accepted because it was represented as benefiting the broader public (Janusek 2008:167). Leaders had downplayed rising social differences for most of Tiahuanaco's history by presenting themselves as "first among equals" (Couture 2004:143) and couching their positions as integral to the efficacy of the ceremonies that took place in the community. They worked for the people, beholden in particular to their respective descent groups. This egalitarian ethos, however, was being stretched to the breaking point as the gap between high-status and low-status groups continued to widen.

A new strategy was therefore employed after AD 800 by Tiahuanaco's leaders that stressed radical class distinctions that crosscut the city's ethnic divisions. A high-status group built homes at this time on top of the Kalasasaya and Akapana platforms (Janusek 2012:135; Manzanilla 1992:54–70), while another group razed the two Putuni compounds to create a highly visible palace and ritual platform (Couture and Sampek 2003:248–259). These and many other efforts transformed the urban core into a space that was ostentatiously dedicated to serving the interests of the settlement's most powerful families (Janusek 2008:148). At the same time, a courtly style developed that linked the city's leaders together into a single elite class, which was now supported by a growing group of bureaucrats and specialists (Burkholder 2002:245; Couture 2004:142–143; Janusek 2008:148–150). Although everyone had ostensibly been equals immediately after Tiahuanaco's founding, after AD 800, any pretense of equality was forgotten.

The growth of elite power during the ninth and tenth century AD derived in large part from the intensification of the ritually charged feasting, drinking, and ceremonies that had periodically brought different groups together (Janusek 2009:171). Elites strove to underwrite these activities through the capture of labor that was now more directly administered rather than cajoled from producers working in compounds throughout the city and beyond. Elites ramped up their sponsorship of the mass production of ceramics and other objects to give away to guests and had more and more of the food and beer consumed at events produced in dedicated kitchen facilities located in the city's monumental core. Elites also likely sought to circumvent well-ensconced intermediaries and directly sponsor more of the llama caravans that brought obsidian, maize, hallucinogens, and prestige goods into the site (Glascock and Giesso 2012:94; Janusek 2008:148–153; Smith and Janusek 2013:13).

Tiahuanaco's ritual festivals, at one time more akin to a potluck where everyone brings something to the table, were reframed as patron-client feasts (e.g., Dietler 2001:82–85 and Jennings and Chatfield 2009:218–221). In return for their lavish hospitality, the newly united elites demanded increasing power over the affairs of those living in and around the city (Janusek 2005:170, 2008:166–167). Life changed in the city, as its previously atomized, largely kin-based political, economic, and social ties were reconfigured. The first clear indications of a Tiwanaku state—one that matches the common definition used in this book—appear in the ninth century AD with the rise of this controlling elite and can best be seen in the reorganization of settlements and subsistence practices in parts of the Titicaca Basin.

Creating a Countryside

At the time Pukara reached its height in the late first millennium BC in the northern Lake Titicaca Basin, the southern part of the basin was quiet. The people who would form Tiahuanaco lived in in mobile groups or in small, dispersed villages that hugged bodies of water and subsisted by fishing, foraging, farming, and hunting (e.g., Moore et al. 1999). Though they came together periodically at small ritual centers like Chiripa, these groups were autonomous and there is no evidence for significant regional economic integration (Bandy 2006:229; Chávez 2012:447). This independence dissipated after AD 200, when increased rainfall in the basin encouraged inland settlement (Abbott et al. 1997:178). As populations moved into the surrounding piedmont and marshy valley bottoms, farming and herding became more important parts of the subsistence economy (Janusek 2008:177). Households after AD 200 still strove to reduce risk by maintaining access to a diverse range of resources, but in a landscape filling in with people there were now greater efforts to improve agricultural and pastoral yields by increasing specialization, decreasing fallow periods, altering grazing schedules, and intensifying the use of once-marginal lands (Bandy 2005:287; Bruno 2014:140; Chávez 2012:448; Stanish 2003:109–110).

The inland villages followed earlier settlement patterns in clustering around newly founded ritual centers like Tiahuanaco (each with populations in the high hundreds) that catered to the needs of both local kin groups and more mobile populations (Bandy 2006:232; McAndrews et al. 1997:71; Smith and Pérez Arias 2015:115). The fact that very few hoes have been found at these small centers suggests that residents were supplied with at least some of their food by surrounding farmers (Giesso 2003:374). Farmers likely voluntarily ramped up their production in order to supply what was needed because of the perceived benefits of the ceremonies that took place in these communities.

Tiahuanaco's growth during the fifth century AD appears to have been fueled by a depopulation of the surrounding area (Mathews 2003:127; McAndrews et al. 1997:73; but see Bandy 2013:84). Why so many people chose to move into this particular ceremonial center at this time remains unclear, but the large-scale abandonment of the land around Tiahuanaco was perhaps the first crisis faced by the leaders of the various groups who were moving into the city. The countryside that began forming around the settlement, as well as another growing center called Lukurmata to the north (Bermann 1994), was a patchwork of locally organized villages, fields, and grazing lands that were likely affiliated with different groups residing in Tiahuanaco (Albarracin-Jordan 1996:204–205, 2003:111; Erickson 1993:33).

The villages in the valleys around Tiahuanaco were organized into clusters that surrounded larger sites that contained platform mounds and sunken courts (Albarracin-Jordan 1996:196). These clusters, at least initially, seem to have operated independently of each other and of Tiahuanaco (Isbell and Burkholder 2002:232; McAndrews et al. 1997:80; Park 2001:126). Iwawi, for example, was a long-established local center on the shore of Lake Titicaca that served as a port for receiving many of the andesite blocks used to build parts of the great monuments of Tiahuanaco (Isbell and Burkholder 2002:231; Janusek et al. 2013). The flow of building material into Tiahuanaco might suggest a close affiliation between it and Iwani, but those living at Iwawi seem to have enjoyed wide-ranging exchange networks that were independent of Tiahuanaco, and they may have even hesitated to embrace Tiwanaku art styles until after AD 600 (Burkholder 1997:223, 225). Whatever misgivings those living at Iwawi may have had about Tiahuanaco's rising clout, they were nonetheless inexorably drawn with the rest of the southern basin into an increasingly specialized regional economy whose center was the city (Isbell and Burkholder 2002:230; Park 2001:125).

As Tiahuanaco grew, settlements throughout the southern Titicaca Basin intensified craft production or concentrated on acquiring greater quantities of a particular resource. Residents of the aptly named Obsidiana, for example, manufactured obsidian tools, while those living in TMV-332 bred guinea pigs for food (Janusek 2008:173). In the case of Iwawi, residents began targeting a particular species of *Orestias* after the founding of Tiahuanaco, although they continued to use traditional fishing methods. Intensified extraction led to overexploitation, evidenced through the increased targeting of smaller-sized fish (Capriles 2013:115). The fish caught at Iwawi were likely exchanged throughout the region in exchange for Tiwanaku-style ceramics, camelid meat, and other items desired by those living in the port (Isbell and Burkholder 2002:232; Park 2001:125).

The resource intensification required to sustain the urban residents of Tiahuanaco and Lukurmata led to widespread landscape modification in the southern Titicaca Basin. The most dramatic of these changes was the introduction of raised agricultural fields across more than 200 square kilometers of marshy lands that had previously been largely unusable for agriculture (Bandy 2005:271). Raised fields had been cultivated before in this part of the basin, but they were not common because of the considerable labor required to dig out water canals and then pile the earth to form platforms on which crops could be grown (Erickson and Candler 1989:239). The need for more food after urbanization, however, encouraged the creation of raised fields, especially since the way in which these fields were irrigated allowed them to be harvested earlier in the year than crops grown on dry land. Additional food could therefore be grown in the region "while minimizing interference with household subsistence activities" (Bandy 2005:290).

The raised fields, like the other intensified and specialized practices that developed in the region during the sixth century AD, seemed to have been locally organized—groups of farmers appear to have independently managed their particular field sections (Erickson 1993:33; Janusek 2008:190). There is no evidence that Tiahuanaco coerced inhabitants of surrounding villages, nor does it seem the rapidly expanding and still deeply subdivided city sought to manage the countryside. Many of those living at Tiahuanaco, as well as the smaller Lukurmata, likely had considerable influence over different groups in the basin by virtue of their kin ties and their association with the city's sacred spaces, yet it appears that urban residents initially survived because many outsiders voluntarily chose to work longer and take on more risky subsistence strategies. In return, they participated in Tiahuanaco's religious events, received Tiwanaku-style wares, and tapped into the long-distance exchange networks that passed through the city (Janusek 2008:203–204).

With subsistence and resource demands outgrowing the production capacity of surrounding valleys by the seventh century AD, Tiahuanaco groups began establishing a number of alliances and colonial enclaves around the lake that could be used to bring in additional resources (Smith and Janusek 2014; Stanish 2003, 2009; Stanish et al. 2005). The most important of these colonies may have been in the Puno Bay on the northwest shore of Lake Titicaca, where a number of distinct groups from the city set up adjacent settlements, each with their own platforms and sunken courts

(Stanish 2003:186–188). Some of the colonists came to the Puno Bay in order to exploit its silver veins (Schultze 2013), but most were likely involved in the creation and cultivation of a vast stretch of raised fields that was expanded after the founding of Tiahuanaco (Erickson 1993).

The relationship of most people living outside of the southern Lake Titicaca Basin to Tiahuanaco was "based on communications and trade rather than direct economic or political control" (Janusek 2008:218; also see Smith and Janusek 2014), and the power of the enclaves themselves was "limited in scope" (Stanish 2009:155). Many of the people living outside colonial enclaves enjoyed occasional access to exotica and regional goods, embraced many of the religious principles espoused in the city, and likely had even been there on a pilgrimage. Those who lived next to Tiahuanaco colonists enjoyed even deeper connections with the city, and their fortunes would have become increasingly entangled with that of the city over time. Local leaders may have tolerated colonial intrusions both because the newcomers were relatively noninvasive in their land use—colonies were often on islands, and colonists may have accessed lands that had been only marginally used before (see Stanish 2003:180–189)—and, more importantly, because they believed that the rituals and other events that they participated in at Tiahuanaco improved their own livelihoods.

Yet the escalating resource demands of Tiahuanaco eventually exceeded the largess of the various groups living in the southern Lake Titicaca Basin (Capriles 2013; Mathews 2003; Seddon 2005). The shift toward a celebration of elite status in the city around AD 800 was paralleled by a radical transformation in Tiahuanaco's relationship with these surrounding groups. To a greater degree than in Cahokia, Harappa, or Jenne-jeno this shift led to outright "overexploitation in land use, material resources, and human labor" (Janusek 2008:191). The biggest change was the dramatic decline of Lukurmata, the sister settlement of Tiahuanaco that had boasted its own monuments and associated settlements. The valley where Lukurmata sat was transformed into "a prime agricultural estate" of Tiahuanaco that was covered with raised fields and inhabited by workers living in "moveable tent-like structures" (Janusek 2004:235–236).

The locally managed countryside that had developed around the city was literally broken apart and reassembled as settlements were abandoned, discrete field systems joined, regional transportation networks created, and storage complexes inaugurated (Janusek 2004:232; 2008:192). To meet their needs, the elites of Tiahuanaco orchestrated a far-reaching economic and political transformation of nearby settlements and subsistence systems. They acquired a significant degree of control over the surrounding region during the ninth century AD and in the process created a well-integrated polity that can be called a state in the way that we have defined it in this book.

The reverberations of state formation on those living elsewhere in the Lake Titicaca Basin remain unclear because of a lack of excavations and inadequate chronological control. It appears that relationship with colonies may have also been increasingly formalized at this time, as more and more resources were required from these locales (Stanish 2003, 2009; Stanish et al. 2005). While places like the Puno Bay were being turned into agricultural estates, the autonomous groups living outside of the southern basin were likely becoming more closely linked to Tiahuanaco through the creation of a "pan-regional pilgrimage complex" that further tied the status of local leaders to their connections to Tiahuanaco's elite (Stanish 2003:201).

The Island of the Sun offers a good example of the form this pilgrimage complex took. The island was an important sacred center that initially had only weak ties to the city (Seddon 1998:464), until after AD 800, when a Tiahuanaco-inspired platform was built over the island's major ritual site. The platform—a miniature version of the Kalasasaya (Seddon 1998:465)—was built at the same time as people on the island began to embrace Tiwanaku-style ceramics and throw incense burners and gold into the lake as offerings (Seddon 2005; Reinhard 1992). The platform provided a ritual space for the all of the island's population, but it also included a prominent enclosed space that local leaders could use to underline their close relationship with Tiahuanaco (Seddon 1998:467).

Tiahuanaco's rise was linked to its populism—it was a site where everyone could participate in religious celebrations—but this embrace of populism was joined in the ninth century AD by a new emphasis on exclusion and elite privilege that resonated with local leaders across the basin who wanted to further solidify their positions through preferential access to Tiwanaku objects and ideas. The conversion of the Island of the Sun into a subsidiary ritual center was in the state's interest, but there is little to indicate that the island's residents were compelled to undertake this conversion through coercion or even economic dependency (Seddon 1998:470). Those in power on the island, as well as colonists and locals elsewhere in the basin (e.g., de la Vega 2005:132; Hill 2013:42), promoted the city's dominant position in the basin's sacred landscape largely out of self-interest—their success and that of the city were becoming increasingly intertwined.

Caravans, Colonization, and the Creation of the Middle Horizon

As Tiahuanaco expanded, more and more resources from the Lake Titicaca Basin were required in order to maintain the city. No amount of regional specialization and resource intensification, however, could provide Tiahuanaco with maize beer and psychotropic drugs, the two critical ingredients in the feasts and rituals that tied the people of the basin to the city. *Anadenanthera colubrine*, *Nicotiana tabacum*, and the other psychotropic plants likely used in the city's ceremonies only grew in the lower elevations of the jungle and eastern flanks of the Andes (Angelo Z. and Capriles 2004:1027–1029), and the maize varieties routinely consumed in the city came from distant valleys that were warmer and wetter than the Altiplano (Hastorf et al. 2006:442–443).

Tiahuanaco's urban expansion in the sixth century AD quickly overwhelmed the preexisting interregional trade networks that brought these and other coveted goods like obsidian, coca, furs, salt, and honey into the basin (Glascock and Giesso 2012:94; Stanish et al. 2010:528). As demand for outside resources grew, the city's "centripetal pull" brought widespread social, political, and economic changes to llama caravan routes (Vining 2011:340; also see Janusek and Smith 2013). The Suches region, for example, is located along what was a well-traveled corridor linking Lake Titicaca to the Pacific Coast. Tiahuanaco's rise led to the fragmentation of villages in Suches; some families from the area moved to the city, while others established independent households in prime pastoral lands (Vining 2011:342). Those who remained in the region were not compelled to change their lifestyles—there is no evidence for intrusive colonies along this corridor, and the few Tiwanaku-style sherds that have been found there are located in what would have been open-air stopover sites for caravans (Stanish et al. 2010:530–531). Suches families instead recognized that they could profit by increasing the size of their llama and alpaca herds in order to provide wool, meat, and transport to those moving up and down the mountains (Vining 2011:346).

The people living to the south along the central Altiplano trade route that connected Lake Titicaca to salt and maize-growing regions likewise responded to Tiahuanaco's growth by placing greater emphasis on camelid pastoralism. They sent high-yield cuts of meat out of their settlements and adjusted their herding strategies to yield older herds in order to optimize transportation and wool production. In return for these products, they enjoyed increased access to Tiwanaku-style ceramics and imported stone (Capriles 2011:319). The changes in the central Altiplano, as in the Suches region, were locally driven "adjustments and responses to the changing political and economic conditions of the south central Andes as opposed to dispositions imposed by the state" (Capriles 2011:319).

Tiahuanaco influence was strongest at the end points of caravan routes, where traders would have spent more time in local communities. In most cases, travelers from the basin did not stay long in these destinations (Beaule 2002:188; Knudson 2007:18; Stovel 2002:388; Nielsen 2013:405; Uribe and Agüero 2002:421). The traders arrived with ceramics, textiles, snuff tablets, and other coveted goods and then returned home laden with maize, honey, and other items produced locally or obtained through traders arriving from other destinations. As the goods produced in or around Tiahuanaco entered regional trade networks, they were widely dispersed, and a cultural horizon was created in the south-central Andes by groups emulating the Tiwanaku style and embracing certain Tiahuanaco ideas regarding status, religion, and cuisine (Browman 1997; Goldstein 2003; Knudson and Torres-Rouff 2014; Nielsen 2013; Salazar et al. 2014; Tarragó 2006; Torres-Rouff 2008) (fig. 8.5).

People from the Lake Titicaca Basin also colonized a handful of locations with particularly high agricultural potential. Although evidence for colonization in some places is equivocal (e.g., Anderson 2009; Higueras-Hare 1996; Lucas 2012), Tiahuanaco-affiliated groups at least settled in the Pacific coast valleys of Azapa and Moquegua by as early as the mid- to late sixth century AD (Goldstein 1996, 2005:132; Rivera Díaz 1987; Focacci Aste 1981; cf. Cassman 1997, Sutter 2005, and Korpisaari et al. 2014, who suggest instead that colonists did not arrive in Azapa before AD 1000). Those moving into Azapa were likely higher-status traders; they founded three small villages in an area that had large local population (Goldstein 1996:68, 2005:108). Tiwanaku styles were widely emulated in Azapa for the next 400 years, and once on the coast, the colonists were able to extend their trade contacts beyond those that they retained with the Lake Titicaca Basin. These connections, coupled with Tiahuanaco's prestige as a ritual center, translated into "a dominant political influence" that was used to ensure access to the valley's agricultural products (Goldstein and Rivera 2004:176).

Extensive research in Moquegua has identified a more dynamic colonial engagement in this region. The valley's first colonists were small groups of mobile pastoralists who settled at the terminus of a caravan route leading up into the mountains. They lived in tentlike structures, stored little, and used a ceramic assemblage quite similar to that used by residents of the southwestern shore of Lake Titicaca (Goldstein 2005:153–154, 2009:290). If these colonists had designs on establishing a trading enclave, then they must have met up with a local population that was not particularly interested in developing a rapport with them (Goldstein 2009:290). Yet the colonists stayed in the region, growing a few crops and frequently returning to where they had grown up.

Figure 8.5. Drinking cups from Cochabamba, Bolivia, that reflect not only strong Tiwanaku stylistic influence but also the acceptance of Tiahuanaco ways of drinking (Karen Anderson).

A second wave of colonists arrived in Moquegua from the Lake Titicaca region by the end of the eighth century AD. Settling adjacent to arable land, these colonists built substantial dwellings, stone-line storage cists, and extensive irrigation systems (Goldstein 2005:211–217). They were not there to trade but rather to grow and export maize (Hastorf et al. 2006:443), as evidenced by both the concentration of processing tools found at the site and the elevated consumption of the crop documented in their bones (Goldstein 2005:218–219; Sandness 1992:51). This new wave of colonists came from a variety of places in the Lake Titicaca Basin. They lived in separate household groups in Moquegua and sent maize, as well as coca and cotton, to contacts in their parent communities (Goldstein 2013:378; Knudson 2008:15).

Moquegua felt the effect of the Tiwanaku state when a sunken court temple complex was constructed in Omo in the ninth century AD (Goldstein 1993). The temple's open courts could be used to host ceremonies that affirmed the spiritual link of all colonists to the city, but its inner chambers were likely reserved for more exclusionary affairs that buttressed local status positions by emphasizing their closer connection to the divine (Goldstein 2005:303–304). The temple was the voice of the state—embodied by an oracle object that was attended by what may have been city-appointed priests (Kjolsing 2013:78)—but it was a voice that could work only through the preexisting social networks that linked Moquegua to a variety of communities in the Lake Titicaca Basin (Goldstein 2013:379). The state could actually do little in either Moquegua or Azapa to compel colonists to increase exports.

Collapse

The Tiahuanaco state fell apart abruptly at the end of the tenth century AD. Construction of the city's monuments—an act of ritual renewal that had gone on in different locales for more than 500 years—ceased circa AD 1000 (Janusek 2008:294; cf. Yaeger and Vranich 2013:143 for an earlier date). At around the same time, the elite residences surrounding the monuments were systematically destroyed after an abrupt abandonment; camelid meat was left unprepared and "literally hundreds of large storage vessels were left behind" (Couture and Sampeck 2003:259). This destruction was part of an "iconoclastic frenzy" that swept across the city, leaving portals and sculptures shattered and defaced (Goldstein 2005:322; also see Owen 2005:71). People left the city over the next 150 years; one neighborhood after the next was abandoned until Tiahuanaco shrank to about 3 percent of its former size (Janusek 2008:294).

The iconoclastic frenzy that toppled the city's elites was felt across the basin as state-affiliated sites were deserted by the beginning of the second millennium AD (Stanish 2003:203). The fury against the state was particularly strong in its most distant colonies. As Paul Goldstein notes, provincials "toppled walls, uprooted idols, smashed the finely cut stones of their own temples and systematically sacked elite tombs in Azapa and Moquegua. Even storage and domestic areas were not immune to this fury, and whole towns were reduced to 'rockpiles' by a systematic process of deliberate destruction" (2005:322). Those living in the colonies, along with perhaps some groups in the Lake Titicaca Basin, then splintered into smaller groups that migrated to different valleys, extending and deepening the Tiwanaku cultural horizon even as the city itself fell into disrepute and its symbolic ties to outside groups withered (Albarracin-Jordan et al. 2015; Korpusaari et al. 2014; Owen 2005).

Why the state collapsed when it did remains unclear. Decreased rainfall beginning near the end of the eleventh century AD may have hastened the final abandonment of Tiahuanaco (Kolata et al. 2000), but there is little evidence that climate change or any other external factor played a major role in the state's demise. Perhaps the roots of the collapse can instead be traced to two centuries earlier when elites consolidated their power and made themselves the primary interlocutors between the public and the divine. Tiahuanaco's success had been built on deeply held traditions of communalism grounded in local kin ties. A hierarchical structure was tolerated as long as higher-status individuals were seen as working for the public's benefit. This "enduring etiquette of social values" was strained as the city's elites sought to monopolize what had previously been community-organized systems of agriculture, long-distance exchange, craft production, and religion (Janusek 2008:298).

To facilitate a rocky societal transformation, elites had chosen to further embellish public ceremonies (Janusek 2009:171). More and more natural resources were therefore being demanded by the city during the ninth and tenth centuries from a region already strained to the breaking point

(Bandy 2005:291; Capriles 2013:115). Producers living outside of the Lake Titicaca Basin—long tied to the city through relationships with particular families or traders—had few allegiances to the state and would have been understandably hesitant to overexploit their own lands for the benefit of those living far away. As conditions worsened in the Lake Titicaca Basin, there was a crisis of faith (Albarracin-Jordan et al. 2015:859; Goldstein 2005:322).

Tiahuanaco's monuments had been constructed to engage with ancestors, local deities, the earth, mountains, and celestial bodies whose collective benevolence ensured a well-functioning society (Kolata 1993). Everyone had come together to build these monuments: they celebrated rituals together and moved en masse through the city's portals, courts, and platforms that linked the monuments to higher powers (Vranich 2009). When high-status individuals first placed their likeness at the heart of these monuments and then restricted access to certain locations altogether, they established a hierarchy that was legitimated through a privileged access to the sacred. As an exhausted Lake Titicaca Basin stopped giving, people would have questioned the efficacy of the rituals conducted at Tiahuanaco. Elites doubled down in reply, sponsoring more outlandish rituals that placed further strain on available resources. Eventually, these elites would bear the brunt of society's rage when urban life proved unsustainable.

A Tiahuanaco Civilization

Alan L. Kolata describes Tiahuanaco and other early cities as "unstable and evanescent," each being composed of "a dynamic congeries of political, economic, and social institutions that is shaped and reshaped by historical circumstances" (1993:87). Kolata's words echo the "the ungainly process of becoming" emphasized in this volume (Kaplan 2012:56), but his book on balance presents a vision of Tiahuanaco that often does not engage with this dynamism. Like many other authors, he instead spends much of his time talking about the city at its height with every structure completed and fully functioning (see Isbell and Vranich 2004:169). Urbanization as a process is obscured in these treatments and what remains is *the* ancient city of Tiahuanaco.

Essentializing Tiahuanaco is understandable. Chronological control, though better than in most regions of the Andes, remains poor for the Lake Titicaca Basin, and blending data from throughout the site's occupation history allows for a more complete picture of the city. Yet the idea of *the* city is often quickly followed by the idea of *the* state and the idea of *the* civilization—an often-unconscious slide that brings us back to a conceptualization of the past in terms of an abrupt, steplike transition to stages of cultural development, which I have suggested is fundamentally flawed. Tiahuanaco scholars often refer to a Tiwanaku civilization, and it did indeed possess many, but not all, of the characteristics in Childe's classic list of traits defining a civilization. Tiwanaku's failure to meet our expectations for civilization should not be surprising at this point in the book, nor should it be surprising that a few of Childe's traits predate the founding of Tiahuanaco by hundreds of years. The civilization concept once again drapes poorly over an unwieldy data set—yet the concept still lingers.

Bruce Trigger's recent repositioning of the civilization concept does little better in the contexts of our case studies. In his civilizations, "class displaced kinship and ethnicity as the main organizing principal of society," "power was based primarily on the control of agricultural surpluses," "centralized governments possessed ultimate control over justice and the use of force," and "the ruling class was able to exert various forms of coercion" (2003:47). This is not what life was like during most of Cahokia's, Harappa's, and Jenne-jeno's occupations. Centralization, coercion, class divisions, and direct control over production, when they occurred at all, often led to the decline of these and other early cities, a phenomena that is most clear with the rise of the state in Tiahuanaco.

Tiahuanaco developed out of a 1,500-year-old tradition of ceremonial centers in the Lake Titicaca Basin. Worship in the region—and one's very identity—was profoundly kin-based and local. When people came together from different communities to participate in feasts, sacrifices, and other events at centers, they celebrated a shared sense of how the world worked and the ways in which the sacred should be engaged. Yet at the same time, these events reinforced existing social differences, since each group worshiped their own particular set of ancestors and deities (Hastorf 2003:327; Roddick et al. 2014:154). Larger centers like Pukara managed to bring together thousands of people, but the basin's population remained divided among many localized, kin-based religious cults until the middle of the first millennium AD (Janusek 2006:486).

Drawing from previous practices in Khonkho Wankane, the creation of the Kalasasaya and subsequent monuments in Tiahuanaco changed the rules of the game by creating a religious cosmology that "meshed imposing natural features with timeless solar cycles" (Janusek 2006:469). Focusing on distant peaks and beyond would lead to the formation of an unprecedented basin-wide Tiwanaku identity in the coming centuries, but this identity was layered on top of a society still very much organized around local, kin-based ties. These were the ties that people leaned on as Tiahuanaco rapidly urbanized during the sixth century AD, and the rich mosaic of ethnicities, craft specializations, and ritual spaces that developed in the settlement is a reflection of the variety of migrants living and working within their own compounds (Janusek 2002, 2003, 2004, 2008). Compartmentalization, as well as ritual elaboration, reduced scalar stress and allowed the city to thrive.

Lineage heads, with privileged access to both sacred knowledge and exotica, enjoyed higher status long before the founding of Tiahuanaco (Stanish 2003:164). As Tiahuanaco grew, the elastic boundaries of kin ties likely stretched—basal-unit sizes expanded—such that more people came under the sway of a particular leader. This person's status was maintained through interactions with his, or perhaps more rarely her, extended kin group. The "ever-tightening spiral of factional competition" in Tiahuanaco pitted these groups against each other in public ceremonies and monument building, which in turn increased production demands on both city residents and those affiliated with the site in the growing countryside (Goldstein 2003:166). Yet there is little evidence for coercion or centralization in Tiahuanaco during its first centuries. Control over the population was instead weak, fragile, and fragmented. Each of the lineage heads were more akin to the Big Men of Oceania, constantly struggling to ensure personal loyalty and amass a "fund of power" through gift giving, spectacle, feasting, marriage, and other means (Malinowski 1921, 1922; Sahlins 1963).

The origins of the Tiwanaku state can be traced back to the efforts of these leaders to create ties between themselves that cut across kinship boundaries. This new set of ties likely grew out of their coordination of public events and would have been reinforced as high-status families began to live in closer proximity to Tiahuanaco's monumental core. As lineage heads found it increasingly difficult to meet escalating demands for local and long-distance products through existing mechanisms during the eight century AD, they appear to have severed many of the kin ties that had brought them to power in order to create a more centralized, extractive political economy that meets both our definition for a state and Trigger's more narrow definition of civilization. This state, however, was short-lived, as efforts to build a strong sense of a class-based community ultimately failed. Beer, drugs, and public spectacles were not enough to keep the city together.

Our deeply held, though often unconscious, adherence to the civilization concept makes us want to see the Tiahuanaco state as having formed when aggregation first began in the region. Yet a critical look at the data from the basin reveals that the state replaced a far more heterarchical, segmentary regional polity that had first grown up around the city. Colonization, the intensification of long-distance exchange, and the extension of a Tiahuanaco cultural horizon were not products of a Tiwanaku state but had instead developed 300 years earlier when people began cobbling together a Tiahuanaco-based polity by reworking preexisting practices to tackle new problems. An abrupt, steplike transition to a civilization stage therefore did not occur at Tiahuanaco. Nor did such a transition occur in Mexico's Monte Albán, our final case study and perhaps *the* type site for 1970s neoevolutionary models of cultural evolution.

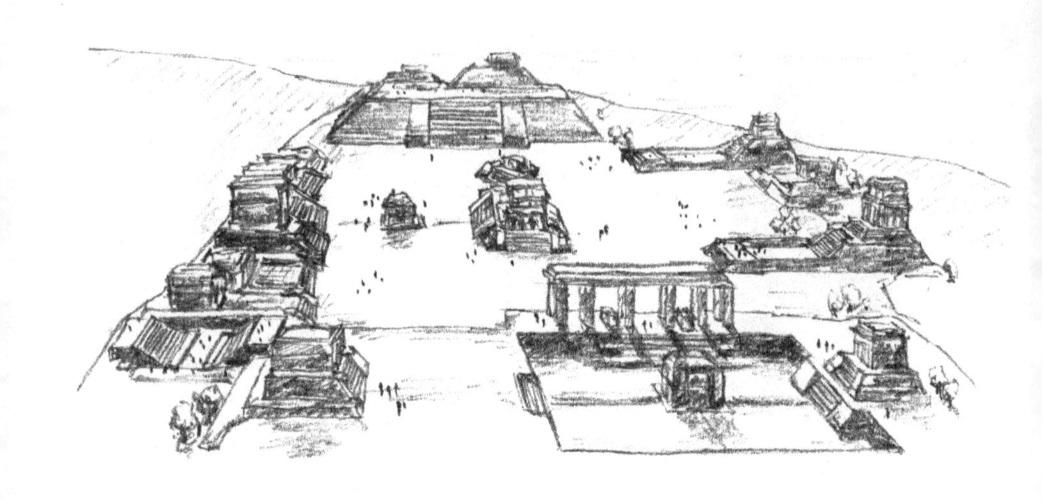

9

MONTE ALBÁN AND THE MAKING OF A ZAPOTEC STATE

MEXICO'S OAXACA VALLEY HAS BEEN CALLED "A LABORATORY for the study of social evolution" (Marcus and Flannery 1996:23). Archaeological research in the well-studied valley started in the nineteenth century, and work in the mid-twentieth century by Alfonso Caso, Ignacio Bernal, and others laid the groundwork for a now well-understood chronological sequence that began with mobile hunter-gatherers and culminated with the rise of the Zapotec state (Blanton et al. 1999; Flannery and Marcus, eds. 1983; Whitecotton 1977). By means of conquest, colonization, and influence, this state impacted life across 20,000 square kilometers of rugged sierra. It was anchored in Monte Albán, a city that in AD 500 was home to as many as 30,000 people (Blanton et al. 1993:9; Marcus and Flannery 1996:206).

The Oaxaca Valley became a laboratory for the study of social evolution in 1966, when Kent Flannery launched a three-decade-long research project in the area (Flannery, ed. 1976, 1986; Flannery and Marcus, eds. 1983; Marcus and Flannery 1996). Flannery was, and remains, a committed evolutionist. He coined the term "step-like" to describe transitions between evolutionary stages that has been frequently referenced in this book (1972:423), and the extensive, well-published accounts of greater Oaxaca fieldwork that were conducted by him, his contemporaries, and two generations of former students all seek to advance the evolutionary paradigm of processual archaeology.

The title of Joyce Marcus and Kent Flannery's popular book on Oaxaca archaeology, *Zapotec Civilization: How Urban Society Evolved in Mexico's*

Oaxaca Valley (1996), holds true to the evolutionary goals that both archaeologists held when they started working in the region. Marcus and Flannery sought a New World civilization with clear local antecedents that could help them further refine a universal model of culture change, and so they exhaustively explored the origins of the city, the state, writing, inequality, and craft specialization in Oaxaca. The creation of the city of Monte Albán was seen as the clearest indicator that the Zapotecs had indeed reached a civilization stage of development, thus making it comparable to Egypt, Mesopotamia, and other Old World examples.

Marcus and Flannery's book, however, is not a spirited defense of universal models and the usefulness of evolutionary stages. After telling the reader to "sit down, reach out for a shot of mescal and a plate of carnitas, and get ready for a surprise," they sketch out an "evolution without stages" that "forces us to investigate the specific cultural and historical contexts in which the actors were shaped and their decisions were made" (1996:236, 244). This monumental shift in theory advanced by two leading evolutionary archaeologists, so bracing as to require a shot of hard liquor, was not absolute—they still saw stages as at least "heuristically useful" (1996:236; also see Flannery and Marcus 2012)—yet it was nonetheless a testament to how the accumulated data from Oaxaca pushed against their long-held preconceptions. Explicitly thinking in discrete stages of cultural development could not be maintained in the face of overwhelming evidence to the contrary.

Marcus and Flannery's newfound focus on individuals, problem solving, and historical context resonates with many of the themes explored in this book. Yet the word "civilization" still lingers in the title of their book, and in this chapter I argue that the civilization concept continues to distort our understanding of Zapotec urbanization, state formation, colonization, and the spread of cultural horizons. Old habits die hard. Though perhaps more hidden from view than in some of our previous case studies, the golem still lumbers onward in Oaxaca, even in the work of those opposed to the application of evolutionary approaches in the region (e.g., Joyce 2004, 2009; Joyce and Winter 1996).

It is important to stress that Zapotec archaeologists have emphasized more than most scholars the unintended consequences of the ungainly becoming of early cities (e.g., Joyce and Winter 1996; Redmond and Spencer 2012). They have pointed to the substantial changes in Monte Albán's urban organization over time (Joyce 2004) and have argued that early raids and colonizations were integral to creating the state (Spencer and Redmond 2006). The full implications of these insights, however, are often left unrealized because the Zapotec data are seen through a stubborn interpretive lens that still links the origins of a civilization to the founding of Monte Albán. Zapotec scholars—often unconsciously—continue to bundle together processes in ways that meet deeply held expectations for what the past *should* be like based on thinking in stages.

The Oaxaca Valley before Monte Albán

The Oaxaca Valley is a rare expanse of arable land within the rugged topography of the southern highlands of Mexico (fig. 9.1). The 95-kilometer-long, Y-shaped valley was heavily forested by 8000 BC, and the people who lived in the valley after this time were mobile hunter-gatherers who exploited a wide variety of wild plants and animals during the course of seasonal rounds. Although living most of the year with next of kin, Oaxaca-based families periodically came together into larger groups for exchanges, rituals, and other activities. The valley's population slowly incorporated corn, beans, squash, and other domesticates into their diet over the next few thousand years. When some groups began shifting their subsistence regimes toward full-time agriculture by 2000 BC, they settled into permanent villages of 50 to 100 residents (Marcus and Flannery 1996:73).

The valley's lower elevation and moister microclimate also attracted agriculturalists from the surrounding region. The earliest villages were located near the floodplain, where the thickest and richest soils were located. New settlers cut down trees to claim other parts of the floodplain, as did splinter groups from already established villages that had grown too big. As time wore on, deforestation and population increases limited the availability of wild resources and pushed people into an even greater reliance on agriculture. With the best land in Oaxaca already spoken for by the second half of the second millennium BC, people had to figure out how to live in larger communities or move into the less desirable piedmont with its sloping terrain and thinner soils. With one prominent exception, people chose to move (Blanton et al. 1993:55, 1999:31; Marcus and Flannery 1996:73–75).

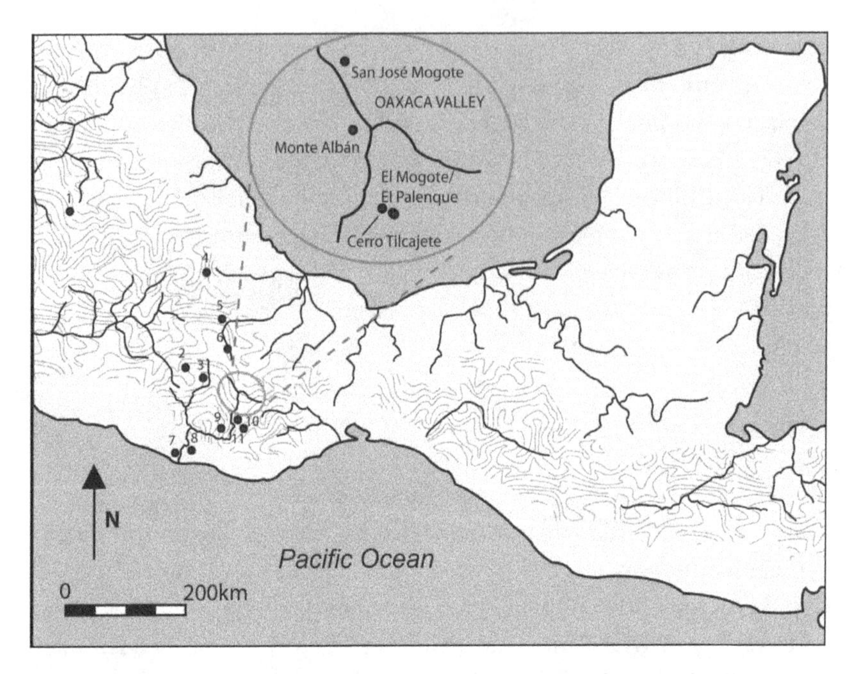

Figure 9.1. Map of Mesoamerica with the location of sites and valleys discussed in the text. The number 1 corresponds to Teotihuacán, 2 to Huamelupan, 3 to Monte Negro, 4 to Tehuacán Valley, 5 to Quiotepec, 6 to Llano Perdido, 7 to Cerro de la Cruz, 8 to Tututepec, 9 to Sola Valley, 10 to Ejutla Valley, and 11 to Miahuatlan Valley (Justin Jennings).

While the other villages in the Oaxaca Valley were composed of no more than 10 households (Flannery 1983:43), there was one much larger collection of family groups at San José Mogote that chose to live together to ensure access to what was the most fertile part of the valley. The settlement, which was located in the northern portion of the valley, grew to cover seven hectares by 1350 BC. The settlement was divided into nine, spatially discrete, residential areas, each of which differed slightly in their artifact assemblages. Some areas, for example, made ornaments primarily out of Pacific shell, while other areas largely used Atlantic shell (Pires-Ferreira 1976:316). Some used more fire serpent motifs on their pots, while others used more jaguar motifs (Pyne 1976:277). The areas, often called "barrios" or "wards" by Zapotec archaeologists, were likely composed of loosely related "corporate kin groups" that would prove to be an enduring organizational structure in Oaxaca (Kowalewski 2003:135). Generations lived in the same house at San José Mogote—next to the same neighbors—burying their dead underfoot and spilling their blood year after year in rituals that took place in the adjacent courtyard (Flannery 1976:336–341; Winter 2002:68–69; for a later example of long-standing wards in Oaxaca see Feinman and Nicholas 2004).

The division of San José Mogote into discrete wards—"each virtually as large as a hamlet elsewhere in the valley" (Marcus and Flannery 1996:87)—was one of the means through which the scalar stress of settlement aggregation was alleviated. Another means of reducing scalar stress was the elaboration of rituals that took place in the site's ceremonial sector (Marcus and Flannery 1996:87). The original location of group rituals was a small open area delineated by wooden posts and stone slabs (Flannery and Marcus 1976:47). This was replaced around 1350 BC by an open space surrounding a four- by six-meter structure that was razed and rebuilt at least eight times. Rituals that took place on the building's steps could be seen by many, but only a subset of San José Mogote's population could be present in the structure's interior, where an altar and storage pit for mixing lime with tobacco were found (Drennan 1983:47–78). Although who attended the more exclusive rituals inside the building remains a matter of speculation, some scholars argue that it may have been elders or other representatives from each of the site's wards (e.g., Blanton et al. 1993:58). The designation of these individuals would have increased the basal units used in decision-making, another method of relieving scalar stress.

Compartmentalization, ritual elaboration, and the increasing of basal-unit size were thus used to help ease tensions as San José Mogote grew to 79 hectares by 850 BC. Although the village was large—half the valley's population lived there (Kowalewski et al. 1989:51)—the settlement was not densely packed like Çatalhöyük and Harappa. San José Mogote was instead a "sprawling community" of only about 1,000 people divided into a number of wards (Marcus and Flannery 1996:86). One-roomed buildings with altars and pits continued to be constructed in the site's ceremonial sector, but these were joined by stepped terraces and platforms in the ninth century BC. The creation of these new structures, which were surrounded by open areas for spectators, suggests an increased emphasis on conducting group rituals that tied wards together as a single community. Yet these terraces and platforms also served as stages for rituals that elevated a chosen few over the rest of the community (Flannery and Marcus 1983a:54).

The increase in basal-unit size slowly eroded antipathy toward status distinctions. As differences between people widened by the beginning of the first millennium BC, some families in the various subunits that made up San José Mogote began living in more elaborate houses. The individuals in these homes were more intensively involved in making stone tools, baskets, and pottery. They had greater access to deer meat, jade, imported pottery, and marine shell. They also wore more jewelry, were buried with more grave goods, and depicted themselves in postures that symbolized authority, at least in later cultures of western Mexico (Marcus and Flannery 1996:96–106). Status differences, however, were only emergent, taking "the form of a continuum from relatively higher to relatively lower status, without a true division into social classes" (Flannery and Marcus 1983a:55).

In the absence of a truly hierarchical society, families within each of San José Mogote's subunits jockeyed for tenuous, still ill-defined social rankings. The preponderance of evidence suggests that San José Mogote was *not* the capital of a centralized chiefdom at this time but rather an inclusive ceremonial center sustained through the voluntary participation of the site's various wards (Blanton et al. 1999:42; cf. Marcus and Flannery 1996:108). This model for aggregation was mimicked by others in the valley, and by 700 BC, San José Mogote was joined by three other ceremonial centers in the Oaxaca Valley that were competing with each other for followers (Blanton et al. 1999:42). Status differences grew more pronounced over time in these centers as wealthier families sponsored feasts, enjoyed privileged access to exotica, orchestrated group rituals, and, in some cases, inched their homes closer to the sites' ceremonial structures.

At San José Mogote, ritual activities were concentrated on Mound 1, a platform built on top of a natural hill. A "long series of superimposed buildings" on the mound culminated in the construction of a waddle-and-daub temple that measured 22 by 29 meters and stood 15 meters above the site (Flannery and Marcus 1983a:57). A fire around 600 BC—so intense that it had to have been set deliberately—consumed this temple (Marcus and Flannery 1996:128). Since burning an enemy's temple would become a common practice during later periods in Mesoamerica, some scholars suggest that this and other intense fires elsewhere in the valley were the result of increasing raiding and pillaging of settlements during this century (Kowalewski et al. 1989:81–82).

One of San José Mogote's leading families took advantage of the chaos following the 600 BC burning of the temple. They and their supporters built a residence on top of Mound 1 in a naked grab for power that was unprecedented in the valley (Marcus and Flannery 1996:131; but see Winter 2011:399–400 for a later dating of these structures). Their attempt to establish a deeply stratified society ultimately failed. Families began leaving San José Mogote, and the settlement lost more than half of its population over the next hundred years (Joyce 2004:196).

Some of those who left San José Mogote likely moved to one of the other established ceremonial centers in the region. A few groups, joining up with families from other places in Oaxaca (Blanton et al. 1993:69; Winter 2004:32–33), pioneered a new site around 500 BC that was located near the center of the valley. The settlement's hilltop location was unusual because of its distance from prime agricultural land, but the settlers may have deliberately chosen the spot because it was a neutral site that was not linked to any of the existing ceremonial sites in Oaxaca (Blanton et al.1993:69). The settlers built three residential wards—each of which are "ethnically distinct" in their artifact assemblages (Blanton 1978:39)— around a main plaza. These first few families were the founders of Monte Albán.

The Making of Monte Albán

As San José Mogote and the other ceremonial centers of the valley withered, Monte Albán grew rapidly through the aggregation of people from across the valley and beyond. Subsistence needs seem to have been initially met at the ward level by the irrigation, damming, and terracing of the more gently sloping piedmont lands that were within a day's walk of Monte Albán (Marcus and Flannery 1996:146–150). The manufacture of a new ceramic type, the tortilla griddle, or comal, also heralded the introduction of a less perishable and highly portable food made from maize that would soon become a staple of the region (Feinman 1986:385). Despite these developments, the "piedmont strategy" of subsistence was soon unable to meet all of the needs of a settlement whose population exceeded 5,000 people within its first few decades (Blanton et al. 1999:57). To make ends meet, each ward also appears to have maintained links to a different part of the valley, calling on their kin still living in outlying settlements for food, ceramics, and other resources (Fargher 2007:327; Kowalewski 2003:133; Kowalewski et al. 1989:96–97).

The household organization of Monte Albán's three wards simply replicated that of the villages the founding families had left behind: a small structure or two was surrounded by an ample open space dotted with storage pits, ovens, and the burials of family members (Winter 1974:982). The grinding stones, pot sherds, and other material remains of Monte Albán's settlers resembles that from previous periods, suggesting that each household in the growing settlement remained "relatively autonomous and self-sufficient" (Winter 1974:983). Status differences were discernable in the earliest material assemblages, just as they are in such assemblages from earlier settlements. The highest-status families, based on excavation data from elsewhere in the valley, were likely spread across Monte Albán, living in larger structures built on top of stone or mud-brick platforms (Winter 1974:984; Blanton et al. 1999:61).

The settlement had "no clear economic focus"; instead, economic activities were diffused across Monte Albán, and roads seem to have been built to serve individual wards rather than to funnel people into one particular place (Marcus 1983a:213; also see Blanton 1978:66, 96). Wards were distinct in terms of craft specialization, spatial organization, and access to foreign goods, and, at least in later periods, were often centered on plazas ringed by public architecture and high-status residences (Blanton 1978:66–100). The city retained an ad hoc, neighborhood-oriented feel throughout its occupation, even as access routes became more formalized and living spaces more compressed (Blanton 1978:99; Winter 1974:983).

The space that united Monte Albán's three wards was a large, relatively flat area at the top of the hill that would become the Great Plaza of the site (fig. 9.2). The plaza was oriented to the cardinal directions and may have been conceived from the start as a communal space for worshiping the gods (Joyce 2009a:34; Winter 2009:509). Although largely obliterated by subsequent constructions, archaeologists have uncovered portions of a few of the earliest structures that were built along the edges of the Great Plaza (Winter 2001:284–286). All of these buildings were ceremonial structures (no high-status residence faced the plaza at this time [Joyce 2009a:38]), each of which may have been built by a different ward (Blanton 1978:69).

The earliest known ceremonial structure from throughout Monte Albán is a platform on the Great Plaza called Building L (Blanton et al. 1999:61) (see fig. 9.2). Building L is famous for its almost 400 *danzantes*, or dancers, that were displayed in a gallery that faced the plaza (fig. 9.3). Since the nude figures, often shown with splayed-out bodies and closed eyes, comprise about 80 percent of the carved monuments ever found at Monte Albán, they are given considerable interpretative weight, and how one interprets the sculptures is a window into how one views Monte Albán's early political organization and the settlement's relationship with outlying areas.

Figure 9.2. Artist's reconstruction of Monte Albán's Great Plaza as it looked near the end of the site's occupation. Three hundred meters separates the North and South Platforms (courtesy of Joyce Marcus and Kent Flannery, University of Michigan).

Figure 9.3. A *danzante* from Building L at Monte Albán (courtesy of Joyce Marcus and Kent Flannery, University of Michigan).

The prevailing interpretation of the dancers is that they represent captives taken in war (Marcus 1976). This interpretation focuses on the acts of violence that were perpetrated against some of the individuals, such as the mutilation of genitals or extraction of hearts, to suggest that Building L was a monument that commemorated victories in battle, a piece of propaganda commissioned by Monte Albán's rulers "to intimidate their enemies and reassure their supporters" (Flannery and Marcus 1983b:90). There is considerable merit in this interpretation. The violence in the sculptures is undeniable, and, when this evidence is combined with similar images from ceramic vessels (Winter 2009:510), a strong argument can be made that the display and sacrifice of captives was an important element of the activities that took place in the Great Plaza. Conceiving of Building L as elite propaganda, however, seems unwarranted.

Few argue a Zapotec state was created in 500 BC—Flannery and Marcus, for example, suggest that the danzantes were carved before Monte Albán's rulers "achieved true statehood and really effective political power" (1983b:90). Yet almost all Zapotec researchers give short shrift to the divisions between and within Monte Albán's wards that would have initially precluded the creation of a ruling class that dictated activities across the site. These scholars tend to project rulers farther into the past, even though there is no iconographic and archaeological evidence for rulers or centralization at Monte Albán during its first few centuries (Spencer and Redmond 2004:453; Winter 2011:404). If San José Mogote collapsed in reaction to the imposition of an overarching social hierarchy, then it seems odd that those who left that center and other sites in the valley would have chosen to immediately recapitulate this failed social experiment at Monte Albán.

Leaders from the settlement's wards were undoubtedly instrumental in organizing the activities that took place in the Great Plaza, but the events were not pitched primarily as affirmations of a still-inchoate elite power. These are instead perhaps better conceived of as community rituals that created "a larger-scale corporate identity" through shared sacrifice (Joyce 2009a:34; also see Orr 2001). Focusing on how incipient hierarchies at Monte Albán were displayed through the danzantes therefore means that important elements of what was happening on the plaza tend to be overlooked. Javier Urcid's more recent interpretation of Building L as commemorating a series of bloodletting rituals perhaps better captures the sense of Monte Albán as a settlement in flux (Urcid 2011; Urcid and Joyce 2014).

According to Urcid's interpretation, the most pervasive social differentiation seen within the danzantes sculptures is between the living and dead, followed by divisions by age. Alongside these more traditional forms of differentiation, however, we find higher-status individuals who the artist has singled out not only by carving earspools, necklaces, and elaborate hairdos on them but also by naming them using some of the earliest glyphs known in Zapotec writing. The stones set into the corner of Building L contain date glyphs—the only glyphs in the writing system that have thus far been deciphered—that suggest that the structure commemorated periodic ceremonies that occurred on the Great Plaza across at least three generations (Urcid 2011:185).

The overarching theme of the danzantes was thus one of *shared* sacrifice. Regardless of social divisions, everyone came together to feed the gods by offering their own blood or, more rarely, the blood of captives (Urcid 2011:225). High-status individuals were making a play for a unique position vis-à-vis the gods in Building L, but—and here I depart from Urcid who sees elite positions as more firmly established by this time—a ranked society was not yet a fait accompli. The social climate still remained hostile to overtly hierarchical positions, especially ones that crosscut the settlement's ward divisions. This hostility would dissipate over time. In the centuries after Monte Albán's founding, a clear disjuncture between commoners and nobles would develop based on "the special role elites played as shamans and sacrificers" (Joyce 2004:203). Sponsoring group rituals, especially the raids that brought sacrificial victims into the city, was one of the means through which emergent elite positions could be slowly strengthened under the guise of community service.

Monte Albán's leaders, likely drawn from the highest-status families of the various districts, strove to place themselves at "the nexus of a sacred covenant between supernaturals and humans while linking that covenant to warfare" (Pool 2013:313). Each feast, bloodletting, and sacrifice that took place in the Great Plaza emphasized the special relationship of emerging elites to the gods and ancestors, and their privileged access to exotics, writing, and timekeeping further highlighted their distinctiveness (Joyce 2009a:34; Joyce and Winter 1996:38). The gradual shift in Zapotec ideology can be most clearly seen in the creation of a cult to Cocijo, a god of fertility and renewal. The cult had roots in earlier, widely held beliefs in the procreative power of fire serpents and earthquakes. Monte Albán leaders in later years would claim a close connection to Cocijo, whose human characteristics made it possible for elites to don masks and vestments to personify the god in public ceremonies (Blanton et al. 1999:107; Sellen 2007:98).

The end result of this ideological shift is perhaps best seen in the contents of an offering that dates to the beginning of the first millennium AD. According to Joyce Marcus and Kent Flannery (2006:187–188), mourners constructed a diorama depicting a deceased Zapotec lord kneeling in his tomb. They then placed a flying figure with Cocijo attributes on top of the lord's tomb and arranged four masked female figures behind the tomb. The flying figure was the Zapotec lord transformed, and the four females—representing clouds, rain, hail, and wind—were the four companions to Cocijo (fig. 9.4). If their interpretation of the scene is correct, then Zapotec lords were seen as becoming at least semidivine in death.

Assemblages like these are one of many indicators of the radical difference between commoners and elites that were in place by the beginning of the first millennium AD in Zapotec society. Yet it is important to emphasize that this ideology became entrenched only centuries *after* Monte Albán was founded. As in Cahokia, Harappa, Jenne-jeno, and Tiahuanaco, the creation of elite positions was a multigenerational process rather than a seismic event that came with the founding of a city.

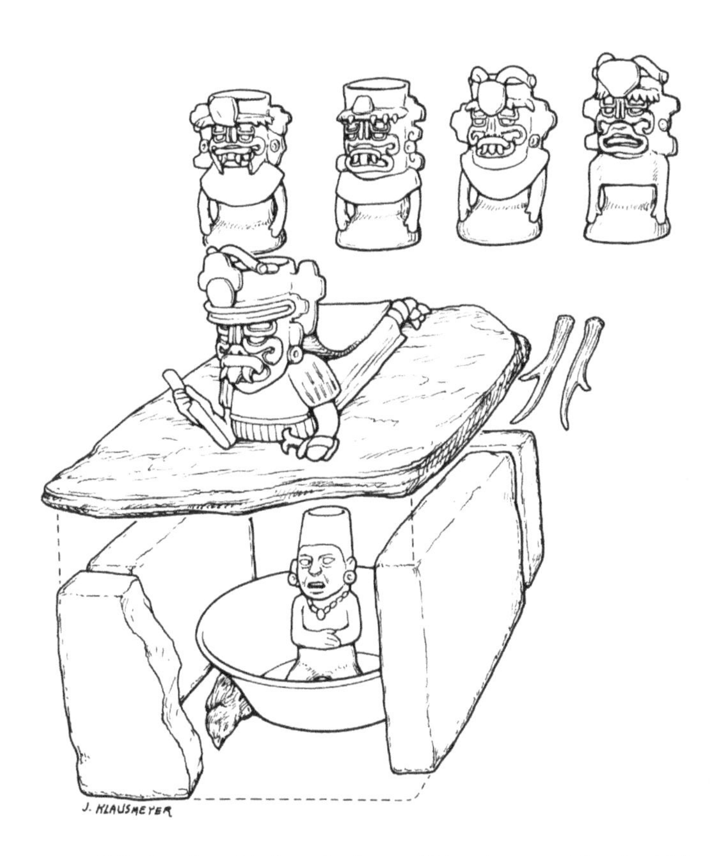

Figure 9.4. Offering found below the floor of Structure 35 at San José Mogote (courtesy of Joyce Marcus and Kent Flannery, University of Michigan).

Monte Albán's population would grow from zero to more than 17,000 people in its first 400 years (Blanton 1993:73). During this time, the city's loose collection of wards was slowly being tied together through events that took place on the Great Plaza. The raids that supported these ceremonies, coupled with the threat of retaliation by those living in other settlements, further helped to create an urban identity, and led to the construction of a wall around the most vulnerable section of the city by at least 100 BC (Blanton 1978:52–54). Raiding had begun as a means to acquire captives and booty, but the city's leaders subsequently used it as a means to gain more secure access to land outside of Monte Albán's immediate environs. They needed to create a countryside that could feed thousands, even as they were still continuing to work toward ensuring their own place within a rapidly changing society (Redmond and Spencer 2012:30; Sherman et al. 2010:280).

Conquest, Colonization, and the Creation of a Zapotec Cultural Horizon

Although many people from the Oaxaca Valley moved into Monte Albán after 500 BC, some groups chose to stay where they were. The initial relationship between those living in villages and in Monte Albán remains unclear. Many families may have at first chosen whether or not to send food, ceramics, and other items to their friends and kin in the city in return for access to both manufactured goods and the public ceremonies that were taking place there (Fargher 2007:327; Kowalewski 2003:133). The leaders of outlying communities also likely sought to strengthen relationships with Monte Albán out of self-interest, as close connections to the city and its sacred space—even if at times these relationships turned antagonistic—would have been useful ideologically as higher-status individuals sought to legitimate the growing social differences that were emerging throughout Oaxaca (Elson 2007:95).

Yet Monte Albán's emphasis on raiding plunged outlying groups into an accelerating cycle of violence that quickly polarized people's relationships to the city. Some people reacted to this violence by migrating into the city or into settlements in the northern portion of the valley that appear to have been closely aligned with Monte Albán. Others, however, moved into or near other expanding ceremonial centers elsewhere in the valley. These few centers, boasting platforms, plazas and other public architecture, were to become the seats of rival polities that would stand in the way of the creation of a countryside around Monte Albán for hundreds of years (Blanton et al. 1993:79; Feinman 1998:128–129; Marcus and Flannery 1996:165; Spencer and Redmond 2001a:207). The armed conflict in Oaxaca led to innovations in political and religious institutions that may have not occurred otherwise—people were more willing to accept change during a time of violent upheaval.

El Mogote, a site near prime agricultural land just 20 kilometers from the city, was one of the centers that resisted the encroaching demands of Monte Albán's population (Spencer and Redmond 2001a, 2004, 2006; Redmond and Spencer 2012) (see fig. 9.1). Though never rivaling Monte Albán in size, the more than 2,000 people living there seem to have relished their oppositional role in valley politics. The organization of their plaza, for example, departed sharply from that of Monte Albán's Great Plaza, and they showed little interest in acquiring the city's elaborate ceramic wares that were gaining cachet elsewhere in the region. Yet El Mogote's "definite social, political, and economic distance and autonomy" from the city proved too dear (Spencer and Redmond 2006:30): it was abandoned after raiders set fire to the settlement around 300 BC.

The community relocated nearby to a higher, more defensible location called El Palenque that maintained a plaza organization similar to that of El Mogote and was protected along its exposed flank by a series of stone-walls (Spencer and Redmond 2006:30). The trauma of the raid, combined with the ongoing need to organize defense, may have led to an acceptance of hierarchical positions there that predated such acceptance in Monte Albán. When El Palenque's new plaza was built, an eight-room residence was constructed on the plaza that was surrounded by platforms and cooking facilities (Spencer and Redmond 2004). The structure's 850-square-meter footprint made it substantially larger than all other residences in El Palenque, and the use of three discrete types of bricks suggests that different work groups were likely involved in its construction (Spencer and Redmond 2004:450). The building is "strikingly similar" in layout to later palaces of the rulers of Monte Albán (Spencer and Redmond 2004:451).

El Palenque boasted not only the earliest palace in Oaxaca but also provided the template for the temple precincts that would become ubiquitous in the valley 200 years later (Redmond and Spencer 2013:E1715; Spencer and Redmond 2006:38). Although it is possible that El Palenque's palace and temple precinct were modeled on existing Monte Albán examples that still remain undetected at the site, the settlement's enmity toward the close-at-hand city had only increased after the raid on El Mogote (e.g., Spencer et al. 2008:336). There would therefore have been little incentive in the context of this hostile environment for El Palenque's rulers to mimic two of Monte Albán's symbols of authority (the palace and temple precinct) while actively rejecting the other (the organization of the plaza). The pressure to transform long-standing institutions would have rather been on El Palenque's residents, who were coming under increasing duress. Since the first-documented palaces and temple complexes at Monte Albán were built just after El Palenque was destroyed at the end of the second century BC, it was perhaps Monte Albán leaders who appropriated architectural designs from their now-defeated rivals.

El Palenque may have been the last of the valley centers to fall under Monte Albán's control. The completion of the conquest of Oaxaca by 100 BC would finally allow for the creation of a well-functioning countryside around the city (Marcus and Flannery 1996:172). Of course, the 17,000 people living in Monte Albán had for years needed food, shell, stone, and other resources and so could not wait for the cessation of intravalley conflict to procure them. The piedmont strategy, raiding, and a shifting network of intravalley political alliances in and of themselves were woefully insufficient mechanisms for supplying a rapidly growing city that had half of the valley aligned against it. To survive, Monte Albán's leaders had to begin looking for resources beyond the Oaxaca Valley during the first centuries after the site's founding, adopting an outward focus perhaps best captured in the more than 50 "conquest slabs" set into Building J on the Great Plaza (Marcus 1983b) (see fig. 9.2).

Most of the slabs used in Building J contain glyph names for places, often accompanied by a human head placed upside down below the glyph. The date of the slabs is unclear—they were reused from an earlier structure and then plastered over soon after Building J was put to use (Peeler and Winter 1995:368)—but they appear to have been made between 300 and 100 BC, when much of much of the Oaxaca Valley still remained inaccessible to city residents (Redmond and Spencer 2012:31). Expanding on

Alfonso Caso's earlier argument (1947), Joyce Marcus has suggested that each slab celebrated a successful conquest (1983b). She links four of these glyphs to toponyms in a sixteenth-century-AD document, and all four of these places were found outside of the Oaxaca Valley (Marcus 1983b:107–108). More recent interpretations of the slabs have tempered such claims by suggesting that the "conquests" celebrated on the slabs may have taken a variety of other forms, such as raiding, colonization, marriage alliances, and trading relationships, all of which would have served to connect outlying regions to the city (Sherman et al. 2010:282; see Urcid and Joyce 2014 for another interpretation).

The various expeditions that were likely commemorated on the conquest slabs appear to have occurred after smaller, far less organized, pulses of colonists left the valley soon after 500 BC to found settlements amid arable land in adjacent valleys or along trade routes that connected Oaxaca to coveted resources zones on the Pacific coast (see fig. 9.1). The first Zapotec families that came to the Sola Valley, for example, were farmers who lived in a single village in the humid bottomlands (Balkansky 2002:84), while there were 21 small farming communities of 8 to 31 inhabitants who settled around this same time in the Ejutla Valley (Feinman and Nicholas 1990:225). The ties between these colonists and the city were at best quite weak—many of these families may have been fleeing the violence in Oaxaca—and the meager movement of resources in the valley were likely "negotiated horizontally by households/individuals" living in these frontier settlements rather than orchestrated by centralized authorities living at Monte Albán (Feinman and Nicholas 1990:228).

Colonial settlements were more closely drawn into the regional economy after the conquest slabs began being made (Balkansky 2002:84–85; Feinman and Nicholas 1990:228, 1992:96–100; Finsten 2002:327; Sherman et al. 2010:285). Groups living in some places like in the Ejutla Valley may have intensified agricultural production independently to meet rising demands in Oaxaca (Feinman and Nicholas 1990:228–230). Other places with more dispersed and poorly organized populations witnessed more direct investments from those living in Monte Albán and perhaps other centers. To return to our Sola Valley example, a series of defensible sites were built between 300 and 200 BC. The largest of these outposts were founded at "strategic entrances to the valley" and the smallest at intervals along a trading route that stretched from Sola to the Pacific Ocean (Balkansky 2002:84). The ceramic assemblages at some of these second-generation outposts hint at strong connections to Monte Albán; some residents were perhaps connected to particular urban wards (Sherman et al. 2010:288).

As Marcus notes, some of the conquest slabs from Monte Albán spoke to relationships with more distant locations. One of the slabs appears to refer to Tututepec, a site near the Pacific coast that was best reached via the Sola Valley (Sherman et al. 2010:291). Zapotec contact with the region is clear—chemical studies demonstrate the arrival of Oaxaca-made ceramics by 300 BC (Joyce et al. 2006:590)—and mass burials at the site of Cerro de la Cruz might be linked to one or more raids into the region by warriors from Monte Albán (Sherman et al. 2010:292–293; cf. Joyce 2010:183–185). Yet the "possibility of a Zapotec conquest . . . appears less and less likely" as more work is done on the coast (Workinger 2013:207; also see Joyce 2010:154–155; Levine 2013:252; Pool 2013:324).

There is no evidence from the Pacific coast for Oaxaca Valley colonists, widespread destruction, or a restructuring of the political economy to meet highland needs. Relations appear instead to have been mutually beneficial, if not always amicable, between the two regions. The goods, ideas, and occasional captives that were brought up from coastal settlements would have sustained Monte Albán's economy and further solidified elite positions. Yet at the same time Monte Albán–affiliated objects and ideas would have been seen as useful to high-status individuals on the coast, who were trying to build on their own still-nascent political authority through activities that took place at highly charged ceremonial sites (Barber 2013:187–188). Access to exotic objects and knowledge helped burnish their authority, and so they appear to have chosen to establish connections with Oaxaca, as well as with other regions (Barber 2013:183; Joyce et al. 2006:591; Workinger 2013:203).

A few of the other conquest slabs that adorned Building J likely depict places in the Mixteca Alta, a mountainous region to the west of Oaxaca (see fig. 9.1). The raids by Monte Albán into this region also did not result in conquest but did spur shifts in settlement patterns that were more striking than those that occurred on the coast. Groups in the Mixteca Alta before 300 BC were organized into small towns surrounded by villages (Balkansky 2004:68–70). The violence in Oaxaca, however, disrupted this arrangement, and most people coalesced in Monte Negro, Huamelupan, and other well-fortified hilltop cities ringed by agricultural terraces that cascaded to the valley floor. The threat of raids thus caused "a chain reaction" that led the residents of these new settlement aggregations "to take a more militaristic posture or risk being consumed" (Balkansky 1998:62; also see Balkansky et al. 2004:55).

The unprecedented size, density, and location of these newly minted cities—some 3,300 people would settle in Monte Negro in less than a hundred years (Balkansky et al. 2004:49)—caused widespread innovations, as people adjusted to life on the fortified mountaintops by tweaking how they made ceramics, farmed, and built their homes. Some of the innovations during this period of urbanism were in situ developments, but many likely were made possible as a result of the knowledge of captives and other contacts that came from Monte Albán or one of the rival centers within the Mixteca Alta (e.g., Cameron 2011). Crosscutting influences reshaped the lifeways of all of the groups involved in these encounters (Balkansky et al. 2004:55).

Those living in Cañada de Cuicatlán had a more one-sided engagement with Monte Albán (see fig. 9.1). Another one of the locations likely depicted on the conquest slabs (Marcus 1983b:108), Cañada de Cuicatlán was a narrow canyon located just to the north of the Valley of Oaxaca. The canyon was home to less than a thousand farmers in 300 BC, its largest site being only nine hectares (Spencer 1982:213). The leading families of Cañada de Cuicatlán had long enjoyed privileged access to imports from Oaxaca and elsewhere, but the volume of interregional trade was minimal, since these families had little need of external resources. Forming alliances with groups living in the canyon was therefore of limited utility to the leaders of Monte Albán, who needed to establish more reliable access to external resource zones. The idea of conquering the population of Cañada de Cuicatlán, in contrast, would have been attractive, since control of the canyon would have opened up a trade corridor to the Tehuacán Valley and, more importantly, have unlocked the canyon's enormous economic potential: it was frost free 12 months of the year, contained tropical fruits and nuts that could not grow at Monte Albán's altitude, and, if properly irrigated, could provide food for almost 10,000 people (Spencer 1982:214–215, 222).

Perhaps with these favorable characteristics in mind, raiders from Monte Albán began entering Cañada de Cuicatlán sometime after 300 BC (Spencer and Redmond 2001b:199). They burned at least one settlement, Llano

Perdido, to the ground, and the canyon's population responded to the violence by dispersing "atop piedmont spurs and ridges" (Spencer 1982:222). Agricultural intensification followed, as villagers built new terraces and irrigation canals in order to make more of the land suitable for agriculture (Spencer 1982:222). The amount of food that was produced—and of tropical fruits in particular (Spencer 1982:227)—far exceeded local needs and was likely bound for Monte Albán.

How the flow of exports to the city was orchestrated remains unclear. The flow of resources from Cañada de Cuicatlán can be seen as the product of "Zapotec imperial administration" over the valley, as Charles Spencer has suggested (1982:226), but repeated raids on a splintered, demoralized population could have also ensured this excess production with far less infrastructural investment. Our best evidence for direct Zapotec administration over Cañada de Cuicatlán's affairs actually comes 300 years after raiding began in the canyon (Flannery and Marcus 2003:11805; Spencer and Redmond 2001b:196–197).

Raised within a context of violent encounters between rival centers, the founders of Monte Albán used raiding as a means to both unite a divided urban population and to acquire captives, exotica, and other goods to strengthen emerging elite positions. Yet there were two other, largely unintended, consequences of the city's militancy. The first was a Zapotec cultural horizon that developed as local populations responded to Monte Albán's incursions and contributed in turn to both the city's and the horizon's development through the sharing of their own ideas, objects, and people (Balkansky 2002:95). This horizon, encompassing an area of 20,000 square kilometers that reached from Cañada de Cuicatlán to the Pacific Coast, was marked most clearly through the spread of a particular kind of grayware ceramic style. This style, though likely pioneered in Monte Albán, was tellingly made in multiple locations and widely exchanged across the cultural horizon (Joyce et al. 2006:591; Levine 2013:255).

The other largely unintended consequence of Monte Albán's raiding and captive taking was the creation of a state (Marcus and Flannery 1996; Redmond and Spencer 2012; Sherman et al. 2010). Archaeologists have on occasion put the cart before the horse, arguing for a Zapotec countryside and administered provinces prior to 100 BC despite a lack of evidence. Yet it is clear that the foundations of a loosely consolidated state were being built during the second half of the first millennium BC, as Monte Albán's leaders coordinated long-distance raids, built colonial outposts, and formed trading alliances. The recalcitrant populations within a portion of the Oaxaca Valley had forced a sustained engagement with neighboring groups, thus exposing emergent elites in Monte Albán to "new forms of social, political, economic, and ritual control" with which to experiment (Sherman et al. 2010:282). These new ideas, when combined with those being generated in rival centers, would eventually form the foundations for a Zapotec state that was anchored by a distinct class of rulers who lived in the Great Plaza of Monte Albán (Joyce 2009a).

The Zapotec State and the Fall of Monte Albán

The Zapotec state that emerged after 100 BC included the Oaxaca Valley, as well as the neighboring Ejutla, Miahuatlan, and Sola valleys (Joyce 2004:205). The clearest evidence for the creation of this state might be the abandonment around this time of 85 percent of the 155 settlements that were located within 15 kilometers of the city (Marcus and Flannery 1996:173–174). Before 100 BC, Monte Albán's survival had depended in large part on the agricultural production of nearby sites, even though these fields were situated on land that was often poorly suited to farming. This piedmont strategy of subsistence, imposed on Monte Albán's residents because they lived adjacent to hostile neighbors, was no longer needed after state formation. Monte Albán's residents could now rely on yields from more productive lands that were located farther away.

The abandonment of many of the villages surrounding Monte Albán was part of a broader shift in settlement patterns that culminated in the creation of a four-tiered settlement hierarchy: the city occupied the highest tier, while more than 400 small villages occupied the lowest (Marcus and Flannery 1996:174). Of particular note were the six Tier II centers with populations ranging in size from 1000 to 2000 people. These centers, along with a few others located just outside the valley (Balkansky 2002:49; Feinman and Nicholas 1992), often contained temples, palaces, platforms, plazas, and ball courts that resembled those being built at the time in Monte Albán. Each of the centers apparently administered its respective environs, encouraging the relocation of people into villages that were situated in such a way as to optimize agricultural production (Kowalewski et al. 1989:156).

Although often considered to be regional administrative centers overseen by Monte Albán (e.g., Marcus and Flannery 1996:174), those living in the city appear to have exercised little control over daily affairs in these settlements and their satellites. As Stephen Kowalewski and his colleagues have argued,

> The elite of the major towns were the local segments of the state hierarchy. Each segment exercised strong and autonomous control over its own commoner population. Segments had comparatively little horizontal integration. Their main ties were vertical, to Monte Albán, in primate center function. Lack of functional integration between segments meant considerable differences in local subsystem organization, potential rivalry, and contradictory centripetal and centrifugal tendencies in political relationships with Monte Albán. (1989:199)

The state was thus loosely consolidated through the flow of tribute and gifts between the city and each regional center. The leaders of each center opted into "different social political and social relationships" with Monte Albán that can be documented archaeologically (Elson 2007:96). San José Mogote's ceremonial core, for example, was radically transformed so that it would mimic Monte Albán; its leaders enjoyed a steady supply of obsidian, jade, and other exotic material that likely came from the city. The architecture of Cerro Tilcajete, in contrast, departed in significant ways from Monte Albán's canon. Those living at Cerro Tilcajete acquired creamware ceramics from the city but had limited access to obsidian (Elson 2007:96–97).

Monte Albán's power in this atomized political landscape was based in part on the threat of violence, but it was sustained more effectively by the creation of an ideology of elite prerogative that was reaffirmed regularly in the rituals, sacrifices, feasts, and other activities that took place in ceremonial spaces. Status differences had been pronounced in Oaxaca for more than a thousand years, but a marked disjuncture between social classes emerged only at the end of the first millennium BC. To solidify this class-based society—one that had failed to take hold centuries earlier at San José Mogote—it was necessary to completely sever the kinship ties between low- and high-ranking families (Elson 2006:45; González Licón 2009:18).

After 100 BC, elites successfully divorced themselves from the rest of society by placing themselves closer to ancestors and the divine. The diorama depicting the transformation of a deceased Zapotec lord into a godlike figure is just one example from a pervasive ideological campaign of social distinction that ultimately created and sustained the position of both a ruling family in Monte Albán and a ranked stratum of nobles that lived both in the city and in regional centers (Marcus 1983c, 1983d).

Elites owed their status positions to links with Monte Albán, where hundreds of years of ritual activities had cemented the Great Plaza's position as an axis mundi connecting the human and supernatural worlds (Joyce 2004:199). Yet these large-scale rituals had also asserted a collective Zapotec identity that at least at times ran counter to the radical social difference elites accorded to themselves (Joyce 2004, 2009; Urcid and Joyce 2014). Because public ceremonies created opportunities for participants to subvert the status quo (e.g., Dirks 1994), the city's ruling families sought to further solidify their newfound political positions by limiting access to the Great Plaza.

A "massive amount of construction" in and around the Great Plaza occurred after 100 BC (Elson 2006:45). The plaza was leveled and plastered, and then workers constructed a large complex on one side called the North Platform that contained a colonnade, sunken patio, and several temples. This platform, accompanied by a row of newly constructed buildings on the eastern side, restricted movement into the Great Plaza and created an exclusive, elite space (Winter 2001:284–290). The plaza, once open to all, was now accessible only via a handful of access points that were possibly guarded by armed soldiers (Martínez López and Markens 2004:96).

Specialists working in and just outside of the now-enclosed plaza made goods from shell, obsidian, and other imported raw materials, along with the ceramics that were highly valued throughout Oaxaca (Martínez López and Markens 2004:93–94; Markens and Martínez López 2009:146). Some of these goods flowed toward the lesser nobles that controlled both Monte Albán's neighborhoods—who by now were presiding over their own public spaces scattered across the settlement (Winter 2001:289)—and the valley's secondary centers. These same nobles would have also attended what were now much more intimate feasts and other elite ceremonies associated with the Great Plaza's various temples (Martínez López and Markens 2004:93). Over time, the space filled in with noble houses and was festooned with images of rulers. The Great Plaza had become a private preserve of a Zapotec elite obsessed with their relationships to ancestors, gods, and fellow elites (Joyce 2009a:41; also see A. Miller 1995; Sellen 2007).

The first Zapotec rulers initially sought to further regularize long-distance relationships. Administrators from the city may have been sent to oversee Pacific trading routes, for example, and the fortress of Quiotepec was established to monitor traffic through the Cuicatlán Cañada (Balkansky 2002:50; Flannery and Marcus 2003:11805). Yet the sharp decline in the Zapotec horizon after AD 200 likely reflects a shift inward, as those living in Monte Albán and surrounding communities became increasingly involved in local affairs. Monte Negro and the other great cities of the Mixteca Alta were abandoned after Zapotec raiding declined, for example, and the state pulled out of Cuicatlán Cañada (Balkansky 2004:49; Spencer 1982:254). With state investment in interregional interaction waning, the descendents of the emerging elites in outlying communities who had coveted Zapotec wares and ideas in past centuries now turned increasingly toward both promulgating their own distinct identities and emulating and importing goods from Teotihuacán and other expansive Mesoamerican powers (Joyce et al. 1995:12; Joyce and Winter 1996:45).

The period from AD 200 to 700 has nonetheless been called the "golden age" of the Zapotec state (Marcus and Flannery 1996:208). Monte Albán's population continued to grow, and this was also the time when many of the most spectacular works of Zapotec art were made. The state's success, however, put considerable strain on those living in Oaxaca. There were as many as 30,000 people crowded into the city during this period (Blanton 1978:58), placing an unsustainably high demand on the region's farmers (Blomster 2008:17). The swelling percentage of nobles within the population also accelerated a trend of conspicuous consumption that caused further environmental degradation and pulled more and more people out of agrarian pursuits (Joyce 2004:211). These and other stresses would have almost certainly caused the Zapotec state to quickly break apart into smaller polities after AD 200. Yet it did not. The state's longevity despite these pressures was likely a product of the external threat of Teotihuacán on Oaxaca's population.

Teotihuacán was a militaristic city of over 100,000 people in the Mexico Valley that had wide-ranging relations with groups across much of Mesoamerica. Although the particular relationship between the two cities remains unclear, a carved stone slab shows a diplomatic meeting between a Zapotec and Teotihuacán noble, and there is some limited evidence suggesting that high-ranking individuals from Teotihuacán lived on Monte Albán's Great Plaza (Marcus and Flannery 1996:233; Winter 2001:291). There was also an enclave in Teotihuacán where people followed Zapotec ritual and funerary traditions (Spence 2002). Isotopic analysis suggests that some of the individuals in this enclave were born in Oaxaca (Price et al. 2008:172).

Monte Albán would have been an effective counterweight to the threat of Teotihuacán expansion, since the ruler had the unique capacity to coordinate activities across Monte Albán's group of lesser nobles, who were often in conflict with each other. When Teotihuacán collapsed during the seventh century AD, the Zapotec state began to break apart, as the leaders of Oaxaca's various wards and secondary centers began asserting their independence. These nobles had by then established their own ritual traditions that legitimated their rule through linkages to their own particular set of powerful gods and ancestors. With positions of power locally grounded, Monte Albán was no longer needed (Joyce 2004:211). The city lost population, and by AD 800 the Zapotec state was replaced in Oaxaca by a fractured political landscape of competing centers (Oudijk 2008).

Civilization and the Zapotecs

In *Zapotec Civilization*, Joyce Marcus and Kent Flannery seek to focus on the "brief phases of rapid evolution" in Oaxacan prehistory rather than "the long, stable periods which gave rise to our typology of stages" (1996:236). Like many of their colleagues working in the region, Marcus and Flannery thus recognize how thinking in stages has occasionally precluded a more serious engagement with what had happened in Oaxaca during the transformative eras of culture change. They are aware that scholars who apply evolutionary theory to the region too often collapse these eras into *moments* of transition between stages, allowing for the creation of just-so stories that sometimes make "humans little more than cogs in a machine" (1996:244).

Marcus and Flannery move away from an engagement with stages and toward a study of the development of individual social and political institutions. Their shift in focus results in a fuller acknowledgment of the more staccato pacing of culture change in Oaxaca—their work and that of others demonstrate that the hallmarks of what is traditionally conceived of as "civilization" did not arrive as a single package (1996:236–237). Perhaps most importantly, they recognize some of the challenges caused by settlement aggregation in Monte Albán and note the 300-year time lag between the founding of the city and the creation of the Zapotec state (1996:241).

Much of the data collected by Marcus, Flannery, and their colleagues therefore fits well with my alternative argument for the origins of cities, states, colonies, and cultural horizons. Yet I suggest that the implications of these data have often gone unrealized by Oaxacan archaeologists because they continue to work within a civilization framework. A reliance on this framework is explicit in the work of Marcus and Flannery; even though they have sought to shift the focus away from stages of cultural development, they do not want to eliminate these stages all together (1996:236). They thus attempt to jettison the idea of near instantaneous change inherited by the late nineteenth-century cultural evolutionists while still somehow maintaining the idea of civilization as a coherent package of traits.

The problem in arguments like these is that you can't have your cake and eat it too. If civilization is understood as a package, then it becomes a latent aspect in all societies—a meta-organism that incubates for millennia in a primordial form before those rare occasions when it unfurls across the landscape. As Marcus and Flannery argue, "In the case of Oaxaca, 'cradle of civilization' is more than a phrase. It implies a period of infancy, then youth, a rapid spurt of adolescent growth, and finally maturity. That image of growth is appropriate, since the Zapotec did not spring into being civilized. They reached civilization only after thousands of years of social evolution" (1996:12). Civilization with a "spurt of adolescent growth" is perhaps an improvement on earlier evolutionary models, but culture change is reduced largely to an unmasking, the great reveal of some *thing* that has been there all along. The past in these models is still based on what we think the civilization stage should look like, and we continue to create teleological arguments that equate the original contexts of innovations with their later uses.

In the case of Oaxaca, the influence of the civilization concept can be most clearly seen in the projection backward of a ranked society. Zapotec archaeologists tend to argue that palaces, temples, and other features commonly associated with civilization "must have existed at Monte Albán itself" hundreds of years before they have been documented in the city (Spencer and Redmond 2004:453). Although state formation is acknowledged to be a later development, scholars often intimate that early Monte Albán was a statelike society writ small, with its early ruling families slowly realizing their imperial ambitions. Even those who have focused on the changing nature of the city still portray Monte Albán at its founding as a settlement organized around nobles and commoners (e.g., Blanton et al. 1999:66; Joyce 2009a:38, 2009b:193).

Mid-first millennium AD Zapotec society *was* organized around class distinctions and, of all our case studies, best fits Bruce Trigger's definition of a civilization (2003:43–46). Social classes, however, were a later development in Oaxaca that had little to do with the earlier process of urbanization, colonization, and the creation of a broad cultural horizon. The tendency to insert status differences as a driver of societal change earlier in Oaxaca prehistory is a product of civilization's enduring influence. State formation, along the marked social distinctions that came with it, was one of the final reactions to the challenges of rapid settlement aggregation at Monte Albán, as well as Tiahuanaco. People in the other regions that we have explored in this book chose different ways to deal with these challenges. One could suggest that only the Tiahuanaco and Zapotec state truly reached "civilization," but to do so would just obscure the commonalities between all of our case studies.

When Monte Albán was founded, it was one of several competing ceremonial centers in the Oaxaca. The site was more cosmopolitan than its rivals—it had been established by groups hailing from different parts of the valley—and this feature, when combined with its central, defensible location, made Monte Albán an attractive place for new settlers. The groups that came into the growing city moved into discrete barrios and participated in the various group rituals that took place in the Great Plaza. Each of these groups, at least in the beginning, may have sponsored the construction of a building on the plaza, a practice similar to that seen at Pukara and the other early ceremonial centers of the Lake Titicaca Basin. The families that organized activities within the barrios and on the Great Plaza accrued greater influence over time in Monte Albán. Though descendents of these families often became nobles generations later, in the beginning Monte Albán would have had the same "continuum from relatively higher to relatively lower status, without a true division into social classes" that was typical of sites in earlier periods (Flannery and Marcus 1983a:55).

The class-based society that developed in Monte Albán was contested across centuries. The danzantes of Building L tell a story of nascent elite positions, but this is only a side note to a far more important message of shared sacrifice and communalism (Urcid 2011; Urcid and Joyce 2014). As population soared, allegiances remained largely at the barrio level, and each group sought to exploit their own particular ties to acquire food and other needed supplies from Oaxaca and farther afield. An urban identity was slowly created through the rituals that took place on the Great Plaza, many of which celebrated successful raids on outlying groups. As Monte Albán's Great Plaza became an increasingly sacred space, aspiring elites found ways to manipulate it to meet their own ends (Joyce 2009a). The Zapotec state, however, is perhaps best seen less as result of primordial elite aspirations and more as an unintended by-product of Zapotec raids, colonizations, and long-distance exchanges. If not for the threat of Teotihuacan, it is doubtful that the tenuous links between nobles that sustained the state would have lasted as long as they did.

Marcus and Flannery, like many of the other scholars discussed in this volume, recognize at least some of the problems with the civilization concept. Yet they still find value in the concept because they feel that it helps them describe "the periods of stability" that are similar across a wide variety of the world's cultural and environmental contexts (1996:245). Their desire to hold on to civilization is understandable. There have been periods of relative political, economic, and social stability in different regions and sometimes striking parallels in institutions. Studying the Zapotec "civilization" allows us to compare it to other designated civilizations like the

Maya, Wari, and Uruk (1996:245). Yet in doing so, we reshape all of these societies so that they fit our understanding of what civilizations should be like, and we preclude comparison to those societies that do not meet our criteria for this stage of development.

Civilization as a concept does not work well in explaining the first centuries of widespread cultural change that followed the founding of Monte Albán—perhaps the type site of processual evolutionary theory—and the concept is of even less use for understanding our other case studies. There *is* considerable value in comparative research, but I argue that this kind of research can be done more effectively without relying on stages of cultural development that produce ill-fitting cardboard caricatures of these dynamic societies. Our reliance on the civilization concept makes it harder to understand the past. It is not an idea worth saving.

10

WITHOUT CIVILIZATION

"CIVILIZATION" IS A WELL-ENSCONCED TERM IN BOTH ACADEMIC and popular writing, and the concept—whether named as such or not—is central to many of the ways that we view the past. Although most of us have misgivings about the concept, there is a tendency to think that whatever harm civilization may cause is dwarfed by its utility as a basic conceptual tool and by the monumental effort that it would take to truly excise the idea from our models of long-term culture change. This book argues that we have both significantly overestimated civilization's value and underestimated its damage. The severe costs of our reliance on the concept are demonstrated by how it has radically distorted our understanding of the relationships between the first cities, states, colonies, and cultural horizons.

Scholars studying the ancient world tend to rely, often unconsciously, on stages of development to help them better understand past societies. This is particularly the case with the earliest cities, states, colonies, and cultural horizons, since they occurred before or just as writing and other kinds of notational systems were being developed. We have huge gaps in our knowledge of all prehistoric cultures, but the civilization concept provides justification for the use of later, far better understood societies to help fill the gaps in our understanding of fellow "civilizations" that occurred earlier in time. The Inca Empire of the fifteenth century AD is routinely employed to better understand that region's Wari phenomena in the eighth century AD, for example, and records from the city of Babylon are often used to help model urban life a thousand years earlier at Uruk-Warka.

These kinds of comparisons, however, often underplay or even ignore the implications of our own data that suggest that there were often substantial economic, political, and social differences between these periods. As most readers would acknowledge, urbanization, state formation, colonization, and the creation of cultural horizons are complex, overlapping processes that unfold over a span of decades, if not centuries. Yet our reliance on the civilization concept leads us to conflate these processes more often then we might realize into a single, steplike transformation at the beginning of a civilization stage. The effort to rid ourselves of civilization *would* be a daunting task, but allowing the concept to linger prevents us from gaining a richer understanding of one of the most pivotal transformations in world history.

Civilization's Other Problems

There are two sets of problems with the civilization concept (Diamond 1974; Goudsblom 2006). This book focuses on the first set of problems that are associated with the imposition since at least the Enlightenment of a staircase structure of cultural development stages on human history. The second set of problems has to do with the term's employment to help justify colonial and racist projects of the nineteenth and early twentieth centuries. This second set of problems has tended to overshadow the damage caused by the first set, as scholars of the ancient world have understandably sought to distance themselves from the idea of civilization as, as Rudyard Kipling puts it, the white man's burden (fig. 10.1).

The negative associations of the term have led to the academic world's often-uncomfortable relationship with the civilization concept over the last hundred years. As arguments for the inherent superiority of Europeans were being discredited during the first decades of the twentieth century, there was mounting concern regarding the use of a lexicon of cultural evolution that was based on the idea of divinely ordained progress. Over time, words in this lexicon like "savage," "primitive," and "Stone Age" were largely banished from academic discourse. The terms were dismissed not only because they were derogatory but also because the ideas behind these terms were shown to be not particularly helpful for understanding past cultures.

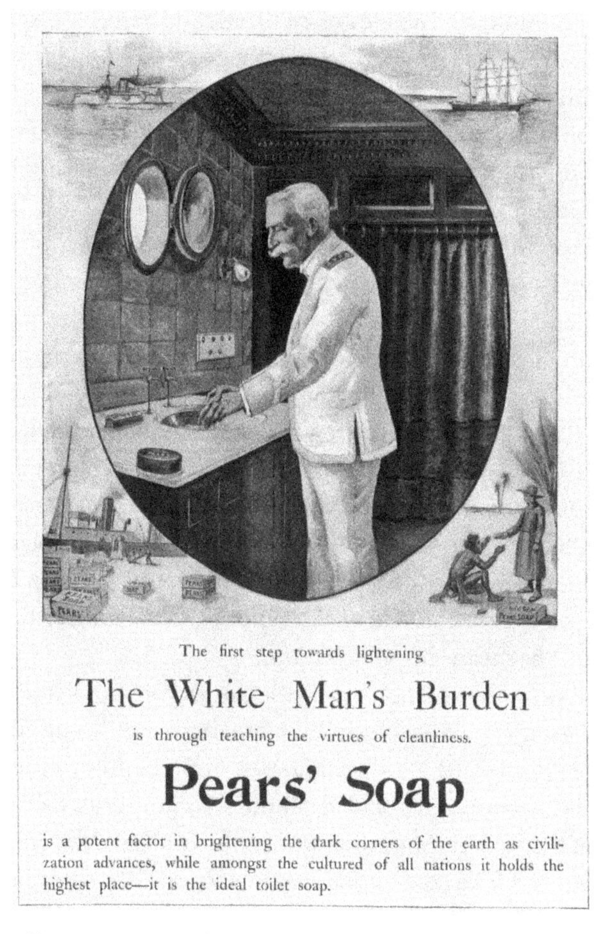

Figure 10.1. An advertisement for Pears' Soap from the 1890s that links cleanliness to civilization.

The term "civilization," in contrast, has remained in widespread use. Its resiliency perhaps reflects our nagging belief that the concept remains valuable. We think that the idea of civilization, once shorn of its racist and colonial undertones, can help us identify a group of similarly organized societies like the Maya, Moche, and Hittites and allow us to compare them in ways that bridge cultural, regional, and temporal divides. Many therefore argue that the case of civilization is different from that of the other words such as "savage." The idea of civilization is perceived to have value despite its baggage, and so many scholars suggest we should not throw out the baby with the bathwater. We should instead rehabilitate the concept by replacing the term "civilization" with "urban societies" or "state-level societies" or else find a way to retain the word in our writing while also acknowledging how the it was misused in the past.

Our unease with the ugly connotations of civilization has often resulted in the concept's second set of structural problems being left unexamined. Bruce Trigger, to his great credit, devotes an entire chapter of his *Understanding Early Civilization* to defining the term (2003:40–52). Most of us, however, choose to avoid dwelling on the concept. A good example of our uneasy relationship with addressing the civilization concept head on can be found in David Wengrow's important and wide-ranging book *What Makes Civilization? The Ancient Near East and Future of the West* (2011). Wengrow attacks the notion that civilizations emerged in splendid isolation and eloquently details the myriad of connections between Mesopotamia and Egypt before the rise of the state. Yet he is tongue-tied when it comes to what he means by "civilization."

Wengrow defines civilization in the beginning of his book as "the highest cultural grouping of people and the broadest level of cultural identity people have short of which distinguishes humans from other species" (2010:9). This inclusive, open-ended definition is not very useful—both the extension of the Roman Empire as well as the first bands of *Homo habilis* that came out of Africa could be seen as instances of the spread of civilization on this definition—and Wengrow's actual use of the word throughout the rest of the book cleaves more closely to civilization's more traditional associations with such traits as cities, states, social classes, and writing.

Wengrow's solution to the civilization problem in *What Makes Civilization?* is thus to redefine the term in a more inclusive way in the book's opening pages and then return implicitly to the idea of civilization as a more narrow societal type in the body of his argument. Some reviewers notice this sleight of hand, but they tend to critique his use of the word "civilization" because of the term's baggage rather than the damage that the concept does through its insistence on a well-defined, distinct stage of cultural development. In his review of the book, Jason Ur, for example, notes that what is

> missing is a thorough discussion of what is meant by "civilization." This term has been abandoned by archaeologists of the processual school because of its origins in Western self-glorification and the corresponding denigration of non-Western societies as barbarous or savage. Civilization is back, but without its cousins, and often, as it is here, without being defined explicitly. (2011:608)

Ur's solution to civilization problems, echoed by many of his colleagues, has thus been to avoid the term because of its negative associations. Yet the "processual school" of archaeology that he refers to in his review still embraces the staircase model of cultural evolution. Avoiding the term, jettisoning its Eurocentric ideas of progress, and even identifying alternative "pathways to power" is not the same as getting rid of the concept (Price and Feinman 2010; also see Lull and Mico 2011). As explored at length in chapter 2, civilization's structuring principle—the concept's original set of problems—has become more exacerbated over the last few decades, even as use of the term "civilization" has declined.

The problems associated with civilization's imposition of a steplike model of cultural development can be traced back to before the origins of the concept. Earlier classificatory schemes, including many still in use today, were often built around stages of cultural development. The past was organized into ages of man in classical Greece; the Aztecs had five suns, and early Hindu writings describe four yugas. The concept of stages was also employed to more easily categorize and rank the bewildering range of societies that were being identified during the age of discovery from the fifteenth to the eighteenth century. This classificatory endeavor was fundamental to Enlightenment scholarship, and even Carl Linnaeus, the Swedish naturalist famous for the binomial nomenclature used to name all living things, divided humans into subgroups based in part on presumed achievements (1741:20–24).

Linnaeus, like some Enlightenment scholars, believed that human subgroups were fixed, but others suggested that people could quickly advance from one societal type to the next given the proper conditions. The highest level of development—typically associated with the urban centers of the West—became known as civilization. The work of Darwin, Lyell, and others in the early to mid-nineteenth century made untenable the biblical chronology used during the Enlightenment and thereby shifted the debate regarding human progress. Adding untold years to the earth's age opened up the possibility for much more gradual change.

Lewis Henry Morgan and other early anthropologists of this era offered more developed models of cultural evolution in the late nineteenth century that tried to accommodate the implications of a far deeper history with the already well-worn stages of savagery, barbarism, and civilization that they had inherited from Enlightenment thinkers. Ultimately, these anthropologists chose to give a nod to gradualism but they largely spent their energies elaborating on how previously defined stages of cultural development could remain stable over long periods of time. The evolutionary models that they developed, though differing in detail from each other, would all share the same basic structure—a staircase composed of treads of relative stasis (the stages of cultural development) punctuated by moments of sweeping change that propelled a group from one type of society to the next.

Because the early cultural evolutionists also tended to argue that cultures would have changed slowly over thousands of years, they had misgivings about the staircase structure of their models. They were prescient, in that the model—often referred to as the ladder of progress—is now held up for censure in introductory anthropology courses. The idea of a single path of societal development has been thoroughly debunked. Professors regularly criticize the fanciful structure of the staircase and celebrate the complexities of all cultures while throwing cold water on the argument that "the West is the best." Like the model's original architects, no one today really *believes* in instantaneous, totalizing culture change or in millennia-long periods during which everything stays the same. We recognize, as Gary Feinman notes with respect to the global increase in polity size over time, that the actual trends are far "more jagged" than these early models allowed (1998:99).

Yet work over the last century has also demonstrated that the rhythms of history are more similar to a staircase than Lewis Henry Morgan and his colleagues may have realized (fig. 10.2). There *were* revolutions, to use Childe's term (1951b), that sometimes quickly propelled people from a hunting-gathering to a more agricultural existence or pushed them from small, scattered villages into a teeming city. Since these revolutions often seem reminiscent of the risers in the evolutionary staircase, scholars have actually become more comfortable than the nineteenth-century evolutionists with "step-like" changes between stages, especially when it comes to the creation of cities and states (Flannery 1972:423). Research has also demonstrated that there have been eras of relative stasis, despite considerable fluctuations within these periods (e.g., Anderson 1996; Marcus 1998), when certain economic, political, and social practices have remained more constant—creating relative plateaus of sociopolitical complexity that also seemingly hearken back to the treads of the evolutionary staircase.

The basic structure of the civilization concept therefore lingers, despite its ugly associations, because the cultural evolution framework is a time-tested, simple way of organizing the past that *almost* works. We realize that the staircase is a gross oversimplification, but it remains a handy one that

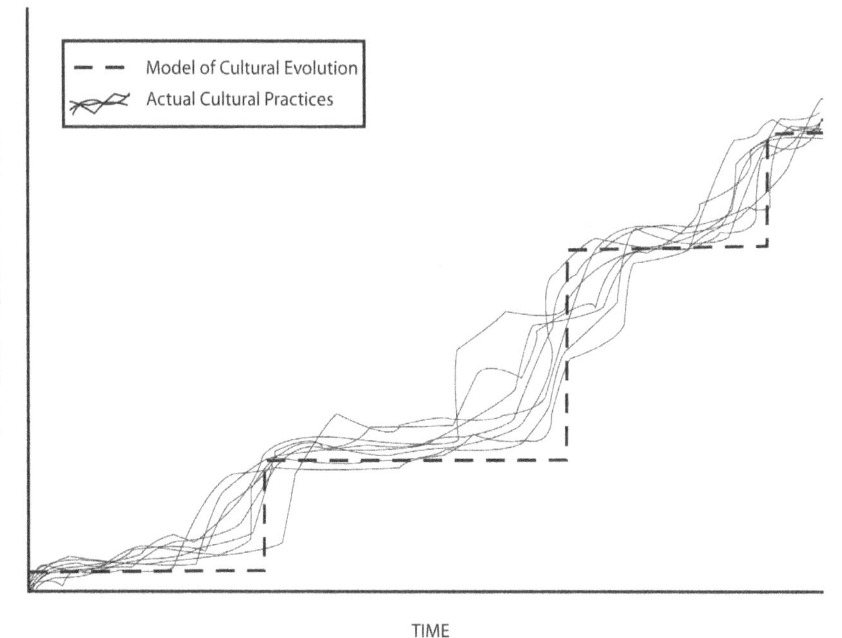

Figure 10.2. Rising social complexity over time in a fanciful region of the world. Note how the staircase model of cultural evolution roughly approximates far more complicated processes of culture change that are occurring (Justin Jennings).

simplifies the complexities of a myriad of comingled, sometimes conflicting, cultural processes that are often quite difficult to track archaeologically. By positing a civilization stage that more or less fits with the data, we can cut through the clutter and more easily compare groups cross-culturally. What then is the problem of using the civilization concept—to dip into archaeology lingo—as an expedient tool? We can use the idea for the quick and dirty job of classification, then toss it away and employ the finer-tuned machinery of analysis at our disposal to study these related societies in greater detail.

The problem is that the "clutter" of the various processes that the civilization concept cuts through is constitutive. How societies in different regions of the world reached periods of relative cultural stasis determined how these societies were structured. By thinking in stages, we tend to conflate an array of social, political, and economic processes into a single moment of cultural change at the beginning of each stage (or more rarely generalize these processes across an earlier, formative period). This conflation results in scholars using conditions from later societies—when certain political, economic, and social structures were well established—to understand what was happening when the earliest cities formed. We fill in the gaps in our knowledge with civilization-appropriate widgets.

One of the more common reactions to the shortcomings of the concept of civilization has been to try to make it more and more inclusive—a trend that perhaps reached its zenith in Wengrow's expansive definition of the term. These and other efforts to rehabilitate the concept have tended to focus on the term's association with progress and its employment within racist and colonial agendas of the nineteenth and early twentieth centuries. Our efforts to save the term reflect a deep-seated desire to hold on to at least the top step of a staircase structure of world history. The concept, after all, almost seems to work. So it is constantly tinkered with, often unconsciously, in order to adjust the civilization stage so that it covers a wider range of past societies.

This book argues that we have failed to see the true scope of the damage done by thinking in stages—the destruction left in the golem's wake. There is seductiveness in the comparative power of the civilization concept since it helps us to break free from the narrow confines of historical particularism. Yet, civilization's power is based in large part on its reshaping of the complex histories of different regions to fit into a single mold (or, on occasion, set of molds). We see the past more easily by employing the concept, but it is a counterfeit past profoundly shaped by our expectations for what civilizations should be like. I agree that comparative research is important, but there are more effective means to compare societies without resorting to stages (e.g., Dietler 2010 and Knappett 2011).

Reconsidering Origins

The cost of our continued reliance on the civilization concept can be perhaps best seen in its distortion of the origins of the world's first cities, states, colonies, and cultural horizons. When we think in stages, there is a tendency to populate our models with the rulers, bureaucrats, peasants, and artists that we expect to see in all civilizations. Yet these roles—and the structural relations that they entailed—were only the occasional end results of complicated, uneven, processes that stretched across generations. Although most of us acknowledge their existence, these processes are given short shrift in a staged model of cultural development that examines change through mechanistic, atemporal models that by their nature insufficiently engage with the hope, tears, and occasional bloodshed of the formative years of urban centers and regionally organized polities.

This book attempts to disentangle the civilization concept from the origins of the earliest cities, states, colonies, and cultural horizons. Using case studies from around the world, I have argued that much of what we think of as civilization is better conceived as the sporadic, often unintended, by-products of rapid settlement aggregation. People, using skill sets largely developed in a world of small-scale agriculturalists, mobile pastoralists, and hunter-gatherers, tried to solve the wide array of novel problems that occur as a result of increasing population size and density. Creating a city proved to be exceptionally difficult, and the stress caused by aggregation broke most settlements apart before the population could climb into the low thousands. In those rare cases when people stayed together, they did so only by making fundamental changes to nearly every facet of their lives. These changes, often haltingly and reluctantly made, had wide repercussions, spurring the creation of vast interaction networks that would transform broad regions of the ancient world (also see Jennings 2011).

Focusing on the wide-reaching implications of the urbanization process provides us with an alternative model for the development of the first states, colonies, and cultural horizons that is a better fit with the available evidence. Cities cross-culturally can be seen as "social reactors" that provide unparalleled opportunities for networking and economies of scale (Ortman et al. 2014:2). Yet our contemporary case studies from São Paulo, Singapore, Abu Dhabi, and Los Angeles demonstrate that cities are initially quite unstable reactors maintained in large part through a wide range of largely horizontal, segmentary, and often-informal relationships that link a city's residents with both each other and those living in outlying communities.

The earliest cities were also very much works in progress as they grew. Though considerably smaller than today's cities, they were created without the benefit of previous models for urban society. Without a developed countryside, the first colonies and cultural horizons were products of the largely nonhierarchical, decentralized relationships that a budding city's families and neighborhoods initially forged in order to connect with the outside world. The states and other kinds of regional polities that subsequently developed in some of these regions were the results of attempts to simplify, and thus make more legible, the complicated web of relationships that had been used to connect people together during the first decades of urbanization (e.g., Scott 1998).

A focus on the challenges, opportunities, and broad-ranging consequences of urbanization highlights some of the damage that has been caused by our adherence to the civilization concept. In the following pages, I briefly outline four areas where critical trends in the development of the earliest cities, states, colonies, and cultural horizons have been obscured in our models of culture change by the ongoing influence of the civilization stage and its steplike rise.

Enduring Aversion to Hierarchy

In an article written more than 40 years ago, Robert Carneiro noted that increasing scale, both at the settlement and at the societal level, demanded the elaboration of more hierarchical relationships (1967:239). This drive toward greater centralization and inequality—a central tenant of social evolutionary theory (e.g., Flannery and Marcus 2012; Price and Feinman 2010)—is seen in all of our case studies. People had to find better ways to get along as settlements grew in size, and introducing more hierarchy, along with ritual elaboration, greater compartmentalization, and larger basal-unit size, were the means through which the stress of aggregation could be relieved. Yet our reliance on a civilization stage of development has led to an overemphasis on the role of hierarchical relationships, especially in the context of early urbanizations.

In these first cities, greater hierarchization was usually the most odious of the available choices. Residents had come from mobile groups or much smaller villages where relations were typically governed by a far more egalitarian ethos that was designed to "actively repress prestige competition" (Ames 2010:37). Most people in a community sought to limit social changes after aggregation, and, as the chapter describing Çatalhöyük demonstrates, they often worked incredibly hard to maintain the feel of "a very very large village" even as population climbed into the thousands (Hodder 2006:98). In Çatalhöyük, families created a house-based society that resisted structural change by focusing attention inward (Hodder and Cessford 2004), while those living in other places favored a mix of other methods to reduce scalar stress.

As settlements get bigger, it becomes increasingly difficult to resolve the stress of aggregation without sacrificing household power and autonomy. People in the Neolithic Near East repeatedly refused to make the kinds of changes that would result in a more hierarchical society (Kuijt 2000:97), and indeed resistance to creeping hierarchy is a typical reason for village fission cross-culturally (Bandy 2004; Fletcher 1995). There were, of course, wealth differences between families. Certain people also had long enjoyed higher-status positions owing to their possession of occult knowledge, their access to long-distance trading partners, or their prowess in warfare. The power of these slightly higher-status individuals over others, however, was often quite limited—they had wide influence, but they could not compel others to do their will.

Periods of rapid settlement growth disrupted the status quo and presented higher-status individuals with opportunities to further advance their positions in society. In most cases, the machinations of these aggrandizers were largely counterbalanced by existing leveling mechanisms that minimized social differences. The resulting status differences, like those seen in Çatalhöyük's neighborhoods, thus remained minor. As sites got bigger, however, there were often more chances to further social differences. Aggrandizers seized these opportunities and reshaped society to their benefit. Yet it is important to emphasize that their success was often short-lived because the rest of the population tended to react negatively to these changes. In the Titicaca Basin, for example, Pukara's leaders were briefly able to restrict access onto the main platform, and a family in San José Mogote managed to build its house on top of the ruins of Mound 1's temple. However, both of these growing sites quickly went into decline; after residents were confronted with an unmistakable grab for power that violated long-standing traditions, they chose to settle elsewhere.

The aversion to pronounced hierarchical relations in small-scale societies is well documented, as are the variety of mechanisms used to maintain relative egalitarianism in the face of those seeking to institutionalize inequalities (e.g., Angelbeck and Grier 2012; Ames 2010; Bird and Bleige-Bird 2009; Eerkens 2009; Wiessner 1996, 2002, 2009). This aversion, if anything, was heightened in the hurly-burly of early urbanization, when many more possibilities for individual aggrandizement presented themselves. The early cities discussed in this book all began as centers of worship and/or exchange and served functions that were seen as beneficial to most members of society. The gap between groups widened quickly in these communities, but in each case these differences were initially downplayed—hidden behind high compound walls like those found at Tiahuanaco—or nipped in the bud like with the segregation of blacksmithing and smelting at Jenne-jeno.

Uneasy about abdicating their decision-making to nonkin, residents tended to try other means first to relieve scalar stress. They became more specialized, lived in discrete neighborhoods, threw themselves into more ostentatious rituals, and even allowed the size of basal units to creep upward. A critical aspect of the early years of these cities was thus the struggle of most residents to create a city *without* simultaneously creating an overarching hierarchical structure. In places like Cahokia, the struggle was short-lived and destructive. In other places like Harappa, residents managed to preserve the feel of a very very large village for centuries by confining hierarchical relationships to certain sectors. Highly stratified societies would eventually become the norm in all of the regions covered in this book, but projecting this stratification back to each city's first moments is a product of thinking in stages that ignores the "the ungainly process of becoming" of densely occupied places (Kaplan 2012:56).

Atypical, Late, and Unstable Early States

If people in the world's first cities resisted the creation of overarching hierarchal relationships, then one would think that states would be uncommon, that they would come late in the process of urbanization, and that they would be quick to collapse. Our data suggest that this was the case. Yet cities are often seen as "a feature of state societies" (Renfrew 2008:34), and those in disagreement with this position tend to argue for the existence of alternative urban-level societies that could also support cities (e.g., Kenoyer 2008a; McIntosh and McIntosh 2003). In either case, there is a reliance on an evolutionary stage that depicts a city and its countryside as effectively unchanging across hundreds of years. The process of urbanization is therefore obscured, as are the broader effects of this process on people living far beyond a city's limits.

I defined states in chapter 1 as regionally organized societies with a professional ruling class, commoner class, and a highly centralized and internally specialized government. Of the five early cities discussed in this book, only two—Tiahuanaco and Monte Albán—eventually became the capitals of polities that meet these criteria (though one might perhaps argue that the Zapotec state was never "highly centralized"). Cahokia, on the other hand, collapsed soon after it was founded, breaking apart into rival fiefdoms, while Harappa and Jenne-jeno would go on to create long-lasting regional polities that were based primarily on specialization, horizontal interdependence, and shared cultural and religious values. There were hierarchical relations within segments of Harappa and Jenne-jeno, but they were never organized in the kind of overarching system that would warrant their designations as states under our definition.

The processes that led to the creation of states and other kinds of regional polities were a reaction to the needs of a growing, increasingly diverse, urban population. When polities began to form, people in these settlements were *already* circulating goods, ideas, and services among themselves and outside groups. These relationships tended to be personal, segmentary, and horizontal, because they were built on the connections that had been previously established in a world of more dispersed villages and mobile groups. The populations in these growing communities were thus attempting to scale up their earlier practices to meet the demands of a new environment. The first regionally organized political organizations in all of our case studies were built from this tinkering, as coalitions came together to bridge divisions between neighborhoods or clusters.

The increase in basal-unit size in these urbanizing settlements allowed for groups defined by their neighborhood, compound, or household group to be represented by a smaller number of people. In all of our case studies, group leaders would eventually seek to secure elite prerogatives and to restructure the political economy in an attempt to buttress their positions. In each case, residents pushed back, maintaining as best they could the more horizontal and fragmented relations that were currently in place. At first glance, the polities that initially formed around early cities look to be based on a fragile compromise, uneasily balanced between an egalitarian ethos and the drive for more hierarchical decision-making. Yet these more bottom-up political structures often proved to be remarkably stable, lasting for hundreds of years.

This balance tilted over time toward greater centralization and stratification. In some cases like Cahokia, this shift happened over the course of just a couple of generations. The result, however, was the fracturing of the city before a state could form, as leaders of plaza groups competed with each other for followers. In most cases, the movement was far more subtle; leading families slowly made a case for their exceptionalism until they were finally emboldened to materialize radical class differences hundreds of years later (e.g., DeMarrais et al. 1996). These materializations of power seem to have often actually led to the *decline* of early urban centers. The Great Hall in Harappa and the enclosure wall in Jenne-jeno, for instance, were likely late attempts to more clearly mark a group of leaders as distinct. Both cities began breaking apart soon after these constructions were finished—people left before further inroads could be made to consolidate elite power.

States only formed midway through the occupations of Tiahuanaco and

Monte Albán. Although considerable effort was made to recast many of the more horizontal, segmentary, and kin-based links that had previously organized relationships in both regions, the process of state formation was in part additive, as new structures were placed on top of existing ones. States, as Joyce Marcus has noted, tend to be short-lived because of the "difficulty of maintaining large-scale inegalitarian structures for long periods of time" (1998:94). This was particularly the case for the earliest states, since those in power were attempting to reconfigure the existing, more egalitarian, structures of the regional polities that had organized around cities during their first years of development. States built on these foundations were inherently unstable, but, once they were created, there was no going back, since the breakdown of these polities did not lead to the reestablishment of earlier ways of living (e.g., Feinman 1998). Society instead was forever restructured, and it was far easier—even in those places where states had not emerged in the wake of early urbanizations—to subsequently develop polities based on more hierarchical and centralized relationships.

Using second- and third-generation states to understand first-generation states (or worse other kinds of regionally organized polities) is therefore a flawed exercise based in thinking in stages. It is flawed because we tend to treat the end stage, when a state was well developed, as similar to the beginning stage, when society was still very much in flux. It is also flawed because we fill in the gaps in our knowledge with "sets of clues" from later states, making earlier polities more statelike in the process (Flannery 1998:54). The final flaw in thinking in stages is that the first generation of regionally organized polities emerged within a far different, more egalitarian-oriented urban context than that found in later cities, where rank and power were regarded as well-established social facts (e.g., Durkheim 1935 [1895]).

Colonization and the State

Colonization tends to be seen as "a process uniquely characteristic of complex societies—almost exclusively states and empires" (Stein 2005:12), and the first colonies are often described as having been founded "immediately following" state formation (Algaze 1993b:304). This association of colonization and the state expansion has been taken largely as a given, and debates have centered on the ability of ancient states to project power over distance and on the interplay between "imperial agendas and local agency" (Schreiber 2005; also see chapters in Stein 1999). The assumed link between the state and colonization betrays, once again, the malign influence of the civilization concept. Scholars recognize, as our case studies also demonstrate, that colonization tends to occur soon after settlement aggregation begins. Yet they tend to conflate the first moments of urbanism with the creation of a well-organized regional polity because they want to argue that the first colonies were the result of state-sponsored activities.

Although a number of the earliest colonies would become state installations, they did not begin that way. Rapid settlement aggregation created enormous supply problems, especially since many of the surrounding villages were depopulated as people migrated into the city. These supply problems were exacerbated by the rising demands for exotica and raw material caused by increasing specialization and status differences. Some of the first colonists may have been accidental ones—families like those in the Sola Valley who escaped the upheaval around Monte Albán only to be pulled back into exchange relationships with the city. Other early colonies, such as the Indus Valley settlement at Shortughaï, were founded by entrepreneurs who sought more direct access to valued resources. Still others seem to have had more evangelical roots, like the colonies established soon after Monks Mound was constructed at Cahokia.

These early colonists had no ties to the state (or any other kind of well-organized regional polity) simply because the state did not yet exist. The people living in urbanizing settlements responded to the challenges and opportunities of aggregation through an evolving patchwork of solutions. To get what they needed, residents leaned on their kin, spent considerable time in fields and pastures far away from home, and fought to create a market for their manufactured goods. The set of tactics used to make ends meet were likely different across the still-atomized neighborhoods, compounds, and clusters that composed growing cities. Colonization was one of these tactics. There were undoubtedly efforts to coordinate colonization and other activities by leading families, and perhaps even some loose coordination across the city, but to argue that colonies were the result of state-led actions is to deny the turbulent beginnings of urban centers witnessed in both our ancient and modern case studies.

The data from the Lake Titicaca Basin colonies in the Moquegua Valley provide insights into the impetuses for early colonization and suggests something of the form of later efforts that were made to draw colonies into more formal relationships with a developing state. The valley's first colonists were small groups of mobile pastoralists who likely came from the southwestern shore of Lake Titicaca during the mid- to late sixth century AD. They maintained contact with their homeland and sent a few coastal products home (Goldstein 2005:153–154, 2009:290). A second wave of colonists arrived in the valley a hundred years later. These colonists, coming from variety of places in the Lake Titicaca Basin, settled in distinct enclaves and farmed a far greater quantity of maize and other coastal crops than the first group. Much of this food was sent back to the basin, with each subgroup coordinating transport with their own kin and other contacts who still lived in the mountains (Goldstein 2013:378; Knudson 2008:15). It was only in the ninth century AD that the state intervened in Moquegua by having a sunken court temple complex built there (Goldstein 1993). The temple gave Tiahuanaco's elite a voice in Moquegua, but the state still had little control over the circulation of goods from the highland to the coast.

The data from Moquegua are mirrored by our other case studies. Monte Albán elites, for example, reorganized the existing colonial settlements stretching through the Sola Valley (Balkansky 2002), while those already living in the colony of Ghola Dora began specializing in the production of shell bangles after the intervention of the powerful traders who lived in the Indus Valley cities (Chase 2011:531). These data suggest that administrators of states and other well-organized regional polities sought to modify preexisting colonial networks to meet their own needs. The earliest colonies therefore did not begin as state projects but were established when social stratification was still weak and centralization nearly nonexistent. The colonists who founded these settlements largely pursued their own agendas, and their relationships to the city were personal rather than bureaucratic. Linking the establishment of the first colonies to the expansion of the earliest state is thus another erroneous product of our adherence to civilization's steplike rise.

CHAPTER 10

Simplification and Cultural Horizons

In *Seeing like a State*, James Scott provides examples of how modern state officials "took exceptionally complex, illegible, and local social practices . . . and created a standard grid whereby it could be centrally recorded and monitored" (1998:2). These efforts to simplify relationships to facilitate more centralized planning often ended in failures—the reality on the ground was too complex and dynamic—but they nonetheless managed in aggregate to create a more standardized society within which more heads could be counted, property recorded, and trade monitored. The relentless drive toward greater simplification was also a feature of the ancient world: those who controlled earlier states, as well as other kinds of regional polities, needed to make sense of the world around them, just as modern bureaucrats do (Yoffee 2001). With their reach more limited, they picked their battles carefully, perhaps overseeing the trade in obsidian cores or restricting access to sacred spaces. Yet a general trend toward greater centralization and oversight can nonetheless still be seen in the archaeological record.

There is a tendency to map this push for simplification onto a longstanding, largely implicit assumption in studies of the ancient world that "there must be congruence between horizon and polity" (Schaedel 1993:247–248). This assumption, on the surface, makes sense, as cultural horizons often create commonalities between previously disparate groups—through shared styles, systems of measurement, and language—that would seemingly be in keeping with a state's drive toward simplicity. Scholars thus tend to focus on the geographic rather than temporal aspects of the horizon/polity assumption by debating the limits of a polity's reach within a broader cultural horizon (e.g., Algaze 2008; Stein 1999). The generative role of the state in the spread of cultural horizons, however, is left unquestioned in these debates; the link between the spread of horizons and the "expansionary dynamics" of early states is taken for granted, reflecting once again our reliance on the civilization concept and its steplike rise (Algaze 1993b:304).

I suggest that cultural horizons, like colonies, are the result of widespread interaction networks that tie groups together through the flow of ideas, objects, and people (Jennings 2011). These networks, created via a wide variety of mechanisms, including trade, warfare, intermarriage, and proselytizing, were formed decades, and often centuries, *before* the regionally organized polities discussed in our case studies were created. Tiahuanaco objects, for example, were circulated in the southern Andes via llama caravans almost 200 years before the Tiahuanaco state formed, and Indus Valley specialists came to reside in Mesopotamia quite early in Harappa's urbanization. The increasing standardization and homogenization that created a common idiom for interaction within the earliest cultural horizons were thus products of the initial responses of residents to rapid settlement aggregation rather than of the implementation of state policy.

Our Cahokia example underlines the connection between the first moments of aggregation and the spread of a cultural horizon. The city expanded rapidly after the creation of Monks Mound in AD 1050, growing from 2,000 to more than 20,000 people in a hundred years (Pauketat and Lopinot 1997:118). Efforts were made to consolidate the region by, for example, founding new settlements such as the Grossman site (Alt 2010), but the city began breaking apart before a regionally organized polity could form. A cultural horizon was nonetheless being created during that century, as an interaction network formed across the American midcontinent through the activities of colonists, pilgrims, marriage partners, captives, traders, and other travelers (Pauketat 2004:120–124).

Our assumption that cultural horizons were products of regionally organized polities is another symptom of our reliance on the civilization concept. Cultural horizons followed quickly on the heels of settlement aggregation largely *because* these budding cities lacked a functioning countryside. Without a regionally organized political economy, residents cast the net wide, relying on a diffuse and shifting array of connections with outlying groups to acquire needed resources. States, as well as other kinds of regionally organized polities, thus developed within an existing web of relationships that had come into being during the first years of urbanization. The drive to simplify was first directed toward making sense of these already established relationships; administrators sought to circumscribe the long-distance flow of ideas, objects, and people in order to strengthen ties with local food producers and those living farther away in a few critical resource zones. In some cases, like in our Zapotec example, polity formation actually resulted in the weakening of cultural horizons, as connections to many outlying areas dwindled once the polity had been established.

Becoming a City

Looking out my office window, the only tangential reminders of Toronto's eighteenth-century beginnings that I can see are a few condominium towers near where the settlement's grid was first laid. Since then some six million people have migrated to the city, creating a landscape of bricks, concrete, and steel that would have been unimaginable to the Mississauga who witnessed the first settlers struggling through a Canadian winter. Very few people would use today's Toronto to understand what life was like in the city 300 years ago, but we remain quite comfortable with using a later instantiation of an ancient city to understand its beginnings (e.g., Marcus and Sabloff 2008).

The tendency to think in terms of *the* ancient city or *the* archaic state is a product of a civilization concept that does great injustice to the processes related to culture change. Cities both today and in the past were often the products of rapid, largely unforeseen, aggregation. Residents were not prepared for this transition, and they tried their best to find on-the-fly solutions to the myriad of problems that occur when many people live together in one place (Birch 2013). We know this. Yet we still often ignore these first decades of urban life in our models or treat these rapidly changing settlements as simply smaller versions of the cities that they would become. Our failure to more deeply engage with urbanization as an extended process has had widespread repercussions.

This book argues that colonization, the creation of cultural horizons, and the formation of states and other regionally organized polities were the final results of piecemeal, sometimes ad hoc, often-self-interested decisions made during the formative years of the world's earliest cities. A mathematical model recently developed by Tom Froese and his colleagues suggests that a self-managing city can "spontaneously emerge from purely localized social interaction given the right kinds of conditions" (2014:10). The data presented here support this assertion, as do the experiences of the millions of people who have witnessed the development of urban centers over the last 200 years. Those who first came together into swiftly aggregating communities were not working off of a blueprint for urbanization, and whatever plans they may have had were reshaped by shifting realities. Some of these early cities would eventually become—to echo the title of Paul Wheatley's famous book (1971)—pivots of the four corners, but these kinds of well-defined positions within urbanized landscapes were later achievements.

Treating the final iterations of the world first's cities as commensurate with their origins as Wheatley and many others have done returns us to the image of Athena that opened this book. My daughters did not spring forth from my head with thunderous war cries, and few would argue that cities just appeared fully formed at the knife's edge of civilization. Yet just such a miraculous birth is implicit within the civilization concept. Despite its manifest shortcomings, the concept's insidious simplicity has beguiled scholars for at least 300 years. Allowing civilization to frame how we view world history has significantly warped our understanding of the origins of early cities, states, colonies, and cultural horizons. The concept is not worth keeping—it's time to kill civilization.

REFERENCES CITED

Abbott, Mark, Michael W. Binford, Mark Brenner, and Kerry Kelts

1997 A 4500 14C Yr High-Resolution Record of Water-Level Changes in Lake Titicaca, Bolivia-Peru. *Quaternary Research* 47:169–180.

Abdo, Rudayna

2010 Redrawing Lines in the Sand. *Planning* 76(5):20–23.

Abshire, Jean A.

2011 *The History of Singapore*. Greenwood, Santa Barbara, California.

Adams, Robert McCormick

1956 Some Hypotheses on the Development of Early Civilizations. *American Antiquity* 21:227–232.

2001 Complexity in Ancient States. *Journal of Anthropological Archaeology* 20:345–360.

2004 Reflection on the Early Southern Mesopotamian Economy. In *Archaeological Perspectives on Political Economies*, edited by Gary M. Feinman and Linda M. Nichols, pp. 41–59. University of Utah Press, Salt Lake City.

Adovasio, J. M., and David Pedler

2005 The Peopling of North America. In *North American Archaeology*, edited by Timothy R. Pauketat and Diana DiPaolo Loren, pp. 30–55. Blackwell, Malden, Massachusetts.

Albarracin-Jordan, Juan

1996 Tiwanaku Settlement System: The Integration of Nested Hierarchies in the Lower Tiwanaku Valley. *Latin American Antiquity* 7:183–210.

2003 Tiwanaku: A Pre-Inca, Segmentary State in the Andes. In *Urban and Rural Archaeology*, Vol. 2 of *Tiwanaku and Its Hinterland: Archaeology and Paleoecology of an Andean Civilization*, edited by Alan L. Kolata, pp. 95–11. Smithsonian Books, Washington, DC.

Albarracin-Jordan, Juan, José M. Capriles, and Melanie J. Miller

2014 Transformations in Ritual Practice and Social Interaction on the Tiwanaku Periphery. *Antiquity* 88:851–862.

Alberti, Gianmarco

2014 Modeling Group Size and Scalar Stress by Logistic Regression from an Archaeological Perspective. *PLoS ONE* 9(3):e91510.

Al Fahim, Mohammed

1995 *From Rags to Riches: A Story of Abu Dhabi*. London Centre of Arab Studies, London.

REFERENCES CITED

Algaze, Guillermo

1993a The Expansionary Dynamics of Some Early Pristine States. *American Anthropologist* 95:303–333.

1993b *The Uruk World System: The Dynamics of Expansion of Early Mesopotamian Civilization*. University of Chicago Press, Chicago, Illinois.

2005 *The Uruk World System: The Dynamics of Expansion of Early Mesopotamian Civilization*. 2nd ed. University of Chicago Press, Chicago, Illinois.

2008 *Ancient Mesopotamia and the Dawn of Civilization: The Evolution of an Urban Landscape*. University of Chicago Press, Chicago, Illinois.

Alt, Susan M.

2001 Cahokian Change and the Authority of Tradition. In *The Archaeology of Tradition: Agency and History Before and After Columbus*, edited by Timothy R. Pauketat, pp. 141–156. University Press of Florida, Gainesville.

2002 Identities, Traditions, and Diversity in Cahokia's Uplands. *Midcontinental Journal of Archaeology* 27:217–235.

2006 The Power of Diversity: Settlement in the Cahokian Uplands. In *Leadership and Polity in Mississippian Society*, edited by Brian M. Butler and Paul M. Welch, pp. 289–308. Southern Illinois University, Carbondale.

2008 Unwilling Immigrants: Culture, Change, and the "Other" in Mississippian Societies. In *Invisible Citizens: Captives and Consequences*, edited by Catherine M. Cameron, pp. 205–222. University of Utah Press, Salt Lake City.

2010 Complexity in Action(s): Retelling the Cahokia Story. In *Ancient Complexities: New Perspectives in Precolumbian North America*, edited by Susan M. Alt, pp. 119–137. University of Utah Press, Salt Lake City.

Alt, Susan M. and Timothy R. Pauketat

2011 Why Wall Trenches? *Southeastern Archaeology* 30:108–122.

Alt, Susan M., Jeffrey D. Krutchen, and Timothy R. Pauketat

2010 The Construction and Use of Cahokia's Grand Plaza. *Journal of Field Archaeology* 35:131–146.

Ambrose, Stanley H., Jane Buikstra, and Harold W. Krueger

2003 Status and Gender Differences in Diet at Mound 72, Cahokia, Revealed by Isotopic Analysis of Bone. *Journal of Anthropological Archaeology* 22:217–226.

Ameri, Marta

2013 Regional Diversity in the Harappan World: The Evidence of the Seals. In *Connections and Complexity: New Approaches to the Archaeology of South Asia*, edited by Shinu Anna Abraham, Praveena Gullapalli, Teresa P. Raczek, and Uzma Z. Rizvi, pp. 355–374. Left Coast Press, Walnut Creek, California.

Ames, Kenneth M.

2010 On the Evolution of the Human Capacity for Inequality and/or Egalitarianism. In *Pathways to Power: New Perspectives of the Evolution of Social Inequality*, edited by T. Douglas Price and Gary M. Feinman, pp. 15–44. Springer, New York.

REFERENCES CITED

Anderson, Atholl

2002 Faunal Collapse, Landscape Change and Settlement History in Remote Oceania. *World Archaeology* 33:375–390.

Anderson, David G.

1994 *The Savannah River Chiefdoms: Political Change in the Late Prehistoric Southeast.* University of Alabama Press, Tuscaloosa.

1996 Fluctuations between Simple and Complex Chiefdoms: Cycling in the Late Prehispanic Southeast. In *Political Structure and Change in the Prehistoric Southeastern United States*, edited by John F. Scarry, pp. 231–252. University Press of Florida, Gainesville.

Anderson, Karen

1999 Tiwanaku Influence on Local Drinking Patterns in Cochabamba, Bolivia. In *Drink, Power, and Society in the Andes*, edited by Justin Jennings and Brenda J. Bowser, pp. 167–199. University Press of Florida, Gainesville.

Andrews, George Reid

1988 Black and White Workers: São Paulo, Brazil, 1888–1928. *Hispanic American Historical Review* 68:491–524.

Angelbeck, Bill, and Colin Grier

2012 Anarchism and the Archaeology of Anarchic Societies: Resistance to Centralization in the Coast Salish Region of the Pacific Northwest Coast. *Current Anthropology* 53:547–587.

Angelo Z., Dante, and José M. Capriles

2004 La importancia de las plantas psicotrópicas para la economía de intercambio y relaciones de interacción en el altiplano sur Andino. *Chungará* 36 (S2):1023–1035.

Aplin, N. G., and Quek Jin Jong

2002 Celestials in Touch: Sport and the Chinese in Colonial Singapore. *International Journal of the History of Sport* 19:67–98.

Aristotle

1999 *Nicomachean Ethics.* Translated by W. D. Ross. Batoche Books, Kitchener, Ontario.

Arnold, Denise Y., and Christine A. Hastorf

2008 *Heads of State: Icons, Power, and Politics in the Ancient and Modern Andes.* Left Coast Press, Walnut Creek, California.

Asad, Talal (editor)

1995 *Anthropology and the Colonial Encounter.* Humanity Books, Amherst, New York.

Asouti, Eleni

2006 Beyond the Pre-Pottery Neolithic B Interaction Sphere. *Journal of World Prehistory* 20:87–126.

Atalay, Sonya, and Christine A. Hastorf

2006 Food, Meals, and Daily Activities: Food *Habitus* at Neolithic Çatalhöyük. *American Antiquity* 71:283–319.

REFERENCES CITED

Austen, Ralph A.

2010 *Trans-Saharan Africa in World History.* Oxford University Press, New York.

Axelrod, Jeremiah B.

2007 "Keep the 'L' out of Los Angeles": Race, Discourse, and Urban Modernity in 1920s Southern California. *Journal of Urban History* 34:3–37.

Bahn, Paul G.

1996 *The Cambridge Illustrated History of Archaeology.* Cambridge University Press, New York.

Baird, Douglas

2005 The History of Settlement and Social Landscapes in the Early Holocene in the Çatalhöyük Area. In *Çatalhöyük Perspectives: Reports from the 1995–99 Seasons*, edited by Ian Hodder, pp. 55–74. McDonald Institute for Archaeological Research and the British Institute at Ankara, Cambridge.

2007 The Boncuklu Project: The Origins of Sedentism, Cultivation, and Herding in Central Anatolia. *Anatolian Archaeology* 16:9–11.

Baird, Douglas, Denise Carruthers, Andrew Fairbairn, and Jessica Pearson

2011 Ritual in the Landscape: Evidence from Pinarbaşi in the Seventh-Millennium cal BC Konya Plain. *Antiquity* 85:380–394.

Baires, Sarah E.

2014 Cahokia's Rattlesnake Causeway. *Midcontinental Journal of Archaeology* 39:145–162.

Baker, Lee D.

2004 Franz Boas out of the Ivory Tower. *Anthropological Theory* 4:29–51.

Balkansky, Andrew K.

1998 Urbanism and Early State Formation in the Huamelulpan Valley of Southern Mexico. *Latin American Antiquity* 9:37–67.

2002 *The Sola Valley and the Monte Albán State: A Study of Zapotec Imperial Expansion.* Memoirs No. 36. Museum of Anthropology, University of Michigan, Ann Arbor.

2004 Monte Albán y su impacto en la urbanización Mixteca. In *Estructuras políticas en Oaxaca antiguo: Memoria de la tercera mesa redonda de Monte Albán*, edited by Nelly M. Robles García, pp. 63–73. Instituto nacional de antropología e historia, Mexico City.

Balkansky, Andrew K., Verónica Pérez Rodríguez, and Stephen A. Kowalewski

2004 Monte Negro and the Urban Revolution in Oaxaca, Mexico. *Latin American Antiquity* 15:33–60.

Baltus, Melissa R., and Sarah E. Baires

2012 Elements of Ancient Power in the Cahokian World. *Journal of Social Archaeology* 12:167–192.

Bandy, Matthew S.

2001 Population and History in the Ancient Titicaca Basin. Unpublished Ph.D. dissertation, University of California, Berkeley.

2004 Fissioning, Scalar Stress, and Social Evolution in Early Village Societies. *American Anthropologist* 106:322–333.

2005 Energetic Efficiency and Political Expediency in Titicaca Basin Raised Field Agriculture. *Journal of Anthropological Archaeology* 24:271–296.

2006 Early Village Society in the Formative Period in the Southern Lake Titicaca Basin. In *Andean Archaeology III: North and South*, edited by William H. Isbell and Helaine Silverman, pp. 210–236. Springer, New York.

2008 Global Patterns of Early Village Development. In *The Neolithic Demographic Transition and Its Consequences*, edited by Jean-Pierre Bocquet-Appel and Ofer Bar-Yosef, pp. 333–358. Springer, New York.

2010 Population Growth, Village Fissioning, and Alternative Early Village Trajectories. In *Becoming Villages: Comparing Early Village Societies*, edited by Matthew S. Bandy and Jake R. Fox, pp. 19–36. University of Arizona Press, Tucson.

2013 Demographic Dimensions of Tiwanaku Urbanism. In *Advances in Titicaca Basin Archaeology*, Vol. 2, edited by Alexei Vranich and Abigail R. Levine, pp. 79–87. Cotsen Institute of Archaeology, University of California, Los Angeles.

Bandy, Matthew S., and Jake R. Fox

2010 Becoming Villagers: The Evolution of Early Village Societies. In *Becoming Villages: Comparing Early Village Societies*, edited by Matthew S. Bandy and Jake R. Fox, pp. 1–16. University of Arizona Press, Tucson.

Banning, Edward B.

2003 Housing Neolithic Farmers. *Near Eastern Archaeology* 66:4–21.

2011 So Fair a House: Göbekli Tepe and the Identification of Temples in the Pre-Pottery Neolithic of the Near East. *Current Anthropology* 52:619–660.

Barber, Sarah B.

2013 Defining Community and Status at Outlying Sites during the Terminal Formative Period. In *Polity and Ecology in Formative Period Coastal Oaxaca*, edited by Arthur A. Joyce, pp. 165–192. University Press of Colorado, Boulder.

Bardolph, Dana N.

2014 Evaluating Cahokian Contact and Mississippian Identity Politics in the Late Prehistoric Central Illinois River Valley. *American Antiquity* 79:69–89.

Barth, Frederick (editor)

1969 *Ethnic Groups and Boundaries: The Social Organization of Culture Difference.* Universiteforlaget, Bergen.

Bar-Yosef, Ofer

2011 Climatic Fluctuations and Early Farming in West and East Asia. *Current Anthropology* 52(S4):175–193.

Beaule, Christine Denise

2002 Late Intermediate Period Political Economy and Household Organization at Jachakala, Bolivia. Unpublished Ph.D. dissertation, University of Pittsburgh, Pittsburgh, Pennsylvania.

Beck, Robin A., Jr.
2003 Consolidation and Hierarchy: Chiefdom Variability in the Mississippian Southeast. *American Antiquity* 68:641–661.
2004 Architecture and Polity in the Formative Lake Titicaca Basin, Bolivia. *Latin American Antiquity* 15:323–343.

Beck, Robin A., Jr. (editor)
2007 *The Durable House: House Society Models in Archaeology.* Center for Archaeological Investigations, Southern Illinois University, Carbondale.

Bedaux, Rogier
1980 The Geographic Distribution of Footed Bowls in the Upper and Middle Niger Region. In *West African Cultural Dynamics: Archaeological and Historical Perspectives,* edited by B. K. Swartz and Raymond Dumett, pp. 247–258. Mouton, The Hague.

Bedaux, Rogier, Kevin MacDonald, Alain Person, Jean Polet, Kléna Sanogo, Annette Schmidt, and Samuel Sidibé
2001 The Dia Archaeological Project: Rescuing Cultural Heritage in the Inland Niger Delta (Mali). *Antiquity* 75:837–848.

Belcher, William R.
2003 Fish Exploitation of the Indus Valley Tradition. In *Indus Ethnobiology: New Perspectives from the Field,* edited by Steven A. Weber and William R. Belcher, pp. 95–174. Lexington Books, Lanham, Maryland.

Belfer-Cohen, Anna, and Ofer Bar-Yosef
2000 Early Sedentism in the Near East: A Bumpy Ride to Village Life. In *Life in Neolithic Farming Communities: Social Organization, Identity, and Differentiation,* edited by Ian Kuijt, pp. 19–37. Kluwer, New York.

Bender, Barbara
1992 Theorizing Landscape and the Prehistoric Landscapes of Stonehenge. *Man* 27:735-55.

Benitez, Leonardo
2009 Descendents of the Sun: Calendars, Myth, and the Tiwanaku State. In *Tiwanaku: Papers from the 2005 Mayer Center Symposium at the Denver Art Museum,* edited by Margaret Young-Sánchez, pp. 49–81. Denver Art Museum, Denver, Colorado.

Bermann, Marc
1994 *Lukurmata: Household Archaeology in Prehispanic Bolivia.* Princeton University Press, Princeton, New Jersey.

Bernardini, Wesley
2004 Hopewell Geometric Earthworks: A Case Study in the Referential and Experiential Meaning of Monuments. *Journal of Anthropological Archaeology* 23:331–356.

Berryman, Carrie Anne
2010 Food, Feasts, and the Construction of Identity and Power in Ancient Tiwanaku: A Bioarchaeological Perspective. Unpublished Ph.D. dissertation, Vanderbilt University, Nashville, Tennessee.

REFERENCES CITED

Bettinger, Robert L., and Jelmer W. Eerkens

1999 Point Typologies, Cultural Transmission, and the Spread of Bow-and-Arrow Technology in the Prehistoric Great Basin. *American Antiquity* 64:231–242.

Bhan, Kuldeep K., V. H. Sonawane, Pottentavida Ajithprasad, and S. Pratapchandran

2005 A Harappan Trading and Craft Production Centre at Gola Dhoro (Bagasra). *Antiquity* 79, www.antiquity.ac.uk/projgall/bhan304, accessed July 17, 2013.

Binford, Lewis R.

1962 Archaeology as Anthropology. *American Antiquity* 28:217–225.

Binford, Michael W., and Alan R. Kolata

1996 The Natural and Human Setting. In *Agroecology*, vol. 1 of *Tiwanaku and Its Hinterland: Archeology and Paleoecology of an Andean Civilization*, edited by Alan L. Kolata, pp. 23–56. Smithsonian Books, Washington, DC.

Birch, Jennifer

2013 Between Villages and Cities: Settlement Aggregation in Cross-Cultural Perspective. In *From Prehistoric Villages to Cities: Settlement Aggregation and Community Transformation*, edited by Jennifer Birch, pp. 1–22. Routledge, New York.

Birch, Jennifer, and Ronald F. Williamson

2013 Organizational Complexity in Ancestral Wendat Communities. In *From Prehistoric Villages to Cities: Settlement Aggregation and Community Transformation*, edited by Jennifer Birch, pp.153–178. Routledge, New York.

Bird, Douglas W., and Rebecca Bliege Bird

2009 Competing to Be Leaderless: Food Sharing and Magnanimity among Martu Aborigines. In *The Evolution of Leadership: Transitions in Decision Making from Small-Scale to Middle-Range Societies*, edited by Kevin J. Vaughn, Jelmer W. Eerkens, and John Kantner, pp. 21–49. School for Advanced Research, Santa Fe, New Mexico.

Birmingham, Robert A., and Lynne G. Goldstein

2005 *Aztalan: Mysteries of an Ancient Indian Town*. Historical Society Press, Madison, Wisconsin.

Blanton, Richard E.

1978 *Monte Albán: Settlement Patters at the Ancient Zapotec Capital*. Academic Press, New York.

Blanton, Richard E., and Lane Fargher

2008 *Collective Action in the Formation of Pre-Modern States*. Springer, New York.

Blanton, Richard E., Gary M. Feinman, Stephen A. Kowalewski, and Linda M. Nicholas

1999 *Ancient Oaxaca*. Cambridge University Press, New York.

Blanton, Richard E., Gary M. Feinman, Stephen A. Kowalewski, and Peter N. Peregrine

1996 A Dual-Processual Theory for the Evolution of Mesoamerican Civilization. *Current Anthropology* 37:1–14.

Blanton, Richard E., Stephen A. Kowalewski, Gary M. Feinman, and Laura M. Finsten.
1993 *Ancient Mesoamerica: A Comparison of Change in Three Regions.* 2nd ed. Cambridge University Press, New York.

Blitz, John H.
1993 Big Pots for Big Shots: Feasting and Storage in a Mississippian Community. *American Antiquity* 58:80–96.
1999 Mississippian Chiefdoms and the Fission-Fusion Process. *American Antiquity* 64:577–592.

Blitz, John H., and Karl G. Lorenz
2002 The Early Mississippian Frontier in the Lower Chattahoochee-Apalachicola River Valley. *Southeastern Archaeology* 21:117–135.

Blom, Deborah D., and John Wayne Janusek
2004 Making Place: Humans as Dedications in Tiwanaku. *World Archaeology* 36:123–141.

Blomster, Jeffrey P.
2008 Changing Cloud Formations: The Sociopolitics of Oaxaca in Late Classic/Postclassic Mesoamerica. In *After Monte Albán: Transformation and Negotiation in Oaxaca, Mexico*, edited by Jeffrey P. Blomster, pp. 3–46. University Press of Colorado, Boulder.

Boas, Franz
1911 *The Mind of Primitive Man.* Macmillan, New York.
1940 *Race, Language, and Culture.* New York: Macmillan.
1989 *A Franz Boas Reader: The Shaping of American Anthropology, 1883–1911.* Edited by George W. Stocking Jr. University of Chicago Press, Chicago, Illinois.

Bocquet-Appel, Jean-Pierre
2002 Paleoanthropological Traces of a Neolithic Demographic Transition. *Current Anthropology* 43:637–650.
2008 Explaining the Neolithic Demographic Transition. In *The Neolithic Demographic Transition and Its Consequences*, edited by Jean-Pierre Bocquet-Appel and Ofer Bar-Yosef, pp. 35–56. Springer, New York.

Boehm, Christopher
1999 *Hierarchy in the Forest: The Evolution of Egalitarian Behavior.* Cambridge University Press, Cambridge.

Bogaard, Amy, Michael Charles, Katheryn C. Twiss, Andrew Fairbairn, Nurcan Yalman, Dragana Filipović, G. Arzu Demirergi, Füsun Ertuğ, Nerissa Russell, and Jennifer Henecke
2009 Private Pantries and Celebrated Surplus: Storing and Sharing Food at Neolithic Çatalhöyük, Central Anatolia. *Antiquity* 83:649–668.

Boivin, Nicole
2000 Life Rhythms and Floor Sequences: Excavating Time in Rural Rajasthan and Neolithic Çatalhöyük. *World Archaeology* 31:367–388.

REFERENCES CITED

Boucher de Perthes, Jacques

1847–1864 *Antiquités celtiques et antédiluviennes.* 3 vols. Treuttel and Wurtz, Paris.

Bourdieu, Pierre

1977 *Outline of a Theory of Practice.* Cambridge University Press, Cambridge.

Bowman, Lynne

1974 *Los Angeles: Epic of a City.* Howell-North, Berkeley, California.

Braidwood, Robert J., and Gordon R. Willey

1962 *Courses towards Urban Life: Archaeological Consideration of Some Cultural Alternates.* Aldine, Chicago.

Brent, Michael

1996 The Rape of Mali. In *Archaeological Ethics,* edited by Karen Vitelli, pp. 163–177. AltaMira, Walnut Creek, California.

Brill, Robert H.

1995 Chemical Analyses of Some Glasses from Jenné-Jeno. In *Excavations at Jenné-Jeno, Hambarketolo, and Kaniana (Inland Niger Delta, Mali): The 1981 Season,* edited by Susan Keech McIntosh, pp. 252–263. University of California Press, Berkeley.

Bristol-Rhys, Jane

2007 Weddings, Marriage and Money in the United Arab Emirates. *Anthropology of the Middle East* 2:20–36.

Browman, David L.

1997 Political Institutional Factors Contributing to the Integration of the Tiwanaku State. In *Emergence and Change in Early Urban Societies,* edited by Linda Manzanilla, pp. 229–244. Plenum Press, New York.

Brown, James A.

1996 *The Spiro Ceremonial Center: The Archaeology of Arkansas Valley Caddoan Culture in Eastern Oklahoma.* University of Michigan, Museum of Anthropology Memoir 29, Ann Arbor.

2006 The Shamanic Element in Hopewellian Period Ritual. In *Recreating Hopewell,* edited by Douglas K. Charles and Jane E. Buikstra, pp. 475–488. University Press of Florida, Gainesville.

2010 Cosmological Layouts of Secondary Burials as Political Instruments. In *Mississippian Mortuary Practices: Beyond Hierarchy and the Representationist Perspective,* edited by Lynne P. Sullivan and Robert C. Mainfort Jr., pp. 30–53. University Press of Florida, Gainesville.

Brown, James A., and John E. Kelly

2000 Cahokia and the Southeastern Ceremonial Complex. In *Mounds, Modoc, and Mesoamerica: Papers in Honor of Melvin L. Fowler,* pp. 469–510. Scientific Papers Series, Vol. 38. Illinois State Museum, Springfield.

Brumfiel, Elizabeth M.

1992 Breaking and Entering the Ecosystem—Gender, Class, and Faction Steal the Show. *American Anthropologist* 94:551–567.

Brumfiel, Elizabeth, and Timothy Earle

1987 Specialization, Exchange, and Complex Societies: An Introduction. In *Specialization, Exchange, and Complex Societies*, edited by Elizabeth Brumfiel and Timothy Earle, pp. 1–9. Cambridge University Press, New York.

Bruno, Maria C.

2014 Beyond Raised Fields: Exploring Farming Practices and Processes of Agricultural Change in the Ancient Lake Titicaca Basin of the Andes. *American Anthropologist* 116:130–145.

Buckler, Edward S., IV, Deborah M. Pearsall, and Timothy P. Holtsford

1998 Climate, Plant Ecology, and Central Mexican Archaic Subsistence. *Current Anthropology* 39:152–164.

Buikstra, Jane E., and George R. Milner

1991 Isotopic and Archaeological Interpretations of Diet in the Central Mississippi Valley. *Journal of Archaeological Science* 18:319–329.

Burger, Richard L., and Robert M. Rosenwig (editors)

2012 *Early New World Monumentality.* University Press of Florida, Gainesville.

Burkholder, JoEllen

1997 Tiwanaku and the Anatomy of Time: A New Ceramic Chronology from the Iwawi Site, Department of La Paz, Bolivia. Unpublished Ph.D. dissertation, State University of New York, Binghamton.

2002 La cerámica de Tiwanaku: ¿Qué indica su variabilidad? *Boletín de Arqueología PUCP* 5:217–250.

Byrd, Brian F.

2005 Reassessing the Emergence of Village Life in the Near East. *Journal of Archaeological Research* 13:231–290.

Cameron, Catherine

2011 Captives and Culture Change: Implications for Archaeologists. *Current Anthropology* 52:169–209.

Cangi, Ellen C.

1993 Civilizing the People of Southeast Asia: Sir Stamford Raffles' Town Plan for Singapore, 1819–23. *Planning Perspectives* 8:166–187.

Capriles, José M.

2011 The Economic Organization of Early Camelid Pastoralism in the Andean Highlands of Bolivia. Unpublished Ph.D. dissertation, Washington University, St. Louis, Missouri.

2013 State of the Fish: Changing Patterns in Fish Exploitation and Consumption during Tiwanaku (AD 500–1100) in Iwawi, Bolivia. In *Advances in Titicaca Basin*

Archaeology, Vol. 2, edited by Alexei Vranich and Abigail R. Levine, pp. 105–116. Cotsen Institute of Archaeology Press, University of California, Los Angeles.

Carli, Gian Rinaldo

1792 *Della disuguaglianza fisica, morale e civile fra gli uomini*. Tipografia del seminario, Padua.

Carneiro, Robert L.

1967 On the Relationship between Size of Population and Complexity of Social Organization. *Southwestern Journal of Anthropology* 23:234–243.

1970 A Theory of the Origin of the State. *Science* 169:733–738.

Carter, Tristan, James Conolly, and Ana Spasojević

2005 The Chipped Stone. In *Changing Materialities at Çatalhöyük: Reports from the 1995–1999 Seasons*, edited by Ian Hodder, pp. 221–283. McDonald Institute of Archaeology and the British Institute at Ankara, Cambridge.

Carter, Tristan, Stéphan Duberner, Rachel King, François-Xavier Le Bourdonnec, Marian Milić, Gérard Poupeau, and M. Steven Shackley

2008 Eastern Anatolian Obsidians at Çatalhöyük and the Reconfiguration of Regional Interaction in the Early Ceramic Neolithic. *Antiquity* 82:900–909.

Carter, Tristan, Gérard Poupeau, Céline Bressy, and Nicholas J. G. Pearce

2006 A New Programme of Obsidian Characterization at Çatalhöyük, Turkey. *Journal of Archaeological Science* 33:893–909.

Casey, Joanna

2010 Between the Forests and the Sudan: The Dynamics of Trade in Northern Ghana. In *West African Archaeology: New Developments, New Perspectives*, edited by Phillip Allsworth-Jones, pp. 83–92. British Archaeological Reports International Series 2164. Archaeopress, Oxford.

Cashdan, Elizabeth A. (editor)

1990 *Risk and Uncertainty in Tribal and Peasant Economies*. Westview Press, Boulder, Colorado.

Caso, Alfonso

1947 Calendario y estructura de las antiguas culturas de Monte Albán. In *Obras completas de Miguel Othón de Mendizábal*, Vol. 1. Taller gráficos de la nación, Mexico City.

Cassman, Vicki

1997 A Reconsideration of Prehistoric Ethnicity and Status in Northern Chile: The Textile Evidence. Unpublished Ph.D. dissertation, Arizona State University, Phoenix.

Cessford, Craig

2005 Estimating the Neolithic Population of Çatalhöyük. In *Inhabiting Çatalhöyük: Reports from the 1995–1999 Seasons*, edited by Ian Hodder, pp. 323–328. McDonald Institute for Archaeological Research and the British Institute at Ankara, Cambridge.

2007 Overall Discussion of Buildings 1 and 5. In *Excavating Çatalhöyük: South, North and KOPAL Area Reports from the 1995–1999 Seasons*, edited by Ian Hodder, pp. 531–549. McDonald Institute for Archaeological Research and the British Institute at Ankara, Cambridge.

Chagnon, Napoleon A.

2012 *The Yąnomamö*. Cengage Learning, New York.

Charles, Michael, Chris Doherty, Eleni Asouti, Amy Bogaard, Elizabeth Henton, Clark Spencer Larsen, Chrisopher B. Ruff, Philippa Ryan, Joshua W. Sadvari, and Katheryn C. Twiss.

2014 Landscapes and Taskscapes at Çatalhöyük: An Integrated Perspective. In *Integrating Çatalhöyük: Themes from the 2000–2008 Seasons*, edited by Ian Hodder, pp. 71–90. Cotsen Institute of Archaeology, University of California, Los Angeles.

Chase, Brad

2010 Social Change at the Harappan Settlement of Gola Dhoro: A Reading from Animal Bones. *Antiquity* 84:528–543.

Chase, Brad, P. Ajithprasad, S. V. Rajesh, Ambika Patel, and Bhanu Sharma

2014 Materializing Harappan Identities: Unity and Diversity in the Borderlands of the Indus Civilization. *Journal of Anthropological Archaeology* 35:63–78.

Chávez, Sergio J.

2012 Agricultural Terraces as Monumental Architecture in the Titicaca Basin: Their Origins in the Yaya-Mama Religious Tradition. In *Early New World Monumentality*, edited by Richard L. Burger and Robert M. Rosenwig, pp. 431–453. University Press of Florida, Gainesville.

Childe, V. Gordon

1950 The Urban Revolution. *Town Planning Review* 21:3–17.

1951a *Social Evolution*. Schuman, New York.

1951b [1936] *Man Makes Himself*. New American Library, New York.

1954 Prehistory. In *The European Inheritance*, edited by Ernest Barker, Geoffrey Clark, and Paul Vaucher, pp. 3–155. Oxford University Press, Oxford.

Chilton, Elizabeth

2005 Farming and Social Complexity in the Northeast. In *North American Archaeology*, edited by Timothy R. Pauketat and Diana DiPaolo Loren, pp. 138–160. Blackwell, Malden, Massachusetts.

Chin, Tamara T.

2010 Defamiliarizing the Foreigner Sima Qian's Ethnography and Han-Xiongnu Marriage Diplomacy. *Harvard Journal of Asiatic Studies* 70:311–354.

Cisse, Mamadou

2010 Archaeological Investigations of Early Trade and Urbanism at Gao Saney (Mali). Unpublished Ph.D. dissertation, Rice University, Houston, Texas.

Claessen, H. J. M., and Peter Skalník

1978 *The Early State*. Mouton, The Hague.

Clark, John E., Jon L. Gibson, and James Zeidler
2010 First Towns in the Americas: Searching for Agricultural, Population Growth, and Other Enabling Conditions. In *Becoming Villages: Comparing Early Village Societies*, edited by Matthew S. Bandy and Jake R. Fox, pp. 165–183. University of Arizona Press, Tucson.

Clark, Mary Elizabeth
2003 Archaeological Investigations at the Jenne-jeno Settlement Complex, Inland Niger Delta, Mali, West Africa. Unpublished Ph.D. dissertation, Southern Methodist University, Dallas, Texas.

Clarke, David
1973 Archaeology: The Loss of Innocence. *Antiquity* 47:6–18.

Cleuziou, Serge, and Maurizano Tozi
1994 Black Boats of Magan: Some Thoughts on Bronze-Age Water Transport in Oman and Beyond from the Impressed Bitumen Slabs of Ra's al Junayz. In *South Asian Archaeology 1993*, Vol. 2, edited by Asko Parpola and Petteri Koskikallio, pp. 645–761. Soumalainene Tiedakatemia, Helsinki.
2000 Ras al-Jinz and the Prehistoric Coastal Cultures of the Ja'alan. *Journal of Oman Studies* 11:19–73.

Cobb, Charles R.
2003 Mississippian Chiefdoms: How Complex? *Annual Review of Anthropology* 32:63–84.

Cobb, Charles R. and Adam King
2005 Re-Inventing Mississippian Tradition at Etowah Georgia. *Journal of Archaeological Method and Theory* 12:167–193.

Cohen, Amanda B.
2010 Ritual and Architecture in the Titicaca Basin: The Development of the Sunken Court Complex in the Formative Period. Unpublished Ph.D. dissertation, University of California, Los Angeles.

Cohen, Ronald
1984 Warfare and State Formation: Wars Make States and States Make Wars. In *Warfare, Culture, and Environment*, edited by R. Brian Ferguson, pp. 329–358. Academic Press, New York.

Cole, Douglas
1999 *Franz Boas: The Early Years, 1858–1906*. University of Washington Press, Seattle.

Commins, David
2012 *The Gulf States: A Modern History*. I. B. Tauris, New York.

Condorcet, Jean-Antoine-Nicolas de Caritat
1933 [1795] *Esquisse d'un tableau historique des progrès de l'esprit humain*. Boivin, Paris.

Coningham, Robin, and Mark Manuel
2009 Priest-Kings or Puritans? Childe and Willing Subordination in the Indus. *European Journal of Archaeology* 12:167–180.

Conklin, William J.
1991 Tiahuanaco and Huari: Architectural Comparisons and Interpretations. In *Huari Administrative Structures: Architecture and State Governance*, edited by William H. Isbell and Gordon F. McEwan, pp. 281–291. Dumbarton Oaks, Washington, DC.

Connah, Graham
2004 *Forgotten Africa: An Introduction to Its Archaeology*. Routledge, London.

Conolly, James
1999 Technical Strategies and Technical Change at Neolithic Çatalhöyük, Turkey. *Antiquity* 73:791–800.
2003 The Çatalhöyük Obsidian Hoards: A Contextual Analysis of Technology. In *Lithic Studies for the New Millennium*, edited by Norah Moloney and Michael Shott, pp. 55–78. Institute of Archaeology, London.

Conrad, Lawrence
1991 The Mississippian Cultures of the Central Illinois Valley. In *Cahokia and the Hinterlands: Mississippian Cultures of the Midwest*, edited by Thomas E. Emerson and Robert B. Lewis, pp. 119–156. University of Chicago Press, Chicago, Illinois.

Constantini, Lorenzo
1984 The Beginning of Agriculture in the Katchi Plain: The Evidence of Mehrgarh. In *South Asian Archaeology 1987*, edited by Bridget Allchin, pp. 29–33. Cambridge University Press, Cambridge.

Cooper, Lisa
2006 *Early Urbanism on the Syrian Euphrates*. Routledge, London.

Cork Edward
2011 *Rethinking the Indus: A Comparative Re-Evaluation of the Indus Civilization as an Alternative Paradigm in the Organization and Structure of Early Complex Societies*. British Archaeological Reports International Series 2213. Archaeopress, Oxford.

Cornwall, Ian
1981 The Pre-Pottery Neolithic Burials. In *Excavations at Jericho 3: The Architecture and Stratigraphy of the Tell*, edited by Thomas Holland, pp. 395–406. British School of Archaeology in Jerusalem, London.

Cortesi, Elisa, Maurizio Tosi, Alessandra Lazzari, and Massimo Vidale
2008 Cultural Relationships beyond the Iranian Plateau: The Helmland Civilization, Baluchistan and the Indus Valley in the 3rd Millennium BCE. *Paléorient* 34(2):5–35.

Courty, M. A.
1995 Late Quaternary Environmental Changes and Natural Constraints to Ancient Land Use (Northwest India). In *Ancient Peoples and Landscapes*, edited by Eileen Johnson, pp. 105–126. Museum of Texas Tech University, Lubbock.

Couture, Nicole C.

2002 The Construction of Power: Monumental Space and Elite Residence at Tiwanaku, Bolivia. Unpublished Ph.D. dissertation, University of Chicago, Chicago, Illinois.

2003 Ritual, Monumentalism, and Residence at Mollo Kontu, Tiwanaku. In *Urban and Rural Archaeology*, Vol. 2 of *Tiwanaku and Its Hinterland: Archaeology and Paleoecology of an Andean Civilization*, edited by Alan L. Kolata, pp. 202–225. Smithsonian Books, Washington, DC.

2004 Monumental Space, Courtly Style and Elite Life at Tiwanaku. In *Tiwanaku: Ancestors of the Inca*, edited by Margaret Young-Sánchez, pp. 127–149. University of Nebraska Press, Lincoln.

Couture, Nicole C., and Kathryn Sampek

2003 Putuni: A History of Palace Architecture at Tiwanaku. In *Urban and Rural Archaeology*, Vol. 2 of *Tiwanaku and Its Hinterland: Archaeology and Paleoecology of an Andean Civilization*, edited by Alan L. Kolata, pp. 226–263. Smithsonian Books, Washington, DC.

Cowgill, George C.

2003 Teotihuacan: Cosmic Glories and Mundane Needs. In *The Social Construction of Ancient Cities*, edited by Monica L. Smith, pp. 37–55. Smithsonian Institution Press, Washington, DC.

2004 Origins and Development of Urbanism: Archaeological Perspectives. *Annual Review of Anthropology* 33:525–549.

Creekmore Andrew T., III

2014 The Social Production of Space in Third-Millennium Cities of Upper Mesopotamia. In *Making Ancient Cities: Space and Place in Early Urban Societies*, edited by Andrew T. Creekmore III and Kevin D. Fisher, pp. 32–73. Cambridge University Press, New York.

Creese, John L.

2012 The Domestication of Personhood: A View from the Northern Iroquoian Longhouse. *Cambridge Archaeological Journal* 22:365–386.

Crown, Patricia L., Thomas E. Emerson, Jiyan Gu, W. Jeffrey Hurst, Timothy R. Pauketat, and Timothy Ward.

2012 Ritual Black Drink Consumption at Cahokia. *Proceedings of the National Academy of Sciences* 109:13944–13949.

Crumley, Carole L.

1995 Heterarchy and the Analysis of Complex Societies. In *Heterarchy and the Analysis of Complex Societies*, edited by Robert M. Ehrenreich, Carole L. Crumley, and Janet E. Levy, pp. 1–5. American Archaeological Association, Arlington, Virginia.

Culver, Lawrence

2010 *The Frontier of Leisure: Southern California and the Shaping of Modern America*. Oxford University Press, Oxford.

Cusik, James G. (editor)
1998 *Studies in Culture Contact: Interaction, Culture Change, and Archaeology.* Center for Archaeological Investigations, Southern Illinois University, Carbondale.
Dalan, Rinita A.
1997 The Construction of Mississippian Cahokia. In *Cahokia: Domination and Ideology in the Mississippian World*, edited by Timothy R. Pauketat and Thomas E. Emerson, pp. 89–102. University of Nebraska Press, Lincoln.
Dalan, Rinita A., George R. Holley, William I. Wood, Harold W. Watters Jr., and John A. Koepke
2003 *Envisioning Cahokia: A Landscape Perspective.* Northern Illinois University Press, DeKalb.
Dales, George F., and Jonathan Mark Kenoyer
1991 Summaries of Five Seasons of Research at Harappa (District Sahiwal, Punjab, Pakistan) 1986–1990. In *Harappa Excavations 1986–1990: A Multidisciplinary Approach to Third Millennium Urbanism*, edited by Richard H. Meadow, pp. 185–262. Prehistory Press, Madison, Wisconsin.
Darwin, Charles
1859 *On the Origin of Species by Means of Natural Selection, or the Preservation of Favoured Races in the Struggle for Life.* John Murray, London.
Davidson, Christopher M.
2007 The Emirates of Abu Dhabi and Dubai: Contrasting Roles in the International System. *Asian Affairs* 38:33–48.
2009 *Abu Dhabi: Oil and Beyond.* London: Hurst.
DeBoer, Warren
1993 Like a Rolling Stone: The Chunkey Game and Political Organization in Eastern North America. *Southeastern Archaeology* 12:83–92.
Delaney-Rivera, Colleen
2004 From Edge to Frontier: Early Mississippian Occupation of the Lower Illinois River Valley. *Southeastern Archaeology* 23:41–56.
de la Vega, Edmundo
2005 Excavations at Sillumocco-Huaquina. In *Advances in Titicaca Basin Archaeology,* Vol. 1, edited by Charles Stanish, Amanda B. Cohen, and Mark S. Aldenderfer, pp. 115–134. Cotsen Institute of Archaeology, University of California, Los Angeles.
DeMarrais, Elizabeth, Luis Jaime Castillo, and Timothy Earle
1996 Ideology, Materialization, and Power Strategies. *Current Anthropology* 27:15–31.
Demirergi, G. Arzu, Kathryn C. Twiss, Amy Bogaard, Laura Green, Philippa Ryan, and Shahina Farid.
2014 Of Bins, Basins, and Banquets: Storing, Handling, and Sharing at Neolithic Çatalhöyük. In *Integrating Çatalhöyük: Themes from the 2000–2008 Seasons*, edited by Ian Hodder, pp. 91–108. Cotsen Institute of Archaeology, University of California, Los Angeles.

REFERENCES CITED

Dhavalikar, M. K.

1992 Kuntasi: A Harappan Port in Western India. In *South Asian Archaeology 1989*, edited by Catherine Jarrige, pp. 73–81. Prehistory Press, Madison, Wisconsin.

Diamond, Stanley

1974 *In Search of the Primitive: A Critique of Civilization*. Transaction Books, New Brunswick, New Jersey.

Dickens, Charles

1867 [1834] *The Adventures of Oliver Twist*. Chapman and Hall, London.

Dietler, Michael

2001 Theorizing the Feast: Rituals of Consumption, Commensal Politics, and Power in African Contexts. In *Feasts: Archaeological and Ethnographic Perspectives on Food, Politics, and Power*, edited by Michael Dietler and Brian Hayden, pp. 65–114. Smithsonian Books, Washington, DC.

2005 The Archaeology of Colonization and the Colonization of Archaeology: Theoretical Challenges from an Ancient Mediterranean Colonial Encounter. In *The Archaeology of Colonial Encounters: Comparative Perspectives*, edited by Gill J. Stein, pp. 33–68. School of American Research Press, Santa Fe, New Mexico.

2010 *Archaeologies of Colonialism: Consumption, Entanglement, and Violence in Ancient Mediterranean France*. University of California Press, Berkeley.

Dirks, Nicholas B.

1994 Ritual and Resistance: Subversion as Social Fact. In *Culture/Power/History: A Reader in Contemporary Social Theory*, edited by Nicholas B. Dirks, Geoff Eley, and Sherry B. Ortner, pp. 483–503. Princeton University Press, Princeton, New Jersey.

Dobres, Marcia-Anne, and John E. Robb (editors)

2000 *Agency in Archaeology*. Routledge, London.

Drennan, Robert D.

1983 Ritual and Ceremonial Development at the Early Village Level. In *The Cloud People: Divergent Evolution of the Zapotec and Mixtec Civilizations*, edited by Kent V. Flannery and Joyce Marcus, pp. 46–50. Academic Press, New York.

1991 Pre-Hispanic Chiefdom Trajectories in Mesoamerica, Central America, and Northern South America. In *Chiefdoms: Power, Economy, and Ideology*, edited by Timothy Earle, pp. 263–287. Cambridge University Press, New York.

2000 *Las sociedades prehispánicas del Alto Magdalena*. Instituto Colombiano de antropología e historia, Bogota.

Drennan, Robert D., and Christian E. Peterson

2006 Patterned Variation in Prehistoric Chiefdoms. *Proceedings of the National Academy of Sciences* 103:3960–3967.

2012 Challenges for Comparative Study of Early Complex Societies. In *The*

Comparative Archaeology of Complex Societies, edited by Michael E. Smith, pp. 62–87. Cambridge University Press, New York.

Dueppen, Stephen A.

2012a *Egalitarian Revolution in the Savanna: The Origins of a West African Political System*. Equinox, Bristol, United Kingdom.

2012b From Kin to Great House: Inequality and Communalism at Iron Age Kirikongo, Burkina Faso. *American Antiquity* 77:3–39.

2012c Cattle in the West African Savanna: Evidence from 1st Millennium CE Kirikongo. *Journal of Archaeological Science* 39:92–101.

2015 Expressing Difference: Inequality and House-Based Potting in a First-Millennium AD Community (Burkina Faso, West Africa). *Cambridge Archaeological Journal* 25:17–43.

Duffy, Paul R. William A. Parkinson, Attila Gyucha, and Richard W. Yerkes

2013 Coming Together, Falling Apart: A Multiscalar Approach to Prehistoric Aggregation and Interaction on the Great Hungarian Plain. In *From Prehistoric Villages to Cities: Settlement Aggregation and Community Transformation*, edited by Jennifer Birch, pp. 44–62. Routledge New York.

Dunnell, Robert C.

1970 *Systematics in Prehistory*. Free Press, New York.

1980 Evolutionary Theory and Archaeology. *Advances in Archaeological Method and Theory* 3:35–99.

Dunnell, Robert C., and Robert J. Wenke

1980a Cultural and Scientific Evolution: Some Comments on "The Decline and Rise of Mesopotamian Civilization." *American Antiquity* 45:605–609.

1980b If You've Nothing Better to Do, Honk. *American Antiquity* 45:612–613.

Düring, Bleda S.

2007 Reconsidering the Çatalhöyük Community: From Households to Settlement Systems. *Journal of Mediterranean Archaeology* 20:155–182.

2013 The Anatomy of a Prehistoric Community: Reconsidering Çatalhöyük. In *From Prehistoric Villages to Cities: Settlement Aggregation and Community Transformation*, edited by Jennifer Birch, pp. 23–43. Routledge, New York.

Düring, Bleda S., and Arkadiusz Marciniak

2006 Household and Communities in the Central Anatolian Neolithic. *Archaeological Dialogues* 12:165–187.

During Caspers, E. C. L.

1992 Intercultural/Mercantile Contacts Between the Arabian Gulf and South Asia at the Close of the Third Millennium B.C. *Proceedings of the Seminar for Arabian Studies* 22:3–28.

Durkheim, Émile

1938 [1895] *The Rules of Sociological Method*. University of Chicago Press, Chicago, Illinois.

1984 [1893] *The Division of Labor in Society*. Free Press, New York.

Earle, Timothy K.
1977 A Reappraisal of Redistribution: Complex Hawaiian Chiefdoms. In *Exchange Systems in Prehistory*, edited by Timothy K. Earle and Jonathan E. Ericson, pp. 213–229. Academic Press, New York.
1987 Chiefdoms in Archaeological and Ethnohistorical Perspective. *Annual Review of Anthropology* 16:279–308.
2000 Archaeology, Property, and Prehistory. *Annual Review of Anthropology* 29:39–60.

Eerkens, Jelmer W.
2009 Privatization of Resources and the Evolution of Prehistoric Leadership Strategies. In *The Evolution of Leadership: Transitions in Decision Making from Small-Scale to Middle-Range Societies*, edited by Kevin J. Vaughn, Jelmer W. Eerkens, and John Kantner, pp. 73–94. School for Advanced Research, Santa Fe, New Mexico.

Ehrenfeucht, Renia
2012 Precursors to Planning: Regulating the Streets of Los Angeles, California, c 1880–1920. *Journal of Planning History* 11:107–123.

Ekholm, Kajsa, and Jonathan Friedman
1979 "Capital" Imperialism and Exploitation in Ancient World Systems. In *Power and Propaganda*, edited by Mogens Trolle Larsen, pp. 41–58. Akademish forlag, Copenhagen.

Eldgridge, Niles and Stephen Jay Gould
1972 Punctuated Equilibria: An Alternative to Phyletic Gradualism. In *Models in Palaeobiology*, edited by Thomas M. Schopf, pp. 82–115. Freeman Cooper, San Francisco, California.

Elkind, Sarah S.
2012 Oil in the City: The Fall and Rise of Oil Drilling in Los Angeles. *Journal of American History* 99:82–90.

El Mallakh, Ragaei
1970 The Challenge of Affluence: Abu Dhabi. *Middle East Journal* 24:135–146.

Elson, Christina M.
2006 Intermediate Elites and the Political Landscape of the Early Zapotec State. In *Intermediate Elites in Pre-Columbian States and Empires*, edited by Christina M. Elson and R. Alan Covey, pp. 44–67. University of Arizona Press, Tucson.
2007 *Excavations at Cerro Tilcajete: A Monte Albán II Administrative Center in the Valley of Oaxaca*. Memoirs No. 42. Museum of Anthropology, University of Michigan, Ann Arbor.

Emerson, Thomas E.
1997 *Cahokia and the Archaeology of Power*. University of Alabama Press, Tuscaloosa.
2003 Materializing Cahokia Shamans. *Southeastern Archaeology* 22:135–154.

Emerson, Thomas E., and Jeffrey S. Girard
2004 Dating Gahagan and Its Implications for Understanding Cahokia-Caddo Interactions. *Southeastern Archaeology* 23:57–64.

Emerson, Thomas E., and Eve Hargrave
2000 Strangers in Paradise? Recognizing Ethnic Mortuary Diversity on the Fringes of Cahokia. *Southeastern Archaeology* 19:1–23.
Emerson, Thomas E., and Randall E. Hughes
2000 Figurines, Flint Clay Sourcing, the Ozark Highlands, and Cahokian Acquisition. *American Antiquity* 65:79–101.
Emerson, Thomas E., Randall E. Hughes, Mary R. Hynes, and Sarah U. Wisseman
2003 The Sourcing and Interpretation of Cahokia-Style Figurines in the Trans-Mississippi South and Southeast. *American Antiquity* 68:297–313.
Erickson, Clark L.
1993 The Social Organization of Prehispanic Raised Field Agriculture in the Lake Titicaca Basin. In *Economics Aspects of Water Management in the Prehispanic New World*, edited by Vernon L. Scarborough and Barry L. Isaac, pp. 369–426. JAI Press, Greenwich, Connecticut.
Erickson, Clark L., and Kay L. Candler
1989 Raised Fields and Sustainable Agriculture in the Lake Titicaca Basin of Peru. In *Fragile Lands of Latin America: Strategies for Sustainable Development*, edited by John O. Browder, pp. 230–248. Westview Press, Boulder, Colorado.
Erickson, Paul A., and Liam D. Murphy
1998 *A History of Anthropological Theory*. Broadview Press, Peterborough, Ontario.
Escalante, Javier
2003 Residential Architecture in La K'araña. In *Urban and Rural Archaeology*, Vol. 2 of *Tiwanaku and Its Hinterland: Archaeology and Paleoecology of an Andean Civilization*, edited by Alan L. Kolata, pp. 316–326. Smithsonian Books, Washington, DC.
Evans-Pritchard, Edward Evans
1940 *The Nuer: A Description of the Modes of Livelihood and Political Institutions of a Neolithic People*. Clarendon Press, Oxford, United Kingdom.
Fagan, Brian (editor)
1996 *The Oxford Companion to Archaeology*. Oxford University Press, Oxford.
Fairbairn, Andrew
2005 A History of Agricultural Production at Neolithic Çatalhöyük East, Turkey. *World Archaeology* 37:197–210.
Fairbairn, Andrew, Julie Near, and Daniéle Martinoli
2005 Macrobotanical Investigation of the North, South and KOPAL Area Excavations at Çatalhöyük East. In *Inhabiting Çatalhöyük: Reports from the 1995–99 Seasons*, edited by Ian Hodder, pp. 137–202. McDonald Institute for Archaeological Research and the British Institute at Ankara, Cambridge.
Fargher, Lane E.
2007 A Microscopic View of Ceramic Production: An Analysis of Thin-Sections from Monte Albán. *Latin American Antiquity* 18:313–332.

Feinman, Gary M.
1986 The Emergence of Specialized Ceramic Production in Formative Oaxaca. In *Economic Aspects of Prehispanic Highland Mexico*, edited by Barry L. Isaac. Research in Economic Anthropology, Supp. 2, pp. 347–373. JAI Press, Greenwich, Connecticut.
1998 Scale and Social Organization: Perspectives on the Archaic State. In *Archaic States*, edited by Gary M. Feinman and Joyce Marcus, pp. 95–133. School for Advanced Research, Santa Fe, New Mexico.
2008 Variability in States: Comparative Frameworks. *Social Evolution and History* 7:54–66.
2012 Comparative Frames for the Diachronic Analysis of Complex Societies: Next Steps. In *The Comparative Archaeology of Complex Societies*, edited by Michael E. Smith, pp. 21–43. Cambridge University Press, New York.
Feinman, Gary M., and Joyce Marcus (editors)
1998 *Archaic States*. School of Advanced Research, Santa Fe, New Mexico.
Feinman, Gary M., and Linda M. Nicholas
1990 At the Margins of the Monte Albán State: Settlement Patterns in the Ejutla Valley, Oaxaca, Mexico. *Latin American Antiquity* 1:216–246.
1992 Pre-Hispanic Interregional Interactions in Southern Mexico: The Valley of Oaxaca and the Ejutla Valley. In *Resources, Power, and Interregional Interaction*, edited by Edward M. Schortman and Patricia A. Urban, pp. 75–116. Plenum Press, New York.
2004 Una perspectiva desde abajo hacia arriba de los sitios con terrazas en el periodo Clásico en el valle de Oaxaca. In *Estructuras políticas en Oaxaca antiguo: Memoria de la tercera mesa redonda de Monte Albán*, edited by Nelly M. Robles García, pp. 101–119. Instituto nacional de antropología e historia, Mexico City.
Finsten, Laura
2002 Archaeological Survey in the Mixteca Sierra. In *Archaeology: Original Readings in Method and Practice*, edited by Peter R. Peregrine, Carol R. Ember, and Melvin Ember, pp. 317–336. Prentice-Hall, Upper Saddle River, New Jersey.
Flad, Rowan K.
2007 Divination and Power: A Multiregional View of the Development of Oracle Bone Divination. *Current Anthropology* 49:403–437.
Flannery, Kent V.
1972 The Cultural Evolution of Civilizations. *Annual Review of Ecology and Systematics* 3:399–426.
1976 Contextual Analysis of Ritual Paraphernalia from Formative Oaxaca. In *The Early Mesoamerican Village*, edited by Kent V. Flannery, pp. 333–345. Academic Press, New York.
1983 The Tierras Largas Phase and the Analytical Units of the Early Oaxacan Village.

In *The Cloud People: Divergent Evolution of the Zapotec and Mixtec Civilizations*, edited by Kent V. Flannery and Joyce Marcus, pp. 43–46. Academic Press, New York.
1986 *Guilá Naquitz: Archaic Foraging and Early Agriculture in Oaxaca, Mexico.* Academic Press, New York.
1999 Process and Agency in Early State Formation. *Cambridge Archaeological Journal* 9:3–21.
2006 On the Resilience of Anthropological Anthropology. *Annual Review of Anthropology* 35:1–13.

Flannery, Kent V. (editor)
1976 *The Early Mesoamerican Village*, edited by Kent V. Flannery. Academic Press, New York.

Flannery, Kent V., and Joyce Marcus
1976a Evolution of the Public Building in Formative Oaxaca. In *Cultural Change and Continuity: Essays in Honor of James Bennett Griffin*, edited by Charles E. Cleland, pp. 205–221. Academic Press, New York.
1976b Formative Oaxaca and the Zapotec Cosmos. *American Scientist* 64:374–383.
1983a The Growth of Site Hierarchies in the Valley of Oaxaca, Pt. 1. In *The Cloud People: Divergent Evolution of the Zapotec and Mixtec Civilizations*, edited by Kent V. Flannery and Joyce Marcus, pp. 53–64. Academic Press, New York.
1983b The Earliest Public Buildings, Tombs, and Monuments of Monte Albán, with Notes on the Internal Chronology of Period 1. In *The Cloud People: Divergent Evolution of the Zapotec and Mixtec Civilizations*, edited by Kent V. Flannery and Joyce Marcus, pp. 87–91. Academic Press, New York.
2003 The Origin of War: New 14C Dates from Ancient Mexico. *Proceedings of the National Academy of Sciences* 100:11801–11805.
2012 *The Creation of Inequality: How Our Prehistoric Ancestors Set the Stage for Monarchy, Slavery, and Empire.* Harvard University Press, Cambridge, Massachusetts.

Flannery, Kent V., and Joyce Marcus (editors)
1983 *The Cloud People: Divergent Evolution of the Zapotec and Mixtec Civilizations*, edited by Kent V. Flannery and Joyce Marcus. Academic Press, New York.

Fletcher, Roland
1995 *The Limits of Settlement Growth: A Theoretical Outline.* Cambridge University Press, New York.
2009 Low-Density, Agrarian Based Reform Urbanism: A Comparative View. *Insights* 2(4):1–19.

Focacci Aste, Guillermo
1981 Nuevos fechados para la época del Tiahuanaco en la arqueología del norte del Chile. *Chungará* 8:63–77.

Fogelson, Robert M.
1967 *The Fragmented Metropolis: Los Angeles, 1850–1930.* Harvard University Press, Cambridge, Massachusetts.

Font, Mauricio A.

1990 *Coffee, Contention, and Change in the Making of Modern Brazil*. Blackwell, Cambridge, United Kingdom.

1992 City and Countryside in the Onset of Brazilian Industrialization. *Studies in Comparative International Development* 27(3):26–56.

Fortes, Meyers, and Edward Evan Evans-Pritchard

1940 *African Political Systems*. Oxford University Press, Oxford.

Fortier, Andrew C.

2001 A Tradition of Discontinuity: American Bottom Early and Middle Woodland Culture History Reexamined. In *The Archaeology of Tradition: Agency and History Before and After Columbus*, edited by Timothy R. Pauketat, pp. 174–194. University Press of Florida, Gainesville.

Fortier, Andrew C., and Douglas K. Jackson

2000 The Formation of a Late Woodland Heartland in the American Bottom, Illinois, cal A.D. 650–900. In *Late Woodland Societies: Tradition and Transformation across the Midcontinent*, edited by Thomas E. Emerson, Dale L. McElrath, and Andrew C. Fortier, pp. 123–147. University of Nebraska Press, Lincoln.

Foster, Mark S.

1975 The Model-T, the Hard Sell, and Los Angeles's Urban Growth: The Decentralization of Los Angeles during the 1920s. *Pacific Historical Review* 44:459–484.

Fourchard, Laurent

2011 Between World History and State Formation: New Perspectives on African Cities. *Journal of African History* 52:223–248.

Fowler, Melvin L.

1991 Mound 72 and the Early Mississippian at Cahokia. In *New Perspectives on Cahokia: Views from the Periphery*, edited by James B. Stoltman, pp. 1–28. Prehistory Press, Madison, Wisconsin.

Fowler, Melvin L., Jerome Rose, Barbara Vander Leest, and Steven A. Ahler

1999 *The Mound 72 Area: Dedicated and Sacred Space in Early Cahokia*. Reports of Investigation 54. Illinois State Museum, Springfield.

Francfort, Henri-Paul

1984 The Harappan Settlement in Shortughai. In *Frontiers of the Indus Civilization*, edited by Braj B. Lal and Swarajya P. Gupta, pp. 301–310. Indian Archaeological Society, Janakpuri.

1989 *Fouilles de Shortughai: Recherches sur l'Asie Centrale protohistorique*. Diffusion de Boccard, Paris.

Frasch, Tilman

2012 Tracks in the City: Technology, Mobility, and Society in Colonial Rangoon and Singapore. *Modern Asian Studies* 46:97–118.

Fried, Morton

1967 *The Evolution of Political Society*. Random House, New York.

Friedman, Jonathan
1982 Catastrophe and Continuity in Social Evolution. In *Theory and Explanation in Archaeology, the Southampton Conference*, edited by Colin Renfrew, Michael J. Rowlands, and Barbara A. Seagraves, pp. 175–196. Academic Press, New York.

Friedman, Jonathan, and Michael J. Rowlands (editors)
1977 *The Evolution of Social Systems*, edited by Jonathan Friedman and Michael J. Rowlands. Duckworth, London.

Froese, Tom, Carlos Gershenson, and Linda R. Manzanilla
2014 Can Government Be Self-Organized? A Mathematical Model of the Collective Social Organization of Ancient Teotihuacan, Central Mexico. *PLoS ONE* 9(10):e109966.

Frost, Mark Ravinder
2005 Emporium in Imperio: Nanyang Networks and Straits Chinese in Singapore, 1919–1914. *Journal of Southeastern Asian Studies* 36:29–66.

Frost, Mark Ravinder, and Yu-Mei Balasingamchow
2009 *Singapore: A Biography*. Hong Kong University Press, Singapore.

Gasco, Alejandra V., and Erik J. Marsh
2013 Hunting, Herding, and Caravanning: Osteometeric Identifications of Camelid Morphotypes at Khonkho Wankane, Bolivia. *International Journal of Osteoarchaeology*, DOI: 10.002/oa.2331, www.onlinelibrary.wiley.com/doi/10.1002/oa.2331/pdf, accessed May 20, 2015.

Gebel, Hans Georg K.
2004 There Was No Center: The Polycentric Evolution of the Near Eastern Neolithic. *Neo-Lithics* 1/04:28–32.

Giesso, Martin
2003 Stone Tool Production in the Tiwanaku Heartland. In *Urban and Rural Archaeology*, Vol. 2 of *Tiwanaku and Its Hinterland: Archaeology and Paleoecology of an Andean Civilization*, edited by Alan L. Kolata, pp. 363–383. Smithsonian Books, Washington, DC.

Gifford-Gonzalez, Diane
2000 Animal Disease Challenges to the Emergence of Pastoralism in Sub-Saharan Africa. *African Archaeological Review* 17:95–139.

Giosan, Liviu, Peter D. Clift, Mark G. Macklin, Dorian Q. Fuller, Stefan Constantescu, Julie A Durcan, Thomas Stevens, Geoff A. T. Duller, Ali R. Tabrez, Kavita Gangal, Ronojoy Adhikari, Anwar Alizai, Florin Fillip, San VanLaningham, and James P. M. Syvitski.
2012 Fluvial Landscapes of the Harappa Civilization. *Proceedings of the National Academy of Science* 109:E1688-E1694.

Gladwell, Malcolm
2000 *The Tipping Point: How Little Things Can Make a Big Difference*. Little Brown, New York.

Glascock, Michael D., and Martin Giesso

2012 New Perspectives on Obsidian Procurement and Exchange at Tiwanaku, Bolivia. In *Obsidian and Ancient Manufactured Glasses*, edited by Ioannis Liritzis and Christopher M. Stevenson, pp. 86–96. University of New Mexico Press, Albuquerque.

Glazebrook, George Parkin de Twenebroker

1971 *The Story of Toronto*. University of Toronto Press, Toronto.

Golden, Charles, and Andrew K. Scherer

2013 Territory, Trust, and Collapse in Classic Period Maya Kingdoms. *Current Anthropology* 54:397–435.

Goldstein, Lynne

1991 The Implications of Aztalan's Location. In *New Perspectives on Cahokia: Views from the Periphery*, edited by John B. Stoltman. pp. 209–228. Prehistory Press, Madison, Wisconsin.

2000 Mississippian Ritual as Viewed Through the Practice of Secondary Disposal of the Dead. In *Mounds, Modoc, and Mesoamerica: Papers in Honor of Melvin L. Fowler*, edited by Steven R. Ahler, pp. 193–205. Scientific Papers Series, Vol. 28. Illinois State Museum, Springfield.

Goldstein, Paul S.

1993 Tiwanaku Temples and State Expansion: A Tiwanaku Sunken Court Temple in Moquegua, Peru. *Latin American Antiquity* 4:22–47.

1996 Tiwanaku Settlement Patterns of the Azapa Valley, Chile: New Data, and the Legacy of Percy Dauelsberg. *Dialogo andino* 14–15:57–73.

2003 From Stew-Eaters to Maize-Drinkers: The Chicha Economy and the Tiwanaku Expansion. In *The Archaeology and Politics of Food and Feasting in Early States and Empires*, edited by Tamara L. Bray, pp. 143–172. Kluwer, New York.

2005 *Andean Diaspora: The Tiwanaku Colonies and the Origins of South American Empire*. University Press of Florida, Gainesville.

2009 Disaporas within the Ancient State: Tiwanaku and Ayllus in Motion. In *Andean Civilization: A Tribute to Michael E. Moseley*, edited by Joyce Marcus and Patrick Ryan Williams, pp. 277–302. Cotsen Institute of Archaeology, University of California, Los Angeles.

2013 Embedded Andean Economic Systems and the Expansive Tiwanaku States: A Case for a State without Market Exchange. In *Merchants, Markets, and Exchange in the Pre-Columbian World*, edited by Kenneth G. Hirth and Joanne Pillsbury, pp. 361–388. Dumbarton Oaks, Washington, DC.

Goldstein, Paul S., and Mario A. Rivera

2004 Arts of Greater Tiwanaku: An Expansive Culture in Historical Context. In *Tiwanaku: Ancestors of the Inca*, edited by Margaret Young-Sánchez, pp. 150–185. University of Nebraska Press, Lincoln.

González Licón, Ernesto

2009 Ritual and Social Stratification at Monte Albán, Oaxaca: Strategies from a

Household Perspective. In *Domestic Life in Prehispanic Capitals: A Study of Specialization, Hierarchy, and Ethnicity*, pp. 7–20. Memoirs No. 46. Museum of Anthropology, University of Michigan, Ann Arbor.

Good, Irene L., Jonathan M. Kenoyer, and Richard H. Meadows

2009 New Evidence for Early Silk in the Indus Civilization. *Archaeometry* 51:457–466.

Gosden, Chris

2004 *Archaeology and Colonialism: Culture Contact from 5000 BC to the Present.* Cambridge University Press, New York.

Goudsblom, Johan

2006 Civilization: The Career of a Controversial Concept. *History and Theory* 45:288–297.

Gouin, Philippe

1990 Rapes, jarres et faisselles: La production et l'exportation des produits laiters dans l'Indus du 3e millénaire. *Paléorient* 16(2):37–54.

Greene, Kevin

1999 V. Gordon Childe and the Vocabulary of Revolutionary Change. *Antiquity* 73:97–109.

Greenfield, Michael

1980 The Development of the Underdeveloped City: Public Sanitation in São Paulo, Brazil, 1885–1913. *Luso-Brazilian Review* 17:107–118.

Grimaldi, Frances Antonio

1958 [1799] *Riflessioni sopra l'inequalglizanza tra gli uomini, in Illuministi italiane*, Vol. 5, edited by Franco Venturi. Riccardo Riccardi, Milan.

Gugler, Josef (editor)

1997 *Cities in the Developing World: Issues, Theory, and Policy.* Oxford University Press, Oxford.

Haas, Jonathan

1982 *The Evolution of the Prehistoric State.* Columbia University Press, New York.

Håland, Randi

1980 Man's Role in the Changing Habitat of Mema during the Old Kingdom of Ghana. *Norwegian Archaeological Review* 13:31–46.

Hall, Edith

1989 *Inventing the Barbarian: Greek Self-Definition through Tragedy.* Oxford University Press, Oxford.

Hall, Robert L.

1991 Cahokia Identity and Interaction Models of Cahokia Mississippians. In *Cahokia and the Hinterlands: Mississippian Cultures of the Midwest*, edited by Thomas E. Emerson and Robert B. Lewis, pp. 3–34. University of Chicago Press, Chicago, Illinois.

Hann, Chris

2011 Back to Civilization. *Anthropology Today* 27(6):1–2.

Haour, Anne
2005 Power and Permanence in Precolonial Africa: A Case Study from the Central Sahel. *World Archaeology* 37:552–565.
Harding, Thomas G., David Kaplan, Marshall D. Sahlins, and Elman R. Service
1960 *Evolution and Culture*. University of Michigan Press, Ann Arbor.
Harn, Alan
1991 The Everland Site: Inroads to Spoon River Mississippian Society. In *New Perspectives on Cahokia: Views from the Periphery*, edited by James B. Stoltman, pp. 129–153. Prehistory Press, Madison, Wisconsin.
Hastorf, Christine A.
1993 *Agriculture and the Onset of Political Inequality Before the Inka*. Cambridge University Press, New York.
2003 Community with the Ancestors: Ceremonies and Social Memory in the Middle Formative at Chiripa, Bolivia. *Journal of Anthropological Archaeology* 22:305–322.
2005 The Upper (Middle and Late) Formative in the Titicaca Region. In *Advances in Titicaca Basin Archaeology*, Vol. 1, edited by Charles Stanish, Amanda B. Cohen, and Mark S. Aldenderfer, pp. 65–94. Cotsen Institute of Archaeology, University of California, Los Angeles.
Hastorf, Christine A., William T. Whitehead, Maria C. Bruno, and Melanie Wright
2006 The Movements of Maize into Middle Horizon Tiwanaku, Bolivia. In *Histories of Maize: Multidisciplinary Approaches to the Prehistory, Linguistics, Biogeography, Domestication, and Evolution of Maize*, edited by John Staller, Robert Tykot, and Bruce Benz, pp. 429–448. Academic Press, New York.
Hastorf, Christine A. (editor)
1999 *Early Settlement at Chiripa, Bolivia: Research of the Taraco Archaeological Project*. University of California Archaeological Research Facility, Berkeley.
Hawking, Stephen
1998 *A Brief History of Time*. Bantam, New York.
Hayden, Brian
1995 Pathways to Power: Principles for Creating Socioeconomic Inequalities. In *Foundation of Social Inequality*, edited by T. Douglas Price and Gary M. Feinman, pp. 15–86. Plenum, New York.
Hedman, Kristin M.
2006 Late Cahokian Subsistence and Health: Stable Isotope and Dental Evidence. *Southeastern Archaeology* 25:257–274.
Helms, Mary W.
1993 *Craft and the Kingly Ideal: Art, Trade, and Power*. University of Texas Press, Austin.
Hemphill, Brian E., John R. Lukacs, and Kenneth A. R. Kennedy
1991 Biological Adaptions and Affinities of Bronze Age Harappans. In *Harappa Excavations 1986–1990: A Multidisciplinary Approach to Third Millennium*

Urbanism, edited by Richard H. Meadow, pp. 137–182. Prehistory Press, Madison, Wisconsin.

Henige, David P.

1974 *The Chronology of Oral Traditions: Quest for a Chimera.* Clarendon Press, Oxford, United Kingdom.

2005 *Historical Evidence and Argument.* University of Wisconsin Press, Madison.

Henry, Donald O.

2004 Assessing the Degree of Supra-Regional Homogeneity in Cultural Elements within the Near Eastern Neolithic. *Neo-Lithics* 1/04:32–33.

Herder, Johann Gottfried

2007 *Herder: Philosophical Writings.* Edited by Desmond M. Clarke and Michael N. Forster. Cambridge University Press, Cambridge.

Higueras-Hare, Álvaro

1996 Prehispanic Settlement and Land Use in Cochabamba, Bolivia. Unpublished Ph.D. dissertation, University of Pittsburgh, Pittsburgh, Pennsylvania.

Hill, James N.

1977 Social Systems and the Explanations of Change. In *The Explanation of Culture Change*, edited by James N. Hill, pp. 59–104. University of New Mexico Press, Albuquerque.

Hill, James N. (editor)

1977 *The Explanation of Culture Change*, edited by James N. Hill. University of New Mexico Press, Albuquerque.

Hill, Kevin Bassett

2013 Evidence for the Intensification of Ritual Activity: State Strategy at the Tiwanaku Colony of Isla Esteves, Puno, Peru. Unpublished master's thesis, University of California, Los Angeles.

Hise, Greg

2009 Industry, Political Alliances and the Regulation of Urban Space in Los Angeles. *Urban History* 36:473–497.

Hobbes, Thomas

2010 [1651] *Leviathan; or, The Matter, Forme, and Power of a Common-Wealth Ecclesiasticall and Civill*, edited by Ian Shapiro. Yale University Press, New Haven, Connecticut.

Hodder, Ian

1982 *Symbols in Action: Ethnoarchaeological Studies of Material Culture.* Cambridge University Press, New York.

1985 Postprocessual Archaeology. *Advances in Archaeological Method and Theory* 8:1–26.

2004 Women and Men at Çatalhöyük. *Scientific American* 290:77–83.

2006 *The Leopard's Tale: Revealing the Mysteries of Çatalhöyük.* Thames and Hudson, London.

2007 Çatalhöyük in the Context of the Middle Eastern Neolithic. *Annual Review of Anthropology* 36:105–120.

2012 *Entangled: An Archaeology of the Relationships between Humans and Things.* Wiley-Blackwell, Malden, Massachusetts.

2014a Mosaics and Networks: The Social Geography of Çatalhöyük. In *Integrating Çatalhöyük: Themes from the 2000–2008 Seasons*, edited by Ian Hodder, pp. 149–167. Cotsen Institute of Archaeology, University of California, Los Angeles.

2014b Temporal Trends: The Shapes and Narratives of Cultural Change at Çatalhöyük. In *Integrating Çatalhöyük: Themes from the 2000–2008 Seasons*, edited by Ian Hodder, pp. 169–183. Cotsen Institute of Archaeology, University of California, Los Angeles.

2014c Çatalhöyük: The Leopard Changes its Spots. A Summary of Recent Work. *Anatolian Studies* 64:1–22.

Hodder, Ian, and Craig Cessford

2004 Daily Practice and Social Memory at Çatalhöyük. *American Antiquity* 69:17–40.

Hodder, Ian, Craig Cessford, and Shahina Farid

2007 Introduction to Methods and Approach. In *Excavating Çatalhöyük: South, North and KOPAL Area Reports from the 1995–1999 Seasons*, edited by Ian Hodder, pp. 3–24. McDonald Institute for Archaeological Research and the British Institute at Ankara, Cambridge.

Hodder, Ian, and Lynne Meskell

2010 The Symbolism of Çatalhöyük in Its Regional Context. In *Religion in the Emergence of Civilization: Çatalhöyük as a Case Study*, edited by Ian Hodder, pp. 32–72. Cambridge University Press, New York.

Holley, George R.

2006 Perspectives from the Edge of Looking Glass Prairie: The Scott Joint-Use Archaeological Project. *Southeastern Archaeology* 25:301–328.

Holloway, Thomas H.

1978 Creating the Reserve Army? The Immigration Program of São Paulo, 1886–1930. *International Migration Review* 12:187–209.

Horace

1863. *The Works of Horace.* Translated by Christopher Smart. Harper and Brothers, New York.

Huang, Yang

2010 Invention of Barbarian and Emergence of Orientalism: Classical Greece. *Journal of Chinese Philosophy* 37:556–566.

Huff, W. G.

1993 The Development of the Rubber Market in Pre-World War II Singapore. *Journal of Southeast Asian Studies* 24:285–306.

Insoll, Timothy

1996 *Islam, Archaeology, and History: Gao Region (Mali) ca. AD 900–1250.* Cambridge Monographs in African Archaeology 39. British Archaeological Reports International Series 647. Tempvs Reparatvm, Oxford.

2000 Conclusions: Gao in Context. In *Urbanism, Archaeology, and Trade (Further Observations on the Gao Region (Mali)): The 1996 Field Season Results*, edited by Timothy Insoll, pp. 150–152. British Archaeological Reports International Series 829. J. and E. Hedges, Oxford.

Isbell, William H., and JoEllen Burkholder

2002 Iwawi and Tiwanaku. In *Variations in Sociopolitical Organization*, Vol. 1 of *Andean Archaeology*, edited by William H. Isbell and Helaine Silverman, pp. 199–241. Kluwer, New York.

Isbell, William H., and Alexei Vranich

2004 Experiencing the Cities of Wari and Tiwanaku. In *Andean Archaeology*, edited by Helaine Silverman, pp. 167–182. Blackwell, Malden, Massachusetts.

Isik, Murat, and Madhu Khanna

2003 Stochastic Technology, Risk Preferences, and Adoption of Site-Specific Technologies. *American Journal of Agricultural Economics* 85:305–317.

Jacobs, Jane

1969 *The Economy of Cities*. Vintage, New York.

Jacobs, Margaret C. C.

2000 *The Enlightenment: A Brief History with Documents*. Bedford/St. Martin's, New York.

Jansen, Michael

1993 *Mohenjo-Daro: City of Wells and Drains; Water Splendour 4500 Years Ago*. Frontinus Society Publications, Bergisch Gladbach, Germany.

Janusek, John Wayne

2002 Out of Many, One: Style and Social Boundaries in Tiwanaku. *Latin American Antiquity* 13:35–61.

2003 The Changing Face of Tiwanaku Residential Life: State and Local Identity in an Andean City. In *Urban and Rural Archaeology*, Vol. 2 of *Tiwanaku and Its Hinterland: Archaeology and Paleoecology of an Andean Civilization*, edited by Alan L. Kolata, pp. 264–295. Smithsonian Books, Washington, DC.

2004a *Identity and Power in the Ancient Andes: Tiwanaku Cities through Time*. Routledge, London.

2004b Collapse as Cultural Revolution: Power and Identity in the Tiwanaku to Pacajes Transition. In *Foundations of Power in the Prehispanic Andes*, edited by Kevin J. Vaughn, Dennis Ogburn, and Christina A. Conlee, pp. 175–209. American Archaeological Association, Arlington, Virginia.

2005 Residential Diversity and the Rise of Complexity in Tiwanaku. In *Advances in Titicaca Basin Archaeology*, Vol. 1, edited by Charles Stanish, Amanda B. Cohen, and Mark S. Aldenderfer, pp. 143–172. Cotsen Institute of Archaeology, University of California, Los Angeles.

2006 The Changing "Nature" of Tiwanaku Religion and the Rise of an Andean State. *World Archaeology* 38:469–492.

2008 *Ancient Tiwanaku.* New York University Press, Cambridge.

2009 Residence and Ritual in Tiwanaku: Hierarchy, Specialization, Ethnicity, and Ceremony. In *Domestic Life in Prehispanic Capitals: A Study of Specialization, Hierarchy, and Ethnicity*, edited by Linda R. Manzanilla and Claude Chapdelaine, pp. 159–179. Memoirs No. 36. Museum of Anthropology, University of Michigan, Ann Arbor.

2012 Understanding Tiwanaku Origins: Animistic Ecology in the Andean Altiplano. In *The Past Ahead: Language, Culture, and Identity in the Neotropics*, edited by Christian Isendahl, pp. 111–138. Uppsala University, Uppsala.

Janusek, John Wayne, Patrick Ryan Williams, Mark Golitko, and Carlos Lémuz Aguirre

2013 Building Taypikala: Telluric Transformations in the Lithic Production of Tiwanaku. In *Mining and Quarrying in the Ancient Andes: Sociopolitical, Economic, and Symbolic Dimensions*, edited by Nicholas Tripcevich and Kevin J. Vaughn, pp. 65–98. Springer, New York.

Jarrige, Catherine, Jean-François Jarrige, Richard H. Meadow, and Gonzague Quivron (editors)

1995 *Mehrgarh Field Reports 1974–1985: From Neolithic Times to the Indus Civilization.* Department of Culture and Tourism, Karachi.

Jarrige, Jean-François

1993 Excavations at Mehrgarh: Their Significance for Understanding the Background of the Harappan Civilization. In *Harappan Civilization: A Recent Perspective*, 2nd ed., edited by Gregory L. Possehl, pp. 79–84. American Institute of Indian Studies, New Delhi.

1995 Introduction. In *Mehrgarh Field Reports 1974–1985: From Neolithic Times to the Indus Civilization*, edited by Catherine Jarrige, Jean-François Jarrige, Richard H. Meadow, and Gonzague Quivron, pp. 1–95. Department of Culture and Tourism, Karachi.

Jarrige, Jean-François, Catherine Jarrige, and Gonzague Quivron

2005 Mehrgarh Neolithic: The Updated Sequence. In *South Asian Archaeology 2001*, edited by Catherine Jarrige and Vincent Lefévre, pp. 128–141. Éditions recherche sur les civilizations-ADPF, Paris.

Jarrige, Jean-François, and Gonzague Quivron

2008 The Indus Valley and the Indo-Iranian Borderlands at the End of the 3rd Millennium and the Beginning of the 2nd Millennium BC. In *South Asian Archaeology* 1999, edited by Ellen M. Raven, pp. 61–83. Egbert Forsten, Groningen, Netherlands.

Jenkins, Paul Christy

2000 The Pottery from Cemetery R37: Chronology and the Changing Social Structure of Harappa Society. In *South Asian Archaeology 1997*, edited by Maurizo

Taddei and Guiseppe De Marco, pp. 35–53. Istituto italiano per l'Africa e l'Oriente, Rome.

Jennings, Justin

2011 *Globalizations and the Ancient World.* Cambridge University Press, New York.

Jennings, Justin, and Melissa Chatfield

2009 Pots, Brewers, and Hosts: Women's Power and the Limits of Central Andean Feasting. In *Drink, Power, and Society in the Andes,* edited by Justin Jennings and Brenda J. Bowser, pp. 200–231. University Press of Florida, Gainesville.

Johnson, Allen W., and Timothy Earle

1987 *The Evolution of Complex Societies.* Stanford University Press, Stanford, California.

Johnson, Gregory A.

1978 Information Sources and the Development of Decision-Making Organizations. In *Social Archaeology: Beyond Subsistence and Dating,* edited by Charles Redman, pp. 87–112. Academic Press, New York.

1982 Organizational Structure and Scalar Stress. In *Theory and Explanation in Archaeology,* edited by Colin Renfrew, Michael Rowlands, and Brian Seagraves, pp. 389–421. Academic Press, New York.

Johnson, Matthew

2010 *Archaeological Theory: An Introduction.* 2nd ed. Wiley-Blackwell, Malden, Massachusetts.

Joyce, Arthur A.

2004 Sacred Space and Social Relations in the Valley of Oaxaca. In *Mesoamerican Archaeology: Theory and Practice,* edited by Julia A. Hendon and Rosemary A. Joyce, pp. 192–216. Blackwell, Malden, Massachusetts.

2009a The Main Plaza of Monte Albán: A Life History of Place. In *The Archaeology of Meaningful Places,* edited by Brenda J. Bowser and María Nieves Zedeño, pp. 32–52. University of Utah Press, Salt Lake City.

2009b Theorizing Urbanism in Ancient Mesoamerica. *Ancient Mesoamerica* 20:189–196.

2010 *Mixtecs, Zapotecs, and Chatinos: Ancient Peoples of Southern Mexico.* Wiley-Blackwell, Malden, Massachusetts.

Joyce, Arthur A., Michael Elam, Michael D. Glascock, Hector Neff, and Marcus Winter

1995 Exchange Implications of Obsidian Source Analysis from the Lower Rio Verde Valley, Oaxaca, Mexico. *Latin American Antiquity* 6:3–15.

Joyce, Arthur A., Hector Neff, Mary S. Thieme, Marcus Winter, J. Michael Elam, and Andrew Workinger

2006 Ceramic Production and Exchange in Late/Terminal Formative Period Oaxaca. *Latin American Antiquity* 17:579–594.

Joyce, Arthur A., and Marcus Winter

1996 Ideology, Power, and Urban Society in Pre-Hispanic Oaxaca. *Current Anthropology* 37:33–47.

Joyce, Rosemary A.
2000 *Gender and Power in Prehispanic Mesoamerica*. University of Texas Press, Austin.
2004 Unintended Consequences? Monumentality as a Novel Experience in Formative Mesoamerica. *Journal of Anthropological Method and Theory* 11:5–29.
2011 What Should an Archaeology of Religion Look Like to a Blind Archaeologist? In *Beyond Belief: The Archaeology of Religion and Ritual*, edited by Yorke M. Rowan, pp. 180–188. American Archaeological Association, Arlington, Virginia.
2012 Life with Things: Archaeology and Materiality: In *Archaeology and Anthropology: Past, Present and Future*, edited by David Shankland, pp. 119–132. Berg, Oxford, United Kingdom.

Kahrl, William L.
1976 The Politics of California Water: Owens Valley and the Los Angeles Aqueduct, 1900–1927. *California Historical Quarterly* 55:98–120.

Kaplan, David
2000 The Darker Side of the "Original Affluent Society." *Journal of Anthropological Research* 56:301–324.

Kaplan, Robert D.
2012 The Vietnam Solution. *Atlantic* 309:54–62.

Kelly, John E.
1990a The Emergence of Mississippian Culture in the American Bottom Region. In *The Mississippian Emergence*, edited by Bruce D. Smith, pp. 113–152. Smithsonian Institution Press, Washington, DC.
1990b Range Site Community Patterns and the Mississippian Emergence. In *The Mississippian Emergence*, edited by Bruce D. Smith, pp. 67–112. Smithsonian Institution Press, Washington, DC.
1991a Cahokia and its Role as a Gateway Center in Interregional Exchange. In *Cahokia and Hinterlands: Middle Mississippian Cultures of the Midwest*, edited by Thomas E. Emerson and R. Barry Lewis, pp. 61–80. University of Illinois Press, Urbana.
1991b The Evidence for Prehistoric Exchange and Its Implications for the Development of Cahokia. *New Perspectives on Cahokia: Views from the Periphery*, edited by John B. Stoltman, pp. 65–92. Prehistory Press, Madison, Wisconsin.
2000 The Nature and Context of Emergent Mississippian Cultural Dynamics in the Greater American Bottom. In *Late Woodland Societies: Tradition and Transformation across the Midcontinent*, edited by Thomas E. Emerson, Dale L. McElrath, and Andrew C. Fortier, pp. 163–175. University of Nebraska Press, Lincoln.
2002 Woodland Period Archaeology in the American Bottom. In *The Woodland Southeast*, edited by David G. Anderson and Robert C. Mainfort Jr., pp. 134–161. University of Alabama Press, Tuscaloosa.

Kennedy, Kenneth A. R.

2000 *God-Apes and Fossil Men: Paleoanthropology in South Asia.* University of Michigan Press, Ann Arbor.

Kenoyer, Jonathan Mark

1991 Urban Process in the Indus Tradition: A Preliminary Model from Harappa. In *Harappa Excavations 1986–1990: A Multidisciplinary Approach to Third Millennium Urbanism*, edited by Richard H. Meadow, pp. 29–60. Prehistory Press, Madison, Wisconsin.

1995 Ideology and Legitimation in the Indus State as Reveled through Symbolic Objects. *Archaeological Review* 4:87–131.

1997 Trade and Technology of the Indus Valley: New Insights from Harappa, Pakistan. *World Archaeology* 29:262–280.

1998 *Ancient Cities of the Indus Valley Civilization.* Oxford University Press, Karachi.

2000 Wealth and Socioeconomic Hierarchies of the Indus Valley Civilization. In *Order, Legitimacy, and Wealth in Ancient States*, edited by Janet Richards and Mary Van Buren, pp. 88–109. Cambridge University Press, New York.

2003 Uncovering the Keys to the Lost Indus Cities. *Scientific American* 289:66–75.

2005 Bead Technologies at Harappa, 3300–1900 BC: A Comparative Summary. In *South Asian Archaeology 2001*, edited by Catherine Jarrige and Vincent Lefévre, pp. 157–170. Éditions recherche sur les civilisations-ADPF, Paris.

2008a Indus Urbanism: New Perspectives on Its Origins and Character. In *The Ancient City: New Perspectives on Urbanism in the Old and New World*, edited by Joyce Marcus and Jeremy A. Sabloff, pp. 183–208. School for Advanced Research, Santa Fe, New Mexico.

2008b Indus and Mesopotamian Trade Networks: New Insights from Shell and Carnelian Artifacts. In *Intercultural Relations between South and Southwest Asia: Studies in Commemoration of E. C. L. During Caspers (1934–1996)*, edited by Eric Olijdam and Richard H. Spoor, pp. 19–28. British Archaeological Reports International Series 1826. Archaeopress, Oxford.

2010 Measuring the Harappan World: Insights into the Indus Order and Cosmology. In *The Archaeology of Measurement: Comprehending Heaven, Earth, and Time in Ancient Societies*, edited by Iain Morley and Colin Renfrew, pp. 106–121. Cambridge University Press, New York.

2011 Changing Perspectives of the Indus Civilization: New Discoveries and Challenges. *Purātattva: Journal of the Indian Archaeological Society* 41:1–18.

Kenyoer, Jonathan Mark, and Richard H. Meadow

2000 The Ravi Phase: A New Cultural Manifestation at Harappa. In *South Asian Archaeology* 1997, edited by Maurizo Taddei and Guiseppe De Marco, pp. 55–76. Istituto italiano per l'Africa e l'Oriente, Rome.

2008 The Early Indus Script at Harappa: Origins and Development. In *Intercultural Relations between South and Southwest Asia: Studies in Commemoration of*

E. C. L. During Caspers (1934–1996), edited by Eric Olijdam and Richard H. Spoor, pp. 124–131. British Archaeological Reports International Series 1826. Archaeopress, Oxford.

Kenoyer, Jonathan Mark, and Heather M. L. Miller

1999 Metal Technologies of the Indus Valley Tradition in Pakistan and Western India. In *The Archaeometallurgy of the Asian Old World*, edited by Vincent C. Piggot, pp. 5–151. MASCA Research Reports in Papers in Science and Archaeology, Vol. 16. University of Pennsylvania Museum, Philadelphia.

Kenoyer, Jonathan Mark, T. Douglas Price, and James H. Burton

2013 A New Approach to Tracking Connections between the Indus Valley and Mesopotamia: Initial Results of Strontium Isotope Analyses from Harappa and Ur. *Journal of Archaeological Science* 40:2286–2297.

King, Adam

2007 Whither SECC? In *Southeastern Ceremonial Complex: Chronology, Content, Context*, edited by Adam King, pp. 251–258. University of Alabama Press, Tuscaloosa.

2010 Multiple Groups, Overlapping Symbols, and the Creation of a Sacred Space at Etowah's Mound C. In *Mississippian Mortuary Practices: Beyond Hierarchy and the Representationist Perspective*, edited by Lynne P. Sullivan and Robert C. Mainfort Jr., pp. 54–73. University Press of Florida, Gainesville.

King, Adam (editor)

2007 The Southeastern Ceremonial Complex: From Cult to Complex. In *Southeastern Ceremonial Complex: Chronology, Content, Context*, edited by Adam King, pp. 1–14. University of Alabama Press, Tuscaloosa.

Kjolsing, Jason Michael

2013 The Political Strategies of Tiwanaku Leaders in Moquegua, Peru: An Analysis of Tiwanaku Priests and the Inner Chambers of the Omo Temple. Unpublished master's thesis, University of California, San Diego.

Klarich, Elizabeth A.

2005 From the Monumental to the Mundane: Defining Early Leadership Strategies at Late Formative Pukara, Peru. Unpublished Ph.D. dissertation, University of California, Santa Barbara.

2009 Pukara: Investigaciones de la temporada 2001 y un nuevo modelo para el desarrollo del sitio. In *Arqueológica del área centro sur Andina: Actas del simposio internacional 30 de junio–2 de julio de 2005, Arequipa, Perú*, edited by Mariusz S. Ziółkowski, Justin Jennings, Luis Augusto Belan Franco, and Andrea Drusini, pp. 283–305. ANDES: Boletín del centro de estudios precolombinos de la Universidad de Varsovia 7. University of Warsaw.

2012 Producción, papas, y proyectiles: evaluado los factores principales en el desarrollo de Pukara. In *Arqueología de la Cuenca del Titicaca, Perú*, edited by Luis Flores Blanco and Henry Tantaleán, pp. 195–216. Instituto francés de estudios andinos, Lima.

Klarich, Elizabeth A., and Nancy Román Bustinza

2012 Scale and Diversity at Late Formative Period Pukara. In *Advances in Titicaca Basin Archaeology*, Vol. 3, edited by Alexei Vranich, Elizabeth Klarich, and Charles Stanish, pp. 105–120. Cotsen Institute of Archaeology, University of California, Los Angeles.

Knappett, Carl

2011 *An Archaeology of Interaction: Network Perspectives on Material Culture and Society*. Oxford University Press, Oxford.

Knight, Vernon James, Jr.

1990 Social Organization and the Evolution of Hierarchy in Southeastern Chiefdoms. *Journal of Anthropological Research* 46:1–23.

Knudson, Kelly J.

2007 La influencia de Tiwanaku en San Pedro de Atacama: Una investigación utilizando el análisis de isótopos del estroncio. *Estudios Atacameños: Arqueología y antropología Surandinas* 33:7–24.

2008 Tiwanaku Influence in the South Central Andes: Strontium Isotope Analysis and Middle Horizon Migration. *Latin American Antiquity* 19:3–23.

Knudson, Kelly J., and Christina Torres-Rouff

2014 Cultural Diversity and Paleomobility in the Andean Middle Horizon: Radiogenic Strontium Isotope Analysis in the San Pedro de Atacama Oases of Northern Chile. *Latin American Antiquity* 25:170–188.

Kohl, Philip L.

2007 *The Making of Bronze Age Eurasia*. Cambridge University Press, New York.

Kohl, Philip L., and Bertille Lyonnet

2008 By Land and By Sea: The Circulation of Materials and Peoples, *ca*. 3500–1800 B.C. In *Intercultural Relations Between South and Southwest Asia: Studies in Commemoration of E. C. L. During Caspers (1934–1996)*, edited by Eric Olijdam and Richard H. Spoor, pp. 29–42. British Archaeological Reports International Series 1826. Archaeopress, Oxford.

Kohler, Timothy A., and Mark D. Varien

2010 A Scale Model of Seven Hundred Years of Farming Settlements in Southwestern Colorado. In *Becoming Villages: Comparing Early Village Societies*, edited by Matthew S. Bandy and Jake R. Fox, pp. 37–61. University of Arizona Press, Tucson.

Koons, Michele L.

2013 Reexamining Tiwanaku's Urban Renewal through Ground-Penetrating Radar and Excavation: The Results of Three Field Seasons. In *Advances in Titicaca Basin Archaeology*, Vol. 2, edited by Alexei Vranich and Abigail R. Levine, pp. 147–165. Cotsen Institute of Archaeology, University of California, Los Angeles.

Kolata, Alan L.

1993 *The Tiwanaku: Portrait of an Andean Civilization*. Blackwell, Malden, Massachusetts.

Kolata, Alan L., Michael W. Binford, Mark Brenner, John W. Janusek, and Charles Ortloff

2000 Environmental Thresholds and the Empirical Reality of State Collapse: A Response to Erickson (1999). *Antiquity* 74:424–426.

Korpisaari, Antti, Markku Oinonen, and Juan Chacama

2014 A Reevaluation of the Absolute Chronology of Cabuza and Related Ceramic Styles of the Azapa Valley, Northern Chile. *Latin American Antiquity* 25:409–426.

Kowalewski, Stephen A.

2003 Internal Subdivisions of Communities in the Prehispanic Valley of Oaxaca. In *Factional Competition and Political Development in the New World*, edited by Elizabeth M. Brumfiel and John W. Fox, pp. 127–137. Cambridge University Press, New York.

2006 Coalescent Societies. In *Light on the Path: The Anthropology and History of the Southeastern Indians*, edited by Thomas J. Pluckhahn and Robbie Ethridge, pp. 94–122. University of Alabama Press, Tuscaloosa.

2013 The Work of Making Community. In *From Prehistoric Villages to Cities: Settlement Aggregation and Community Transformation*, edited by Jennifer Birch, pp. 201–218. Routledge, New York.

Kowalewski, Stephen A., Gary M. Feinman, Laura Finsten, Richard E. Blanton, and Linda M. Nichols.

1989 *Prehispanic Settlement Patterns in Tlacolula, Etla, and Ocotlan, the Valley of Oaxaca, Mexico*. Pt. 2 of *Monte Albán Hinterland*. Memoirs No. 23. Museum of Anthropology, University of Michigan, Ann Arbor.

Kramer, Karen L., and James L. Boone

2002 Why Intensive Agriculturists Have Higher Fertility: A Household Energy Budget Approach. *Current Anthropology* 43:511–517.

Kroeber, Alfred L.

1944 *Configurations of Cultural Growth*. University of California Press, Berkeley.

Kuijt, Ian

1996 Negotiating Equality through Ritual: A Consideration of Late Natufian and Pre-Pottery Neolithic A Period Mortuary Practices. *Journal of Anthropological Archaeology* 15:313–336.

2000 People and Space in Early Agricultural Villages: Exploring Daily Lives, Community Size, and Architecture in the Late Pre-Pottery Neolithic. *Journal of Anthropological Archaeology* 19:75–102.

2008 The Regeneration of Life: Neolithic Structures of Symbolic Remembering and Forgetting. *Current Anthropology* 49:171–197.

Kuijt, Ian, and Nigel Goring-Morris
2002 Foraging, Farming, and Social Complexity in the Pre-Pottery Neolithic of the South-Central Levant: A Review and Synthesis. *Journal of World Prehistory* 16:361–440.
Kuznar, Lawrence A.
2001 Risk Sensitivity and Value Among Andean Pastoralists: Measures, Models, and Empirical Tests. *Current Anthropology* 42:432–440.
Kuznesof, Elizabeth Anne
1980 Household Composition and Headship as Related to Changes in Mode of Production: São Paulo, 1765 to 1836. *Comparative Studies in Society and History* 22:78–108.
Lansing, J. Stephen
2003 Complex Adaptive Systems. *Annual Review of Anthropology* 32:183–204.
LaViolette, Adria, and Jeffrey Fleisher
2004 The Archaeology of Sub-Saharan Urbanism: Cities and Their Countrysides. In *African Archaeology: A Critical Introduction*, edited by Ann Brower Stahl, pp. 327–352. Blackwell, Malden, Massachusetts.
Law, Randall W.
2005a Regional Interaction in the Prehistoric Indus Valley: Initial Results of Rock and Mineral Sourcing Studies at Harappa. In *South Asia Archaeology 2001*, edited by Catherine Jarrige and Vincent Lefévre, pp. 179–190. Éditions recherche sur les civilizations-ADPF, Paris.
2005b A Diachronic Examination of Lithic Exchange Networks during the Urban Transformation of Harappa. In *South Asian Archaeology 2003*, edited by Ute Franke-Vogt and Hans-Joachim Weisshaar, pp. 111–121. Linden Soft, Aachen, Germany.
2006 Moving Mountains: The Trade and Transport of Rocks and Minerals within the Greater Indus Valley Region. In *Space and Spatial Analysis in Archaeology*, edited by Elizabeth C. Robertson, Jeffrey D. Seibert, Deepika C. Fernandez, and Marc U. Zeder, pp. 301–313. University of Calgary Press, Calgary.
Lee, Richard B.
1984 *The Dobe !Kung*. New York, Harcourt Brace.
Levine, Abigail R.
2012 Conflict and Cooperation in the Northern Titicaca Basin. *Backdirt: Annual Review of the Cotsen Institute of Archaeology*:137–147.
Levine, Abigail, R., Charles Stanish, P. Ryan Williams, Cecilia Chávez, and Mark Golitko
2013 Trade and Early State Formation in the Northern Titicaca Basin, Peru. *Latin American Antiquity* 24:289–308.
Levine, Marc N.
2013 Examining Ceramic Evidence for the Zapotec Imperialism Hypothesis in the Lower Río Verde Region of Oaxaca, Mexico. In *Polity and Ecology in Formative Period Coastal Oaxaca*, edited by Arthur A. Joyce, pp. 227–264. University Press of Colorado, Boulder.

Lévi-Strauss, Claude
1983 *The Raw and the Cooked.* University of Chicago Press, Chicago, Illinois.
Lewis, R. Barry, and Charles Stout (editors)
1998 *Mississippian Towns and Sacred Spaces: Searching for an Architectural Grammar.* University of Alabama Press, Tuscaloosa.
Lewis-Williams, David
2003 Constructing a Cosmos: Architecture, Power, and Domestication in Çatalhöyük. *Journal of Social Archaeology* 4:28–59.
Linnaeus, Carolus
1758 *Systema naturae per regna naturae, secundum classes, ordines, genera, species, cum characteribus, differentiis, synonymis,* Bk. 1. 10th ed. Laurentius Salvius, Stockholm.
Locke, John
1956 [1690] *The Second Treatise of Government: An Essay Concerning the True Original, Extent and End of Civil Government, and A Letter Concerning Toleration.* Blackwell, Oxford, United Kingdom.
Logan, Amanda L., Christine A. Hastorf, and Deborah M. Pearsall
2012 "Let's Drink Together": Early Ceremonial Use of Maize in the Titicaca Basin. *Latin American Antiquity* 23:235–258.
Lowie, Robert H.
1920 *Primitive Society.* Boni and Liveright, New York.
Lubbock, John
1865 *Pre-Historic Times, as Illustrated by Ancient Remains, and the Manners and Customs of Modern Savages.* William and Norgate, Edinburgh.
Lucas, Cristin A.
2012 People on the Move: Examining Tiwanaku State Expansion in the Cochabamba Valley through Strontium Isotope Analysis. Unpublished master's thesis, Northern Arizona University, Flagstaff.
Lucretius
1916 [50 BC] *Of the Nature of Things.* Translated by William Ellery Leonard. Dent, London.
Lull, Vincente, and Rafael Mico
2011 *Archaeology of the Origin of the State.* Oxford University Press, Oxford.
Lyell, Charles
1830–1833 *Principles of Geology, Being an Attempt to Explain the Former Changes of the Earth's Surface, by Reference to Causes Now in Operation.* John Murray, London.
MacDonald, Kevin C.
1995 Analysis of the Mammalian, Avian, and Reptilian Remains. In *Excavations at Jenné-Jeno, Hambarketolo, and Kaniana (Inland Niger Delta, Mali): The 1981 Season,* edited by Susan Keech McIntosh, pp. 291–318. University of California Press, Berkeley.

1997 Korounkorokalé Revisited: The Pays Mande and the West African Microlithic Technocomplex. *African Archaeological Review* 14:161–200.

1999 Invisible Pastoralists: An Inquiry into the Origins of Nomadic Pastoralism in the West African Sahel. In *The Prehistory of Food: Appetites for Change*, edited by Chris Gosden and Jon Hather, pp. 333–349. Routledge, London.

MacDonald, Kevin C., and R. H. MacDonald

2000 The Origins and Development of Domesticated Animals in West Africa. In *The Origins and Development of African Livestock: Archaeology, Genetics, Linguistics, and Ethnography*, edited by Roger Blench and Kevin C. MacDonald, pp. 127–162. University College London Press, London.

Madella, Marco, and Dorian Q. Fuller

2006 Paleoecology and the Harappan Civilization of South Asia: A Reconsideration. *Quaternary Science Reviews* 25:1283–1301.

Mahajan, Naha, Margaret A. Martinez, Nathashya L. Guitierrez, Gil Diesendruck, Mahrazin R. Banaji, and Laurie R. Santos

2011 The Evolution of Intergroup Bias: Perceptions and Attitudes in Rhesus Macaques. *Journal of Personality and Social Psychology* 100:387–405.

Malinowski, Bronislaw

1921 The Primitive Economics of the Trobriand Islanders. *Economic Journal* 31:1–16.

1922 *Argonauts of the Western Pacific*. E. P. Dutton, New York.

Manzanilla, Linda

1992 *Akapana: Una pirámide en el centro del mundo*. Universidad nacional autónoma de México, Instituto de investigaciones anthrológicas, Mexico City.

1997 Early Urban Societies: Challenges and Perspectives. In *Emergence and Change in Early Urban Societies*, edited by Linda Manzanilla, pp. 3–39. Plenum Press, New York.

Marcoux, Jon Bernard

2007 On Reconsidering Display Goods Production and Circulation in the Moundsville Chiefdom. *Southeastern Archaeology* 26:232–245.

Marcoux, Jon Bernard, and Gregory D. Wilson

2010 Categories of Complexity and the Preclusion of Practice. In *Ancient Complexities: New Perspectives in Precolumbian North America*, edited by Susan M. Alt, pp. 138–152. University of Utah Press, Salt Lake City.

Marcus, Joyce

1976 *Emblem and State in the Classic Maya Lowlands: An Epigraphic Approach to Territorial Organization*. Dumbarton Oaks, Washington, DC.

1983a On the Nature of the Mesoamerican City. In *Prehistoric Settlement Patterns: Essays in Honor of Gordon R. Wiley*, edited by Evon Z. Vogt and Richard M. Leventhal, pp. 195–242. Peabody Museum of Archaeology and Ethnology, Cambridge, Massachusetts.

1983b The Conquest Slabs of Building J, Monte Albán. In *The Cloud People: Divergent Evolution of the Zapotec and Mixtec Civilizations*, edited by Kent V. Flannery and Joyce Marcus, pp. 106–108. Academic Press, New York.

1983c Stone Monuments and Tomb Murals of Monte Albán IIIa. In *The Cloud People: Divergent Evolution of the Zapotec and Mixtec Civilizations*, edited by Kent V. Flannery and Joyce Marcus, pp. 137–143. Academic Press, New York.

1983d Rethinking the Zapotec Urns. In *The Cloud People: Divergent Evolution of the Zapotec and Mixtec Civilizations*, edited by Kent V. Flannery and Joyce Marcus, pp. 144–148. Academic Press, New York.

1998 The Peaks and Valleys of Ancient States: An Extension of the Dynamic Model. In *Archaic States*, edited by Gary M. Feinman and Joyce Marcus, pp. 59–94. School for Advanced Research, Santa Fe, New Mexico.

Marcus, Joyce, and Gary M. Feinman

1998 Introduction. In *Archaic States*, edited by Gary M. Feinman and Joyce Marcus, pp. 3–14. School for Advanced Research, Santa Fe, New Mexico.

Marcus, Joyce, and Kent V. Flannery

1994 Ancient Zapotec Ritual and Religion: An Application of the Direct Historical Approach. In *The Ancient Mind: Elements of Cognitive Archaeology*, edited by Colin Renfrew and Ezra B. Zubrow, pp. 55–74. Cambridge University Press, New York.

1996 *Zapotec Civilization: How Urban Society Evolved in Mexico's Oaxaca Valley.* Thames and Hudson, London.

Marcus, Joyce, and Jeremy A. Sabloff (editors)

2008 *The Ancient City: New Perspectives on Urbanism in the Old and New World.* School for Advanced Research, Santa Fe, New Mexico.

Markens, Robert, and Cira Martínez López

2009 El sistema de producción cerámica en Monte Albán durante el Preclásico tardío y el Clásico tardío. In *Bases de la complejidad social en Oaxaca: Memoria de la cuarta mesa redonda de Monte Albán*, edited by Nelly M. Robles García, pp. 123–152. Instituto nacional de antropología e historia, Mexico City.

Marsh, Erik J.

2012a A Bayesian Re-Assessment of the Earliest Radiocarbon Dates from Tiwanaku, Bolivia. *Radiocarbon* 54:203–218.

2012b The Emergence of Tiwanaku: Domestic Practices and Regional Traditions at Khonkho Wankane and Kk'araña. Unpublished Ph.D. dissertation, University of California, Santa Barbara.

2012c The Founding of Tiwanaku: Evidence from Kk'araña. *Ñawpa Pacha: Journal of Andean Archaeology* 32:169–188.

Marshall, John

1931 *Mohenjo-daro and the Indus Civilization*. Probsthain, London.

Martínez, López, and Robert Markens

2004 Análisis de la función político-económica del conjunto Plataforma Norte lado poniente de la Plaza Principal de Monte Albán. In *Estructuras políticas en Oaxaca antiguo: Memoria de la tercera mesa redonda de Monte Albán*, edited by Nelly M. Robles García, pp. 75–99. Instituto nacional de antropología e historia, Mexico City.

Marx, Karl
1977 [1875] Critique of the Gotha Programme. In *Karl Marx: Selected Writings*, edited by David McLellan, pp. 564–570. Oxford University Press, Oxford.

Marx, Karl, and Frederick Engels
1906 [1848] *Manifesto of the Communist Party*. Charles H. Kerr, Chicago, Illinois.

Maschner, Herbert D. G. (editor)
1996 *Darwinian Archaeologies*. Springer New York.

Mathews, James Edward
2003 Prehistoric Settlement Patterns in the Middle Tiwanaku Valley. In *Urban and Rural Archaeology*, Vol. 2 of *Tiwanaku and Its Hinterland: Archaeology and Paleoecology of an Andean Civilization*, edited by Alan L. Kolata, pp. 112–128. Smithsonian Institution Press, Washington, DC.

Matthews, Wendy
1996 Surface Scraping and Planning. In *On the Surface of Çatalhöyük 1993–1995*, edited by Ian Hodder, pp. 79–99. McDonald Institute for Archaeological Research and the British Institute of Archaeology at Ankara, Cambridge.
2005 Micromorphological and Microstratigraphic Traces of Uses and Concepts of Space. In *Inhabiting Çatalhöyük: Reports from the 1995–99 Seasons*, edited by Ian Hodder, pp. 355–398. McDonald Institute for Archaeological Research and the British Institute at Ankara, Cambridge.

Mattingly, David J.
2010 *Imperialism, Power, and Identity: Experiencing the Roman Empires*. Princeton University Press, Princeton, New Jersey.

Mattoon, Robert H., Jr.
1977 Railroads, Coffee, and the Growth of Big Business in São Paulo, Brazil. *Hispanic American Historical Review* 57:273–295.

Mauch, Karl
1971 *Karl Maunch: African Explorer*, edited by F. O. Bernhard. C. Struik, Cape Town.

Mayor, Anne, Eric Huysecom, Alain Gallay, Michel Rasse, and Ariz Ballouche
2005 Population Dynamics and Paleoclimate over the Past 3000 Years in the Dogon Country, Mali. *Journal of Anthropological Archaeology* 24:25–61.

Mayor, Anne, Eric Huysecom, Sylvain Ozainne, and Sonja Magnavita
2014 Early Social Complexity in the Dogon Country (Mali) as Evidenced by a New Chronology of Funerary Practices. *Journal of Anthropological Archaeology* 34:17–41.

Mazlish, Bruce
2004 *Civilization and Its Contents*. Stanford University Press, Stanford, California.

McAndrews, Timothy L., Juan Albarracin-Jordan, and Marc Bermann
1997 Regional Settlement Patterns in the Tiwanaku Valley of Bolivia. *Journal of Field Archaeology* 24:67–83.

McElrath, Dale L., and Andrew C. Fortier
2000 The Early Late Woodland Occupation of the American Bottom. In *Late Woodland Societies: Tradition and Transformation across the Midcontinent*, edited by Thomas E. Emerson, Dale L. McElrath, and Andrew C. Fortier, pp. 97–121. University of Nebraska Press, Lincoln.
McIntosh, Roderick J.
1983 Geomorphology and Human Occupation of the Upper Inland Delta of the Niger. *Geographical Journal* 149:182–201.
1991 Early Urban Clusters in China and Africa: The Arbitration of Social Ambiguity. *Journal of Field Archaeology* 18:199–212.
1993 The Pulse Model: Genesis and Accommodation of Specialization in the Middle Niger. *Journal of African History* 34:181–212.
1998 *The Peoples of the Middle Niger: The Islands of Gold*. Blackwell, Malden, Massachusetts.
2000 Social Memory in Mande. In *The Way the Wind Blows: Climate, History, and Human Action*, edited by Roderick J. McIntosh, Joseph A. Tainter, and Susan Keetch McIntosh, pp. 141–180. Columbia University Press, New York.
2005 *Ancient Middle Niger: Urbanism and the Self-Organizing Landscape*. Cambridge University Press, New York.
McIntosh, Roderick J., and Susan Keech McIntosh
1988 From *Siécles Obscurs* to Revolutionary Centuries on the Middle Niger. *World Archaeology* 20:141–165.
1995 Stratigraphy, Features and Chronology. In *Excavations at Jenné-Jeno, Hambarketolo, and Kaniana (Inland Niger Delta, Mali): The 1981 Season*, edited by Susan Keech McIntosh, pp. 27–129. University of California Press, Berkeley.
2003 Early Urban Configurations on the Middle Niger: Clustered Cities and Landscapes of Power. In *The Social Construction of Cities*, edited by Monica L. Smith, pp. 103–120. Smithsonian Books, Washington, DC.
McIntosh, Susan Keech
1995a Conclusion: The Sites in Regional Context. In *Excavations at Jenné-Jeno, Hambarketolo, and Kaniana (Inland Niger Delta, Mali): The 1981 Season*, edited by Susan Keech McIntosh, pp. 360–411. University of California Press, Berkeley.
1995b Pottery. In *Excavations at Jenné-Jeno, Hambarketolo, and Kaniana (Inland Niger Delta, Mali): The 1981 Season*, edited by Susan Keech McIntosh, pp. 130–213. University of California Press, Berkeley.
1995c Metals. In *Excavations at Jenné-Jeno, Hambarketolo, and Kaniana (Inland Niger Delta, Mali): The 1981 Season*, edited by Susan Keech McIntosh, pp. 264–290. University of California Press, Berkeley.
1999 Modeling Political Organization in Large-Scale Settlement Clusters: A Case Study from the Inland Niger Delta. In *Beyond Chiefdoms: Pathways to Complexity in Africa*, edited by Susan Keech McIntosh, pp. 66–79. Cambridge University Press, New York.

McIntosh, Susan Keetch (editor)
1995 *Excavations at Jenné-Jeno, Hambarketolo, and Kaniana (Inland Niger Delta, Mali): The 1981 Season*. University of California Press, Berkeley.
McIntosh, Susan Keetch, and Roderick J. McIntosh
1980 *Prehistoric Investigations at Jenne, Mali*. Cambridge Monographs in African Archaeology 2. British Archaeological Reports International Series 89. British Archaeological Reports, Oxford.
1993 Cities Without Citadels: Understanding Urban Origins along the Middle Niger. In *The Archaeology of Africa: Food, Metals, and Towns*, edited by Thurtan Shaw, Paul Sinclair, Bassey Andah, and Alex Okpoko, pp. 622–641. Routledge, New York.
1995 Background to the 1981 Research. In *Excavations at Jenné-Jeno, Hambarketolo, and Kaniana (Inland Niger Delta, Mali): The 1981 Season*, edited by Susan Keech McIntosh, pp. 1–26. University of California Press, Berkeley.
Meadow, Richard H.
1989 Continuity and Change in the Agriculture of the Greater Indus Valley: The Paleoethnobotanical and Zooarchaeological Evidence. In *Old Problems and New Perspectives in the Archaeology of South Asia*, edited by Jonathan Mark Kenoyer, pp. 61–74. Wisconsin Archeological Reports 2. Department of Anthropology, University of Wisconsin, Madison.
1993 Animal Domestication in the Middle East: A Revised View from the Eastern Margin. In *Harappan Civilization: A Recent Perspective*, 2nd ed., edited by Gregory L. Possehl, pp. 295–320. American Institute of Indian Studies, New Delhi.
1998 Pre- and Proto-historic Agricultural and Pastoral Transformation in Northwestern South Asia. *Review of Archaeology* 19(2):12–21.
Meadow, Richard H. (editor)
1991 *Harappa Excavations 1986-1990*. Prehistory Press, Madison, Wisconsin.
Meadow, Richard H., and Jonathan Mark Kenoyer
1997 Excavations at Harappa 1994–1995: New Perspectives on the Indus Script, Craft Activities, and City Organization. In *South Asia Archaeology 1995*, edited by Raymond Allchin and Bridget Allchin, pp. 139–172. Oxford and IBH Publishing, New Delhi.
2005 Excavations at Harappa 2000-2001: New Insights on Chronology and City Organization. In *South Asian Archaeology 2001*, edited by Catherine Jarrige Vincent Lefévre, pp. 207–224. Éditions recherche sur les civilisations-ADFP, Paris.
2008 Harappa Excavations 1998–1999: New Evidence for the Development and Manifestations of the Harappan Phenomenon. In *South Asian Archaeology 1999*, edited by Ellen M. Raven, pp. 85–110. Egbert Forsten, Groningen, Netherlands.
Meadow, Richard H., and Ajita K. Patel
2003 Prehistoric Pastoralism in Northwestern South Asia from the Neolithic

through the Harappan Period. In *Indus Ethnobiology: New Perspectives from the Field*, edited by Steven A. Weber and William R. Belcher, pp. 65–93. Lexington Books, Lanham, Maryland.

Mehrer, Mark W.

1995 *Cahokia's Countryside: Household Archaeology, Settlement Patterns, and Social Power.* Northern Illinois University Press, DeKalb.

Mehrer, Mark W., and James M. Collins

1995 Household Archaeology at Cahokia and Its Hinterlands. In *Mississippian Communities and Households*, edited by J. Daniel Rogers and Bruce D. Smith, pp. 32–57. University of Alabama Press, Tuscaloosa.

Mellaart, James

1967 *Çatal Hüyük: A Neolithic Town in Anatolia.* Thames and Hudson, London.

Mery, Sophie, and M. James Blackman

2005 Socio-Economic Patterns of a Ceramic Container: The Harappan Black Slipped Jar. In *South Asian Archaeology 2001*, edited by Catherine Jarrige and Vincent Lefévre, pp. 227–235. Éditions recherche sur les civilizations-ADPF, Paris.

Meskell, Lynne, and Rosemary A. Joyce

2003 *Embodied Lives: Figuring Ancient Egypt and the Classic Maya.* Routledge, London.

Mesoudi, Alex, and Michael J. O'Brien

2009 Placing Archaeology within a Unified Science of Cultural Evolution. In *Patterns and Process in Cultural Evolution*, edited by Stephen Shennan, pp. 21–32. University of California Press, Berkeley.

Miller, Arthur G.

1995 *The Painted Tombs of Oaxaca, Mexico: Living with the Dead.* Cambridge University Press, New York.

Miller, Daniel

1985 Ideology and the Harappan Civilization. *Journal of Anthropological Archaeology* 4:34–71.

Miller, Daniel, and Christopher Tilley (editors)

1984 *Ideology, Power, and Prehistory.* Cambridge University Press, Cambridge.

Miller, Heather M.-L.

1999 Pyrotechnology and Society in the Cities of the Indus Valley. Unpublished Ph.D. dissertation, University of Wisconsin, Madison.

2007 Associations and Ideologies in the Locations of Urban Craft Production at Harappa, Pakistan (Indus Civilization). In *Rethinking Craft Specialization in Complex Societies: Archaeological Analyses of the Social Meaning of Production*, edited by Zachary X. Hruby and Rowan K. Flad. *Archaeological Papers of the American Anthropological Association* 17: 37–51.

2008 Issues in the Determination of Ancient Value Systems: The Role of Talc (Steatite) and Faience in the Indus Civilization. In *Intercultural Relations between*

South and Southwest Asia: Studies in Commemoration of E. C. L. During Caspers (1934–1996), edited by Eric Olijdam and Richard H. Spoor, pp. 145–157. British Archaeological Reports International Series 1826. Archaeopress, Oxford.

2013 Weighty Matters: Evidence for Unity and Regional Diversity from the Indus Civilization Weights. In *Connections and Complexity: New Approaches to the Archaeology of South Asia*, edited by Shinu Anna Abraham, Praveena Gullapalli, Teresa P. Raczek, and Uzma Z. Rizvi, pp. 161–176. Left Coast Press, Walnut Creek, California.

Miller, Laura J.

2003 Secondary Products and Urbanism in South Asia: The Evidence for Traction at Harappa. In *Indus Ethnobiology: New Perspectives from the Field*, edited by Steven A. Weber and William R. Belcher, pp. 251–326. Lexington Books, Lanham, Maryland.

2004 Urban Economies in Early States: The Secondary Products Revolution in the Indus Civilization. Unpublished Ph.D. dissertation, New York University.

Milner, George R.

1984 *The Robinson's Lake Site*. University of Illinois Press, Urbana.

1998 *The Cahokia Chiefdom: The Archaeology of a Mississippian Society*. Smithsonian Institution Press, Washington, DC.

Mirabeau, Victor Riqueti

1756 *L'ami des hommes ou traité sur la population*. A. Avignon, Paris.

Mohammad, Robina, and James D. Sidaway

2012 Spectacular Urbanization amidst Variegated Geographies of Globalization: Learning from Abu Dhabi's Trajectory through the Lives of South Asian Men. *International Journal of Urban and Regional Research* 36:606–627.

Monsma, Karl

2006 Symbolic Conflicts, Deadly Consequences: Fights between Italians and Blacks in Western São Paulo, 1888–1914. *Journal of Social History* 39:1123–1152.

Montesquieu, Charles de Secondat

1951 [1748] De l'esprit des lois. In *Oeuvres complètes*, 2 vols., edited by Roger Callois, pp. 1:1–19. Bibliothèque de la Pléiade, Paris.

Moore, Katherine M., David Steadman, and Susan DeFrance

1999 Herds, Fish, and Fowl in the Domestic and Ritual Economy of Formative Chiripa. In *Early Settlement at Chiripa, Bolivia: Research of the Taraco Archaeological Project*, edited by Christine A. Hastorf, pp. 105–116. University of California Archaeological Research Facility, Berkeley.

Morgan, Lewis Henry

1963 [1877] *Ancient Society; or, Researches in the Lines of Human Progress from Savagery through Barbarism to Civilization*. Meridian Books, New York.

Morrison, Kathleen D.

1994 The Intensification of Production: Archaeological Approaches. *Journal of Archaeological Method and Theory* 1:111–159.

Morse, Richard M.
1974 *From Community to Metropolis: A Biography of São Paulo, Brazil.* Octagon Books, New York.

Moses, Daniel Noah
2009 *The Promise of Progress: The Life and Work of Lewis Henry Morgan.* University of Missouri Press, Columbia.

Mughal, M. Rafique
1990 Further Evidence of the Early Harappan Culture in the Greater Indus Valley: 1971–90. *South Asian Studies* 6:175–199.
1994 The Harappan Nomads of Cholistan. In *Living Traditions: Studies in the Ethnoarchaeology of South Asia*, edited by Bridget Allchin, pp. 53–68. Oxford and IBH Publishing, New Delhi.
1997a A Preliminary Review of Archaeological Surveys in Punjab and Sindh: 1993–1995. *South Asian Studies* 13:241–249.
1997b *Ancient Cholistan: Archaeology and Architecture.* Ferozsons Limited, Lahore, Pakistan.

Mumford, Lewis
1961 *The City in History: Its Origins, Its Transformations, and Its Prospects.* Harcourt, Brace and World, New York.

Murdock, George Peter
1959 *Africa: Its Peoples and Their Culture History.* McGraw-Hill, New York.

Netting, Robert M.
1993 *Smallholders, Householders: Farm Families and the Ecology of Intensive, Sustainable Agriculture.* Stanford University Press, Stanford, California.

Nielsen, Axel L.
2013 Circulating Objects and the Constitution of South Andean Society (500 BC–AD 1550). In *Merchants, Markets, and Exchange in the Pre-Columbian World*, edited by Kenneth G. Hirth and Joanne Pillsbury, pp. 389–418. Dumbarton Oaks, Washington, DC.

Nmadu, Job N., G. P. Eze, and Abigail J. Jirgi
2012 Determinants of Risk Status of Small Scale Farmers in Niger State, Nigeria. *British Journal of Economics, Management and Trade* 2:92–108.

Nordhoff, Charles
1873 *California: For Health Pleasure, and Residence.* Harper and Brothers, New York.

O'Brien, Michael J., and R. Lee Lyman
2002 Evolutionary Archeology: Current Status and Future Prospects. *Evolutionary Anthropology* 11:26–36.

Oka, Rahul, and Chapurukha M. Kusimba
2008 The Archaeology of Trading Systems: Towards a New Trade Synthesis. Pt. 1. *Journal of Archaeological Research* 16:339–395.

Orlove, Ben
2002 *Lines in the Water: Nature and Culture at Lake Titicaca.* University of California Press, Berkeley.

Orr, Heather S.
2001 Procession Rituals and Shrine Sites: The Politics of Sacred Space in the Late Formative Valley of Oaxaca. In *Landscape and Power in Ancient Mesoamerica*, edited by Rex Koontz, Kathryn Reese-Taylor, and Annabeth Headrick, pp. 55–80. Westview Press, Boulder, Colorado.

Ortman, Scott G., Andrew H. F. Cabaniss, Jennie O. Strum, and Luís M. A. Bettencourt
2014 The Pre-History of Urban Scaling. *PLoS One* 9(2):e87902.

Orwell, George
1945 *Animal Farm: A Fairy Story*. Secker and Warburg, London.

Oudijk, Michel R.
2008 The Postclassic Period in the Valley of Oaxaca: The Archaeological and Ethnohistorical Record. In *After Monte Albán: Transformation and Negotiation in Oaxaca, Mexico*, edited by Jeffrey P. Blomster, pp.95–118. University Press of Colorado, Boulder.

Owen, Bruce D.
2005 Distant Colonies and Explosive Collapse: The Two Stags of the Tiwanaku Diaspora in the Osmore Drainage. *Latin American Antiquity* 61:45–80.

Owensby, Brian P.
1999 *Intimate Ironies: Modernity and the Making of Modern Brazil*. Stanford University Press, Stanford, California.

Özdoğan, Mehmet
2002 Defining the Neolithic of Central Anatolia. In *The Neolithic of Central Anatolia: Internal Developments and External Relations during the 9th–6th Millennium cal BC*, edited by Frédéric Gérard and Laurens Thissen, pp. 253–261. Ege Yayınları, Istanbul.

Pagden, Anthony
1988 The "Defense of Civilization" in Eighteenth Century Social Theory. *History of Human Sciences* 1:33–45.

Park, Douglas Post
2010 Prehistoric Timbuktu and Its Hinterland. *Antiquity* 84:1076–1088.
2011 Climate Change, Human Response, and the Origins of Urbanism at Timbuktu: Archaeological Investigations into the Prehistoric Urbanism of the Timbuktu Region on the Niger Bend, Mali, West Africa. Unpublished Ph.D. dissertation, Yale University, New Haven, Connecticut.

Park, Jang-Sik, and Vasant Shinde
2014 Characterization and Comparison of the Copper-Base Metallurgy of the Harappan Sites at Framana in Haryana and Kuntasi in Gujarat, India. *Journal of Archaeological Science* 50:126–138.

Park, Julie Eunju
2001 The Iwawi Site and Tiwanaku Political Economy from a Faunal Perspective. Unpublished master's thesis, Simon Frasier University, Burnaby.

Parkinson, William A. (editor)
2002 *The Archaeology of Tribal Societies.* International Monographs in Prehistory, Ann Arbor, Michigan.
Parpola, Simo, Asko Parpola, and Robert H. Brunswig Jr.
1977 The Meluhha Village: Evidence of Acculturation of Harappan Traders in Late Third Millennium Mesopotamia? *Journal of the Economic and Social History of the Orient* 20:129–165.
Parsons, Jeffrey R.
1968 An Estimate of the Size and Population for Middle Horizon Tiahuanaco, Bolivia. *American Antiquity* 33:243–245.
Pauketat, Timothy R.
1994 *The Ascent of Chiefs: Cahokia and Mississippian Politics in Native North America.* University of Alabama Press, Tuscaloosa.
1997a Cahokian Political Economy. In *Cahokia: Domination and Ideology in the Mississippian World*, edited by Timothy R. Pauketat and Timothy E. Emerson, pp. 30–51. University of Nebraska Press, Lincoln.
1997b Specialization, Political Symbols, and Crafty Elite of Cahokia. *Southeastern Archaeology* 16:1–15.
1998 Refiguring the Archaeology of Greater Cahokia. *Journal of Archaeological Research* 6:45–89.
2003 Resettled Farmers and the Making of a Mississippian Polity. *American Antiquity* 68:39–66.
2004 *Ancient Cahokia and the Mississippians.* Cambridge University Press, Cambridge.
2007 *Chiefdoms and other Archaeological Delusions.* AltaMira Press, Lanham, Maryland.
2013 *Archaeology of the Cosmos: Rethinking Agency and Religion in Ancient America.* Routledge, New York.
Pauketat, Timothy R., and Susan M. Alt
2003 Mounds, Memories, and Contested Mississippian History. In *Archaeologies of Memory*, edited by Ruth M. Van Dyke and Susan E. Alcock, pp. 151–179. Blackwell, Malden, Massachusetts.
2005 Archaeology in a Postmold? Physicality and the Archaeology of Culture Making. *Journal of Archeological Method and Theory* 12:213–236.
Pauketat, Timothy R., and Thomas E. Emerson
1991 The Ideology of Authority and the Power of the Pot. *American Anthropologist* 93:919–941.
Pauketat, Timothy R., Andrew C. Fortier, Susan M. Alt, and Thomas E. Emerson
2013 A Mississippian Conflagration at East St. Louis and Its Political-Historical Implications. *Journal of Field Archaeology* 38:210–226.

Pauketat, Timothy R., Lucretia S. Kelly, Gayle J. Fritz, Neal H. Lopinot, Scott Elias, and Eve Hargrave

2002 The Residues of Feasting and Public Ritual at Early Cahokia. *American Antiquity* 67:57–279.

Pauketat, Timothy R., and Neal H. Lopinot

1997 Cahokian Population Dynamics. In *Cahokia: Domination and Ideology in the Mississippian World*, edited by Timothy R. Pauketat and Thomas E. Emerson, pp. 103–123. University of Nebraska Press, Lincoln.

Pauketat, Timothy R., and Diana D. Loren

2005 Alternative Histories and North American Archaeology. In *North American Archaeology*, edited by Timothy R. Pauketat and Diana D. Loren, pp. 1–29. Blackwell, Oxford, United Kingdom.

Pearson, Jessica

2013 Human and Animal Diet as Evidenced by Stable Carbon and Nitrogen Isotope Analysis. In *Çatalhöyük Excavations: Humans and Landscapes of Çatalhöyük*, edited by Ian Hodder, pp. 271–298. Cotsen Institute of Archaeology, University of California, Los Angeles.

Pearson, Jessica, Hijlke Buitenhuis, Robert E. M. Hedges, Louise Martin, Nerissa Russell, and Katheryn C. Twiss

2007 New Light on Early Caprine Herding Strategies from Isotope Analysis: A Case Study from Neolithic Anatolia. *Journal of Archaeological Science* 34:2170–2179.

Peeler, Damon E., and Marcus Winter

1995 Building J at Monte Albán: A Correction an Reassessment of the Astronomical Hypothesis. *Latin American Antiquity* 6:362–369.

Peixoto-Mehrtens, Cristina

2010 *Urban Spaces and National Identity in Twentieth Century São Paulo, Brazil: Crafting Modernity.* Palgrave Macmillan, New York.

Peregrine, Peter N.

2012 Power and Legitimization: Political Strategies, Typologies, and Cultural Evolution: In *Comparative Archaeology of Complex Societies*, edited by Michael E. Smith, pp. 165–191. Cambridge University Press, New York.

Peters, Stuart M.

1980 Comments on the Analogy between Biological and Cultural Evolution. *American Antiquity* 45:696–601.

Pines, Yuri

2005 Beasts or Humans: Pre-Imperial Origins of Sino-Barbarian Dichotomy. In *Mongols, Turks and Others: Eurasian Nomads and the Sedentary World*, edited by Reuven Amitai and Michael Biran, pp. 59 -102. Brill, Leiden.

Pires-Ferreira, Jane W.

1976 Shell and Iron-Ore Mirror Exchange in Formative Mesoamerica, with Comments on Other Commodities. In *The Early Mesoamerican Village*, edited by Kent V. Flannery, pp. 311–326. Academic Press, New York.

Plog, Fred

1977 Explaining Change. In *The Explanation of Prehistoric Change*, edited by James N. Hill, pp. 17–57. University of New Mexico Press, Albuquerque.

Plourde, Aimée M.

2006 Prestige Goods and Their Role in the Evolution of Social Ranking: A Costly Signalling Model with Data from the Late Formative Period of the Northern Lake Titicaca Basin. Unpublished Ph.D. dissertation. University of California, Los Angeles.

Pool, Christopher A.

2013 Coastal Oaxaca and Formative Developments in Mesoamerica. In *Polity and Ecology in Formative Period Coastal Oaxaca*, edited by Arthur A. Joyce, pp. 301–329. University Press of Colorado, Boulder.

Porubcan, Paula J.

2000 Human and Nonhuman Surplus Display at Mound 72, Cahokia. In *Mounds, Modoc, and Mesoamerica: Papers in Honor of Melvin L. Fowler*, edited by Steven R. Ahler, pp. 207–225. Scientific Papers Series, Vol. 28. Illinois State Museum, Springfield.

Possehl, Gregory L.

1990 Revolution in the Urban Revolution: The Emergence of Indus Urbanization. *Annual Review of Anthropology* 19:261–282.

1991 A Short History of Archaeological Discovery at Harappa. In *Harappa Excavations 1986–1990: A Multidisciplinary Approach to Third Millennium Urbanism*, edited by Richard H. Meadow, pp. 5–11. Prehistory Press, Madison, Wisconsin.

1993 The Harappan Civilization: A Contemporary Perspective. In *Harappan Civilization: A Recent Perspective*. 2nd ed. Edited by Gregory L. Possehl, pp. 15–28. American Institute of Indian Studies and Oxford and IBH Publishing, New Delhi.

1997 The Transformation of the Indus Civilization. *Journal of World Prehistory* 11:425–472.

1998 Sociocultural Complexity Without the State: The Indus Civilization. In *Archaic States*, edited by Gary M. Feinman and Joyce Marcus, pp. 261–291. School of Advanced Research, Santa Fe, New Mexico.

1999 *Indus Age: The Beginning.* University of Pennsylvania Press, Philadelphia.

2002 *The Indus Civilization: A Contemporary Perspective*. AltaMira Press, Lanham, Maryland.

2007 The Middle Asian Interaction Sphere: Trade and Contact in the 3rd Millennium BC. *Expedition* 49:40–42.

Possehl, Gregory L., and Raval, M. H.

1989 *Harappan Civilization and Rojdi.* Brill, New York.

Potts, Daniel T.

1993a Tel Abraq and the Harappan Tradition in Southeastern Arabia. In *Harappan Civilization: A Recent Perspective*, 2nd ed., edited by Gregory L. Possehl,

pp. 323–333. American Institute of Indian Studies and Oxford and IBH Publishing, New Delhi.
1993b Patterns of Trade in Third-Millennium BC Mesopotamia and Iran. *World Archaeology* 24:379–402.

Prasad, Vandana, Anjum Farooqui, Anupam Sharma, Binita Phartiyal, Supriyo Chakraborty, Subhash Bhandari, Rachna Raj, and Abha Sing
2014 Mid-Late Holocene Monsoonal Variations from Mainland Gujarat, India: A Multi-Proxy Study for Evaluating Climate Culture Relationship. *Paleogeography, Paleoclimatology, Paleoecology* 397:38–51.

Prentice, Deborah A., and Dale T. Miller (editors)
1999 *Cultural Divides: Understanding and Overcoming Group Conflict.* Russell Sage Foundation, New York.

Price, T. Douglas, and Ofer Bar-Yosef
2011 The Origins of Agriculture: New Data, New Ideas. *Current Anthropology* 52(S4):163–174.

Price, T. Douglas, James H. Burton, Paul D. Fullagar, Lori E. Wright, Jane E. Buikstra, and Vera Tiesler
2008 Strontium Isotopes and the Study of Human Mobility in Ancient Mesoamerica. *Latin American Antiquity* 19:167–180.

Price, T. Douglas, James H. Burton, and James B. Stoltman
2007 Place of Origin of Prehistoric Inhabitants of Aztalan, Jefferson Co., Wisconsin. *American Antiquity* 72:524–538.

Price, T. Douglas, and Gary M. Feinman (editors)
2010 *Pathways to Power: New Perspectives on the Emergence of Social Equality.* Springer, New York.

Protzen, Jean-Pierre, and Stella Nair
2013 *The Stones of Tiahuanaco: A Study of Architecture and Construction.* Cotsen Institute of Archaeology, University of California, Los Angeles.

Pyne, Nanette M.
1976 The Fire-Serpent and Were-Jaguar in Formative Oaxaca. A Contingency Table Analysis. In *The Early Mesoamerican Village*, edited by Kent V. Flannery, pp. 272–280. Academic Press, New York.

Rabi, Uzi
2006 Oil Politics and Tribal Rulers in Eastern Arabia: The Reign of Skakhbut (1928–1966). *British Journal of Middle Eastern Studies* 33:37–50.

Radcliffe-Brown, Alfred R.
1952 *Structure and Function in Primitive Society.* Free Press, Glencoe, New York.

Rathje, William L.
1971 The Origin and Development of Lowland Classic Maya Civilization. *American Antiquity* 36:275–285.

Ratnagar, Sherren
1993 The Location of Harappa. In *Harappan Civilization: A Recent Perspective*,

2nd ed., edited by Gregory L. Possehl, pp. 261–264. American Institute of Indian Studies and Oxford and IBH Publishing, New Delhi.
2004 *Trading Encounters: From the Euphrates to the Indus in the Bronze Age*. Oxford University Press, New Delhi.

Ratzel, Friedrich
1891 *Anthropogeographie*. Englehorn, Stuttgart.

Redmond, Elsa M., and Charles S. Spencer
2012 Chiefdoms at the Threshold: The Competitive Origins of the Primary State. *Journal of Anthropological Archaeology* 31:22–37.
2013 Early (300–100 B.C.) Temple Precinct in the Valley of Oaxaca, Mexico. *Proceedings of the National Academy of Science* 110:e1707–1715.

Reinhard, Johan
1992 Underwater Archaeological Research in Lake Titicaca, Bolivia. In *Ancient Americas: Contributions to New World Archaeology*, edited by Nicholas Saunders, pp. 117–143. Oxford Books, Oxford, United Kingdom.

Renfrew, Colin
1978 The Anatomy of Innovation. In *Approaches to Social Archaeology*, edited by Colin Renfrew, pp. 390–419. Harvard University Press, Cambridge, Massachusetts.
2008 The City through Time and Space: Transformations of Centrality. In *The Ancient City: New Perspectives on Urbanism in the Old and New World*, edited by Joyce Marcus and Jeremy A. Sabloff, pp. 29–52. School for Advanced Research, Santa Fe, New Mexico.

Renfrew, Colin (editor)
1973 *The Explanation of Culture Change, Models in Prehistory: Proceedings of a Meeting of the Research Seminar in Archaeology and Related Subjects Held at the University of Sheffield*. Duckworth, London.

Resek, Carl
1960 *Lewis Henry Morgan: American Scholar*. University of Chicago Press, Chicago, Illinois.

Rick, John
2005 The Evolution of Authority and Power at Chavín de Huántar, Peru. In *Foundations of Power in the Prehispanic Andes*, edited by Kevin J. Vaughn, Dennis Ogburn, and Christina A. Conleee, pp. 71–89. American Archaeological Association, Arlington, Virginia.

Rissman, Paul
1988 Public Displays and Private Values: A Guide to Buried Wealth in Harappan Archaeology. *World Archaeology* 20:209–228.

Rivera Casanovas, Claudia
2003 Ch'iji Jawira: A Case of Ceramic Specialization in the Tiwanaku Periphery. In *Urban and Rural Archaeology*, Vol. 2 of *Tiwanaku and Its Hinterland:*

Archaeology and Paleoecology of an Andean Civilization, edited by Alan L. Kolata, pp. 296–315. Smithsonian Books, Washington, DC.

Rivera Díaz, Mario A.

1987 Tres Fechados radiométricos de Pampa Alto de Ramírez, norte de Chile. *Chungará* 18:7–14.

Roberts, Neil, Stuart Black, Peter Boyer, Warren J. Eastwood, H. I. Griffiths, Henry F. Lamb, Melanie J. Leng, Randall Parrish, Jane M. Reed, David Twigg, and Hakan Yiğitbaşioğlu.

1999 Chronology and Stratigraphy of Late Quaternary Sediments in the Konya Basin, Turkey: Results from the KOPAL Project. *Quaternary Science Review* 18:611–630.

Roberts, Neil, and Arlene Rosen

2009 Diversity and Complexity in Early Farming Communities of Southwest Asia: New Insights into the Economic and Environmental Basis of Neolithic Çatalhöyük. *Current Anthropology* 50:393–402.

Robinson, Jennifer

2006 *Ordinary Cities: Between Modernity and Development*. Routledge, New York.

Roddick, Andrew P.

2013 Temporalities of the Formative Period Taraco Peninsula, Bolivia. *Journal of Social Archaeology* 13:287–309.

Roddick, Andrew P., Maria C. Bruno, and Christine A. Hastorf

2014 Political Centers in Context: Depositional Histories at Formative Period Kala Uyuni, Bolivia. *Journal of Anthropological Archaeology* 36:140–157.

Roddick, Andrew P., and Christine A. Hastorf

2010 Tradition Brought to the Surface: Continuity, Innovation, and Change in the Late Formative Period, Taraco Peninsula, Bolivia. *Cambridge Archeological Journal* 20:157–178.

Rogers, J. Daniel

1995 Dispersed Communities and Integrated Households: A Perspective from Spiro and the Arkansas Basin. In *Mississippian Communities and Households*, edited by J. Daniel Rogers and Bruce D. Smith, pp. 81–98. University of Alabama Press, Tuscaloosa.

Rogers, J. Daniel, and Bruce D. Smith (editors)

1995 *Mississippian Communities and Households*. University of Alabama Press, Tuscaloosa.

Rollefson, Gary O.

1996 The Neolithic Devolution: Ecological Impact and Cultural Compensation at 'Ain Ghazal, Jordan. In *Retrieving the Past: Essays on Archaeological Research and Methodology in Honor of Gus W. Van Beek*, edited by Joe D. Seger, pp. 219–230. Eisenbrauns, Winona Lake, Indiana.

Rose, Jerome C.

1999 Mortuary Data and Analysis. In *The Mound 72 Area: Dedicated and Sacred Space* in *Early Cahokia*, edited by Melvin L. Fowler, Jerome Rose, Barbara Vander Leest and Steven A. Ahler, pp. 63–82. Reports of Investigation 54. Illinois State Museum, Springfield.

Rosen, Arlene M.

2005 Phytolith Indicators of Plant and Land Use at Çatalhöyük. In *Inhabiting Çatalhöyük: Reports from the 1995–99 Seasons*, edited by Ian Hodder, pp. 203–212. McDonald Institute for Archaeological Research and the British Institute at Ankara, Cambridge.

Rosen, Arlene M., and Neil Roberts

2005 The Nature of Çatalhöyük: People and Their Changing Environments on the Konya Plain. In *Çatalhöyük Perspectives: Reports from the 1995–99 Seasons*, edited by Ian Hodder, pp. 39–53. Cambridge: McDonald Institute for Archaeological Research and the British Institute at Ankara, Cambridge.

Rosenberg, Michael

1998 Cheating at Musical Chairs: Territoriality and Sedentism in an Evolutionary Context. *Current Anthropology* 39(5):653–681.

Rousseau, Jean Jacques

2007 [1755] *A Discourse Upon the Origin and the Foundation of the Inequality among Mankind*. Filiquarian Publishing, Minneapolis, Minnesota.

Roy, Ben

2000 The Beads. In *Urbanism, Archaeology, and Trade (Further Observations on the Gao Region (Mali)): The 1996 Fieldseason Results*, edited by Timothy Insoll, pp. 98–126. British Archaeological Reports International Series 829. J. and E. Hedges, Oxford.

Russell, Nerissa, Louise Martin, and Hijlke Buitenhuis

2005 Cattle Domestication at Çatalhöyük Revisited. *Current Anthropology* 46(S5):101–108.

Russell, Nerissa, and Amy Bogaard

2010 Subsistence Actions at Çatalhöyük. In *Agency and Identity in the Ancient Near East: New Paths Forward*, edited by Sharon E. Steadman and Jennifer C. Ross, pp. 63–79. Equinox London.

Russell, Nerissa, Katherine I. Wright, Tristan Carter, Sheena Ketchum, Philippa Ryan, Nurcan Yalman, Roddy Regan, Mirjana Stevanović, and Marina Milić

2014 Bringing Down the House: House Closing Deposits at Çatalhöyük. In *Integrating Çatalhöyük: Themes from the 2000–2008 Seasons*, edited by Ian Hodder, pp. 109–121. Cotsen Institute of Archaeology, University of California, Los Angeles.

Sahlins, Marshall

1963 Poor Man, Rich Man, Big-Man, Chief: Political Types in Melanesia and Polynesia. *Comparative Studies in Society and History* 5:285–303.

1972 *Stone Age Economics*. Aldine, Hawthorne, New York.

Salazar, Diego, Hermann M. Niemeyer, Helena Horta, Valentina Figueroa, and Germán Manríquez

2014 Interaction, Social Identity, Agency and Change during Middle Horizon San Pedro de Atacama (Northern Chile): A Multi-Dimensional and Interdisciplinary Perspective. *Journal of Anthropological Archaeology* 35:135–152.

Sanderson, Stephen K.

2007 *Evolutionism and Its Critics: Deconstructing and Reconstructing an Evolutionary Interpretation of Human Society.* Paradigm Publishers, Boulder, Colorado.

Sandhu, Kernial Singh

1969 Some Aspects of Indian Settlements in Singapore, 1819–1969. *Journal of Southeast Asian History* 10:193–201.

Sandness, Karin L.

1992 Temporal and Spatial Dietary Variability in the Osmore Drainage, Southern Peru: The Isotopic Evidence. Unpublished master's thesis, University of Nebraska, Lincoln.

Sassen, Saskia

2001 *The Global City: New York, London, Tokyo.* 2nd ed. Princeton University Press, Princeton, New Jersey.

Saw Swee-Hock

1969 Population Trends in Singapore, 1819–1967. *Journal of Southeast Asian History* 10:36–49.

Scarborough, Vernon L., and Lisa J. Lucero

2010 The Non-Hierarchical Development of Complexity in the Semitropics: Water and Cooperation. *Water History* 2:185–205.

Scarry, John F.

2007 Connections between the Etowah and Lake Jackson Chiefdoms: Patterns in the Iconographic and Material Evidence. In *Southeastern Ceremonial Complex: Chronology, Content, Context*, edited by Adam King, pp. 134–150. University of Alabama Press, Tuscaloosa.

Scarry, John F. (editor)

1996 *Political Structure and Change in the Prehistoric Southeastern United States.* University Press of Florida, Gainesville.

Schaedel, Richard P.

1993 Congruence of Horizon with Polity: Huari and the Middle Horizon. In *Latin American Horizons: A Symposium at Dumbarton Oaks*, edited by Don Stephen Rice, pp. 225–261. Dumbarton Oaks, Washington, DC.

Schilling, Timothy

2012 Building Monks Mound, Cahokia, Illinois, A.D. 800–1400. *Journal of Field Archaeology* 37:302–313.

Schmidt, Klaus

2000a Göbekli Tempe, Southeastern Turkey: A Preliminary Report on the 1995-1999 Excavations. *Paléorient* 26(1): 45–54.

2001 Göbekli Tepe and the Early Neolithic Sites of the Urfa region: A Synopsis of New Results and Current Views. *Neo-Lithics* 1:9–11.

2006 *Sie bauten die ersten Tempel: Das rätselhafte Heiligtum der Steinzeitjäger.* Beck, Munich.

Schneider, Jane

1977 Was There a Pre-Capitalist World System? *Peasant Studies* 6:20–29.

Schreiber, Katharina J.

2005 Imperial Agendas and Local Agency: Wari Colonial Strategies. In *The Archaeology of Colonial Encounters: Comparative Perspectives*, edited by Gill J. Stein, pp. 237–262. School of American Research Press. Santa Fe, New Mexico.

Schroeder, Sissel

2004a Power and Place: Agency, Ecology, and History in the American Bottom, Illinois. *Antiquity* 78:812–827.

2004b Current Research on Late Precontact Societies of the Midcontinental United States. *Journal of Anthropological Research* 12:311–372.

Schug, Gwen Robbins, Kelsey Gray, V. Mushrif-Tripathy, and A. R. Sankhyan

2012 A Peaceful Realm? Trauma and Social Differentiation at Harappa. *International Journal of Paleopathology* 2:136–147.

Schuldenrein, Joseph, Rita P. Wright, M. Rafique Mughal, and M. Afzal Khan

2004 Landscapes, Soils, and Mound Histories of the Upper Indus Valley, Pakistan: New Insights on the Holocene Environment near Ancient Harappa. *Journal of Archaeological Science* 31:777–797.

Schultze, Carole A.

2013 Silver Mines of the Northern Lake Titicaca Basin. In *Mining and Quarrying in the Ancient Andes: Sociopolitical, Economic, and Symbolic Dimensions*, edited by Nicholas Tripcevich and Kevin J. Vaughn, pp. 231–352. Springer, New York.

Schwartz, Glen M., and Steven E. Falconer

1994 Rural Approaches to Social Complexity. In *Archaeological Views from the Countryside: Village Communities in Early Complex Societies*, edited by Glenn M. Schwartz and Steven E. Falconer, pp. 1–18. Smithsonian Institution, Washington, DC.

Scott, James C.

1998 *Seeing like a State: How Certain Schemes to Improve the Human Condition Have Failed.* Yale University Press, New Haven, Connecticut.

Seddon, Matthew T.

1998 Ritual, Power, and the Development of a Complex Society. Unpublished Ph.D. dissertation, University of Chicago, Chicago, Illinois.

2005 The Tiwanaku Occupation on the Island of the Sun. In *Advances in Titicaca Basin Archaeology*, Vol. 1, edited by Charles Stanish, Amanda B. Cohen, and Mark S. Aldenderfer, pp. 135–142. Cotsen Institute of Archaeology, University of California, Los Angeles.

Sellen, Adam T.

2007 *El cielo compartido: deidades y ancestros en las vasijas efigie Zapotecas*. Universidad nacional autónoma de México, Mérida.

Service, Elman R.

1962 *Primitive Social Organization*. Random House, New York.

1975 *Origins of the State and Civilization*. Norton, New York.

Shanks, Michael, and Christopher Tilley

1987 *Re-Constructing Archaeology: Theory and Practice*. Wiley, London.

Shaw, Brent D.

2000 Rebels and Outsiders. In *The High Empire, A.D. 70–192*, edited by Alan K. Bowman, Peter D. A Garnsey, and Dominic Rathborne, pp. 361–403. Cambridge University Press, Cambridge.

Shen, Chen

2003 Compromises and Conflicts: Production and Commerce in the Royal Cities of Eastern Zhou, China. In *The Social Construction of Ancient Cities*, edited by Monica L. Smith, pp. 290–310. Smithsonian Institution Press, Washington, DC.

Sherman, Jason R., Andrew K. Balkansky, Charles S. Spencer, and Brian D. Nicholls

2010 Expansionary Dynamics of the Nascent Monte Albán State. *Journal of Anthropological Archaeology* 29:278–301.

Sherratt, Andrew

2004 Material Resources, Capital, and Power: The Coevolution of Society and Culture. In *Archaeological Perspectives on Political Economies*, edited by Gary M. Feinman and Linda M. Nicholas, pp. 79–103. University of Utah Press, Salt Lake City.

Sherwood, Sarah C., and Tristram R. Kidder

2011 The DaVincis of Dirt: Geoarchaeological Perspectives on Native American Mound Building in the Mississippi River Basin. *Journal of Anthropological Archaeology* 30:69–97.

Shinnie, Peter L., and François J. Kense

1989 *Archaeology of Gonja, Ghana: Excavations at Daboya*. University of Calgary Press, Calgary.

Simmons, Alan H.

2007 *The Neolithic Revolution in the Near East: Transforming the Human Landscape*. University of Arizona Press, Tucson.

Simon, Mary L.

2002 Red Cedar, White Oak, and Bluestem Grass: The Colors of Mississippian Construction. *Midcontinental Journal of Archaeology* 27:273–308.

Simpson, David

1993 *Romanticism, Nationalism, and the Revolt against Theory*. University of Chicago Press, Chicago, Illinois.

Slater, Philip A., Kristin M. Hedman, and Thomas E. Emerson
2014 Immigrants at the Mississippian Polity of Cahokia: Strontium Isotope Evidence for Population Movement. *Journal of Archaeological Science* 44:117–127.
Smith, Adam
1970 [1776] *The Wealth of Nations*. Penguin, Harmondsworth, United Kingdom.
Smith, Michael E.
2004 The Archaeology of Ancient State Economies. *Annual Review of Anthropology* 33:73–102.
2006 Review of *Ancient Middle Niger: Urbanism and the Self-Organizing Landscape*, by Roderick J. McIntosh. *Journal of African Archaeology* 4:357–359.
2007 Form and Meaning in the Earliest Cities: A New Approach to Ancient Urban Planning. *Journal of Planning History* 6:3–47.
2009 Just How Comparative is Comparative Urban Geography? A Perspective from Archaeology. *Urban Geography* 30:113–117.
2010 Sprawl, Squatters, and Sustainable Cities: Can Archaeological Data Shed Light on Modern Urban Issues? *Cambridge Archaeological Journal* 20:229–253.
Smith, Michael E., and Peter Peregrine
2012 Approaches to Comparative Analysis in Archaeology. In *The Comparative Archeology of Complex Societies*, edited by Michael E. Smith, pp. 4–20. Cambridge University Press, New York.
Smith, Monica L.
2003 Introduction: The Social Construction of Cities. In *The Social Construction of Ancient Cities*, edited by Monica L. Smith, pp. 1–36. Smithsonian Books, Washington, DC.
2013 The Substance and Symbolism of Long-Distance Exchange: Textiles as Desired Trade Goods in the Bronze Age Middle Asian Interaction Sphere. In *Connections and Complexity: New Approaches to the Archaeology of South Asia*, edited by Shinu Anna Abraham, Praveena Gullapalli, Teresa P. Raczek, and Uzma Z. Rizvi, pp. 143–160. Left Coast Press, Walnut Creek, California.
Smith, Scott C., and John Wayne Janusek
2014 Political Mosaics and Networks: Tiwanaku Expansion into the Upper Desaguadero Valley, Bolivia. *World Archaeology* 46:681–704.
Smith, Scott C., and Maribel Pérez Arias
2015 From Bodies to Bones: Death and Mobility in the Lake Titicaca Basin, Bolivia. *Antiquity* 89:106–121.
Soja, Edward W.
2000 *Postmetropolis: Critical Studies of Cities and Regions*. Blackwell, Oxford, United Kingdom.
Southall, Aidan
1998 *The City in Time and Space*. Cambridge University Press., New York.

Spence, Michael W.
2002 Domestic Ritual in Tlailotlacan, Teotihuacan. In *Domestic Ritual in Ancient Mesoamerica*, edited by Patricia Plunket, pp. 53–66. Cotsen Institute of Archaeology, University of California, Los Angeles.

Spencer, Charles S.
1982 *The Cuicatlán Cañada and Monte Albán: A Study of Primary State Formation.* Academic Press, New York.
1990 On the Tempo and Mode of State Formation: Neoevolutionism Reconsidered. *Journal of Anthropological Archaeology* 9:1–30.
1997 Evolutionary Approaches in Archaeology. *Journal of Anthropological Research* 5:209–264.
1998 A Mathematical Model of Primary State Formation. *Cultural Dynamics* 10:5–20.
2003 War and Early State Formation in Oaxaca, Mexico. *Proceedings of the National Academy of Sciences* 100:11185–11187.
2010 Territorial Expansion and Primary State Formation. *Proceedings of the National Academy of Sciences* 107:7119–7126.

Spencer, Charles S., and Elsa M. Redmond
2001a Multilevel Selection and Political Evolution in the Valley of Oaxaca, 500–100 B.C. *Journal of Anthropological Archaeology* 20:195–229.
2001b The Chronology of Conquest: Implications of New Radiocarbon Analyses from the Cañada de Cuicatlán, Oaxaca. *Latin American Antiquity* 12:182–201.
2004 A Late Monte Albán I Phase (300–100 B.C.) Palace in the Valley of Oaxaca. *Latin American Antiquity* 15:441–455.
2006 Resistance Strategies and Early State Formation in Oaxaca. In *Intermediate Elites in Pre-Columbian States and Empires*, edited by Christina M. Elson and R. Alan Covey, pp. 21–43. University of Arizona Press, Tucson.

Spencer, Charles S., Elsa M. Redmond, and Christina M. Elson
2008 Ceramic Microtypology and the Territorial Expansion of the Early Monte Albán State in Oaxaca, Mexico. *Journal of Field Archaeology* 33:321–341.

Squier, Ephraim G.
1877 *Peru, Incidents of Travel and Exploration in the Land of the Incas.* Macmillan, London.

Squier, Ephraim G., and Edwin H. Davis
1848 *Ancient Monuments of the Mississippi Valley: Comprising the Results of Extensive Original Surveys and Explorations.* Smithsonian Institution Press, Washington, DC.

Stahl, Ann Brower
2004 Comparative Insights into the Ancient Political Economies of West Africa. In *Archaeological Perspectives on Political Economies*, edited by Gary M. Feinman and Linda M. Nicholas, pp. 253–270. University of Utah Press, Salt Lake City.

Stanford, Craig B.

2001 *The Hunting Apes: Meat Eating and the Origins of Human Behavior.* Princeton University Press, Princeton, New Jersey.

Stanish, Charles

2003 *Ancient Titicaca: The Evolution of Complex Society in Southern Peru and Northern Bolivia.* University of California Press, Berkeley.

2004 The Evolution of Chiefdoms: An Economic Anthropological Model. In *Archaeological Perspectives on Political Economies*, edited by Gary M. Feinman and Linda M. Nicholas, pp. 7–24. University of Utah Press, Salt Lake City.

2009 The Tiwanaku Occupation of the Northern Titicaca Basin. In *Andean Civilization: A Tribute to Michael E. Moseley*, edited by Joyce Marcus and Patrick Ryan Williams, pp. 145–164. Cotsen Institute of Archaeology, University of California, Los Angeles.

Stanish, Charles, Edmundo de la Vega, Michael Moseley, Patrick Ryan Williams, Cecilia Chávez J., Benjamin Vining, and Karl LaFavre

2010 Tiwanaku Trade Patterns in Southern Peru. *Journal of Anthropological Archaeology* 29:524–532.

Stanish, Charles, Kirk Lawrence Frye, Edmundo de la Vega, and Matthew T. Seddon

2005 Tiwanaku Expansion into the Western Titicaca Basin, Peru. In *Advances in Titicaca Basin Archaeology*, Vol. 1, edited by Charles Stanish, Amanda B. Cohen, and Mark S. Aldenderfer, pp. 103–114. Cotsen Institute of Archaeology, University of California, Los Angeles.

Stanish, Charles, and Abigail Levine

2011 War and Early State Formation in the Northern Titicaca Basin. *Proceedings of the National Academy of Sciences* 108:13901–13906.

Stanner, W. E. H.

1933 Ceremonial Economics of the Mulluk Mulluk and Madngella Tribes of the Daly River, North Australia: A Preliminary Paper. *Oceania* 4:156–175.

Steadman, Sharon E.

2010 Agency, Architecture, and Archaeology: Prehistoric Settlements in Central Anatolia. In *Agency and Identity in the Ancient Near East: New Paths Forward*, edited by Sharon E. Steadman and Jennifer C. Ross, pp. 27–46. Equinox, London.

Stein, Gill J.

1999 *Rethinking World-Systems: Diasporas, Colonies, and Interaction in Uruk Mesopotamia.* University of Arizona Press, Tucson.

2002 Colonies without Colonialism: A Trade Diaspora Model of Fourth Millennium BC Mesopotamian Enclaves in Anatolia. In *The Archaeology of Colonialism*, edited by Claire L. Lyons and John K. Papadopoulos, pp. 27–64. Getty Research Institute, Los Angeles, California.

2005 Introduction: The Comparative Archaeology of Colonial Encounters. In *The Archaeology of Colonial Encounters*, edited by Gill J. Stein, pp. 3–32. School of American Research, Santa Fe, New Mexico.

Stein, Gill J. (editor)
2005 *The Archaeology of Colonial Encounters*, School of American Research, Santa Fe, New Mexico.
Stephens, John L., and Frederick Catherwood
1841 *Incidents of Travel in Central America, Chiapas, and Yucatan*. Harper and Brothers, New York.
Stevens, J. W.
1970 Changing Agricultural Practice in an Arabian Oasis: A Case Study of the Al 'Ain Oasis, Abu Dhabi. *Geographic Journal* 132:410–418.
Steward, Julian H.
1955 *Theory of Culture Change*. University of Illinois Press, Urbana.
Stolcke, Verena, and Michael M. Hall
1983 The Introduction of Free Labour on São Paulo Coffee Plantations. *Journal of Peasant Studies* 10(2–3):170–200.
Stoltman, James B., Danielle M. Berden, and Robert F. Boszhardt
2008 New Evidence in the Upper Mississippi Valley for Pre-Mississippian Cultural Interaction with the American Bottom. *American Antiquity* 73:317–336.
Storey, Glenn (editor)
2006 *Urbanism in the Preindustrial World: Cross Cultural Approaches*. University of Alabama Press, Tuscaloosa.
Stovel, Emily
2002 Patrones funerarios de San Pedro de Atacama y el problema de la presencia de los contextos Tiwanaku. *Boletín de Arqueología PUCP* 5:375–396.
Sullivan, Lynne P., and Timothy R. Pauketat
2007 Cahokia's Mound 31: A Short-Term Construction at a Long-Term Site. *Southeastern Archaeology* 26:12–31.
Sutter, Richard C.
2006 The Test of Competing Models for the Prehistoric Peopling of the Azapa Valley, Northern Chile, Using Matrix Correlations. *Chungará* 38:63–82.
Sweeney, Megan, and Susan McCouch
2007 The Complex History of the Domestication of Rice. *Annals of Botany* 100:951–957.
Tantaleán, Henry, Michiel Zegarra, Alex Gonzales, and Carlos Zapata Benites
2012 Qaluyu y Pukara: Una perspectiva desde el valle del río Quilcamayo-Tintiri, Azángaro. In *Arqueología de la Cuenca del Titicaca, Perú*, edited by Luis Flores Blanco and Henry Tantaleán, pp. 155–194. Instituto francés de estudios andinos, Lima.
Tarragó Myriam
2006 Espacios surandinos y la circulación de bienes en época de Tiwanaku. In *Esferas de interacción prehistóricas y fronteras nacionales modernas: Los Andes sur centrales*, edited by Heather Lechtman, pp. 331–369. Instituto francés de estudios andinos, Lima.

Taylor, Peter J.
2012 Extraordinary Cities: Early "City-ness" and the Origins of Agriculture and the State. *International Journal of Urban and Regional Research* 36:415–447.

Tellier, Luc-Normand
2009 *Urban World History: An Economic and Geographical Perspective.* Presses de l'Université du Québec, Quebec.

Thompson, Andrew S.
2013 Odontometric Determination of Sex at Mound 72, Cahokia. *American Journal of Physical Anthropology* 151:408–419.

Togola, Tereba
2008 *Archaeological Investigations of Iron Age Sites in the Mema Region, Mali (West Africa).* British Archaeological Reports International Series 1736. Archaeopress, Oxford.

Torres, Constantino M.
2002 Iconigrafía Tiwanaku en la paraphernalia inhalatoria de los Andes centro-sur. *Boletín de Arqueología PUCP* 5:427–454.

Torres-Rouff, Christina
2008 The Influence of Tiwanaku on Life in the Chilean Atacama: Mortuary and Bodily Perspectives. *American Anthropologist* 110:325–337.

Torres-Rouff, David
2012 Water Use, Ethnic Conflict, and Infrastructure in Nineteenth-Century Los Angeles. *Pacific Historical Review* 75:119–140.

Trigger, Bruce G.
1989 *A History of Archaeological Thought.* Cambridge University Press, New York.
2003 *Understanding Early Civilizations.* Cambridge University Press, New York.
2008 Early Cities: Craft Workers, Kings, and Controlling the Supernatural. In *The Ancient City: New Perspectives on Urbanism in the Old and New World*, edited by Joyce Marcus and Jeremy A. Sabloff, pp. 53–66. School for Advanced Research, Santa Fe, New Mexico.

Trubitt, Mary Beth D.
2000 Mound Building and Prestige Goods Exchange: Changing Strategies in the Cahokia Chiefdom. *American Antiquity* 65:669–690.

Turgot, Jacques
1973 A philosophical review of the successive advances of the human mind. In *Turgot on Progress, Sociology, and Economics*, edited by Ronald L. Meeks, pp. 41-59. Cambridge University Press, Cambridge.

Turnbull, Colin M.
1989 *A History of Singapore, 1819–1988.* Oxford University Press, New York.

Tylor, Edward B.
1881 *Anthropology: An Introduction to the Study of Man and Civilization.* Appleton, New York.

Uesugi, Akinori

2012 Development of the Inter-Regional Interaction System in the Indus Valley and Beyond—A Hypothetical View towards the Formation of an Urban Society. In *Cultural Relations between the Indus and the Iranian Plateau during the Third Millennium BCE*, edited by Toshiki Osada and Michael Witzel, pp. 359–380. Harvard University Press, Cambridge, Massachusetts.

Upham, Steadman

1990 Decoupling the Processes of Political Evolution. In *The Evolution of Political Systems*, edited by Steadman Upham, pp. 1–17. Cambridge University Press, New York.

Ur, Jason

2011 The Myth of Isolated Civilizations. *Current Anthropology* 52:607–608.

2014 Households and the Emergence of Cities in Ancient Mesopotamia. *Cambridge Archaeological Journal* 24: 249–268.

Urcid, Javier

2011 Los oráculos y la guerra: el papel de las narrativas pictóricas en el desarrollo temprano de Monte Albán (500 a.C.-200 d.C.). In *Monte Albán en la encrucijada regional y disciplinaria: Memoria de la quinta mesa redonda de Monte Albán*, edited by Nelly M. Robles García and Ángel L. Rivera Guzmán, pp. 163–237. Instituto nacional de anthropología e historia, Mexico City.

Urcid, Javier, and Arthur A. Joyce

2014 Early Transformations of Monte Álban's Main Plaza and Their Political Implications, 500 BC–AD 200. In *Mesoamerican Plazas: Arenas of Community and Power*, edited by Kenchiro Tsukamoto and Takeshi Inomata, pp. 149–167. University of Arizona Press, Tucson.

Uribe, Mauricio, and Carolina Agüero

2002 Alfarería, textiles, y la integración del Norte grande de Chile a Tiwanaku. *Boletín de Arqueología PUCP* 5:397–426.

Valliéres, Claudine

2012 A Taste of Tiwanaku: Daily Life in an Ancient Andean Urban Center as Seen through Cuisine. Unpublished Ph.D. dissertation, McGill University, Montreal.

Van Neer, Wim

1995 Analysis of the Fish Remains. In *Excavations at Jenné-Jeno, Hambarketolo, and Kaniana (Inland Niger Delta, Mali): The 1981 Season*, edited by Susan Keech McIntosh, pp. 319–347. University of California Press, Berkeley.

Vaughn, Kevin J., Jelmer W. Eerkens, and John Katner (editors)

2010 *The Evolution of Leadership: Transitions in Decision Making from Small-Scale to Middle-Range Societies*. School of Advanced Research Press, Santa Fe, New Mexico.

Vayda, Andrew V.

1967 Pomo Trade Feasts. In *Tribal and Peasant Economics*, edited by George Dalton, pp. 494–500. Natural History Press, Garden City, New York.

Vidale, Massimo
1989 Specialized Producers and Urban Elites: On the Role of Craft Industries in Mature Harappan Urban Contexts. In *Old Problems and New Perspectives in the Archaeology of South Asia*, edited by Jonathan Mark Kenoyer, pp. 171–181. Wisconsin Archaeological Reports 2. Department of Anthropology, University of Wisconsin, Madison.
2010 Aspects of Palace Life at Mohenjo-Daro. *South Asian Studies* 26:59–76.

Vidale, Massimo, and Heather M.-L. Miller
2000 On the Development of Indus Technical Virtuosity and Its Relation to Social Structure. In *South Asian Archaeology 1997*, edited by Maurizo Taddei and Guiseppe De Marco, pp. 115–132. Istituto italiano per l'Africa e l'Oriente, Rome.

Vining, Benjamin R.
2011 Ruralism, Land Use History and Holocene Climate Change in the Suches Highlands, Peru. Unpublished Ph.D. dissertation, Boston University, Boston, Massachusetts.

Voltaire
1759 *An Essay on Universal History, the Manners, and Spirit of Nations: From the Reign of Charlemaign to the Age of Lewis XIV*, translated by Thomas Nugent. London: J. Nourse.

Vranich, Alexei
2009 The Development of the Ritual Core of Tiwanaku. In *Tiwanaku: Papers from the 2005 Mayer Center Symposium at the Denver Art Museum*, edited by Margaret Young-Sánchez, pp. 11–34. Denver Art Museum, Denver, Colorado.

Wallerstein, Immanuel
1974 *The Modern World System*, Vol. 1. Academic Press, San Diego, California.
1990 The Renewed Concern with Civilization(s). *Thesis Eleven* 25:107–113.

Warren, John Francis
1990 Prostitution and the Politics of Venereal Diseases: Singapore, 1870–98. *Journal of Southeast Asian Studies* 21:360–383.

Watson, Robert J.
2000 Sacred Landscapes at Cahokia: Mound 72 and the Mound 72 Precinct. In *Mounds, Modoc, and Mesoamerica: Papers in Honor of Melvin L. Fowler*, edited by Steven R. Ahler, pp. 227–243. Scientific Papers Series, Vol. 28. Illinois State Museum, Springfield.

Weber, Max
1949 [1904] The "Objectivity" of Knowledge in Social Science and Social Policy. In *The Methodology of the Social Sciences*, edited by Edward A. Shils and Henry A. Finch, pp. 49–112. Free Press, Glencoe, New York.
1958 [1921] *The City*. Translated and edited by Don Martindale and Gertrud Neuwirth. Free Press, Glencoe, New York.

Weber, Steven A.

1999 Seeds of Urbanism: Paleoethnobotany and the Indus Civilization. *Antiquity* 73:813–826.

2003 Archaeobotany at Harappa: Indications for Change. In *Indus Ethnobiology: New Perspectives from the Field*, edited by Steven A. Weber and William R. Belcher, pp. 175–198. Lexington Books, Lanham, Maryland.

Wengrow, David

2010 *What Makes Civilization? The Ancient Near East and the Future of the West.* Oxford University Press, New York.

Wiessner, Polly

1996 Leveling the Hunter: Constraints on the Status Quest in Foraging Societies. In *Food and the Status Quest*, edited by Polly Wiessner and Wulf Schiefenhovel, pp. 171–191. Berghahn, Oxford, United Kingdom.

2002 The Vines of Complexity: Egalitarian Structures and the Institutionalization of Inequality among the Enga. *Current Anthropology* 43:233–269.

2009 The Power of One? Big Men Revisited. In *The Evolution of Leadership: Transitions in Decision Making from Small-Scale to Middle-Range Societies*, edited by Kevin J. Vaughn, Jelmer W. Eerkens, and John Kantner, pp. 195–222. School for Advanced Research, Santa Fe, New Mexico.

Wheatley, Paul

1972 *The Pivot of the Four Quarters: A Preliminary Enquiry into the Origins and Character of the Ancient Chinese City.* Aldine, Chicago, Illinois.

White, Charles

1799 *An Account of the Regular Gradation in Man, and in Different Animals, and Vegetables.* Dilley, London.

White, Christine R., Rebecca Storey, Michael W. Spence, and Fred J. Longstaffe

2004 Immigration, Assimilation, and Status in the Ancient City of Teotihuacan: Isotopic Evidence from Tlajinga 33. *Latin American Antiquity* 15:176–198.

White, Leslie

1945 "Diffusion vs. Evolution": An Anti-Evolutionist Fallacy. *American Anthropologist* 47:339–356.

1949 *The Science of Culture.* Farrar, Straus and Giroux, New York.

1959 *The Evolution of Culture.* McGraw-Hill, New York.

Whitecotton, Joseph W.

1977 *The Zapotecs: Princes, Priests, and Peasants.* University of Oklahoma Press, Norman.

Wilford, John Noble

2011 Lewis Binford, Leading Archaologist, Dies at 79. *New York Times.* April 23:A17.

Wilkinson, T. J.

2007 Urbanization within a Dynamic Environment: Modeling Bronze Age Communities in Upper Mesopotamia. *American Anthropologist* 109:52–68.

Wilson, Gregory D.
1999 The Production and Consumption of Mississippian Fineware in the American Bottom. *Southeastern Archaeology* 18:98–109.
Winter, Marcus
1974 Residential Patters at Monte Albán, Oaxaca, Mexico. *Science* 186:981–987.
2001 Palacios, templos, y 1,300 años de vida urbana en Monte Albán. In *Reconstruyendo la ciudad Maya: El urbanismo en las sociedades antiquas*, edited by Andrés Ciudad Ruiz, María Josefa Iglesias Ponce de León, and María del Carmen Martínez Martínez, pp. 277–301. Sociedad española de estudios Mayas, Madrid.
2002 Monte Albán: Mortuary Practices as Domestic Ritual and Their Relation to Community Religion. In *Domestic Ritual in Ancient Mesoamerica*, edited by Patricia Plunket, pp. 67–82. Cotsen Institute of Archaeology, University of California, Los Angeles.
2004 Monte Albán: Su organización e impacto político. In *Estructuras políticas en Oaxaca antiguo: Memoria de la tercera mesa redonda de Monte Albán*, edited by Nelly M. Robles García, pp. 27–59. Instituto nacional de antropología e historia, Mexico City.
2009 La religión, el poder y las bases de la complejidad social en Oaxaca prehispánica. In *Bases de la complejidad social en Oaxaca: Memoria de la cuarta mesa redonda*, pp. 504–532. Instituto nacional de antropología e historia, Mexico City.
2011 Social Memory and the Origins of Monte Albán. *Ancient Mesoamerica* 22:393–409.
Winterhalder, Bruce, and Douglas J. Kennett
2006 Behavioral Ecology and the Transition from Hunting and Gathering to Agriculture. In *Behavioral Ecology and the Transition to Agriculture*, edited by Douglas J. Kennett and Bruce Winterhalder, pp. 1–22. University of California Press, Berkeley.
Wirth, Louis
1938 Urbanism as a Way of Life. *American Journal of Sociology* 44:1–24.
Wolfe, Joel
1991 Anarchist Ideology, Worker Practices: The 1917 General Strike and the Formation of São Paulo's Working Class. *Hispanic American Historical Review* 71:809–846.
1993 *Working Women, Working Men: São Paulo and the Rise of Brazil's Industrial Working Class, 1900–1950*. Duke University Press, Durham, North Carolina.
Wong Lin Ken
1978 Singapore: Its Growth as an Entrepot Port, 1819–1941. *Journal of Southeast Asian Studies* 9:50–84.
Workinger, Andrew
2013 Coastal/Highland Interaction in Oaxaca, Mexico: The Perspective from San

Francisco de Arriba. In *Polity and Ecology in Formative Period Coastal Oaxaca*, edited by Arthur A. Joyce, pp. 193–226. University Press of Colorado, Boulder.

Wright, Katherine I.

1994 Ground Stone Tools and Hunters and Gatherer Subsistence in Southwest Asia: Implications for the Transition to Farming. *American Antiquity* 59:238–263.

2014 Domestication and Inequality? Households, Corporate Groups, and Food Processing Tools at Neolithic Çatalhöyük. *Journal of Anthropological Archaeology* 33:1–33.

Wright, Melanie F., Christine A. Hastorf, and Heidi A. Lennstrom

2003 Pre-Hispanic Agriculture and Plant Use at Tiwanaku: Social and Political Implications. In *Urban and Rural Archaeology*, Vol. 2 of *Tiwanaku and Its Hinterland: Archaeology and Paleoecology of an Andean Civilization*, edited by Alan L. Kolata, pp. 384–403. Smithsonian Books, Washington, DC.

Wright, Rita P.

2010 *The Ancient Indus: Urbanism, Economy, and Society*. Cambridge University Press, New York.

2012 Perspectives from the Indus: Contexts of Interaction in the Late Harappa/Post-Urban Period. *Fifty Years of Emirates Archeology: Proceedings of the Second International Conference on the Archaeology of the United Arab Emirates*, edited by Daniel T. Potts and Peter Hellyer, pp. 100–111. Motivate Publishing, Abu Dhabi.

Wright, Rita P., Reid A. Bryson, and Joseph Schuldenrein

2008 Water Supply and History: Harappa and the Beas Regional Survey. *Antiquity* 82:37–48.

Wright, Rita P., Joseph Schuldenrein, M. Afzal Khan, and M. Rafique Mughal

2005a The Emergence of Satellite Communities along the Beas Drainage: Preliminary Results from Lahoma Lal Tibba and Chak Purbane Syal. In *South Asia Archaeology 2001*, edited by Catherine Jarrige and Vincent Lefévre, pp. 327–335. Éditions recherche sur les civilizations-ADPF, Paris.

Wright Rita P., Joseph Schuldenrein, M. Afzal Khan, and S. Malin-Boyce

2005b The Beas River Landscape and Settlement Survey: Preliminary Results from the Site of Vainiwal. In *South Asian Archaeology 2003*, edited by Ute Franke-Vogt and Hans-Joachim Weisshaar, pp. 101–110. Linden Soft, Aachen, Germany.

Yaeger, Jason, and Alexei Vranich

2013 A Radiocarbon Chronology of the Pumapunku Complex and a Reassessment of the Development of Tiwanaku, Bolivia. In *Advances in Titicaca Basin Archaeology*, Vol. 2, edited by Alexei Vranich and Abigail R. Levine, pp. 127–146. Cotsen Institute of Archaeology, University of California, Los Angeles.

Yen Ching-Hwang

1981 Early Chinese Clan Organization in Singapore and Malaysia, 1819–1911. *Journal of Southeast Asian History* 12:62–92.

Yépez Álvarez, Willy, and Justin Jennings (editors)
2012 *Wari en Arequipa: Análisis de los contextos funerarios de La Real.* Museo arqueológica José María Morante, Universidad nacional de San Agustín, Arequipa.
Yerkes, Richard W.
1989 Mississippian Craft Specialization on the American Bottom. *Southeastern Archaeology* 8:93–106.
1991 Specialization in Shell Artifact Production at Cahokia. In *New Perspectives on Cahokia: Views from the Periphery,* edited by John B. Stoltman, pp. 49–64. Prehistory Press, Madison, Wisconsin.
2005 Bone Chemistry, Body Parts, and Growth Marks: Evaluating Ohio Hopewell and Cahokia Mississippian Seasonality, Subsistence, Ritual, and Feasting. *American Antiquity* 70:241–265.
Yoffee, Norman
1979 The Decline and Rise of Mesopotamian Civilization: An Ethnoarchaeological Perspective on the Evolution of Social Complexity. *American Antiquity* 44:5–35.
1980a Do You See Yonder Cloud That's Almost in the Shape of a Camel? Reply to Peters. *American Antiquity* 45:601–604.
1980b Honk If You Know Darwin: Brief Reply to Dunnell and Wenke. *American Antiquity* 45:610–612.
1993 Too Many Chiefs? (Or Safe Texts for the '90s). In *Archaeological Theory: Who Sets the Agenda?,* edited by Norman Yoffee and Andrew Sherratt, pp. 60–78. Cambridge University Press, New York.
2001 The Evolution of Simplicity. *Current Anthropology* 42:767–769.
2005 *Myths of the Archaic State: Evolution of the Earliest Cities, States, and Civilizations.* Cambridge University Press, New York.
2009 Making Ancient Cities Plausible. *Reviews in Anthropology* 38:264–289.
Young, Bilone W., and Melvin L. Fowler
2000 *Cahokia: The Great Native American Metropolis.* University of Illinois Press, Urbana.
Young-Sánchez, Margaret (editor)
2004 *Tiwanaku: Ancestors of the Inca.* University of Nebraska Press, Lincoln.
Zeder, Melinda A.
1991 *Feeding Cities: Specialized Animal Economy in the Ancient Near East.* Smithsonian Institution, Washington, DC.

INDEX

Page numbers in italic text indicate illustrations.

CPSIA information can be obtained
at www.ICGtesting.com
Printed in the USA
LVHW040434230723
753122LV00001B/93